The Psalms in the N

The New Testament and the Scriptures of Israel

The Psalms in the New Testament (2004)
Isaiah in the New Testament (2005)
Deuteronomy in the New Testament (2006)

The Psalms in the New Testament

Edited by
STEVE MOYISE
and
MAARTEN J. J. MENKEN

T&T CLARK INTERNATIONAL
A Continuum imprint
LONDON • NEW YORK

T&T Clark International, an imprint of Continuum

The Tower Building   15 East 26th Street
11 York Road   New York
London SE1 7NX   NY 10010

www.tandtclark.com

First published 2004

British Library Cataloguing-in-Publication Data
A catalogue record for this book is available from the British Library

ISBN 0567089134 (HB)
ISBN 0567089142 (PB)

Typeset by Tradespools, Frome, Somerset
Printed and bound by The Cromwell Press Ltd, Trowbridge, Wiltshire

Contents

Abbreviations

AB	Anchor Bible
AGJU	Arbeiten zur Geschichte des antiken Judentums und des Urchristentums
ALGHJ	Arbeiten zur Literatur und Geschichte des hellenistischen Judentums
AnBib	Analecta biblica
ANRW	Hildegard Temporini and Wolgang Haase, eds, *Aufstieg un der Niedergang der römischen Welt: Geschichte und Kultur Roms im Spiegel der neueren Forschung* (Berlin: W. de Gruyter, 1972–)
AUSS	*Andrews University Seminary Studies*
BBR	*Bulletin for Biblical Research*
BETL	Bibliotheca ephemeridum theologicarum lovaniensium
BHT	Beiträge zur historischen Theologie
Bib	*Biblica*
BJS	Brown Judaic Studies
BNTC	Black's New Testament Commentaries
BU	Biblische Untersuchungen
BWANT	Beiträge zur Wissenschaft vom Alten und Neuen Testament
BZ	*Biblische Zeitschrift*
BZNW	Beihefte zur ZNW
CBET	Contributions to Biblical Exegesis and Theology
CBQ	*Catholic Biblical Quarterly*
CBQMS	*Catholic Biblical Quarterly*, Monograph Series
CRINT	Compendia rerum iudaicarum ad Novum Testamentum
DJD	Discoveries in the Judaean Desert
DRev	*Downside Review*
DSD	*Dead Sea Discoveries*
EKKNT	Evangelisch-katholischer Kommentar zum Neuen Testament
ExpT	*Expository Times*
FAT	Forschungen zum Alten Testament
FRLANT	Forschungen zur Religion und Literatur des Alten und Neuen Testaments

HTKAT	Herders theologischer Kommentar zum Alten Testament
HTKNT	Herders theologischer Kommentar zum Neuen Testament
HTKNTSup	Herders theologischer Kommentar zum Neuen Testament, Supplement band
ICC	International Critical Commentary
JBL	*Journal of Biblical Literature*
JETS	*Journal of the Evangelical Theological Society*
JGRCh	*Journal of Greco-Roman Christianity and Judaism*
JJS	*Journal of Jewish Studies*
JSNT	*Journal for the Study of the New Testament*
JSNTSup	Journal for the Study of the New Testament, Supplement Series
JSOT	*Journal of the Study of the Old Testament*
JSOTSup	Journal for the Study of the Old Testament, Supplement Series
JSPSup	Journal for the Study of the Pseudepigrapha, Supplement Series
JSS	*Journal of Semitic Studies*
LAB	*Liber Antiquitatum Biblicarum*
MT	Masoretic Text
NA[27]	Nestle and Aland, *Novum Testamentum Graece* (Stuttgart: Deutsche Bibelgesellschaft, 27th edn., 1993)
NCB	New Century Bible
NICNT	New International Commentary on the New Testament
NIV	New International Version
NIVAC	New International Version Application Commentary
NIGTC	The New International Greek Testament Commentary
NJB	New Jerusalem Bible
NovT	*Novum Testamentum*
NovTSup	Novum Testamentum, Supplement Series
NRSV	New Revised Standard Version
NTD	Das Neue Testament Deutsch
NTS	*New Testament Studies*
OLZ	*Orientalistische Literaturzeitung*
OTG	Old Testament Guides
OTL	Old Testament Library
OTP	*Old Testament Pseudepigrapha* (ed. J.H. Charlesworth)
RB	*Revue biblique*
RevQ	*Revue de Qumrân*
RNT	Regensburger Neues Testament
RSV	Revised Standard Version
RTP	*Revue de théologie et de philosophie*
SBL	Society of Biblical Literature
SBLDS	SBL Dissertation Series
SBLEJL	SBL Early Jewish Literature
SBLMS	SBL Monograph Series
SBLSP	SBL Seminar Papers

SNTSMS	Society for New Testament Studies Monograph Series
STDJ	Studies on the Texts of the Desert of Judah
SVTP	Studia in Veteris Testamenti pseudepigrapha
TLZ	Theologische Literaturzeitung
ThWAT	*Theologisches Wörterbuch zum Alten Testament* (eds. G.J. Botterweck and H. Ringgren)
Transeu	Transeuphratène
TynBul	*Tyndale Bulletin*
VT	*Vetus Testamentum*
VTSup	Vetus Testamentum, Supplement Series
UBS[4]	United Bible Societies' *Greek New Testament*, 4th edition
WBC	Word Biblical Commentary
WMANT	Wissenschaftliche Monographien zum Alten und Neuen Testament
WUNT	Wissenschaftliche Untersuchingen zum Neuen Testament
ZAW	*Zeitschrift für die alttestamentliche Wissenschaft*
ZNW	*Zeitschrift für die neutestamentliche Wissenschaft*
ZTK	*Zeitschrift für Theologie und Kirche*

List of Contributors

HAROLD W. ATTRIDGE is Lillian Claus Professor of New Testament and Dean of Yale Divinity School and author of the Hermeneia commentary on Hebrews (Fortress Press, 1989).

GEORGE J. BROOKE is Rylands Professor of Biblical Criticism and Exegesis at the University of Manchester. Among his recent publications are *The Complete World of the Dead Sea Scrolls* (co-authored with P.R. Davies and P. Callaway; Thames and Hudson, 2002) and *Copper Scroll Studies* (co-edited with P.R. Davies; Sheffield Academic Press, 2002).

MARGARET DALY-DENTON is Director of Programmes in Word, Worship and Spirituality at the Newman Institute, Ballina, Co Mayo and author of *David in the Fourth Gospel: The Johannine Reception of the Psalms* (Brill, 2000).

PETER DOBLE is Visiting Fellow, School of Theology and Religious Studies, University of Leeds and author of *The Paradox of Salvation* (Cambridge University Press, 1996) and 'Vile Bodies or Transformed Persons? (Phil 3:21)', *JSNT* 86 (2002).

SYLVIA C. KEESMAAT is Associate Professor of Biblical Studies and Hermeneutics at the Institute for Christian Studies, Toronto and author of *Paul and his Story: (Re)Interpreting the Exodus Tradition* (Sheffield Academic Press, 1999).

MICHAEL LABAHN is Wissenschaftlicher Assistent for New Testament at Martin-Luther University, Halle-Wittenberg and author of *Jesus als Lebensspender: Untersuchungen zu einer Geschichte der johanneischen Tradition anhand ihrer Wundergeschichten* (W. de Gruyter, 1999) and *Offenbarung in Zeichen un der Wort: Untersuchungen zur Vorgeschichte von Joh 6,1–25a und seiner Rezeption in der Brotrede* (Mohr Siebeck, 2000).

MAARTEN J.J. MENKEN is Professor of New Testament Exegesis at the Catholic Theological University, Utrecht and author of *2 Thessalonians* (Routledge, 1994) and *Old Testament Quotations in the Fourth Gospel* (Kok Pharos, 1996).

THORSTEN MORITZ is Professor of New Testament at Bethel Seminary, Minnesota and author of *A Profound Mystery: The Use of the Old Testament in Ephesians* (Brill, 1996).

STEVE MOYISE is Principal Lecturer at University College, Chichester and author of *The Old Testament in the Book of Revelation* (Sheffield Academic Press, 1995) and *The Old Testament in the New* (Continuum, 2001).

RIKK WATTS is Associate Professor in New Testament at Regent College, Vancouver and author of *Isaiah's New Exodus in Mark* (Mohr Siebeck, 1997).

H.H. DRAKE WILLIAMS, III is adjunct faculty member at Eastern Baptist Theological Seminary/Biblical Theological Seminary, Pennsylvania and author of *The Wisdom of the Wise: The Presence and Function of Scripture within 1 Cor 1:18–3:23* (Brill, 2001).

SUE WOAN is Chaplain of Bournemouth and Poole College of Further Education, tutor for the Salisbury diocese Board of Ministry and PhD candidate at the University of Exeter.

Introduction

The use of the Old Testament in the New Testament is a topic that receives much attention nowadays, not only in academic biblical scholarship, but at the more popular level as well.[1] It is a topic that deserves attention, because it brings us right into the heart of early Christian religion and theology. To first-century Jews such as Jesus of Nazareth and his first followers, the collection of writings that we use to call the 'Old Testament', was Holy Scripture, a divine revelation that was relevant to their past, present and future. As Holy Scripture, it provided them with their religious imagery and their religious language. As soon as Jesus' followers tried to express the significance of the message and person of Jesus, they did so largely in terms derived from Scripture, and they considered the Jesus event and its effects to be the 'fulfilment' of Scripture.

Among the various writings of the Old Testament, the book of Psalms, traditionally ascribed to King David, enjoyed a special position. As a collection of prayers, hymns, laments and similar poetic genres, it was capable of giving expression to various religious experiences. Feelings of joy, of gratitude, of guilt, of distress, of abandonment, even of rebellion, could be channelled into the words of the Psalms. This happened not only in public worship (in the synagogue liturgy and before 70 CE, in the Jerusalem temple as well), but also in private piety. There is eloquent evidence of this in *4 Maccabees*, a book that was probably written sometime between 19 and 54 CE. A large part of it concerns the story of the martyrdom of a mother and her seven sons under the Syrian king Antiochus IV Epiphanes, who took a series of vehement anti-Jewish measures in the period between 167 and 164 BCE. When the mother reminds her sons of their deceased father, one of the many things she says about him is: 'He used to sing to you the psalmist David who says: Many are the afflictions of the righteous' (*4 Macc.* 18:15, quoting Ps. 34:20). A clause from a psalm ascribed to David is immediately applied to the situation of a family suffering persecution under Antiochus Epiphanes. Jews and Christians

---

[1] See, e.g., R.N. Longenecker, *Biblical Exegesis in the Apostolic Period* (Grand Rapids: Eerdmans; Vancouver: Regent College Publishing, 2nd edn, 1999); S. Moyise, *The Old Testament in the New: An Introduction* (London: Continuum, 2001); J.M. Court, ed., *New Testament Writers and the Old Testament: An Introduction* (London: SPCK, 2002).

have continued to apply psalm words to themselves and the situations they face, with similar immediacy.

No wonder then that the book of Psalms is – together with Isaiah – the most extensively used Old Testament book in the New Testament. It is the source of many quotations and allusions, and it has provided the language for songs and prayers.[2] It should be stressed, however, that there is much diversity in how the Psalms are used in the New Testament, both in terms of selection and function and the amount of agreement with specific Hebrew or Greek sources. This is not surprising for while there are common elements shared by all or most of the New Testament writings, we must also say that every New Testament author has his own concerns and his own ideas, and this individuality also extends to the reception of the Old Testament, including the Psalms.

Thus there is reason to study the reception of the Psalms in the various New Testament writings. The reception of the Old Testament by a specific New Testament author (such as Matthew, John or Paul) has been studied intensively, and there has also been attention to the use of one Old Testament writing in a specific New Testament book.[3] Less attention has been paid to the study of the use of *one* Old Testament book, with its own distinct profile, in a *range* of New Testament writings.[4] The present collection of essays aims to meet this need, bringing to light the diverse ways in which the New Testament authors made use of the Psalms.

It does not aim to cover the entire New Testament. Philippians, 1 and 2 Thessalonians, the Pastoral Epistles, Philemon, James, 2 Peter, the Johannine Epistles and Jude are absent, because overt references to the Psalms in the form of marked or unmarked quotations are missing from these writings.[5] On the other hand, Q, the name given to the hypothetical document that Matthew and Luke may have used to expand Mark, is included, because it is thought to contain quotations from the Psalms, and also because recent research has shown that it is worthwhile to study Q in its own right. There is also an introductory chapter on the Psalms in early Jewish literature, especially in the Dead Sea Scrolls, for the early Christian reception of the Psalms started in the context of and even as part of the early Jewish reception of the Psalms. Nor

---

[2] The two well-known canticles in Luke 1 (*Magnificat*, 1:46–55; *Benedictus*, 1:68–79), for instance, were heavily influenced by the Psalter.

[3] Examples of studies in the latter category that concern the Psalms are: S.J. Kistemaker, *The Psalm Citations in the Epistle to the Hebrews* (Amsterdam: van Soest, 1961); M. Daly-Denton, *David in the Fourth Gospel: The Johannine Reception of the Psalms* (AGJU 47; Leiden: Brill, 2000).

[4] A. Vis, *The Messianic Psalm Quotations in the New Testament: A Critical Study of the Christian 'Testimonies' in the New Testament* (Amsterdam: Hertzberger, 1936), does not show much interest in the variety of receptions of the Psalms in the New Testament – which is perhaps not too surprising, given the date of publication of the book.

[5] Colossians is only included because of its relationship to Ephesians.

should we forget that the historical Jesus prayed with the words of the Psalms (see esp. Mk 15:34), and that his disciples no doubt did the same.

The authors of the chapters that have been collected in this volume are specialists in the use of the Old Testament in the particular New Testament document on which they are writing. And just as there is variety in the reception of the Psalms in the New Testament, so there is variety among scholars writing on this subject. Some focus on the textual form of the Old Testament passages that have been quoted; others on the role or function that they have in the new work. Some assume that when a New Testament author made use of part of a psalm, he presupposed that his audience knew the entire psalm; others are more reluctant to make this assumption. Some make use of terminologies deriving from theories of intertextuality; others keep to the more 'classical' terminology. However, these differences do not detract from the common commitment to elucidate how various New Testament authors have made use of the Psalms. The essential point is that it becomes possible to compare these various ways of dealing with the Psalms, to detect agreements and differences, and so come to view them in their proper relations and proportions.

This volume originates from the seminar on 'The Use of the Old Testament in the New Testament', which is annually held at Hawarden (North Wales, UK),[6] and also from a similar seminar which has taken place within the annual conferences of the European Association for Biblical Studies (Utrecht, Rome, Berlin). We are grateful to all the participants of these seminars, whose constructive comments and suggestions have been an important factor in the revision of the papers for publication. There continues to be a great deal of interest in the reception of the Old Testament in the New Testament and a further volume on the use of Isaiah in the New Testament is already underway.

---

[6] For the history of this seminar, see J.L. North, 'ΚΑΙΝΑ ΚΑΙ ΠΑΛΑΙΑ: An Account of the British Seminar on the Use of the Old Testament in the New Testament', in S. Moyise, ed., *The Old Testament in the New Testament* (FS J.L. North; JSNTSup 189; Sheffield: Sheffield Academic Press, 2000), pp. 278–81. In recent years, the seminar has increasingly gained a more international profile.

The Psalms in Early Jewish Literature in the Light of the Dead Sea Scrolls

George J. Brooke

Introduction

The purpose of this study is to present in a summary form some of the significant implications of the psalms manuscripts from the eleven Qumran caves together with some information about the presentation, re-presentation and use of the psalms in some other early Jewish literature, including the writings of Philo. Although what is offered here in a limited space is selective and partial, it is hoped that this short description and analysis will serve both to set the abundance of evidence from the eleven Qumran caves in a broader Jewish context and also to provide ways of reading the early Jewish evidence which may be of benefit to those studying the use of the psalms in the New Testament writings.

The Psalms at Qumran

Psalms and the Variety of Psalters

The advantage of beginning with the evidence for psalms and psalters from Qumran is that it throws into sharp relief all that we thought we knew about the psalter in the late Second Temple period.[1] Ever since the 1965 publication of 11QPs[a] by J.A. Sanders,[2] it has been necessary for scholars to consider whether at least one group of Jews in the late Second Temple period had more than one psalter. The debate has ranged widely and is well known.[3] In brief, the two poles of the debate can be summed up as follows. On the one hand, some have argued that 11QPs[a] is a secondary collection of psalms, perhaps put

---

[1] See R.T. Beckwith, 'The Early History of the Psalter', *TynBul* 46 (1995), pp. 1–27; E. Zenger ed., *Der Septuaginta-Psalter: Sprachliche und theologische Aspekte* (Herders biblische Studien 32; Freiburg im Breisgau: Herder, 2001).

[2] J.A. Sanders, *The Psalms Scroll of Qumrân Cave 11 (11QPs^a)* (DJD 4; Oxford: Clarendon Press, 1965).

[3] See J.C. VanderKam, *The Dead Sea Scrolls Today* (Grand Rapids, MI: Eerdmans; London: SPCK, 1994), pp. 135–39; H.-J. Fabry, 'Der Psalter in Qumran', in E. Zenger, ed., *Der Psalter in Judentum und Christentum* (Herders biblische Studien 18; Freiburg im Breisgau: Herder, 1998), pp. 137–63; P.W. Flint, 'The Book of Psalms in the Light of the Dead Sea Scrolls', *VT* 48 (1998), pp. 453–72.

together for liturgical use, which in many ways reflects the psalter as known in its later form in the MT. On the other hand, some have argued that 11QPs[a] is a fully-fledged authoritative psalter. There seemed to be no way of settling the argument, but the publication of all the psalms manuscripts from Qumran's Cave 4[4] has resulted in the debate swinging in favour of those who reckon that the Hebrew psalter existed in at least two forms in late Second Temple Palestine.

The most accessible list of the several psalms manuscripts found at Qumran and at other sites in the vicinity of the Dead Sea has been provided by P.W. Flint.[5] Flint's list is highly informative, but it is worth noting that elements of it could have been organized in several other ways. Some of his headings are oriented exclusively towards the Masoretic Text, such as 'Different order from MT', 'Includes compositions not in MT', 'Range of contents (using order of MT)'. It could be that this is done out of necessity, but the uninitiated reader should be wary of supposing that the form of the Hebrew psalter as now known in the MT was presupposed as exclusively normative in the three centuries before the fall of the temple in 70 CE.

In fact, nobody is more aware of the problems of aligning manuscripts alongside the MT than Flint himself,[6] and on the basis of the evidence of the scrolls he has become an advocate for the existence of three editions of the psalter: (1) Psalms 1/2–89, (2) what he calls the '11QPs[a]-Psalter' (Psalms 1–89 plus the arrangements found in 11QPs[a], which is also found in 11QPs[b] and 4QPs[e]),[7] and (3) the 'MT-150 Psalter' (Psalms 1–89 plus 90–150, attested most clearly by MasPs[b]). When each manuscript is considered in its own right, it

---

[4] P.W. Skehan, E. Ulrich and P.W. Flint, 'Psalms', in E. Ulrich, *et al.*, eds, *Qumran Cave 4.XI: Psalms to Chronicles* (DJD 16; Oxford: Clarendon Press, 2000), pp. 7–170.

[5] P.W. Flint, 'Appendix: Psalms Scrolls from the Judaean Desert', in J.H. Charlesworth and H.W.L. Reitz, eds, *The Dead Sea Scrolls, Hebrew, Aramaic, and Greek Texts with English Translations: Pseudepigraphic and Non-Masoretic Psalms and Prayers* (Princeton Theological Seminary Dead Sea Scrolls Project 4A; Tübingen: Mohr Siebeck; Louisville, KY: Westminster John Knox Press, 1997), pp. 287–90. This Appendix contains a useful list of some of the chief characteristics of the manuscripts containing psalms, such as how much is preserved, what the original contents might have been, what compositions the extant fragments of each manuscript contained, the format of the scrolls (whether stichometric or in prose), notes on titles and superscriptions, comparative datings, and major disagreements with the Masoretic psalter. There is also a useful select bibliography which should form the basis of any research into the psalms in the Dead Sea Scrolls. Flint's list of manuscripts in that Appendix now has to be updated in light of his own further research and that of others as that has been published in the principal edition of DJD 16 (see n. 4): basically, since 1997, 4QPs[s] has been separated into two manuscripts (4QPs[s] and 4QPs[t]) with the result that 4QPs[t] is now 4QPs[u] (in DJD 16), 4QPs[u] is now 4QPs[v] (in DJD 16), 4QPs[w] is now the designation for two fragments (4QUnidC frg. 1 and 4QToharot E[b]) containing part of Psalm 112, and 4QPs[w] is now 4QPs[x] (in DJD 16).

[6] As he has made known in several publications, not least the published version of his doctoral dissertation *The Dead Sea Psalms Scrolls and the Book of Psalms* (STDJ 17; Leiden: Brill, 1997).

[7] P.W. Flint, 'The "11QPs[a]-Psalter" in the Dead Sea Scrolls, Including the Preliminary Edition of 4QPs[e]', in C.A. Evans and S. Talmon, eds, *The Quest for Context and Meaning: Studies in Biblical Intertextuality in Honor of James A. Sanders* (Biblical Interpretation Series 28; Leiden: Brill, 1997), pp. 173–96.

could well be concluded that there are even more options than those promulgated by Flint, not least because the very presentation of the psalms varies from manuscript to manuscript. Such variety can be discerned, for example, in whether or not a manuscript is laid out stichometrically, in consideration of the size of the manuscript, both in terms of height and length, and in such matters as how superscriptions are presented and used. Nevertheless, it is likely that there was indeed the kind of variety for which Flint has argued.

With regard to the use of the psalms in much late Second Temple Jewish literature, this variety poses the issue of which form of psalter may lie behind the quotation or adaptation of the psalm, and whether that matters. With regard to the New Testament a similar issue may need to be kept in mind, even though the overwhelming view of the evidence suggests that the New Testament authors were heavily dependent upon the LXX version of the psalter.[8]

Psalms Manuscripts: Psalters or Excerpted Texts?

The manuscripts from the Judaean wilderness which contain one or more psalms have provided us with a wide range of insights into how the psalms were viewed, not least raising the question whether all uses of the psalms depended directly on complete collections such as are now found in the MT or LXX. Many introductory chapters on the so-called biblical manuscripts found at Qumran, and at a number of other sites, list the number of copies of biblical books.[9] Surprisingly, few of the authors of such chapters pause to consider whether all the manuscripts to which they make reference are what they have considered them to be.

In many instances it is simply no longer possible to determine whether the remains of a particular manuscript indicate either that a whole collection of psalms was originally written on it or whether the manuscript contained just one or a few selected psalms. Thus, one of the first matters to consider is the character of each manuscript, not only to determine whether or not its contents might be deemed to merit the label 'biblical' and so carry some kind of authority, but also to see whether there are clear features which can indicate how the psalm or psalms may have been understood and used. Such considerations will broaden the context within which the use of the psalms by other contemporary authors can be suitably understood.

---

[8] It is possible that there are indications of an alternative form of the psalter in the minority reading of 'in the first psalm' to introduce what is known as Psalm 2 at Acts 13:33. This might imply the absence of Psalm 1 from such a version (and possibly the other psalm which concerns the Law, Psalm 119, which is barely visible in the NT).

[9] E.g., G. Vermes, *An Introduction to the Complete Dead Sea Scrolls* (London: SCM Press, 1999), p. 173: under 'Writings' Vermes states straightforwardly that there are 36 manuscript copies of the psalms.

Thus it is very likely that 4QPs^g and 4QPs^h were both manuscripts which contained Psalm 119 alone (as also possibly 5QPs). These manuscripts should not be seen as regular collections of psalms, as psalters, but as something else. The particular devoted care given to copying their contents indicates something special about the psalm's significance within the context in which it was copied and preserved.

4QPs^g is extant in six fragments; Psalm 119 is presented in full lines stichometrically, with eight lines per column of manuscript and a blank line in between each acrostic stanza. The whole psalm would fit in a manuscript of 25 columns with these dimensions.[10] 4QPs^h is extant in two pieces making one fragment. Like 4QPs^g it appears to have contained Psalm 119 alone because the wide right-hand margin next to the first preserved column of writing almost certainly indicates that this was the start of the manuscript. The psalm is laid out stichometrically in full lines but there is no blank line between stanzas, the separate stanzas being indicated, in the one place where a transition is preserved, by a large marginal *lamed*. Neither of these manuscripts was a psalter proper. Whatever the case, it is clear that Psalm 119 by itself was of considerable interest to some people.[11]

The existence of a diverse range of manuscripts which are excerpted texts has been highlighted in a 1995 study by E. Tov.[12] On fragment 3 of 4QPs^n, Ps. 135:11–12 is directly followed by Ps. 136:23–24 and the transition appears to be deliberate inasmuch as Ps. 135:12a and 12b are both given the phrase *ky l'lm hsdw*, which is used throughout Psalm 136. A new psalm is created, though it is not presented stichometrically. Was it free-standing? We cannot tell, but the question must be asked.

It is also the case that some manuscripts, apparently containing nothing other than copies of certain psalms, represent an intermediate stage in which the collections of psalms are presented in various ways for various purposes. It thus becomes increasingly important for scholars to consider the likely function of any manuscript copy as they consider the psalms manuscripts as a whole as well as just how many kinds of psalter there may have been at Qumran.[13] It is striking how few commentators dare to speak about a manuscript's function, even though it is clear that not all copies of scriptural works were made for the same purpose.

---

[10] Cf. 4QDeut^q (as Ulrich and Flint do in DJD 16), which seems also to be an excerpt of an important passage (the Song of Moses) arranged stichometrically, rather than a copy of Deuteronomy as such.

[11] Cf. J. Genot-Bismuth, 'Zoroastrisme et culture judéenne scribe sous influence perse: archéologie de l'essénisme à la lumière de l'étude comparée du Psaume 119 et du Yasna 45', *Transeu* 13 (1997), pp. 107–21.

[12] E. Tov, 'Excerpted and Abbreviated Biblical Texts from Qumran', *RevQ* 16 (1995), pp. 581–600.

[13] A step in the right direction with regard to the possible function of the LXX form of the psalter has recently been taken by G. Dorival, 'Septante et texte massorétique: le cas des psaumes', in A. Lemaire, ed., *Congress Volume Basel 2001* (VTSup 92; Leiden: Brill, 2002), pp. 139–61.

Books of Psalms?

The special character of 4QPs^g and 4QPs^h (and probably 5QPs) highlights a distinctive role for Psalm 119. This is clearly a psalm about the Law, which is referred to in almost every line, either directly or indirectly. It is often described as a wisdom psalm though it contains elements of several different psalm types. As is well known, A. Weiser, for one, was of the opinion that Psalm 119 concluded an earlier edition of the Psalter, forming an inclusion with Psalm 1 which also stresses the place of the Law.[14] It is unlikely that Weiser's view should be followed precisely, but it is not impossible that the inclusion of Psalm 1 and Psalm 119 in one form of the psalter provided a two-fold key to that form, namely that the collection of psalms should be understood as a Pentateuch, not just in beginning and possibly ending with the Law, but also in having five books, and that as Psalm 1 indicates the texts should be part of the curriculum of any wise person.

As can be seen from Flint's lists, he has concluded overall that at Qumran (and elsewhere) there existed side by side at least three literary editions of the Psalter: Psalms 1/2–89, the 11QPs^a Psalter (1–89 and the arrangement found in 11QPs^a), and the MT-150 Psalter. It is important to stress the phrase 'at least', and recognize that there is possible, even probable evidence, for more editions than three. We have already mentioned the possibility that the special character of Psalm 119 in two or three manuscripts may go some way to vindicating Weiser in seeing yet another edition beginning at Psalm 1 and running to Psalm 119, but the variety of the evidence listed by Flint indicates that there may have been other collections too, not least inasmuch as the relative stability of the first three Books, Psalms 1–89, may imply that they were published separately.

The Great Psalms Scroll from Cave 11 (11QPs^a) has come to be seen as witnessing to a Davidic form of the last two books of the Psalter, which, when added on to the first three in their more or less stable form, would encourage the reader to consider the whole collection as Davidic.[15] The three manuscripts which seem to contain this form of the psalter are 11QPs^a, 11QPs^b and 4QPs^e. All three of these manuscripts are dated to the first half of the first century CE. Even if one allows at least a generation or more for dating error, the manuscripts would still fall into the second half of the occupation of the Qumran site. This might be taken as an indication that a more or less complete psalter of five books was being adapted at a late stage for some

---

[14] A. Weiser, *The Psalms* (OTL; London: SCM Press, 1962), *ad loc.*
[15] This may inform how introductory statements including a reference to David might best be understood; see, e.g., Matt. 22:43; Mk. 12:36; Lk. 20:42; Acts 1:16; 2:25, 34; 4:25; Rom. 4:6; 11:9; Heb. 4:7.

particular purpose, such as a liturgical one. The stress on the figure of David in this collection, however, is suggestive of a correspondence to be noted between these Davidic collection manuscripts and those sectarian manuscripts, also almost exclusively to be dated to the same period, in which there is explicit Davidic messianism. Changing political circumstances and developing messianic views may have encouraged the promulgation of a Davidic psalter, of which there was already some knowledge. Thus it is as easy to see the form of the text as presented in 11QPs^a as suggestive of the ongoing open-endedness of the canonical process as it is to see it as a late aberration for liturgical use only.

The Davidic character of the type of text to be found in 11QPs^a is largely dependent on the pseudepigraphical autobiographical poem of Psalm 151 in column 28 and the prose interlude known as the compositions of David.

> And he [David] wrote psalms: three thousand six hundred; and songs to be sung before the altar over the perpetual offering of every day, for all the days of the year: three hundred and sixty-four; and for the sabbath offerings: fifty-two songs; and for the offering for the beginning of the month, and for all the days of the festivals, and for the day of atonement: thirty songs. And all the songs which he composed were four hundred and forty-six. And songs to be sung over the possessed: four. The total was four thousand and fifty. He composed them all through the spirit of prophecy which had been given to him from before the Most High.[16]

The overall total of 4050 songs which David composed gives plenty of scope for alternative collections of psalms. R. Beckwith and others have suitably pointed out that the number 3600 is 24×150, the number of Levitical courses multiplied by the number of psalms in the MT psalter, and so he justifiably supposes that 11QPs^a presupposes knowledge of a 150 Psalm Psalter.[17] But on that basis and perhaps somewhat illogically Beckwith then proceeds to suppose that the MT-150 Psalter was the only one of any authoritative status from the second century BCE onwards. Flint's more careful analysis of the manuscript leads him to the conclusion that it originally contained 56 compositions, which he takes to be 52 for the weeks of the solar year and four (David's Last Words, David's Compositions, Psalms 151A and 151B) which assert Davidic authorship. Flint proposes that the collection was probably put together as authoritative well before the Qumran settlement was occupied, though all the manuscripts containing this text were copied at Qumran.[18]

Inclusion or Exclusion

Flint's analysis of Psalms manuscripts from Qumran (and elsewhere) appears deceptively comprehensive. In fact, as mentioned, most of his analysis is based

---

[16] 11QPs^a 27:4–11; trans. F. García Martínez, *The Dead Sea Scrolls Translated: The Qumran Texts in English* (Leiden: Brill; Grand Rapids, MI: Eerdmans, 2nd edn, 1996), p. 309.

[17] R. Beckwith, *Calendar and Chronology, Jewish and Christian: Biblical, Intertestamental and Patristic Studies* (AGJU 33; Leiden: Brill, 1996), pp. 141–66.

[18] P.W. Flint, *The Dead Sea Psalms Scrolls and the Book of Psalms*, pp. 172–201.

on the assumption that matters should be discussed in relation to the MT-150 Psalter, even though he is very careful not to give priority to its text-type or ordering in anything that he states. As a result the data about psalms in the Qumran manuscripts is somewhat distorted. Two examples must suffice, though others could be given.

The most obvious text which falls just outside the parameters of the discussion as it is set up by Flint is 4Q448.[19] This peculiarly arranged manuscript contains two columns of a national invocation referring to a King Jonathan, who is identified by a majority of scholars with Alexander Jannaeus.[20] These two columns form a kind of state prayer on behalf of the monarch. However, the manuscript also includes portions of Ps. 154:17–20, which is also to be found in its Hebrew form in 11QPs[a] and together with four other psalms is extant in Syriac manuscripts of the psalter. The Syriac evidence confirms the Palestinian provenance of the material and supports its antiquity.[21] H. Eshel and E. Eshel, the principal editors of 4Q448, have recently argued in a convincing manner that quite possibly Psalm 154, or a tradition based upon it, was known to the author of 4QpIsa[a] and that on the basis of both compositions it is possible to explain why the two columns which speak of Jonathan were added to Psalm 154 in 4Q448;[22] this would give Psalm 154 a status within the community (and possibly in Judaism more broadly) akin to the other psalms now known from the MT-150 collection. Any consideration of the state and status of the psalter in Palestinian Judaism in the late Second Temple period should include detailed discussion of the significance of 4Q448 alongside collections such as 11QPs[a]. Whatever is decided, the point is that the range of evidence is broader than any discussion prejudiced from a Masoretic starting point would seem to allow.

Or again, it is perhaps surprising that Flint's analysis contains no reference to the collections of psalms found in 4Q380 and 4Q381. 4Q380 contains a psalm which has the title 'Prayer (tehillah) of Obadiah'. This has been variously discussed by E. Schuller in her edition of the text and may be a reference either to the prophet or to the steward of the house of Ahab (1 Kings 18).[23] Of

---

[19] E. Eshel, H. Eshel and A. Yardeni, '448. 4QApocryphal Psalm and Prayer', Qumran Cave 4.VI: Poetical and Liturgical Texts, Part 1 (DJD 11; Oxford: Clarendon Press, 1998), pp. 403–25.

[20] The loudest voice against this identification is G. Vermes, 'The So-Called King Jonathan Fragment (4Q448)', JJS 44 (1993), pp. 294–300, who prefers to identify the object of the prayer with Jonathan Maccabee. Those who link these two columns with Alexander Jannaeus are divided as to whether the reference to him should be read positively or negatively.

[21] See A. Lemaire, 'Attestation textuelle et critique littéraire: 4Q448 Col. A et Psalm 154', in L.H. Schiffman, E. Tov and J.C. VanderKam, eds, The Dead Sea Scrolls Fifty Years after their Discovery: Proceedings of the Jerusalem Congress, July 20–25, 1997 (Jerusalem: Israel Exploration Society in cooperation with The Shrine of the Book, Israel Museum, 2000), pp. 12–18, and the notes there.

[22] H. Eshel and E. Eshel, '4Q448, Psalm 154 (Syriac), Sirach 48:20, and 4QpIsa[a]', JBL 119 (2000), pp. 645–59.

[23] E. Schuller, '380. 4QNon-Canonical Psalms A', Qumran Cave 4.VI: Poetical and Liturgical Texts, Part 1 (DJD 11; Oxford: Clarendon Press, 1998), pp. 75–85.

significance in the manuscript is the way in which spacing occurs between psalms, as noted already for some of the manuscripts which are deemed to contain scriptural psalms collections. 4Q380 does not seem to contain any psalms known from other collections, though much of its phraseology echoes or is echoed in known scriptural psalms.

4Q381 contains a collection of psalms which are presented in a way which is standard scribal practice for psalter texts, in terms especially of spacing between poems.[24] The psalms in this manuscript are pseudepigraphically ascribed to biblical figures such as Manasseh, the man of God, a king of Judah. Parts of over a dozen compositions have survived. It could be that the contents are part of a royal collection of texts, with the man of God designating David, though Moses or some other prophetic figure might also merit such a title. On linguistic and other grounds Schuller is inclined to date these compositions to the late Persian or early Hellenistic period, and so it could be that they predate some of the compositions in the MT-150 psalter. The relation of these psalms to those which end up in the canonical MT-150 collection is very complex: for example, the psalm in fragment 15 is very close in its phrasing to Psalms 86 and 89, and the psalm in fragment 24 lines 7–11 imitates Psalm 18 and 2 Samuel 22.[25] In light of compositions such as these it becomes increasingly difficult to be precise about the development of the MT-150 psalter in the Second Temple period. Flint should have included these and other manuscripts with poetic compositions in them as he drew up his theory over the number of psalters and their varying authority in both the pre-Qumran period and at Qumran.

The significance of this for the study of the use of the psalms in other early Jewish literature or in the New Testament is difficult to discern. The presence of Psalm 151 in the LXX psalter indicates that the boundaries between the various forms of the psalter may have been more flexible than is sometimes supposed. At the least it is possible that the psalms in the MT-150 collection retained their influence because in many cases they were mediated to audiences through their use and reuse in such compositions as 4Q380, 4Q381, and 4Q448.

Miqṣat Ma'aśe Ha-Torah and the Authority of the Psalms

At this point it is appropriate to mention the late second century BCE Miqṣat Ma'aśe Ha-Torah (= MMT).[26] In the copies of MMT which preserve what its

---

[24] E. Schuller, '381. 4QNon-Canonical Psalms B', *Qumran Cave 4.VI*, pp. 87–172.

[25] On how the relationship between some of the material in 4Q381 and scriptural counterparts might be conceived, see E. Chazon, 'The Use of the Bible as a Key to Meaning in Psalms from Qumran', in S.M. Paul, R.A. Kraft, L.H. Schiffman and W.W. Fields, eds, *Emanuel: Studies in Hebrew Bible, Septuagint and Dead Sea Scrolls in Honor of Emanuel Tov* (VTSup 94; Leiden: Brill, 2003), pp. 85–96.

[26] The principal edition of the six extant manuscripts is E. Qimron and J. Strugnell, *Qumran Cave 4.V: Miqṣat Ma'aśe Ha-Torah* (DJD 10; Oxford: Clarendon Press, 1994).

editors have labelled in their composite text as C 10–11, there seems to be reference to collections of authoritative texts: 'we have [written] to you so that you may study (carefully) the book of Moses and the books of the Prophets and (the writings of) David [and the]/[events of] ages past'.[27] The text of the manuscripts here is very fragmentary, but the proposed reading of the Hebrew by Qimron and Strugnell has been largely endorsed. However, their understanding of the text as 'a significant piece of evidence for the history of the tripartite division of the Canon' has been more widely challenged.

In the first place, while the contents of the book of Moses may be obvious, it is far from clear what might constitute the books of the Prophets.[28] Furthermore, it is possible that the reconstructed passage refers to four not three groupings of texts: the Torah, the Prophets, the writings associated with David (at least the Psalms), and those books containing the description of the things that happened from generation to generation.[29] Yet others have preferred to see a reference to two groups of texts alone, the Law and the Prophets. Among this group is J. Campbell who has argued that J. Barton's view that authoritative scripture was generally collected under two headings should be applied consistently to the scrolls, Philo, Josephus and the New Testament, so that whenever a third element is introduced, such an element is no more than a clarification of what was included in the broad and open-ended category of the Prophets.[30] T. Lim also now supports a reading of this passage in MMT as endorsing two groups of scriptures, the Law and the Prophets;[31] for him, for the second century BCE the contents of both categories are somewhat unsure, but it is highly likely that Prophets included more than is now contained in that section of the rabbinic Bible.

Provided that it is acknowledged that the dominant way of referring to authoritative scripture in the late Second Temple period was in terms of the Law and the Prophets,[32] then in fact there is little difference between the various understandings of the so-called canon note in MMT. It is clear that the

---

[27] Qimron and Strugnell, *Miqṣat Maʿaśe Ha-Torah*, pp. 58–59:

11 [כתב]נו אליכה שתבין בספר מושה [ו]בספר[י] הנ[ביאים ובדוי[ד
12 [במעשי] דור ודור [

[28] I raised this problem in my brief comments in my study 'The Explicit Presentation of Scripture in 4QMMT', in M. Bernstein, F. García Martínez and J. Kampen, eds, *Legal Texts and Legal Issues: Proceedings of the Second Meeting of the International Organization for Qumran Studies, Cambridge 1995, Published in Honour of Joseph M. Baumgarten* (STDJ 23; Leiden: Brill, 1997), pp. 85–6.

[29] First argued, to my knowledge, by G. Brin in his review of the principal edition of MMT in *JSS* 40 (1995), pp. 341–42; to support his proposal Brin looks to 2 Macc. 2:13–15 which speaks of 'the books about the kings and the prophets'.

[30] J. Campbell, '4QMMTᵈ and the Tripartite Canon', *JJS* 51 (2000), pp. 181–90; depending largely upon J. Barton, *Oracles of God* (London: Darton, Longman and Todd, 1986). Campbell's approach was anticipated by A.E. Steinmann, *The Oracles of God* (St Louis, MO: Concordia Academic Press, 1999), pp. 70–71.

[31] T.H. Lim, 'The Alleged Reference to the Tripartite Division of the Hebrew Bible', *Revue de Qumrân* 20.1 (2001), pp. 23–37.

[32] As has been forcefully argued by S.B. Chapman, *The Law and the Prophets: A Study of Old Testament Canon Formation* (FAT 27; Tübingen: Mohr Siebeck, 2000).

text gives some further precision to the two categories of authoritative scripture by mentioning David, whether his psalms or an account of his deeds, and possibly some other writings which might have been associated with him as a royal figure (such as Chronicles). What is important for our purposes is the implication of the text that at least two groups of Jews in the second century BCE could debate various topics by reference to collections of written authorities and that such debate almost certainly involved some kind of written works associated with David. If Flint's argument is correct that 11QPs[a] represents a Davidic collection of psalms that belongs at least to the second century BCE, then the reference to David in MMT could be to such a Davidic collection rather than to the MT-150 collection as such. This would support his view that the collection of Psalms in 11QPs[a], 11QPs[b] and 4QPs[e] date at least to the second century BCE.

Discussing the Qumran evidence both in relation to what was held in common with the rest of Judaism and from the point of view of what was peculiarly authoritative for the sect highlights the possibility that the same dual perspective could be apparent among other groups of Jews or in some measure regionally. Greek-speaking Egyptian Judaism seems to have developed a collection of authoritative scriptures somewhat at odds with what was found in Palestine. The status of the various books of the Apocrypha remains very unclear, but the variations in the Egyptian Jewish canon can certainly be identified in the form of the psalms.

We can conclude that by the end of the second century most Jews acknowledged the authority of the Law and the Prophets, the Law as a relatively well-demarcated collection of five books, the Prophets as more open-ended. The open-ended character of the Prophets gave rise to a wide-ranging set of clarifications, some of which may have been prompted by Gentile activity with regard to Homer.[33] On this basis there was much in common between Ben Sira's grandson (in his Prologue to his grandfather's work), the author of MMT, and what Philo reports about the Therapeutae: 'Laws and oracles given by inspiration through Prophets and the Psalms and the other books whereby knowledge and piety are increased and completed' (*Contempl. Life* 25), as well as in the hints of the division of authorities in 2 Macc. 2:13–15; and this is broadly confirmed in Lk. 24:44 and, of course, by Josephus (*Against Apion* 1:37–43). Nevertheless, the questions of precisely how many categories of authoritative scriptures there should be, which books should be assigned to which category, and the issue concerning which form any book might take, must remain open for the whole of the period that Qumran was occupied.

---

[33] A. de Pury, 'Qohéleth et le Canon des *Ketubim*', *RTP* 131 (1999), pp. 163–98, locates the emergence of the collection of the Writings in the second century BCE as a reflection of Hellenistic activity, though the collection itself was the result of two earlier more limited collections, the Psalms and the so-called 'humanist writings' (the wisdom books).

Historicization

The role of David in the process of the collecting and sorting of the psalms can be linked in several ways with the development of the superscriptions of many of the psalms. Those that involve David commonly juxtapose a timeless poem with a particular event of David's life, thus providing for a reading of the psalm as if it referred to a historical event. A similar shift can be identified in the commentaries on the psalms in which a general sentiment in a psalm is identified with particular circumstances in the community's experiences.

This historicization may have several features. Part of this shift from poetry to history is the way in which the psalms are viewed as some kind of oracular text, which is unfulfilled. David, says the section on David's compositions in 11QPs[a], spoke through (the spirit of) prophecy which had been given to him before the Most High. Those with a particular eschatological perspective on life are able to recognize that if these oracular texts are ever to be fulfilled, their meaning must lie in the present (or immediate past or immediate future). The same goes for unfulfilled blessings, curses and promises.

Within an eschatological frame of reference part of the shift from poetry to history involves the figure of David in a typological fashion. As some superscripts identify the subject matter of many poems with their author David, so the eschatological reader is able to recognize the typological implications of what the psalm may say in relation to the Davidic messiah. More than most texts, probably because of their associations with David, the psalms become the scriptural basis for messianic fulfilment, seen in the New Testament in the historicized proof-texting of the passion narratives, as well as in such works as the Epistle to the Hebrews.

The Psalms in Other Early Jewish Literature

In a short study of this kind it is not possible to present an overall survey of the use of the Psalms in all extant early Jewish literature, but it is important in providing a context within Judaism on the use of the Psalms to consider at least a few examples from some of the major genres of early Jewish writing to see if any trends in the use of the psalms can be detected, especially in light of the issues which the psalms materials in the Dead Sea Scrolls have enabled us to see more clearly. Thus this section will consider examples of apocalyptic (the *Apocalypse of Abraham*), of narrative (Tobit), of wisdom literature (Wisdom of Solomon), and of testamentary writings (*Testament of Levi*). Since there is virtually no explicit use of the psalms in any of these writings,[34] it is also

---

[34] D. Dimant, 'Use and Interpretation of Mikra in the Apocrypha and Pseudepigrapha', in M.J. Mulder, ed., *Mikra* (CRINT 2/1; Assen: Van Gorcum; Philadelphia: Fortress Press, 1988), pp. 385 and 390–91, notes just two explicit quotations of the Psalms in the whole of the Apocrypha: Ps. 79:2–3 in 1 Macc. 7:16–17 and Ps. 34:20 in *4 Macc.* 18:15. Dimant comments that the use of Ps. 79:2–3 in 1 Macc. 7:16–17 is an 'example of the exegetical procedure of actualization' in

instructive to look at some early Jewish literature which contains explicit quotations of the psalms. The writings of Philo will be used for this purpose; here it is a matter of analysing the writings of a known author whose exegetical concerns and prejudices are well known.

The Psalms in an Apocalypse: The Apocalypse of Abraham[35]

No separate study of the use of the Psalms in the *Apocalypse of Abraham* exists, so the few comments offered here are put together with the assistance of a number of resources and commentaries on the *Apocalypse of Abraham*.[36] Since the themes of the *Apocalypse* concern Israel's election and the covenant with God and the leading subject of the *Apocalypse* is Abraham, it is not surprising that the scriptural bases of the *Apocalypse* are to be found principally in Genesis and other parts of the Torah. The visionary materials in parts of the *Apocalypse* are also heavily dependent on Ezekiel 1 and 10.

The most common use of the Psalms seems to lie in the divine epithets which are used at various points throughout the work, most especially in the song of *Apoc. Ab.* 17, where God is most high (17:11; cf. Ps. 47:3), protector (17:14; cf. Ps. 121:4, 5), merciful (17:12; cf. Pss 86:15; 145:8), redeemer (17:17; cf. Pss 19:15; 78:35), the one who makes light shine (17:18, 22; cf. Pss 97:11; 104:2), and the one who receives prayer (17:20; cf. Ps. 6:10). In the divine speech in *Apoc. Ab.* 9:4 a few words in which God describes himself as protector and helper echo the same description in Ps. 20:3. There need be no conscious recollection of the contexts of each epithet; rather, this represents a standard use of scriptural forms of address to God. Other aspects of divine activity may also echo parts of the Psalms: God judges with justice (27:11; cf. Pss 9:9; 96:13; 98:9), he is known by his creative word (9:9; 22:2; cf. Pss 33:6, 148:5), he pre-exists all things (9:3; cf. Pss 55:20; 119:152), he is a jealous God (27:7; cf. Ps. 79:5).

Some allusions concern the heavens and what takes place there. The heavenly cult of *Apoc. Ab.* 12:9 and 15:6–7 may generally reflect Pss 11:4 and 89:6–8 as much as any other apocalyptic tradition. The fate of the bodies of the righteous (13:10) may be described in terms which depend on Ps. 16:9–10, verses which are used to attest the resurrection of Jesus in Acts 2:25–31 and 13:34–37. Abraham's ascent with the winds (*Apoc. Ab.* 15:4) may reflect the

---

which the quotation is applied to a real historical event. Within the narrative the quotation expresses reflection on the story-line, rather than forming a part of it; the psalm is cited with minor adjustments freely made to the text.

[35] Detailed bibliography on the *Apocalypse of Abraham* can be found in L. DiTommaso, *A Bibliography of Pseudepigrapha Research 1850–1999* (JSPSup 39; Sheffield: Sheffield Academic Press, 2001), pp. 135–44.

[36] See especially, R. Rubinkiewicz, 'Apocalypse of Abraham', *OTP*, I, pp. 681–705; *idem, L'Apocalypse d'Abraham en vieux slave: Introduction, texte critique, traduction et commentaire* (Lublin: Société des Lettres et des Sciences de l'Université Catholique de Lublin, 1987).

description of the wings of the wind in Ps. 18:11. The fullness of the universe in *Apoc. Ab.* 12:10 may reflect the language of Pss 24:1, 50:12 and 89:12. Abraham is sent to enter into his inheritance (*Apoc. Ab.* 29:22; cf. Ps. 79:1). The elect one of *Apoc. Ab.* 31:1 is best understood as a reference to the messiah (cf. David in Ps. 89:4). The descriptive phrase 'holy heights' is used in *Apoc. Ab.* 13:4 (cf. Ps. 102:20; also 93:4; 148:1). Some allusions refer to the earth and what lies beneath it. Pss 18:6, 49:15, 55:16, 89:49 and 116:3 all use Sheol to describe the abode of the dead; this terminology seems to be reflected, perhaps directly from a Semitic source, in *Apoc. Ab.* 21:3. The furnace of *Apoc. Ab.* 14:5 may echo the similar phrasing of Ps. 21:10.[37] Some are apportioned to Azazel (*Apoc. Ab.* 14:6; cf. Ps. 50:18). Leviathan makes an appearance (*Apoc. Ab.* 10:10; cf. Ps. 74:14). Some have taken counsel against God (*Apoc. Ab.* 14:4; cf. Ps. 83:4). The silence referred to in some manuscripts at 24:9 may reflect that of Pss 94:17 and 115:17.

In all this it is not apparent that there is any carefully thought through dependence on the psalms or particular parts of them. The psalms are raided for suitable vocabulary to enhance narrative and other descriptions, both of the heavens and those who reside there, and of the earth and the realm of the dead. The closest thing to systematic use of the psalms is in the song of ch. 17, which seems to be a very conscious imitation of the psalmists, though the addresses are also expanded and elaborated as is to be expected in such new compositions. There does not seem to be any preference for one part of the psalter over against another, nor an undue use of psalms from the first three books of Psalms alone. Perhaps there need be no surprise about this, since the likely date of the *Apocalypse of Abraham* falls after the five books have reached some kind of stability and the variety evident at Qumran has receded.

The Psalms in Narrative: The Book of Tobit[38]

As in the Qumran scrolls, so in more than one apocryphal book there are new poetic compositions which variously rewrite, rework and re-present the scriptural psalms. The most well-known examples of this are the poems at the end of the book of Tobit and at the end of the book of Judith. Tobit 13 does indeed reuse several phrases and ideas from the psalms, such as in the characterization of God in 13:2 (cf. Ps. 89:32–34) and his activities (cf. Ps. 88:12). Many other parts of scripture are also used in the poetic pastiche that emerges. There are other poetic passages in Tobit too. So parts of Tobit's prayer in Tob. 3:1–6 adopt psalmic language, such as in the address of God as merciful and true (cf. Ps. 25:10). Sarah's prayer in Tob. 3:11–15 reworks

---

[37] This is the image which Rubinkiewicz suggests may reflect the eruption of Vesuvius in 79 CE and so may be the closest the *Apocalypse of Abraham* comes to the historicization of the Psalms.

[38] Part of the evidence in this section is derived from C.A. Moore, *Tobit* (AB 40A; New York: Doubleday, 1996) and J.A. Fitzmyer, *Tobit* (Commentaries on Early Jewish Literatures Berlin: W. de Gruyter, 2003).

various tropes from the psalms such as in the invocation to creation to praise God (Tob. 3:11; Ps. 19:1–4). The blessing in Tob. 8:5–7 rewrites various parts of Scripture, not least the psalms: the call to the heavens and all creation to praise God variously replays Pss 19:1–2; 50:6; 93:3; 97:6; 98:7; and especially Psalm 148. The closing Amen in Tob. 8:8 may reflect the structural signal from the end of each section of the psalter.

A second feature of the use of the psalms in Tobit concerns the general acknowledgement of certain motifs which are to be found in them (and also elsewhere). For example, the wisdom teaching of Tob. 4:5–6 echoes the morality espoused by Ps. 1:1–3: in light of the commandments the way of righteousness and the upright is to be chosen over against the path walked by wrongdoers. And the subsequent testamentary advice replays motifs from the psalms: 'make your ways straight' (Tob. 4:19; cf Ps. 5:9); 'let them be erased' (Ps. 69:29); and the concern for present wealth (Ps. 34:11). Or again the sneering of Tobit's friends (Tob. 2:8) recalls the hostility of friends described in Pss 31:12 and 38:12. Tobit's view of the grave as a place of eternal darkness (Tob. 5:10) may reflect the same view in Ps. 88:7.

A third feature of the use of the psalms in Tobit concerns various idioms: 'south of Kedesh' (Tob. 1:2; Ps. 89:13); 'Lord, do not turn your face from me' (Tob. 3:6; Pss 13:1; 27:9; 30:7); 'he said in his heart' (Tob. 4:2; Pss 10:6; 53:1); the patriarchs as 'prophets' (Tob. 4:12; Ps. 105:15); 'the light of my eyes' (Tob. 10:5; Ps. 38:11).

Overall it is not surprising that there is not great use of the psalms in a narrative work such as Tobit. Nevertheless the use of the psalms in the poetic sections of the book, together with the inclusion of several phrases from them is evidence that many of the psalms were a resource for the narrator. In this respect it is worth noting that since Tobit was certainly complete by the end of the third century BCE, it is not surprising that the vast majority of allusions which can be noted with some security can be derived from the psalms that belong now in the first three books of the psalter. Though slight, the use of the psalms in Tobit seems to reflect exactly the process of the stabilization of the psalter which is now found in the evidence from Qumran.

The Psalms in Testamentary Literature: The Testament of Levi[39]

There are no quotations from the psalms in the Testament of Levi and it is rare to find any certain allusions either.[40] Perhaps the most noteworthy reflection of

---

[39] The comments here are based especially on the detailed work of H.W. Hollander and M. de Jonge, The Testaments of the Twelve Patriarchs: A Commentary (SVTP 8; Leiden: Brill, 1985), pp. 129–83.

[40] S. Delamarter's useful index of scriptural references in OTP lists 17 cross-references to the psalms for the whole of the Testaments of the Twelve Patriarchs: S. Delamarter, A Scripture Index to Charlesworth's The Old Testament Pseudepigrapha (London: Sheffield Academic Press, 2002), pp. 23–25.

the psalms in *T. Levi* is the way in which the elaborate new poem in praise of the Law in *T. Levi* 13 echoes in recognizable but independent ways the praise of the Law to be found in Psalm 1. In *T. Levi* 4:2 there seems to be a deliberate adoption of language from Ps. 2:7 ('Son') for describing the priestly heir of Levi. The language of the psalm is thus taken and extended in its referent. It is possible that this takeover is partly sustained through an implicit understanding of the role of the priest in Psalm 110, though that psalm does not use the title 'Son'. Psalm 110 appears to have influenced the description of the new priest in the prophetic poem of *T. Levi* 18.[41]

More straightforward use of psalm language can be discerned in various places. Levi describes the iniquity on the walls of the unrighteous (*T. Levi* 2:3) in a way echoing the language of Ps. 55:11. The description of the angel opening the gates of heaven for Levi at the moment of his vision of the Most High (*T. Levi* 5:1) has echoes of Ps. 24:7–10, and the reference to the 'holy temple' in the same verse echoes the Greek phraseology of Ps. 18:7, while the throne of God is described in Ps. 47:9. In some instances the precise choice of Greek words seems to depend on usage in the psalms. The manifestation of God's majesty with its accompanying shaking (*T. Levi* 3:9) uses the same verbs as in the theophanic passages of Pss. 96:9 and 98:7; the combination with elements of judgement might depend on similar language in Pss. 96:9, 97:2 and 98:7; the additional motif of melting is also to be found in Ps. 97:5. Here are a collection of allusions in a neighbouring set of psalms which could well have influenced the choice of vocabulary of the translator or author of *T. Levi* 3. Or again, in *T. Levi* 7:1 that God 'sets at nought' the Canaanites echoes the verbal usage of Pss 44:6, 53:6 and 108:14. Levi's reference to the risk his children might be of becoming a laughing-stock (*T. Levi* 14:1) echoes the use of the same term in Pss 43:14 and 79:4. The phrase 'light of the law' (*T. Levi* 14:4) is found in Ps. 119:105. God is 'magnified' (applied to Levi's descendant in *T. Levi* 18:3) most especially in Pss 35:27, 40:17, 69:31 and 70:5.

Overall the use of the psalms in the *Testament of Levi* is not very extensive. In one or two instances, which may have also appealed to a Christian redactor, the Greek text seems to suggest that the psalms are being fulfilled in what Levi promises his descendants. But in most cases the psalms are simply a repository of suitable language for use in visionary descriptions of the heavens and various other matters. When particular choices of vocabulary are made with the psalms in mind, then the choice is often suitably based on the use of the word in its original context in the psalms, but that context is not exploited to the full in the construction of new poems.

The questions which are posed by the evidence concerning the psalms in the

---

[41] This poem has sometimes been associated with Hasmonaean priest-kings, since the priesthood is described in language of royal sovereignty; the association would be the expression of hope for an eschatological priest-king far surpassing the merits of any member of the Hasmonean house. Once again, it is possible to notice historical elements in the poetry.

Dead Sea Scrolls barely affect the reading of the use of the psalms in the *Testament of Levi*. Allusions run from throughout the psalter, not principally the first three books. As would be expected, it is the LXX text type which is clearly reflected in the use of certain key phrases rather than any other type of text. There is plenty of new poetry in the *Testament of Levi* but, unlike some of the new poetry in the scrolls, it is not overly dependent in vocabulary or form on the scriptural psalms.

The Psalms in Wisdom: The Wisdom of Solomon[42]

A characteristic trait of Jewish wisdom literature, whether in its scriptural form or in the forms known in the apocrypha and pseudepigrapha, is that it is commonly expressed poetically. Not surprisingly, facets of such poetic compositions are dependent on the psalms. In a detailed study of the psalms in the Wisdom of Solomon, P.W. Skehan confidently asserted that 'there need be, it would seem, no doubt that the author of Wis had knowledge of the complete collection of Pss as we now have it, especially in its Greek form'.[43] Skehan outlines the role of the influence of the psalms in several places in Wisdom where the psalms seem to be the sole or principal scriptural influence on what the author has said.

The first example concerns the opening verse of Wisdom in juxtaposition with Wis. 6:1–2, 21. These verses reflect Ps. 2:10–12. All the technical terms of address and the verbs in Ps. 2:10 feature either in Wis. 1:1 or 6:1 and 11. Together the use of the terminology of the psalm in this way seems to indicate that, as in the psalm, the author of Wisdom intended his work for as wide an audience as possible, even if it was addressed in the first place to fellow Jews. The dependence of these sections of Wisdom on the Psalms is further confirmed by noting that some of the phrasing of Ps. 2:8 (LXX) has also been taken up in Wis. 6:1.[44] Overall the opening sections of Wisdom 1 are dependent on several other psalms too: Wis. 1:2–3 is reminiscent of the distinctive Greek terminology of Ps. 94:9, Wis. 1:12 recalls the justice of man in Ps. 112:3 and 9.[45] In a similar way Wis. 11:2–4 seems to depend heavily upon the thought of Ps. 107:4–6 together with Pss 114:8 and 118:10–12; the passages from the psalms are being used as the basis for the structure of the thought of the passage in Wisdom. A similar structural use of psalm material may take place in Wis. 13:10, 17; 14:11; and 15:5, 6, and 15; these variously play on Pss 115:4–8 and 135:15–18, with the use of Ps. 115:4–7 in Wis. 15:15 as the most explicit.

---

[42] See Dimant, 'Use and Interpretation of Mikra', pp. 410–15.
[43] P.W. Skehan, *Studies in Israelite Poetry and Wisdom* (CBQMS 1; Washington, DC: Catholic Biblical Association of America, 1971), p. 149. Ch. 24 in this collection of essays is entitled 'Borrowings from the Psalms in the Book of Wisdom'; this section of this study is heavily dependent on Skehan's work in combination with a number of other studies.
[44] Skehan also notes that Ps. 148:11 (LXX) seems to have been used in Wis. 6:1.
[45] Cf. the similar idiom in Pss 111:3 and 119:142 applied to God's justice.

Several other passages in Wisdom may reflect the phraseology of the psalms.[46] Most noteworthy, however, is the way several phrases from various psalms have been woven together in Wis. 5:7–8: 'the way of the Lord we have not known' (cf. Pss 95:10; 25:4; 27:11), 'What has our arrogance profited us? And what good has our boasted wealth brought us?' (cf. Pss 49:7; 37:20). In several verses from the same pericope the language of the psalms is also apparent. A further significant reflection of the terminology of the psalms is apparent in Wis. 7:27: Wisdom, 'while remaining in herself, renews all things' (cf. Ps. 104:24, 30). Yet another striking instance is the way Wis. 16:22, 24 reflects the phrasing of Ps. 148:8: the manna is 'snow and ice' in order to show how the same group of forces listed by the psalmist are recognized as at work in the marvellous events of the Exodus.

As with Tobit, it is no surprise that the prayer of Wisdom 9 is based in part on reworking several phrases from the psalms: Wis. 9:3 ('rule the world in holiness and righteousness; and pronounce judgement in uprightness of soul') seems to involve allusions to Ps. 72:1–2, a psalm which has Solomon in its superscription and so may reflect the same process of historicization which we have noted for the role of David in relation to several of the psalms, if not the whole psalter in the scrolls found at Qumran.

The author of Wisdom was well acquainted with the psalms in Greek and used them as a source of phrasing and motifs, but also as the basis for structuring some of his ideas and sequences of thought. Since the work belongs to the end of the first century BCE, it is not surprising to see the author using the full range of the psalms as reflected in the Greek psalter which was probably known to him much as it survives today in the major witnesses.

The Psalms in the Writings of Philo of Alexandria[47]

A survey of Philo's readings of the Psalms has been undertaken by D. Runia.[48] He began by noting the well-known observation that the Judaism whose forms are preserved in Greek was overwhelmingly preoccupied with the Torah. Of

---

[46] Skehan has noted the following by way of example: Wis. 2:10–12 (Pss 10:8–9; 37:12–14); 4:1 (Ps. 112:6); 4:7–18 (Pss 37, 49); 4:17a (Ps. 49:11); 4:17b–c (Ps. 12:6); 4:18b (Pss 2:4; 37:13; 59:9); 10:2 (Ps. 29:11); 10:10 (Ps. 27:11); 10:16 (Ps. 76:13); 10:20 (Ps. 105:3); 10:21 (Ps. 8:3); 15:1 (Ps. 86:5, 15); 16:2 (Pss 65:10; 78:18–20); 16:5 (Pss 74:1; 79:5); 16:7 (Ps. 78:34); 16:12 (Ps. 107:20); 16:13–15 (Ps. 78:34, 39); 16:20 (Ps. 78:25).

[47] On Philo as Bible exegete, see, e.g., P. Borgen, 'Philo of Alexandria', in M.E. Stone, ed., *Jewish Writings of the Second Temple Period* (CRINT 2/2; Assen: Van Gorcum; Philadelphia: Fortress Press, 1984), pp. 259–64; Y. Amir, 'Authority and Interpretation of Scripture in the Writings of Philo', in M.J. Mulder, ed., *Mikra* (CRINT 2/1; Assen: Van Gorcum; Philadelphia: Fortress Press, 1988), pp. 421–53.

[48] D. Runia, 'Philo's Reading of the Psalms', *Studia Philonica* 13 (2001) in D.T. Runia and G.E. Sterling, eds, *In the Spirit of Faith: Studies in Philo and Early Christianity in Honor of David Hay* (BJS 332; Providence: Brown Judaic Studies, 2001), pp. 102–21; based in part on V. Nikiprowetzky, *Le commentaire de l'Écriture chez Philon d'Alexandrie: son caractère et sa portée; observations philologique* (ALGHJ 11; Leiden: Brill, 1977).

Philo's 1161 quotations of scripture, only 41 are texts from outside the Pentateuch, of which 20 are from the Psalms.[49] These 20 quotations are explicitly introduced and follow the text of the LXX very closely in the vast majority of cases. Almost all the quotations are to be found in the Allegorical Commentary and Runia proposes that this is because of the exegetical approach that Philo adopts in that work. That approach is characterized by an explicit introductory formula which in every case, bar one, mentions the Psalms as hymns or hymnody: in three instances the prophetic dimension of the psalmody is emphasized and in three discipleship of Moses is mentioned. Through the terminology that is used in these introductory formulae it is clear that Philo viewed the utterances of those who wrote the Psalms as inspired, being composed with divine assistance. Philo never uses the term ψαλμός which suggests to Runia that 'we have to do with a reflex that can be frequently observed in Philo's writings, namely to avoid terms that are somehow peculiarly biblical and substitute the word that was commonly used in Greek literary contexts'.[50]

Philo's quotations from the Psalms are all very short, nearly all of them of ten words or less. Perhaps this economy suggests he was quoting from memory. Furthermore, there is no reason to suppose that Philo's acquaintance with the Psalms was from some other secondary source. Since there are so few quotations from outside the Pentateuch in Philo's voluminous writings, however, one may wonder why Philo bothers to cite the Psalms at all. Runia suggests that he quotes them to provide evidence or proof of a particularly daring exegesis, or as pertinent illustrations of his exegesis, or in a couple of instances to provide new material which permits him to extend his exegesis. In no case does the psalm quotation control the exegesis; it is always used secondarily. Associated with the principal text of the exegesis through catchword, the psalm quotations commonly concern the relationship of the soul to God, as befits their spiritual character, and their motifs are allegorized as would be expected in Philo's train of thought.

In his description of the Therapeutae (*Contempl. Life* 25) Philo notes that they withdraw to their cells with only laws and oracles pronounced through the prophets and hymns and other things that increase and make knowledge and piety perfect. For Runia it is clear that Philo 'here refers to the tripartite

---

[49] Runia lists these as follows: *Giants* 17 (Ps. 78:49); *Unchangeable* 74 (Ps. 101:1); 77 (Ps. 75:8); 82 (Ps. 62:11); *Agriculture* 50, 52 (Ps. 23:1); *Planting* 29 (Ps. 94:9); 39 (Ps. 37:4); *Confusion* 39 (Ps. 31:19); 52 (Ps. 80:7); *Migration* 157 (Pss 80:6; 42:4); *Heir* 290 (Ps. 84:11); *Flight* 59 (Ps. 113:25); *Names* 115 (Ps. 23:1); *Dreams* 1.75 (Ps. 27:1); 2.242 (Ps. 27:1); 2.245 (Ps. 65:10); 2.246 (Ps. 46:4); *QG* 4.147 (Ps. 69:33); 4.232 (Ps. 65:2). Runia also lists ten indirect allusions to the psalms, mostly in the Exposition of the Law, from which he concludes that the exegetical process in the Exposition of the Law is intriguingly distinct from that found in the Allegorical Commentary.

[50] Runia, 'Philo's Reading of the Psalms', p. 113.

division of the Hebrew Bible into Torah, Prophets and Writings'.[51] As with what may have followed the so-called canon notice in MMT, the 'interpretation of the final phrase, however, cannot be determined with exactitude'.[52] Whatever the case, as in MMT (and Luke 24) the Writings seem to be characterized by the Psalms. Overall, however, Runia concludes that 'the Book of Psalms is thus present in Philo's Judaism, but it is read in a quite distinctive manner, at a considerable remove from the use of the Psalter both in Qumran and in Early Christian Writings'.[53] In light of the psalms in the Dead Sea Scrolls, it should also be noted that all but two of Philo's quotations of the psalms come from the first three books of the Psalms.

Conclusion

Beyond the evidence of the so-called psalms manuscripts from Qumran, evidence which is now widely available in lists and editions, this study has tried to draw out something of the significance of the psalms scrolls from Qumran from a range of perspectives. In some ways the range and diversity of the evidence means that we probably know less than we thought a generation ago. The questions have changed and multiplied as the material has been more closely studied. Beyond matters such as the range of psalters available at Qumran for all or part of its existence, there are issues concerning David and his typological status, issues concerning the oracular and authoritative status of the psalms, issues concerning their suitability for the understanding and interpretation of historical events.

This study has not attempted to reconsider the use of the psalms in the sectarian scrolls found at Qumran, but has rather tried to see whether the kinds of questions posed by the manuscript copies of psalms found in the Qumran caves influence in any significant way how the use of the psalms may be understood in early Jewish literature broadly conceived. There are two ways of summing up the significance of what is presented here. On the one hand, the answer seems to be that those questions offer some suitable issues for reconsidering the background of the use of the psalms. Among those issues are the form of the psalter used, the character of poetic reworking (which is both a pre-canonical and post-canonical affair), and the tendency to historicize the poetry of the psalms. Keeping these issues in mind has offered some insight, such as noticing that Tobit's allusions to the psalms are almost entirely from the first three books of the psalter which were stabilized relatively early. In addition the historicizing tendency that is discernible now in the additional superscriptions of the psalms in Hebrew manuscripts from Qumran and in the

---

[51] Runia, 'Philo's Reading of the Psalms', p. 116.
[52] Runia, 'Philo's Reading of the Psalms', p. 116.
[53] Runia, 'Philo's Reading of the Psalms', p. 119.

role of David has long been recognized as a characteristic of the development of the LXX psalter; this LXX tendency now has a wider frame of reference. On the other hand, because so much of early Jewish literature is from the turn of the era or later and has only been preserved by Christians and in Greek or other versional languages, the dominant influence of the psalter in Greek reduces somewhat the overall significance of what has been learnt from the Qumran psalms manuscripts about the text and transmission of the psalms in the late Second Temple period in Palestine. Philo's use of the Greek psalter is limited in any case.

Nevertheless there are some issues here which are probably of interest to those who study the use of the psalms in the New Testament. The ability of Jewish authors to rework and reuse poetic passages which had become authoritative is important for the better understanding of many of the allusions to the psalms in the poetic passages of the New Testament. The interest in the role of David as prophetic psalmist illuminates several New Testament references to him. The open-ended character of the psalter in Palestine may be discerned in a few places. The choice of psalms in explicit quotations seems to be generally in tune with what has been pointed out here: apart from those which obviously carry a messianic significance, the overwhelming majority of quotations and allusions to the psalms derives from the first three books of the psalter as it now stands. Thus overall the individual concerns of the authors of the New Testament books control much of their use of the psalms, and their writing in Greek often restricts their base material to the psalms as known in the LXX, but the Qumran psalms manuscripts display something of a wider frame of reference for the transmission and use of the psalms which needs to be borne in mind and is occasionally significantly illuminating.

2

The Psalms in Mark's Gospel

Rikk Watts

Introduction

In keeping with the rest of the New Testament, Mark's interest in the Psalms is second only to Isaiah, whose hope of a new exodus – itself heavily influenced by psalmic language[1] – provides the overarching paradigm for his gospel.[2] Four psalms, each cited or alluded to at least twice, play a major role in Mark.[3] There is an allusion to Psalm 2 in the divine attestation during Jesus' baptism in Mark's prologue (Ps. 2:7 in 1:11) and another at the transfiguration in Mark's 'way' section (9:7). However, it is in Mark's final section, Jesus' arrival in Jerusalem, that the heavens open as it were,[4] with more than half of the seven usages being on Jesus' lips. Psalm 118 is cited twice: vv. 25–26 in the popular acclamation during the 'triumphal' entry (11:9–10) and vv. 22–23 at the culmination of the parable of the tenants (12:10–11). Ps. 110:1 is cited as the basis of Jesus' rhetorical question about the Christ being David's son (12:36) and is alluded to when Jesus finally reveals his identity during his trial (14:62). Finally, Psalm 22 dominates Mark's crucifixion scene, with v. 19 'cited' at the division of Jesus' garments (15:24), v. 2 at Jesus' cry of dereliction (15:34), and v. 8 alluded to in the mockery of the passing crowds (15:29).

The approach here will follow a growing body of opinion in assuming that Mark, as other New Testament writers, is not unaware of the original contexts and contemporary understandings of Israel's scriptures and that these often provide hermeneutical clues as to the significance of the surrounding New Testament material. Consequently, both the original sense and first-century interpretations of relevant psalms will be considered. This applies across the board since one assumes that Mark includes material because it serves his purpose regardless of whether it comes from the tradition or his own redaction.

---

[1]   R.N. Whybray, *The Second Isaiah* (OTG; Sheffield: JSOT Press 1983), pp. 20–42.
[2]   R.E. Watts, *Isaiah's New Exodus and Mark*; (WUNT 2/88 (Tübingen: J.C.B. Mohr [Paul Siebeck], 1997 Grand Rapids: Baker, 2000).
[3]   There are possible echoes of Ps. 118:22 in Mk 8:31; Ps. 49:8–9 in 8:37; Ps. 22:7 in 9:12b; and Ps. 22:15 in 10:33–34; but they are not immediately clear. Interestingly, Pss 118 and 22 both appear twice later in Mark, see below.
[4]   E.g. H.C. Kee, 'The Function of Scriptural Quotations and Allusions in Mark 11–16', in E. Earle Ellis and E. Grässer, eds, *Jesus und Paulus* (Göttingen: Vandenhoeck & Ruprecht, 1975), pp. 165–83.

The Prologue

Psalm 2:7 in Mark 1:11

Although Mark's introductory sentence explicitly appeals to Israel's scripture, it has important contacts with Graeco-Roman motifs. His 'good news' and 'son of god' (if original) challenge the claims of the imperial cult.[5] Mark has set the stage for a clash of imperia: Yahweh's kingdom (cf. Jesus' announcement in 1:14) versus Rome (cf. the centurion's confession in 15:39). It is surely significant, then, that at the climax of his prologue, Jesus' baptism, the divine attestation begins with an allusion to Psalm 2, a famous royal psalm which not only designates the addressee as Yahweh's chosen king but does so precisely in the context of a clash of political powers.

It is widely agreed that 'you are my son' (1:11) alludes to Ps. 2:7. The words are almost identical to the LXX/Hebrew, differing only in having a more natural order (cf. the LXX's chiastic 'my son are you'). Although Mark's 'beloved' could allude to Gen. 22:2 (cf. vv. 12, 16), it probably reflects an earlier interpretative trend later found in the *Targum's* 'beloved as a son to his father are you to me'.

Doubtless based on Yahweh's promise to David (2 Sam. 7:14; cf. Ps. 89:26), Psalm 2 is often designated an enthronement psalm (cf. 'today', v. 7).[6] However, not only does v. 7 suggest that the king has already taken his throne – 'I will tell of the decree the Lord *declared* to me' – but the events envisaged seem subsequent to the king's ascension.[7] Taking the opening verses at face value, the psalm is a response to the nations' rebellion against Yahweh's universal kingship, expressed on earth through his anointed (vv. 1–3).[8]

His terrifying anger aroused, the Lord who sits in the heavens mocks the nations' pretensions (v. 4; cf. Isa. 40:15, 17, 22) since he himself has installed 'my king, on Zion, my holy mountain' (v. 6). Sharing in the Lord's universal kingship but faced with this looming conflict, the Davidic scion recalls Yahweh's covenantal promise given by prophetic decree 'You are my son, this day I have begotten you' (v. 7; cf. 2 Sam. 7:14a; 2 Kgs 11:12; Exod. 4:22). That Psalms 1 and 2 were conjoined in some traditions (*b. Ber.* 9b; Acts 13:33) suggests that as Yahweh's son the king must submit to and delight in Yahweh's instruction if he is to enjoy prosperity (Ps. 1:2; cf. 2 Sam. 7:14b).[9]

Recalling Yahweh's promise that he will inherit the nations (v. 8) and

---

[5]   C.A. Evans, 'Mark's Incipit and the Priene Calendar Inscription: From Jewish Gospel to Greco-Roman Gospel', *JGRCh* 1 (2000), pp. 67–81.

[6]   E.g. H.-J. Kraus, *Theology of the Psalms* (trans. Keith Crim; Minneapolis: Augsburg, 1986), pp. 111–22.

[7]   John T. Willis, 'A Cry of Defiance – Psalm 2', *JSOT* 47 (1990), p. 36.

[8]   As Willis admits the accession of a new king would be an ideal time to rebel, but clearly not all rebellions happen at that time ('A Cry of Defiance', pp. 44–46).

[9]   Perhaps explicitly the Deuteronomic Torah (Deut. 17:18–20), W.H. Brownlee, 'Psalms 1–2 as a Coronation Liturgy', *Bib* 57 (1971), pp. 321–36.

shatter their rebellion (v. 9), and because the Lord's powerful intervention is near (v. 12),[10] the king warns them to serve the Lord and give due homage to his anointed (vv. 11–12).[11]

Although the Davidic kingship ceased with the exile, this psalm, along with other royal psalms, was preserved in Israel's psalter probably because the Davidic covenant was eternal (e.g. 2 Sam. 7:16; 22:51; 23:5; cf. Isa. 55:3–5). As such it articulates an eschatological/messianic vision of Yahweh's ultimate victory over the nations. Thus, *Psalms of Solomon* 17 (especially vv. 21–25, 30–32) is almost a commentary on Psalm 2. It emphasizes the destruction of hostile rulers (vv. 22–25) and the subservience of the nations to the messiah (vv. 29–31) whose rule, as in Psalm 2, is itself subordinate to and an extension of Yahweh's kingship (vv. 1–4). Given Judah's dire straights (vv. 5–20), the messianic Davidic king will purge Jerusalem of God's enemies both within and without (vv. 22, 30, 36).

At Qumran, 4QFlor [174] 3:18–19 also understands Ps. 2:1 as referring to 'the end of days' when Yahweh will raise up the fallen branch of David (citing Amos 9:11) to save Israel (3:12–13). The temple will be established (3:3–6, cf. 2 Sam. 7:12–14) and Yahweh will defeat the sons of Belial. He will raise up 'the branch of David' to whom, citing 2 Sam. 7:14, 'I will be a father ... and he will be a son' (3:11; cf. Ps. 2:7; Heb. 1:5). Likewise, 1QSa [28a] 2:11–12 describes the future salvation as the time 'when God begets the Messiah'.

In addition to describing the Davidic king as 'beloved' (v. 7) the *Targum* has Yahweh responding to the Gentiles' rebellion by speaking to them 'in his strength' (v. 5). The Davidic king's responsibility to safeguard the sanctity of the Temple is explicated in v. 6's 'I have anointed my king and set him over my sanctuary'. Finally, the warning in v. 12 includes an admonition to the nations to 'accept instruction' (cf. *Midr. Ps.* 2.9, where the Messiah's victory comes because he occupies himself with Torah, as per the close link between Pss 1 and 2).

Later rabbinic literature appealed frequently to Ps. 2:1–4, often in the context of Yahweh's eschatological victory over Gog and Magog and Israel's defeat of idolaters (e.g. *b. Ber.* 7b; *Exod. R.* 1:1; *Midr. Ps.* 2:2, 4; the latter being an action of Yahweh as warrior citing Isa. 42:13). The psalm's subject is often understood to be the messiah (*b. Sukk.* 52a; *Midr. Ps.* 2:3, 9, 10).[12]

With this background, Mark's use of Psalm 2 takes on greater significance. His opening mixed citation, the rent heavens, and descent of the Spirit already indicate his story's eschatological setting and the imminence of the Lord's

---

[10] H.-J. Kraus, *Psalms 1–59, 60–150* (trans. Hilton C. Oswald; 2 vols.; Minneapolis: Augsburg, 1988, 1989) I, p. 129.

[11] See Peter C. Craigie, *Psalms 1–50* (WBC19; Waco: Word Books, 1983), p. 64.

[12] M.A. Signer, 'King/Messiah: Rashi's Exegesis of Psalm 2', *Prooftexts* 3 (1983), p. 294; cited in Joel Marcus, *The Way of the Lord: Christological Exegesis of the Old Testament in the Gospel of Mark* (Louisville, KY: Westminster/John Knox, 1992), pp. 60–61.

saving intervention (cf. 1:15).[13] And as in the Psalm, God in heaven declares that his Davidic messianic agent is none other than Jesus (cf. 10:47; 11:10; on Ps. 110:1 in 12:36, see below), his beloved and obedient son (e.g. 3:29; 9:7; 12:28–34), through whom the Lord's universal kingship is expressed and whose first public action is the proclamation of the kingdom of God (1:14–15). Not surprisingly, his designation as 'son of God' collides with and repudiates the claims of the Roman imperial cult: God has only one son (cf. again the centurion's confession in 15:39).

At the same time, Mark's opening citation connects Jesus with the coming not of a messianic figure but God himself. The designation 'son of God' is already therefore ambiguous, going beyond the metaphorical language of the Davidic covenant as the demons themselves seem to perceive (1:24; 3:11; 5:7; cf. 2:7–12; 4:41).

In short order conflict also emerges as a major Markan motif. His Jesus promptly engages the hostile demonic forces who hold Israel in bondage (1:21–28, 34, 39; 3:10–11, 15, esp. 22–27; 5:1–20; 6:7, 13; 7:24–30; 9:12–29; cf. 4Q174).[14] The military overtones in the Legion exorcism[15] underscore this motif, even intimating that the Davidic messiah's dominion is now extending 'to the nations' (5:1–20; cf. 7:24–8:10). Interestingly, given the *Targum's* emphasis on Yahweh's strong and terrifying speech (2:5), the signal characteristic of Jesus' conflict with the demons is his powerful word and their terrified response (1:23–27; 5:7–13; cf. 1:7).

But opposition comes from other quarters too. Israel's leadership (2:7, 16, 18, 24;[16] 3:2, 6) and particularly the Jerusalem authorities (3:20; 7:1; 11:18, 28; 12:12–13) quickly align themselves against Jesus (1:22, 27; 2:10; 3:15; 11:28; 12:35–40).[17] Consequently, just as Qumran's vision of the restored Davidic branch focused on the temple (e.g. 1QSa [28a]; cf. *Tg. Ps.* 2:6) and *Psalms of Solomon* 17 on the purging of Jerusalem, so too Mark's Gospel. Finally arriving in Jerusalem, Jesus' intercalated Temple demonstration and fig-tree cursing (11:12–14, 17b, 20–21)[18] is followed by the announcement of the Temple's imminent destruction and apparent replacement with another built around him (13:2; 12:10; see below).

And just as the rebels are urged to 'kiss the son' (Ps. 2:12), or with the *Targum*, 'accept instruction', so too Israel must submit to Jesus' teaching (cf. Mk 3:28–35). Interestingly, it is in the Temple that Jesus' opponents receive the most instruction (seven occasions in 11:17–12:40).

---

[13] Watts, *Isaiah's New Exodus*, pp. 53–121.

[14] Watts, *Isaiah's New Exodus*, pp. 144–64; Marcus, *The way of the Lord*, p. 67.

[15] J.D.M. Derrett, 'Contributions to the Study of the Gerasene Demoniac', *JSNT* 3 (1979), pp. 2–17.

[16] Note the appeal to the example of David, 1 Sam. 21:1–7.

[17] See also J.D. Kingsbury, *Conflict in Mark* (Minneapolis: Fortress Press, 1989).

[18] W.R. Telford, *The Barren Temple and the Withered Tree* (JSNTSup 1; Sheffield: JSOT, 1980) and Watts, *Isaiah's New Exodus*, pp. 310–37.

On the Way

Psalm 2 and the Transfiguration

The next clear allusion to the psalms is again from Ps. 2:7, also as a divine attestation (Mk 9:7). Almost identical to the baptismal voice (though without the Isa. 42:1 allusion) the only modification is the substitution of the demonstrative 'this' for the personal pronoun 'you' because the voice now addresses the disciples.

Immediately following the first passion prediction (8:31), the transfiguration almost begins the second of Mark's three Isaianic new exodus panels, his 'way' section (8:27–10:52). In Isaiah 40–55 the crucial issue in the announcement of salvation was the confrontation between Israel and Yahweh over the manner of her deliverance. Israel's questioning of Yahweh's plan revealed her 'blind and deaf' idolatrous mindset (Isa. 42:18–19; 43:8; cf. 6:9–10). Nevertheless, Yahweh promises to lead his people along a 'way' they do not know (Isa. 42:16). Ultimately Israel refuses and her idolatrous rejection of Yahweh's 'way' means the delay of the new exodus.[19] Deliverance now awaits an obedient 'servant' whose faithful suffering (Isa. 53) will occasion Israel's release from exile (Isa. 52) and restoration to a renewed Jerusalem (Isa. 54).[20]

The issue resurfaces here. Again the nation resists the Lord's way in both the leadership's opposition (Mk 8:31) and Peter's 'demonic' remonstrance (8:15, 33). Like the partially healed man (8:22–26), 'blind' Peter does not 'know' the way the Lord (8:31–38).[21] Bracketing as it were Mark's first section, Psalm 2 again reiterates the Lord's response. Jesus is his beloved S/son whose instruction, as in *Targ. Ps.* 2:12, must be heard (Mk 9:7b). But in a startling reversal both the wielding of the rod of iron (Ps. 2:9) and the new exodus way in which God leads his blind people are centred in the Davidic messiah's death, subsequently developed primarily in terms of Isaiah's 'suffering servant' (Mk 9:12; 10:45).[22]

---

[19] See R.E. Watts, 'Consolation or Confrontation? Isaiah 40–55 and the Delay of the New Exodus', *TynBul* 41 (1990), pp. 31–59; cf. Antje Labahn, 'The Delay of Salvation within Deutero–Isaiah', *JSOT* 85 (1999), pp. 71–84.

[20] Watts, *Isaiah's New Exodus*, pp. 278–79, and the literature cited therein, especially A.R. Ceresko, 'The Rhetorical Strategy of the Fourth Servant Song (Isaiah 52:13–53:12): Poetry and the Exodus-New Exodus', *CBQ* 56 (1994), pp. 42–55.

[21] For a fuller treatment, see Watts, *Isaiah's New Exodus*, pp. 221–57.

[22] With perhaps some influence of Psalms 22 and 118; Watts, 'Jesus' Death, Isaiah 53, and Mark 10:45' in William H. Bellinger, Jr, and William R. Farmer, eds, *Jesus and the Suffering Servant* (Pennsylvania: Trinity Press International, 1998), pp. 125–51; cf. A.Y. Collins, 'The Appropriation of the Individual Psalms of Lament by Mark', in C.M. Tuckett, ed., *The Scriptures in the Gospels* (BETL 131; Leuven: Leuven University Press – Peeters, 1997), pp. 223–41.

In Jerusalem

Psalm 118 and the 'Triumphal Entry'

The first clear citation of a psalm is in the mouths of the exultant crowd as they escort Jesus to Jerusalem. Their acclamation is in chiastic form, (a) 'Hosanna! (b) Blessed is the one who comes in the name of the Lord! (b') Blessed is the coming kingdom of our ancestor David! (a') Hosanna in the highest heaven!' (NRSV; vv. 9b–10), with the first two elements deriving from Psalm 118. 'Hosanna' is a transliteration of the Hebrew, 'save now' (הושיעה נא), taken from v. 25's 'Please, Yahweh, save now; please, Yahweh, prosper now'. The first 'blessed...' refrain is a direct quotation from the first half of v. 26 LXX, which accurately translates the Hebrew. But in a significant departure, whereas the Psalm reads, 'we bless you (LXX: have blessed you) from the house of the Lord' (v. 26b), Mark's crowd blesses the coming Davidic kingdom.

Psalm 118 appears to have been composed as a 'royal song of thanksgiving for military victory' which was then incorporated into a processional liturgy (cf. *Targ. Ps.* 118, *b. Pes.* 119a).[23] Although not explicitly identified, the individual in view destroys the surrounding hostile nations in the name of the Lord, which strongly suggests a Davidic king (vv. 10–12; the *Targ.* is explicit). Recalling how he was threatened on all sides (vv. 10–13; cf. Ps. 2:1–3) and employing the language of the exodus, the psalmist rejoices in Yahweh's mighty intervention on his behalf (vv. 14–18; cf. Exod. 15:2, 6).[24] Fresh from victory (vv. 15–16), he approaches the Temple, asks the gate-keepers to grant him entrance (vv. 19–20), and is joined by the congregation in offering thanksgiving (vv. 19–24). He is then addressed by a group of priests from within the sanctuary. They respond to Yahweh's victorious intervention first with a celebratory request that he continue to bless his people (v. 25) and second by blessing, 'from within the house of the Lord', the king who comes in his name (v. 26; cf. Ps. 2:8). If Psalm 2 celebrates the promise given to the Davidic king in the face of the threatening nations, Psalm 118 is its victorious realization.

Included in the fifth and final book of palms (Pss 107–150), Psalm 118 more specifically concludes that group known as the *Hallel* (Pss 113–118) which was traditionally connected with Passover and subsequently other feasts (*m. Sukk.* 3:9, 11; 4:5; *b. Sukk.* 45a, 45b; *b. 'Arak* 10a; *Pesiq. Rab.* 51:7). This is not surprising since Exodus theology permeates the collection, with Psalm 118 particularly focusing on the Temple as the goal of the eschatological new

---

[23] Leslie C. Allen, *Psalms 101–150* (WBC 21; Waco: Word Books, 1983), p. 124.

[24] Following Mitchell Dahood, *Psalms III: 101–150* (AB 17A; New York: Doubleday, 1970), p. 155; cf. the *Targum's* numerous expansionist references pointing to David (vv. 26, 28; cf. vv. 22–25) and *b. Pes.* 119a.

exodus.[25] Incorporated in the *Hallel* collection, Psalm 118 became a communal anticipation of the nation's future deliverance under a Davidic king. In the context of Passover, itself connected in various traditions with new exodus deliverance,[26] the Markan crowd's blessing on 'the coming kingdom of our ancestor David' is entirely understandable.

The *Hallel* psalms played a significant role in later Jewish eschatological expectation, with Psalm 118 in particular being associated with the last judgement (*Midr. Ps.* 118.10) and, as with Psalm 2, the eschatological war against Gog and Magog (*Midr. Ps.* 118:12; 26:6; *Pesiq. Rab.* 51:7; cf. *y. Ber.* 2:4d.49), Messianic salvation (*Pesiq. Rab.* 36:1; *Midr. Ps.* 118:22; cf. 118:24), and the restoration of Jerusalem (*Lev. R.* 37:4; cf. 30:5).[27] Although some question whether these perspectives were current during the first century, the new exodus aura surrounding the *Hallel* in general, that the central individual in Psalm 118 is almost certainly a Davidic figure, and Mark's unselfconscious messianic application within a new exodus framework,[28] suggests that Psalm 118 was already understood along these lines.

Mark has carefully orchestrated his preceding account to resonate with Psalm 118's new exodus associations. He interprets Jesus' release of the strong man Beelzebul's captives as Yahweh's deliverance of his people from exilic bondage (3:27; Isa. 49:24–26).[29] Jesus' healings in general recall Isaiah's new exodus (Isa. 35:5–6), the feedings the first exodus provision,[30] and his authority over the sea and subsequent drowning of a demonic legion (4:35–5:13), Israel's deliverance at the sea (Exod. 15).[31] Such authority belongs only to Yahweh but then in the psalms the Davidic king's victories are only a participation in and extension of God's power over creation (cf. the Exodus in

---

[25] Especially Jutta Schröten, *Entstehung, Komposition und Wirkungsgeschichte des 118. Psalms* (BBB 95; Weinheim: Beltz, 1995); R.G. Kantz, 'Die Gnade des täglichen Brots: Späte Psalmen auf dem Weg zum Vaterunser', *ZTK* 89 (1992), pp. 36–38; 'Die Tora Davids: Psalm 1 und die doxologische Fünfteilung des Psalters', *ZTK* 93 (1995), pp. 23–28; Erich Zenger, 'The Composition and Theology of the Fifth Book of Psalms, Psalms 107–45', *JSOT* 80 (1998), p. 92.

[26] *Mekilta* on Exod. 12:42, R. Joshua b. Hananiah, c. 90; cf. *Targ. Yer.* I Exod. 21:42; *Targ. Yer.* II Exod. 15:18, and later, *Exod. R.* 18:12 on 12:24.

[27] Cf. Joachim Jeremias, *The Eucharistic Words of Jesus* (trans. N. Perrin; Philadelphia: Fortress; Press, 1977), p. 256 n. 3; and the thorough survey in Michel Berder, 'La Pierre Rejetée par les Bâtisseurs': *Psaume 118, 22–23 et son emploi dans les traditions juives et dans le Nouveau Testament* (EBib n.s. 31; Paris: Gabalda, 1996), pp. 170–241, who notes that in addition to the more common Davidic interpretation the 'stone' was also understood as Abraham, Jacob, Joseph and Israel.

[28] This includes the numerous echoes of Isa. 35 in the Bartimaeus account, Watts, *Isaiah's New Exodus*, p. 309, and its clear linkage with Jesus' arrival, D.R. Catchpole, 'The "Triumphal" Entry' in E. Bammel and C.F.D. Moule, eds, *Jesus and the Politics of His Day* (Cambridge: 1984), pp. 319–21; C.A. Evans, *Mark 8:27–16:20* (WBC 34b; Nashville: Thomas Nelson, 2001), pp. 139–40.

[29] Watts, *Isaiah's New Exodus*, pp. 146–52.

[30] Watts, *Isaiah's New Exodus*, pp. 169–79.

[31] Watts, *Isaiah's New Exodus*, pp. 157–63.

Ps. 89).[32] The nations' defeat in Isaiah's new exodus also reflect Davidic theology[33] with Yahweh's superiority over the nations and their idols again evident in his supreme authority over creation, notably the Exodus (Isa. 43:14–17).[34] As Paul Duff has argued (albeit on different grounds) Jesus' arrival at Jerusalem is in a very real sense the climax of 'the march of the divine warrior'.[35]

For Mark, if at the outset Psalm 2 designates Jesus as the recipient of God's promise of imminent victorious intervention, then at the culmination Psalm 118 fittingly applies to this Davidic messianic S/son of God, who fresh from his astounding new exodus and new creational victories, comes in splendid procession to Jerusalem and its Temple.

But there is also a profound irony. The restoration of Zion and its Temple as the place of prayer for all nations will require its destruction. For unlike the psalm, Israel's response is bitterly divided. The attendant pilgrim crowds rejoice, but ominously the Temple hierarchs offer no blessing from the house of the Lord (cf. Ps. 118:26b) and Israel's unwelcome messianic king returns to Bethany (11:11). This implied censure provides the basis for Mark's second clear citation of a psalm, again Psalm 118.

Psalm 118 and the Rejected Stone

Given Psalm 118's particular focus on the Temple, Mark's chiastic structuring of the two citations around Jesus' Temple demonstration is probably deliberate:

Jesus, the 'triumphant' Davidic king (Ps. 118:25–26)	(11:1–11)
Cursing of the fig-tree	(11:12–14)
Jesus' Temple demonstration (Isa. 56:7/Jer. 7:11)	(11:15–19)
Withered fig-tree, and mountain-moving	(11:20–25)
Jesus, the rejected but vindicated Davidic king	
(Ps. 118:22–23)	(11:27–12:12)

If the first citation is celebratory, the second has darker connotations. From early on opponents have plotted his demise (3:6). This rejection becomes the focus of Mark's 'way' section (ἀποδοκιμασθῆναι 8:31), structured as it is around the three passion predictions (8:31–32; 9:30–31; 10:32–34).[36] Arriving in Jerusalem and in the tradition of such entries, Jesus' first public act is in the

---

[32] J.J.M. Roberts, 'The Enthronement of Yhwh and David: The Abiding Theological Significance of the Kingship Language of the Psalms', *CBQ* 64 (2002), pp. 679–80.

[33] Andrew Wilson, *The Nations in Deutero-Isaiah: A Study in Composition and Structure* (Lewiston: Edwin Mellen, 1986), pp. 48–60.

[34] Watts, *Isaiah's New Exodus*, p. 160, and the literature therein.

[35] P.B. Duff, 'The March of the Divine Warrior and the Advent of the Greco-Roman King: Mark's Account of Jesus' Entry into Jerusalem', *JBL* 111 (1992), pp. 55–71.

[36] For a detailed defence of the literary integrity of this section and its main themes, see Watts, *Isaiah's New Exodus*, pp. 124–32.

Temple.[37] But by refusing to welcome him, the Temple authorities have shown themselves to be insurrectionists (λῃσταί, cf. 11:17b; 15:27). In keeping with (a) entry patterns where a refusal to welcome was considered an act of rebellion,[38] (b) contemporary understandings of Psalm 2 which envisaged the purging of Jerusalem's leadership, and (c) Mark's opening citation of Mal 3:1, it is no surprise that his Jesus performs an acted parable of judgement in the Temple intercalated with the cursing of the fig-tree (11:12–25).[39]

Thus when questioned by a Temple delegation comprised of priests, lawyers and elders as to his authority, Jesus' retort is apposite (11:27–33). Because Israel's leadership rejected John (Mk 9:13; cf. Mal. 3:23), they are unprepared for Yahweh's coming and are now under Malachi's curse (3:24).[40] Far from blessing Israel's rightful messianic king 'from the house of the Lord' (Ps. 118:26), those into whose keeping it was given have challenged and rejected him, the very Lord of the Temple.

This brings us to the parable of the insurrectionist tenants (12:1–12). Drawing on traditional Jewish imagery[41] – particularly Isa. 5:1–7's juridical parable which contrasts Yahweh's provision for his people with their less than faithful response[42] – Jesus' story constitutes a searing condemnation of the nation's leadership. The use of 'vat' and 'tower' (12:1) as metaphors for the altar and the sanctuary in several contemporary sources again highlights the centrality of the Temple (e.g. 4Q500:3–7; t. Me'il. 1:16, citing Isa. 5:2; t. Sukk. 3:15, citing Isa. 5:1–2; Targ. Isa. 5:1–7; cf. 4Q162; 1 En. 89:56, 67, 72–73).[43]

In spite of some recent attempts to argue otherwise, the referents are clear enough: the fenced vineyard with vat and tower is Zion with its Temple and altar, the owner is Yahweh, the vine his people, the tenants Israel's leadership, the servants the prophets, and the owner's 'beloved' son Jesus. 'Beloved' occurs only twice elsewhere in Mark: the two divine attestations which allude to Psalm 2 (1:11; 9:7) and wherein Yahweh affirms his Davidic son's inheritance in the face of insurrection (κληρονομίαν, Ps. 2:8), which inheritance is the focus of the parable (cf. κληρονόμος, 12:7). Israel's new exodus deliverance has been inaugurated through Yahweh's messianic son.

---

[37] E.g. Catchpole, 'The "Triumphal" Entry', pp. 319–21; Duff, 'March of the Divine Warrior' and Evans, Mark, p. 139.

[38] E.g. when Alexander the Great's request for entry and access to the Temple was rebuffed by the Tyrians, he laid siege to their city, see Duff, 'March of the Divine Warrior', 61–2. It seems likely that Mark understands the Jerusalem authorities' rejection of Jesus along similar lines, cf. Mk 13.

[39] See Watts, Isaiah's New Exodus, pp. 310–37.

[40] Telford, The Barren Temple, p. 163.

[41] See e.g. the rabbinic vineyard parables in Midr. Tanh. B. Qed. 6 on Lev. 19:2; Exod. R. 30:17; Midr. Prov. 19:21; and Sipre Deut. p. 312, Evans, Mark, pp. 220–21.

[42] See Evans, Mark, pp. 224–28; cf. Jer. 2:21; Isa. 5:1–7; Ezek. 19:10; Hos. 10:1; Jer. 7:25; 25:4; Amos 3:7; Zech. 1:6.

[43] Watts, Isaiah's New Exodus, p. 342 and n. 279.

But Jerusalem's insurrectionist leaders have rejected him. As Psalm 2 warned and its intertestamental interpreters understood, those who rebel against God's kingship expressed through his anointed would be destroyed whether in David's day or the day of his eschatological son (cf. Isa. 65:6–15; 66:3–4, 14b–16, 24). If in the past Israel's failure to produce fruit incurred judgement (e.g. Isa. 5:5–6; *3 Bar.* 1:2) then so it is now, hence the fig-tree incident (Mal. 3:25).[44]

But there is not only judgement. The superintendence of God's people-vineyard is to be transferred (12:9). But to whom? Mark's Jesus concludes with an appeal to Psalm 118 but this time from earlier in the poem (vv. 22–23): 'A stone which the builders rejected has become the head of the corner. This is from the Lord and it is wonderful in our eyes' (12:10–11). The citation is identical to the LXX which accurately renders the Hebrew (adding only a relative pronoun to aid the syntax).

The oft-remarked Hebrew wordplay between 'son' (בן) and 'stone' (אבן), cf. Exod. 28:9–12, 21; 39:6–7, 14; Lam. 4:1–2; Zech. 9:16; cf. Matt. 3:9 // Lk. 3:8), does not translate into Greek. The 'builders' metaphor is used in Qumran (CD 4:19–20; 8:12), rabbinic (e.g. *b. Shabb.* 114a; *b. Ber.* 64a), and Christian literature (Acts 4:11; 1 Cor. 3:10) of 'scholars' or 'religious leaders' and locates the parable within the larger setting of Jesus' rejection by the Temple authorities.[45] Likewise ἀποδοκιμασθῆναι ('to reject') occurs in Mark only here and in Jesus' first passion prediction where he is 'rejected' by the elders, chief priests and scribes (8:31). The latter, surely significantly, follows immediately after the first public confession of Jesus as the Messiah (8:29) which confession, when echoed by Bartimaeus and the crowds, sets the stage for the present confrontation. The tenants' murder of the son is only the final outcome, to which the passion predictions pointed: the rejection of the messianic son-stone by Israel's teacher-builders (cf. *Targ. Ps.* 2:12).

Given that Mark's Jesus has twice been designated David's messianic son, the later *Targum* to Psalm 118 merits attention. Relating the psalm specifically to David, the *Targum* substitutes 'child' for 'stone' adding that this child 'was among the sons of Jesse and he was worthy to be appointed king and ruler' (v. 22). By adding references throughout to Jesse, his family, David, and even Samuel's offering sacrifice, the *Targum* appears to read the last half of the psalm as a liturgy based in particular on 1 Sam. 16:1–13 where David, although initially passed over, is ultimately appointed king first over the tribes of Judah (2 Sam. 2:1–4; *Targ. Ps.* 118:27b) and then Israel (2 Sam. 5:1–9; *Targ. Ps.*

---

[44] On the issue being the absence, not so much of fruit, but even of the tasty buds that heralded it, R.H. Gundry, *Mark: A Commentary on his Apology for the Cross* (Grand Rapids: Eerdmans, 1993), p. 636.

[45] J.D.M. Derrett, '"The Stone that the Builders Rejected"' in *Studies in the New Testament* vol. 2 (Leiden: Brill, 1978), pp. 60–67; K.R. Snodgrass, *The Parable of the Wicked Tenants* (WUNT 27; Tübingen: J.C.B. Mohr [Paul Siebeck], 1983), p. 96.

118:29). The psalm is thus a celebration of rejected David's inexorable accession to the throne and that with prophetic attestation (cf. the 'servants' in Jesus' parable). If this reflects an earlier tradition, then Mark's appeal to Psalm 118 is even more fitting: Jesus *will* become king over God's vineyard people – unlike Isaiah's parable, it is not the vineyard but the tenants who will be destroyed.

However, Mark's larger context clearly foreshadows the Temple's destruction. The resolution apparently lies with the cornerstone metaphor which resumes the architectural imagery of 'vat' and 'tower' and provides the only hint of rebuilding and that centred on Jesus himself. This is not unlike Qumran where remnant Israel (e.g. CD 1:4–5) constitutes a new Temple. 1QS 8:7–14 describes the faithful as 'an everlasting plantation, a holy house ... and the foundation of the holy of holies ... the precious cornerstone'. In a direct application of Isaiah's new exodus language, they are to prepare in the desert 'the way of the Lord', citing Isa. 40:3, a not insignificant text for Mark. Likewise, 4QFlor [174] 3:1–13 speaks of God's fulfilling his promise to build David a house, understood to be a temple consisting of people, namely, the Qumran community.[46] We have here a combination of Isaiah's new exodus with, in fulfilment of God's promise to David, the building of a people-Temple. In Mark's new exodus it is the rejected Davidic son-stone Jesus who becomes the pre-eminent stone of a new people-Temple (14:58; 1 Pet. 2:4–7; cf. 'stone', 'building', and 'wonder' in Mk 13:1–2).[47] Again, Psalm 118's particular connection with the new exodus restoration of the Temple makes it especially appropriate.

But if Mark's Jesus knows he is to die, how could this be? Given the threefold declarations of his vindication after death (8:31b; 9:31b; 10:34b), it is not unlikely that Mark's Jesus here alludes to his resurrection: the rejected stone *will* become the cornerstone.[48] This would indeed be 'the Lord's doing' and 'wonderful in our eyes' (12:11). Here again, the language of seeing Yahweh's wonderful deeds originates in the defeat of Egypt at the Exodus (Exod. 15:11; 34:10). It is echoed in the celebration of King Yahweh's worldwide victory over the nations in general (LXX Ps. 97:1–2) and provides the basis of their eschatological defeat in Micah's vision of the new exodus (LXX Mic. 7:15–20). At the same time, the new exodus was also understood as a 'resurrection' (Ezek. 37:1–14) in which a Davidic king would oversee a reconstituted people and a new sanctuary (37:15–28).

---

[46] Jacqueline C.R. De Roo, 'David's Deeds in the Dead Sea Scrolls', *DSD* 6 (1999), pp. 50–51. This would still be the case even if such a people-Temple were only anticipatory of the proper future Temple; cf. Rev. 21 and John Kampers, 'The Significance of the Temple in the Manuscripts of the Damascus Document', in Robert A. Kugler and Eileen M. Schuller, eds, *The Dead Sea Scrolls at Fifty* (SBLEJL 15; Atlanta: Scholars Press, 1999), pp. 185–6, 196–7.

[47] See further Marcus, *The Way of the Lord*, pp. 119–25.

[48] Cf. Marcus, *The Way of the Lord*, p. 114.

Psalm 110 and the Question about David's Son

The next two appeals to the psalms are drawn from the same passage – Ps. 110:1 – and both occur at climactic moments in Jesus' final confrontation with the Jerusalem leadership.

Following the parable of the wicked tenants, the first appeal concludes the four Temple controversies (12:13–37).[49] Chiastically arranged around the citation,[50] Mark's account has Jesus, having defeated all comers, taking the offensive by asking his own question (12:35–37). Citing v. 1 he questions the adequacy of the scribes' conception of the Messiah. The citation follows the LXX except that 'under' replaces the LXX's 'footstool of'. Although the Hebrew uses different words to distinguish speaker and recipient (יהוה; אדני) the LXX has only κύριος but preserves the distinction through syntax.

Concluding the short collection ascribed to David found in the fifth book (Pss 108–10), Psalm 110 is yet another royal psalm.[51] The first question concerns the addressee: who is the lord (אדני) of whom the psalmist speaks? Most modern scholars take the addressee to be either David or his royal descendants, possibly at enthronement. The parallels with Psalm 2 are noteworthy and suggest that Psalm 110 is a new interpretation of that material.[52] The primary concern of both is the nations' subjugation (2:1–3, 8–12; 110:1a–2, 5–6), envisaging a shattering of Israel's enemies (2:9; 110:3, 6) and describing Yahweh's anger against opposing kings (2:5a; 110:5). In both victory is assured because the Davidic king shares in, and is yet subordinate to, Yahweh's universal kingship, whether as 'son' (2:7; cf. 110:3) or as one who sits at Yahweh's right hand (110:1; cf. *Midr. Ps.* 2.7).

Nevertheless, Psalm 110 heightens several key features. To sit at Yahweh's right hand is to have the highest possible authority and honour short of usurpation (cf. 1 Chron. 28:5; 29:23; 2 Chron. 9:8) and implies blessing (cf. Gen. 48:13–14) and participation in his power (Exod. 15:6; Pss 80:18; 98:1) and righteousness (Ps. 48:10). This language, though consistent with, is more explicit than Ps. 2:7's 'son'. Whereas in Psalm 2 the nations take counsel against the Lord's anointed, here the king rules in the midst of his enemies, implying that they now surround him. In Psalm 2 Yahweh invites the king to ask for the nations as his inheritance (v. 8) but in Psalm 110 the king sits while the Lord fights for him (v. 1, cf. vv. 5–6). The latter is a common enough holy war motif (e.g. Exod. 14:13; 2 Chron. 20:17; cf. Isa. 7:4–9) and a staple of David's victories (2 Sam. 5:10, 17–25; 8:6, 14). Finally, we move from a warning in Psalm 2 to the rather more grotesque outcome of Yahweh's

[49] Cf. J. Dewey, *Markan Public Debate* (SBLDS 48; California: Scholars Press, 1977), pp. 156–63.

[50] Marcus, *The way of the Lord*, p. 130.

[51] On the considerable debate over form and setting, see Allen, *Psalms 101–150*, p. 83; Kraus, *Theology of the Psalms*, p. 111. However, in order to avoid anachronism I am here assuming Mark's Jesus acceptance of Davidic authorship as representing the common first century view.

[52] Zenger, 'Composition and Theology', p. 90.

intervention: shattered heads and a corpse-filled earth (Ps. 110:5–6; cf. the finale of Isa. 66:24).

What is unique to Psalm 110, however, is the designation of the Davidic king as a priest after Melchizedek.[53] Mentioned only in Gen. 14:18–20 (cf. Josephus, *Ant.* 1:180; Philo, *Leg. All.* 3:79–82), Melchizedek was a priest of 'God most high' whose superiority Abram recognized in being blessed by and tithing to him (cf. *b. Sanh.* 108b where God defeats the kings while Abraham sits at his right hand).

Whatever the origin of this connection, a sacerdotal role is difficult to reconcile with Israel's thorough-going separation of priesthood and kingship. If that separation is assumed, the verse just might refer to the Davidic king's leadership over a priestly nation (Exod. 19:6), his cultic role (2 Sam. 6:14–18; 1 Kgs 8:14, 22, 55, 62–63; Jer. 30:21), and responsibility for the purity of Israel's worship (e.g. 2 Kgs 18:4–5; 22–23; 2 Chron. 17:6; 29–31; 34–35). On the other hand, however difficult, it must be admitted that a fundamental reorientation in Israel's polity could be in view.

It might be these two factors – sitting at God's right hand and the Melchizedekian priest-king connection – that explain the relative absence of this text in intertestamental literature.[54] Nevertheless, there are some indications that both ideas were taken up. Given the military achievements of the priestly Hasmonaeans, Psalm 110's dual royal-priestly reference might lie behind their attempts to legitimate their fusing of priestly and royal roles (e.g. 1 Macc. 14:41; *T. Moses* 6:1, *Jub.* 32:1; cf. Ps. 110:4; *T. Levi* 8:3, 14).[55]

It seems probable too that Psalm 110's unique understanding of exaltation also informs two other important passages: (a) the exaltation of Isa. 52:13's obedient yet suffering servant, understood *sans* suffering as the Messiah in the *Targum*, who will be 'high and lifted up' and which language is elsewhere appropriate only to God (Isa. 6:1; 14:13–14; 33:10), and (b) the exaltation in Dan. 7:9–14 of the suffering saints and/or their representative, one 'like a human being', who will enjoy eternal dominion and glory which is again normally reserved for Yahweh.[56] Interestingly, both texts and their key individuals are connected with Israel's hope of new exodus restoration and with Mark's Jesus (e.g. Mk 8:38; 10:45; 14:62).[57] Given Mark's emphasis on Jesus' suffering it is also intriguing that *T. Job* 33:3 alludes to Ps. 110:1 when the

---

[53] The Hebrew of v. 4, על דברתי, is very difficult; we follow here the LXX's κατὰ τὴν τάξιν Μελχισεδεκ.

[54] Cf. Martin Hengel, *Studies in Early Christology* (Edinburgh: T & T Clark, 1995), p. 179. See further Donald M. Hay, *Glory at the Right Hand* (Nashville: Abingdon, 1973) and David R. Alexander, *The King-Priest of Psalm 110 in Hebrews* (SBL 21; New York: Peter Lang, 2001).

[55] Hay, *Glory*, p. 25.

[56] Hay, *Glory*, p. 26; Hengel, *Studies*, pp. 180–84.

[57] On Mk 10:45 and Isa. 53, see Watts, 'Jesus Death'.

righteous sufferer Job vindicates himself by pointing to his throne at the right hand of God.[58]

The apparently first-century *Similitudes* of *1 Enoch* also reflects the influence of Psalm 110. In a context which combines Isaianic servant and Danielic son of man motifs, it applies them to Yahweh's Elect One who sits on God's throne at the end of days (51:3; 55:4; 61:8; 62:2).[59] Not much later, Rabbi Akiba is rebuked for profaning the divine presence because he understood two thrones in Dan. 7:9, one for God and one for David (*b. Hag.* 14a), again probably under the influence of Psalm 110.[60]

In Qumran 11QMelch [13] describes Melchizedek's return to preside over Israel's new exodus liberation, the final atonement of her sins, judgement of her enemies, and the inauguration of God's kingly reign (Isa. 52:7 in 2:16, 24; cf. *b. Sukk.* 52b where Melchizedek returns in the messianic age). Commonly regarded as an exalted angelic figure there is some warrant for seeing him as a human messiah.[61] If so, his exercising judgement over Israel's enemies (2:13–14) can really only be explained by the influence of Psalm 110 – it could hardly have come from Genesis 14 – in spite of the absence of an explicit citation.[62] Likewise, 4Q491 11 col. 1:12 seems to be drawing on Psalm 110 in its description of a figure who, after victory and the vindication of the priestly community in the eschatological battle, is enthroned among the gods.

The *Targum* applies the psalm to David but eschatologically such that he is to be appointed leader of the age to come because of his righteousness (v. 4). In later rabbinic materials, God defeats the kings while Abraham sits at his right hand (*b. Sanh.* 108b) although *Midr. Ps.* 18:29 has the Messiah sitting at God's right hand while Abraham is relegated to his left (citing Ps. 110:1, 5). *Midr. Ps.* 2:7 cites Ps. 110:1 where the son is true servant Israel, who will be the Messiah, while 2:9 appeals to both Isa. 52:13 and Dan. 7:13–14, texts we already suggested were influenced by Psalm 110.

In summary, Psalm 110 seems to have informed two streams of speculation: the combination of priestly and royal roles (Hasmonaeans; 11QMelch [13]) and the idea of supreme eschatological exaltation, particularly of a messianic/son of man figure and often after tribulation, over God's and his opponents (cf. Isa. 52; Dan. 7; etc.).

---

[58] *T. Levi* 18 describes a new priest who will understand the word of the Lord (v. 2), whose star will rise in the heaven like a king (v. 3; cf. Ps. 110:3), who shall have no successor (v. 8; cf. Ps. 110:4), and who shall bind Beliar and grant to his children authority to trample over wicked spirits (v. 12; cf. Ps. 110:1) but the presence of a number of apparently Christian interpolations (e.g. vv. 6–7, 9) dilutes its relevance.

[59] Including the possible influence of Isa. 52:13 and 53:12, M. Black, 'The Messianism of the Parables of Enoch', in James H. Charlesworth, ed., *The Messiah* (Minneapolis: Fortress Press, 1992), p. 159, *infra.*

[60] Cf. Donald Juel, *Messianic Exegesis: Christological Interpretation of the Old Testament in Early Christianity* (Philadelphia: Fortress Press, 1988), p. 138, but cf. *Midr. Ps.* 18:29.

[61] Paul Rainbow, 'Melchizedek as a Messiah at Qumran', *BBR* 7 (1997), pp. 179–94.

[62] Rainbow, 'Melchizedek', p. 184; Marcus, *The Way of the Lord*, p. 133.

What role does Psalm 110 play in Mark 12? In apparent agreement with the scribes, Mark's Jesus assumes that David is speaking prophetically of the Messiah.[63] Some have suggested that he is questioning the popular assumption that the Christ would be a son of David.[64] But Mark's use of the psalms thus far and his unqualified recording of public Davidic-messiah affirmations clustered conspicuously around Jesus' arrival in Jerusalem (10:47, 48; 11:10) make this highly unlikely.[65] Instead, the point, as πόθεν suggests,[66] is whether the scribes are justified in calling the Messiah 'merely' 'the son of David' when speaking by the Spirit David himself calls him 'lord'.[67] Given the previously noted parallels between Psalms 2 and 110, this also raises questions as to what the former's 'son' (of God) might mean when applied to Mark's Jesus.

This naturally leads to a consideration of Psalm 110's unique combination of priestly and royal integration and highly exalted status. Given Jesus' messianic identity, Mark's prolonged focus on his Temple actions could be to underline his ultimate responsibility over the Temple and the purity of Israel's worship (as noted above). It might also be that Mark highlights Jesus' priestly role in teaching and safeguarding the sanctity of the sanctuary precisely because of Psalm 110's Melchizedek association. If so, the citation implies both Jesus' priestly authority and, by virtue of its Melchizedekian character, that it supersedes that of the present Temple authorities (cf. Heb. 7).

But Mark's Jesus also seems to be after something more. Just as Isa. 52:13–53:12, Dan. 7:9–14, 11QMelch [13], *1 Enoch*, and R. *Akiba* suggest a trajectory of exaltation based on Psalm 110, there is much in Mark that indicates Jesus is indeed far more than David's human son.[68] Mark's Jesus has already identified himself in terms of Isaiah 52–53 and particularly Daniel 7 with their implicit notions of exaltation. All three elements of Mark's opening combined citation – Isa. 40:3; Exod. 23:20; and Mal. 3:1 – are closely associated not with a messianic figure but the presence of God himself. Mark's Jesus exercises a solely divine prerogative in offering forgiveness of sin (2:5–7), behaves like God in his rebuking and then walking on the sea (4:39–41; 6:49–52), commands healings rather than requests them, and silences the demons whose cries of recognition suggest more than a merely human messiah. It appears that Mark has been preparing the reader for this moment all along.

---

[63] The Hebrew נאם (v. 1) is characteristic of prophetic utterances; cf. 2 Sam. 23:2; 11QPs^a [5] 4–11; Acts 1:16; b. *Sukk.* 25a.

[64] E.g. W.H. Kelber, *The Kingdom in Mark* (Philadelphia: Fortress Press, 1974), p. 96; P.J. Achtemeier, "'And He Followed Him'': Miracles and Discipleship in Mark 10:46–52', *Semeia* 11 (1978), pp. 115–45; B.D. Chilton, 'Jesus ben David: Reflections on the *Davidssohnfrage*', *JSNT* 14 (1982), pp. 88–112.

[65] Marcus, *The way of the Lord*, pp. 151–2; Evans, *Mark*, pp. 274–75.

[66] Meaning not negation but an unsettling or surprising fact that requires explanation, Watts, *Isaiah's New Exodus*, p. 287.

[67] Evans, *Mark*, pp. 274–75.

[68] See J. Marcus, 'Mark 14:61: "Are You the Messiah-Son-of-God?"', *NovT* 31 (1989), pp. 136–37.

Finally, if the significance of messianic identity was the only issue in question the first strophe of Ps. 110:1 would have sufficed. But Mark's Jesus adds Yahweh's promise to make the Messiah's enemies his footstool. This is already happening to the demonic hosts (cf. 11QMelch [13] 2:13). But in the language of Ps. 110:2, the mighty sceptre of the Lord from Zion is also evident in Jesus' powerful silencing of Israel's authorities (12:34b).[69] More ominously, this part of Psalm 110 only reinforces the point of the parable of the tenants. Those who refused to bless Jesus from the house of the Lord but instead plotted his death will be shattered and placed under his feet by Yahweh himself.

At his baptism and transfiguration Mark's Jesus was privately designated son of God. But just as Psalm 110 and its trajectories represent a heightening of Psalm 2 so too as Mark's narrative nears its zenith his Jesus publicly discomfits the scribes with the inadequacy of their messianic expectations. Jesus cannot merely be David's messianic son. He is also David's exalted Lord, Son of God, who as Mark's unfolding portrayal of his extraordinary and super-human authority suggests uniquely sits at God's right hand sharing in his blessing, authority and righteousness. Furthermore, God will see to it that he rules in the midst of his enemies, shattering kings in the day of his wrath, and if need be, their Temple-safe house (13:1ff, cf. Jer. 7:11 in Mk 11:17b). Just what this means will soon be revealed when at the final moment of confrontation Mark's Jesus again appeals to Ps. 110:1.

Psalm 110 and Jesus as the Exalted Son of Man

The second appeal to Psalm 110 occurs during Jesus' trial and constitutes the final straw of his confrontation with official Israel (14:53–65; cf. 8:31; 11:27). Without any previous indication Mark records the accusation that Jesus declared he would destroy this Temple (ναόν) made by man and replace it in three days with a different one (ἄλλον) of divine origin – perhaps alluded to in the cornerstone saying. Whatever the full significance of the charge or Jesus' refusal to be drawn, the reference to the ναός is clearly important for Mark (cf. 15:29, 38) and coheres with Psalm 110's combination of royal and priestly prerogatives, Jesus' view of the exalted status of David's son, his action in the Temple, and the Olivet discourse (13:2).

However, the High Priest's question concerning Jesus' messianic identity is clearly pivotal. In Mark's story it seems highly unlikely that Israel's educated elite would have failed to perceive the implications of Jesus' manner of arrival in Jerusalem, his Temple demonstration especially given the Jeremiah 7 justification, his parable of the tenants, or his earlier jibe over Psalm 110. If they are already aware of messianic tempers that pose a threat to their regime and failing to elicit an answer on the temple accusation, it might be that Mark's

[69] Marcus, *The Way of the Lord*, p. 135.

High Priest considers a direct question on the nature of Jesus' messiahship as the way to force the issue. His response suggests that he got everything he hoped for and more.

The debate over what actually constitutes blasphemy is too extensive to canvas here.[70] In my view, it is not so much Jesus' claim to be the Messiah, son of God *simpliciter* (Ps. 2:7),[71] as it is his scriptural gloss including what it implies for his opponents. Universally recognized as an allusion to Ps. 110:1 the first person context necessitates changes in the LXX's second person imperative 'sit' and first person possessive pronoun 'my'. Mark's Jesus substitutes the participle 'sitting' and the circumlocution 'the power' (cf. *1 En.* 62:7; *Sipre Num.* §112). The latter's referent is clear enough given the chiastic arrangement within the Dan. 7:13 allusion which seems designed to stress Jesus' close relationship with God.[72] It might also be a deliberate echo of God's 'powerful' sceptre wielded on behalf of his king in the day of his 'power' so as to stress what is at stake (Ps. 110:2). The combination of Psalm 110 and Daniel 7 (cf. *Midr. Ps.* 2:9) is not surprising seeing the former probably influenced the latter.

While Psalm 110, Daniel 7, and *1 Enoch* allowed that God could choose to endow an individual with extraordinary status, for a mere human to claim such for himself is entirely another matter.[73] To assert that one will sit at God's right hand and thereby arrogate God's prerogatives to oneself is offensive enough. But, after all the preceding tension, to do so at one's own trial by citing Daniel 7 which itself presupposes a courtroom confrontation, wherein a cloud-riding son of man is vindicated over beast-like and idolatrous nations is incendiary. Add to this Psalm 110's Melchizedekian promise with its implication of a change of polity (read demise of the present Temple leadership; cf. 11QMelch [13]) and Yahweh's crushing of the Messiah's enemies, and the lines could hardly be more clearly drawn. Mark's Jesus not only claims the highest possible status for himself but accuses his opponents not only of being Yahweh's enemies but of effectively playing the role of the fourth beast with the High Priest as the little horn. The trajectory of warning in Psalm 2 culminates in a devastating denunciation against a faithless Jerusalem (Mk 13:1ff; Isa. 66:24).

Psalm 22 and the Passion Narrative

Not surprisingly the outraged authorities swiftly orchestrate Jesus' end. Again the psalms are prominent as Mark's passion narrative is replete with echoes of

---

[70] See, e.g., Darrell L. Bock, *Blasphemy and Exaltation in Judaism* (Grand Rapids: Baker, 2000).

[71] Marcus, 'Mark 14:61', sees this as restrictive, meaning a 'son-of-God' rather than a 'son-of-David' version of the Messiah. But his evidence derives from material where an alternative model is explicitly canvassed. Mark has none. Marcus is right to note that son of God in Mark is more than merely a Davidic messiah. But this happens because of Jesus' scriptural response at 14:62, not in the High Priest's question that precedes it. In other words the issue turns not on Jesus' use of son of God but what he means by it.

[72] Cf. Gundry, *Mark*, p. 886.

[73] Bock, *Blasphemy*, pp. 202–206.

what are sometimes called the 'Psalms of the Righteous Sufferer'.[74] Generally, Mark's portrayal of Israel's leadership who plan to take Jesus 'by guile' 'to kill' him (14:1; cf. Ps. 10:7–8) echoes the psalmist's enemies who characteristically operate with guile, slander and false witness as they plot the innocent's demise.[75] Other details from these psalms abound: betrayal by 'one who eats with me' (14:18; Ps. 41:10), Jesus' soul being 'deeply saddened' (14:34; Pss 42:6, 12; 43:6), being 'delivered' into the 'hands' of sinners (14:41; Pss 140:5–9; 36:12; 71:4; 82:4), enemies seeking testimony to put him to death (14:55; Pss 37:32; 54:5), false witnesses (14:57; Pss 27:12; 35:11), Jesus' silence (14:61; 15:4–5; Ps. 38:13–15; cf. Isa. 53:7), the offering of vinegar (15:36; Ps. 69:22), and friends observing from a distance (15:40; Ps. 38:12). Although not all are equally apparent or necessarily intentional, the overall effect strongly suggests that Mark interprets Jesus' suffering in such terms.

Our concern, however, is with Psalm 22's pervasive influence on the crucifixion narrative: the division of Jesus' garments (v. 19; Mk 15:24), mockery and head-shaking (v. 8; 15:29), 'save yourself!' (v. 9; 15:30–31), reviling (v. 7; 15:32), and the cry of dereliction (a citation of v. 2; 15:34). Belonging to the collection attributed to David which constitutes the first book of the Psalms (1–41), Psalm 22 uniquely progresses from the deepest distress and suffering (vv. 1–21b ET) to the farthest-reaching praise and thanksgiving for deliverance (vv. 21c–31).[76]

The opening verses state the singularly terrifying situation: the overwhelming sense of God-forsakenness (vv. 2–3). The sufferer responds with a reaffirmation of God's holiness (v. 4)[77] – an allusion to Yahweh's being enthroned in Zion (Ps. 99:3; Isa. 57:15)[78] – and recalls his past faithfulness in delivering those who trusted in him (vv. 5–7). Even so, the psalmist has been reduced to scorn, his trust parodied in the derision of his enemies (vv. 13–14, 17, 21–22). They see his dehumanizing and extreme suffering (vv. 15–16, 18) as a sign of God's utter abandonment (vv. 8–10)[79] and divide his last shreds of human dignity as though he is already deceased (v. 19).[80] Still, through it all he continues to cry out for divine intervention (vv. 12, 20–22b). Then suddenly, without warning, he declares 'you have answered me!' (v. 22c). Celebrating Yahweh's deliverance the supplicant now calls on an ever-widening audience –

---

[74] I am here indebted to the excellent discussion in Marcus, *The Way of the Lord*, pp. 172–84; see also Douglas J. Moo, *The Old Testament in the Gospel Passion Narratives* (Sheffield: Almond, 1986); Collins, 'Appropriation of the Individual Psalms'.

[75] Kraus, *Theology of the Psalms*, p. 130.

[76] Peter C. Craigie, *Psalms 1–50* (WBC 19; Waco: Word Books, 1983), p. 198.

[77] LXX punctuates differently, reading קָדוֹשׁ, as ἐν ἁγίοις thus 'dwelling in a sanctuary', see Craigie, *Psalms 1–50*, p. 196.

[78] H.-J. Kraus, *Psalms 1–59* (trans. Hilton C. Oswald; Philadelphia: Fortress Press, 1993), p. 295.

[79] Ellen F. Davis, 'Exploding the Limits: Form and Function in Psalm 22', *JSOT* 53 (1992), p. 97.

[80] Cf. Victor C. Matthews and Don C. Benjamin, *Social World of Ancient Israel 1250–587 BCE* (Peabody, MA: Hendrickson, 1993), pp. 147, 203.

Israel, the nations, generations yet unborn, and even the dead[81] – to join him in making known Yahweh's dominion over the nations (v. 29) that all the ends of the earth, in keeping with the Zion traditions of Yahweh's universal kingship,[82] might worship him (v. 28).

The Qumran Hymns (1QH) contain imagery but no direct citations of the 'righteous sufferer' psalms, including Psalm 22.[83] Given the eschatological orientation of the community and of elements within 1QH itself it seems reasonable to suppose that they saw the deliverance envisaged in these psalms as anticipating their eschatological vindication over against Belial and his agents. This would explain why Ps. 22:15–18 is found in 4QPs^f [88], apparently as the prelude to eschatological vindication and the restoration of Zion.[84] Intriguingly, 1QH also echoes material from Isaiah's 'suffering servant', a key figure for Mark's presentation of Jesus.

'Righteous sufferer' motifs are also picked in various pseudepigraphical works (e.g. Wis. Sol. 2:12–20; 5:1–7; 2 Bar. 15:7–8; 48:49–50) where the righteous must suffer but will be vindicated in the eschaton. The later Targum understands the enemies of Psalm 22 to be gentile kings who opposed David (vv. 13–14, 17, 21–22) which is consistent with the allusion to Yahweh's universal kingship that underlies the appeal (v. 2) and the conclusion (vv. 27–28). As Psalm 2 makes clear, Yahweh's honour and glory is at stake when his anointed regent is under threat. Verses 28–31 thus envisage the Gentiles' universal submission and the return of Israel's descendants which suggests an eschatological and perhaps messianic orientation (cf. Midr. Ps. 22:32). Nevertheless, in spite of these indications that the righteous sufferer's vindication had broad eschatological significance, there is no explicit evidence that Psalm 22 itself was understood messianically. Perhaps the notion of utter abandonment and such profound suffering, almost to the point of death, while applicable to Israel (cf. Midr. Ps. 22:7 where David is understood to have prophesied concerning Queen Esther) was deemed outside the bounds of messianic possibilities.[85]

On the other hand, since Mark's Jesus has already included suffering and death in his messianic role that impediment no longer stands. If the vindication of the suffering righteous could be applied to Israel, then why not Israel's representative? And if Psalm 22 described David, why not great David's greater son? The critical question is whether Mark expects the reader to 'fill in the gaps' and anticipate Jesus' vindication. Apart from the difficulty of imagining

---

[81] Davis, 'Exploding the Limits', p. 101.

[82] Kraus, Psalms 1–59, p. 300.

[83] See Moo, The Old Testament, p. 230 n. 3; H-J. Steichele, Der leidende Sohn Gottes (Regensburg: Pustet, 1980), p. 246; Marcus, The Way of the Lord, p. 178.

[84] Marcus, The Way of the Lord, p. 178, also cites Ps. 22:16 in 1 QH 13:31 but it is doubtful if this is an intentional allusion.

[85] Cf. Mk 8:32; and Targ. Isa. 52:13–53.12 where any suffering is either Israel's or the nations' but the Messiah knows only triumph.

where Mark could have included explicit references to the psalm's thanksgiving sections without appearing gauche, everything in his narrative points in this direction.

As we have seen the various contemporary interpretations of Psalms 2, 118 and 110 all testify to Yahweh's eschatological vindication of his messianic king. Given that Mark's employment of these psalms seems to share that perspective, why should his use of Psalm 22 suddenly break rank? On the contrary, in keeping with the vindication expressed in the passion predictions and the son-stone saying, Psalm 22 likewise assumes Yahweh's universal kingship and able protection of his own. Like his father David before him, Mark's Jesus is surrounded by his enemies – who for the first time and with considerable irony refer to him as Israel's King Messiah (15:32). Given his shameful situation, they mockingly conclude that God has abondened him. But it is hard to see how anyone familiar with the 'righteous sufferer' psalms and Psalm 22 in particular could fail to expect that Jesus, David's messianic lord, will know Yahweh's vindication. It is intriguing then to note that after Mk 15:37 and in keeping with the conclusion of Psalm 22, a representative of the Gentiles confesses Jesus to be son of God (15:39; Ps. 22:28), reference is made to God's dominion (15:43; Ps. 22:29), life is regained (16:6; Ps. 22:30c), and proclamation encouraged (16:7; Ps. 22:31–32).[86]

Finally one notes the convergence of the Isaianic 'servant' whose oracle is also patterned on the thanksgiving for deliverance of a righteous sufferer[87] and whose death and vindication inaugurates exiled Israel's deliverance and the coming of light to the nations, with the vindication of great David's greater messianic son which will eventually lead to the nations' submission to Yahweh.

Conclusion

By referencing at least twice each of four psalms traditionally associated with David, Mark integrates his view of Jesus as David's messianic son into his larger Isaianic new exodus schema. The first two allusions, both to Psalm 2, set the agenda. First, in designating Jesus as the Lord's Davidic, messianic son, Mark links him at the baptism with the Isaianic servant messiah (Mk 1:10; *Targ. Isa.* 42:1). It also provides the basis for the seven or so subsequent applications of Davidic psalms to Jesus. But Psalm 2 also presupposes conflict and for its later interpreters was connected, as was Isaiah's new exodus, with the purging and restoration of Jerusalem and its Temple. Not surprisingly the rest of Mark's major psalms' references centre on Jesus' relationship to Jerusalem and the Temple.

If Psalm 2 promised Yahweh's victory then Psalm 118 celebrates its

---

[86] Marcus, *The Way of the Lord*, p. 182.
[87] R.N. Whybray, *Thanksgiving for a Liberated Prophet: An Interpretation of Isaiah Chapter 53* (JSOTSup 4; Sheffield: JSOT Press, 1978).

realization where Jesus as the conquering new exodus Yahweh-warrior processes, in keeping with the psalm and its later eschatological interpretation, to the Temple. At the same time, however, the conflict motif which emerged early in Mark begins to reach its final expression in hierarchs' refusal to welcome him. Consequently the second appeal to Psalm 118 signals their demise and the elevation of the rejected Davidic son-stone to become the centrepiece of a new people-Temple.

Mark's two-fold appeal to the difficult Psalm 110 then functions as the climax of these several trajectories. Again in the face of hostility the first appeal sees the one initially designated as David's messianic son exalted to be David's Lord, sharing God's throne and with God putting his enemies under his feet. In the second reference and at the height of Jesus' trial, the motifs of conflict, of Jesus' exaltation, and the demise of his and God's enemies, now unquestionably the Temple authorities, are fully developed.

But this enthronement will only come after enduring suffering, as Mark's earlier and second reference to Psalm 2 in the context of Jesus' first passion prediction indicated. The Davidic messiah is also Isaiah's suffering servant. Jesus' deliverance of his people and enthronement will only come after descending into the depths as the righteous sufferer. Once one allows for a suffering messiah, Psalm 22, traditionally ascribed to David, with its uniquely heightened images of suffering and vindication, provides the perfect vehicle for marrying together not only the suffering of the righteous servant but also, through its climactic celebration of deliverance, the anticipation of the Lord's intervention on behalf of his Davidic scion, which deliverance will cause the Lord's dominion to be known among the nations. Even, indeed, to Rome (15:39).

3

The Psalms in Q

Michael Labahn

Preliminary Remarks

It is well known that the book of Psalms is one of the most widely used parts of
scripture in early Christianity, particularly for understanding the passion and
crucifixion of Jesus. Since these events are not explicitly mentioned in Q, it
remains to be seen whether the psalms are also important for this document. In
seeking to answer this, the fact that many scholars believe the document to be
composite must first be noted.[1] Indeed, some recent studies suggest either a
shorter document Q^2 or a number of smaller sources that make up the final Q.[3]
The possible inclusion of some texts in Q that derive from the minor
agreements between Matthew and Luke (e.g. the baptism of Jesus) should also
be mentioned. I thus begin with some methodological considerations:

(1) The following investigation uses the classical Two Document Hypothesis
    as a point of departure.[4]
(2) There are some indications that Q was used by Matthew (Q^{Mt}) and Luke
    (Q^{Lk}) in slightly different versions, notably within Jesus' programmatic
    speech on the plain/mountain (Q 6:20–49).[5] Some psalm references may
    have belonged to Q^{Mt}.[6]
(3) This study does not differentiate between layers of Q but analyses the
    reception of the psalms in the final text, without denying that the
    document undoubtedly had a complex pre-history.

---

[1] J.S. Kloppenborg Verbin, *Excavating Q: The History and Setting of the Sayings Gospel* (Edinburgh:
T and T Clark, 2000).

[2] A. Lindemann, 'Die Logienquelle Q: Fragen an eine gut begründete Hypothese', in A.
Lindemann, ed., *The Sayings Source Q and the Historical Jesus* (BETL 158; Leuven: Leuven
University Press Peeters, 2001), pp. 3–26, 4–9, assuming that Q starts in 6:20ff with a
programmatic proclamation of Jesus.

[3] M. Hengel, *The Four Gospels and the One Gospel of Jesus Christ: An Investigation of the Collection and
Origin of the Canonical Gospels* (Harrisburg, PA: TPI, 2000), pp. 169–207.

[4] See U. Schnelle, *The History and Theology of the New Testament Writings* (London: SCM Press,
1998), pp. 166–72.

[5] See G. Strecker, *Die Bergpredigt: Ein exegetischer Kommentar* (Göttingen: Vandenhoeck &
Ruprecht, 1985), 2nd edn, pp. 10–12; U. Schnelle, *History*, pp. 174, 185; U. Luz, 'Sermon on
the Mount/Plain: Reconstruction of QMt and QLk', *SBLSP* 22 (1983), pp. 473–79.

[6] E.g. Matt. 5:5 (Ps. 37:11; cf. Pss 37:22, 29; 25:13); 5:8 (Ps. 24:4); 5:35 (the prohibition to swear
by Jerusalem is motivated by alluding to Ps. 47:3).

(4) Q is a text which can only be reconstructed from its use by Matthew and Luke. Both Matthew and Luke are narrators of a new story and make changes to their source texts. There are obvious differences in the use of scripture between Matthew and Luke[7] which can clearly be seen in those cases where they depend on the same source.

From these remarks a double subject of reconstruction is required: (1) the original wording of Q must be determined and here we will make use of the Critical Edition of Q,[8] while recognizing that it is not beyond critique; and (2) the extent of the references to the psalms must be analysed and the textual version of the source text considered. Methodologically, determining the textual version of the source text has to be the second step and should not be used in the reconstruction of Q, for dependence on the LXX version cannot be claimed in advance.[9]

The Role of Scripture in Q in Recent Scholarship

In recent research, reference to scripture in Q is one of a number of questions concerning the reconstruction, sociology and theology of Q.[10] One main issue is the textual form of the scriptural references. Siegfried Schulz proposes a two stage hypothesis: (1) an early non-apocalyptic Jewish Christian layer; and (2) a later layer which used the LXX for references to scripture.[11] Although his assumptions have been challenged, the use of textual form to discern layers in Q is still practised.[12] Such an argument is difficult to sustain, however, for it cannot be proved that a 'Septuagint-like' quotation could only come from a Greek text unless the Hebrew is significantly different.[13] Further, there was

---

[7] M. Müller, 'The Reception of the Old Testament in Matthew and Luke-Acts: From Interpretation to Proof from Scripture', *NovT* 43 (2001), pp. 315–30.

[8] J.M. Robinson, P. Hoffmann and J.S. Kloppenborg, eds, *The Critical Edition of Q: Synopsis including the Gospels of Matthew and Luke, Mark and Thomas with English, German, and French translations of Q and Thomas* (Hermeneia. Supplement Series; Minneapolis, MN: Fortress Press, 2000); cf. my review in *OLZ* 97 (2002), pp. 769–73. All quotations are taken from this edition unless otherwise indicated.

[9] C. Heil, "Πάντες ἐργάται ἀδικίας" Revisited: The Reception of Ps. 6,9a LXX in Q and in Luke', in R. Hoppe and U. Busse, eds, *Von Jesus zum Christus. Christologische Studien. Festgabe P. Hoffmann* (BZNW 93; Berlin: de Gruyter, 1998), pp. 261–76, 266.

[10] C.M. Tuckett, 'Scripture and Q', in C.M. Tuckett, ed., *The Scriptures in the Gospels* (BETL 131; Leuven: Leuven University Press Peeters, 1997), pp. 3–26, 8–13.

[11] S. Schulz, *Q. Die Spruchquelle der Evangelisten* (Zürich: TVZ, 1972), pp. 27–28; cf. the critical examination by P. Hoffmann in *BZ* 19 (1975), pp. 104–15, 108–109.

[12] A.D. Jacobson, *The First Gospel: An Introduction to Q* (Foundations and Facets; Sonoma, CA: Polebridge, 1992), pp. 87, 112.

[13] It should not be overlooked that there is no fixed text of the Greek Old Testament during the first century (cf. M. Müller, *The First Bible of the Church: A Plea for the Septuagint* [JSOTSup 206; Sheffield: Sheffield Academic Press, 1996], pp. 41ff.). Therefore it is difficult to determine if a Greek reading which is in accordance with the Hebrew text in contrast to a LXX reading may go back to the Hebrew itself or to another Greek version.

hardly any literary layer of Q not written in Greek.[14] Indeed, from the moment that the traditions were transmitted in Greek there is the possibility that the LXX itself has influenced the wording of any quotations or allusions.[15]

Kloppenborg's reconstruction of Q should also be mentioned, since it is an important point of departure in North American Q-research. He distinguishes (1) an early 'sapiential' layer; (2) a 'prophetic' layer with a sharp polemical attitude against 'this generation'; and (3) a reworking of the document with a tendency towards a biographical genre.[16] Old Testament quotations, according to Kloppenborg, are part of the later or even the latest layer,[17] so that some exegetes draw far-reaching conclusions on the meaning of scripture in Q. For example, Wendy Cotter says of the basic layer of Q^1:

> Q^1 sayings do not display much if any explicit reference to specifically Jewish religious traditions. Scripture is never quoted, and, with the exception of Solomon 'in all his glory' (Q 12:27), no Jewish heroes are mentioned at all ... We can only say that the community does not show interest in appealing to Jewish traditions.[18]

Kloppenborg himself judges that the scribes of Q do 'not ... appeal to Torah as the self-evident starting point for argumentation'.[19] Undoubtedly, explicit quotations from scripture with an introductory formula are rare in the document and they occur in passages (Q 4:1–13; 7:27) which many scholars regard as late. However, serious questions need to be raised about this theory,[20] for there are good reasons for accepting the temptation story (Q 4:1–13) as an integral part of Q. If this is so, then quite a different view of Q's use of scripture emerges, for Q 4:1–13 is a programmatic text which depends heavily on argumentation from scripture. Indeed, some scholars understand the fundamental validity of the Torah as a key feature of Q.[21] And Dale Allison's recent study on the use of scripture in Q argues persuasively for the far reaching

---

[14] Kloppenborg Verbin, *Excavating Q*, pp. 72–80.

[15] Tuckett, 'Scripture', pp. 11–12.

[16] J.S. Kloppenborg, *The Formation of Q: Trajectories in Ancient Wisdom Collections* (Studies in Antiquity and Christianity; Harrisburg: TPI, 1999); *idem, Excavating Q*, pp. 143–53.

[17] B.L. Mack, *The Lost Gospel: The Book of Q and Christian Origins* (New York: HarperSan-Francisco, 1993), pp. 143ff.; A. Polag, *Die Christologie der Logienquelle* (WMANT 45; Neukirchen-Vluyn: Neukirchener Verlag, 1977), p. 9; M. Sato, *Q und Prophetie: Studien zur Gattungs- und Traditionsgeschichte der Quelle Q* (Tübingen: Mohr–Siebeck, 1988), pp. 35–36.

[18] W. Cotter, ' "Yes, I Tell You, and More Than a Prophet": The Function of John in Q', in J.S. Kloppenborg, ed., *Conflict and Invention: Literary, Rhetorical, and Social Studies on the Sayings Gospel Q* (Valley Forge, PA: TPI, 1995), pp. 135–50, 135–36.

[19] J.S. Kloppenborg, 'The Sayings Gospel Q: Recent Opinion on the People behind the Document', *CR:B S* 1 (1993), pp. 9–34, 25.

[20] C.M. Tuckett, 'On the Stratification of Q', *Semeia* 55 (1991), pp. 213–22; *idem*, 'Scripture', p. 10.

[21] J. Schröter, *Erinnerung an Jesu Worte: Studien zur Rezeption der Logienüberlieferung in Markus, Q und Thomas* (WMANT 76; Neukirchen-Vluyn: Neukirchener Verlag, 1997), p. 439. See also C.M. Tuckett, *Q and the History of Early Christianity: Studies on Q* (Edinburgh: T & T Clark, 1996), pp. 404–24.

influence of scripture on the document.[22] Thus the question of the importance of the psalms in Q is a suitable topic for investigation.

Quotations

In preparing a catalogue of possible quotations and allusions to the Psalms I have consulted the critical editions UBS[4] and NA[27] and various collections of scriptural references.[23] It is usual to distinguish between marked and unmarked quotations. Marked quotations are texts which are introduced by an introductory formula and show close verbal agreement with a known text; unmarked quotations lack the introductory formula. The study will begin by discussing those texts that fall into these categories. On the other hand, the concept of intertextuality shows that texts relate to one another in all kinds of complex ways, including texts known to a particular reader.[24] There is insufficient space to give this full attention but I will mention some of the more important 'allusions/echoes' that might be significant for the use of psalms in Q, even if there is little verbal affinity.

Q 4:10–11 and Psalm 91:11–12

The first reference to the Psalms marked by an introductory formula is found in Q's temptation story (Q 4:1–13). In the second temptation,[25] Jesus is led to a high place and the devil addresses him with the command to leap into the deep. If Jesus' baptism is mentioned in Q, the conditional sentence 'if you are God's Son' (Q 4:3) clearly refers back to the initial introduction of Q's main

---

[22] D.C. Allison, *The Intertextual Jesus: Scripture in Q* (Harrisburg, PA: TPI, 2000).

[23] E. Hühn, *Die messianischen Weissagungen des israelitisch-jüdischen Volkes bis zu den Targumim historisch-kritisch untersucht und erläutert nebst Erörterung der alttestamentlichen Citate und Reminiscenzen im Neuen Testamente, Band II* (Tübingen: Mohr–Siebeck, 1900); R. Hodgson, 'On the Gattung of Q: A Dialogue with James M. Robinson', *Biblica* 66 (1985), pp. 73–95; Allison, *The Intertextual Jesus*, pp. 157–71.

[24] The term was coined by Julia Kristeva (*Semeiotike: Recherches pour une sémanalyse* [Paris: Editions du Seuil, 1969]) who points to an open world of interrelations of texts. It was taken up by the literary critic Roland Barthes: There is no original text – everything is reception; that means intertextuality is produced by the reader. For a general portrayal of intertextuality, its roots and developments, see G. Allen, *Intertextuality* (The New Critical Idiom; London: Routledge, 2000). Exegetes use the term in a narrower sense for the relationship between the cited text and its new location. See H. Hübner, 'Intertextualität – die hermeneutische Strategie des Paulus? Zu einem neuen Versuch der theologischen Rezeption des Alten Testaments im Neuen', in *idem, Biblische Theologie als Hermeneutik: Gesammelte Aufsätze* (ed. A. Labahn and M. Labahn; Göttingen: Vandenhoeck & Ruprecht, 1995), pp. 252–71.

[25] The reconstruction of the original order of Jesus' temptations is puzzling. The order of Matthew and of Luke both fit well with their actual context. However, it seems to be more plausible that the original order aims at the veneration of the devil; see G. Theissen, *Lokalkolorit und Zeitgeschichte in den Evangelien: Ein Beitrag zur Geschichte der synoptischen Tradition* (Freiburg / Göttingen: Vandenhoeck & Ruprecht, 2nd edn, 1992), pp. 216–17; C.M. Tuckett, 'The Temptation Narrative in Q', in F. van Segbroeck, C.M. Tuckett, G. van Belle and J. Verheyden, eds, *The Four Gospels 1992. FS F. Neirynck* (BETL 100; Leuven: Leuven University Press Peeters, 1992), pp. 479–507, 479.

character: God's voice describes Jesus as his beloved Son (Q 3:22). The devil questions this designation and invites Jesus to put God to the test. As justification, the devil quotes Ps. 91:11–12:

Ps. 91:11–12	Matt. 4:6	Lk. 4:10
For he will command his angels concerning you *to guard you in all your ways.* On their hands they will bear you up, so that you will not dash your foot against a stone.[26]	for it is written, 'He will command his angels concerning you,' and 'On their hands they will bear you up, so that you will not dash your foot against a stone.'	for it is written, 'He will command his angels concerning you, *to guard you,*' and 'On their hands they will bear you up, so that you will not dash your foot against a stone.'

There are two issues here (see italics). First, there appears to be no reason why Matthew would delete 'to guard you' if it were present in his Q-text, so it is likely to be a Lukan addition. Second, the phrase 'in all your ways' does not fit with the situation on the pinnacle of the temple and is therefore not present in either gospel. We may safely conclude that it was not part of Q. The LXX is an accurate rendering of the Hebrew. Thus Q could be dependent on the LXX but the evidence does not allow certainty.

The devil's request is only meaningful if Jesus was the Son of God (cf. Q 3:22; 4:3). Satan quotes a scripture that underlines God's care and fits well with the narrative world of Q. The stressed 'you' of the devil's quest corresponds with the promise of the psalm. The protasis of the quest and its justification strictly correspond to one another, so that Jesus as Son of God is characterized by the protection described in Ps. 91:11a, 12. The connection between the psalm and the narrative situation of Q 4:9–12 can be seen in the act of being carried by the angels, which would prevent the body from falling to the ground. This is of course different to what is envisaged within the psalm itself.

There is a high degree of reflection in the scene which may be characterized as irony. The devil quotes a psalm text which is used in apotropaic collections and in magical papyri to protect people from Satan and demons.[27] The tempter quotes a word from scripture which is intended against him. The irony focuses on the point that scripture will appear true against the speaker's intention, for the Son of God is indeed protected by God and has no need to prove this by agreeing to the devil's request. In Q the absolute godless Satan tempts the Son of God by asking him to bring himself close to death. According to Q, the devil reckons with the saving act by God but wishes to force Jesus to initiate it, thus jeopardizing his obedience as Son of God. This is made clear by Jesus'

[26] All biblical references are from NRSV, except the quotations from Q.
[27] Allison, *The Intertextual Jesus*, p. 159; C. Kähler, 'Satanischer Schriftgebrauch: Zur Hermeneutik von Mt 4,1–11/Lk 4,1–13', *ThLZ* 119 (1994), pp. 857–68, 861; E. Zenger, in F.-L. Hossfeld and E. Zenger, *Ps 50–100* (HThKAT; Freiburg: Herder, 2000), p. 626.

answer taken from Deut. 6:16. It is not the content of the devil's address that is wrong, but his aim is to 'tempt God' and is thus not in accordance with the nature of the Son of God. Reading the context of Psalm 91 we find that the pious one who is searching for God's protection (91:2, 9a) is the one who will be protected; protection is connected with piety and faith. Piety, faith and obedience in Q are evoked by quoting Deuteronomy 6. By refusing the aim of the devil, Jesus is characterized as the true Son of God who is obedient.

In Mk 15:39, the Roman officer under the cross declares Jesus to be 'Son of God'. The gospel tradition reports the taunt that if Jesus were truly the Son of God, he could come down from the cross (Matt. 27:39–43 parr.). There may be a comparable aim in Q.[28] Protection of the Son of God does not mean prevention from suffering, but that he will pass through suffering to resurrection, in accordance with God's will.

Q 13:27 and Psalm 6:9

A much debated passage stems from the beginning of a collection of sayings against Israel (Q 13:24–14:23). Q 13:24–27 is a statement of judgement. The addressees are confronted with the metaphor of the narrow door which opens into the house. The owner of the house closes the door, rejects entrance of the people outside and denies knowledge of the evildoers:

> And he will say to you: I do not know you! Go away (ἀποχωρεῖτε) from me, you evildoers (οἱ ἐργαζόμενοι τὴν ἀνομίαν).

The reconstruction of the Q-text presented here is slightly different from CEQ. First, ἀποχωρεῖτε (go away!) is preferred to Luke's ἀφίστημι, since the latter is a favourite term in Luke, whereas the former is a *hapax legomenon* in Matthew. Second, there seems no good reason why Matthew would change an original πάντες ἐργάται. Third, because of Luke's preference for words in the semantic field δίκαιος, the term ἀνομία may originally be part of Q.[29]

The quotation from Ps. 6:9 ('Depart from me, all you workers of evil') is not marked by any quotation formula but the verbal affinity with the Old Testament is clear.[30] There are, however, two differences of the Q-quotation to the LXX: (1) the word 'all' is omitted; and (2) it uses a different verb, though with much the same meaning. Since the LXX is an accurate rendering of the Hebrew of Ps. 6:9, no decisions can be taken about the source of Q's citation.

---

[28] T. Söding, 'Der Gehorsam des Gottessohnes: Zur Christologie der matthäischen Versuchungserzählung (4,1–11)', in C. Landmesser, H.-J. Eckstein and H. Lichtenberger, eds, *Jesus Christus als Mitte der Schrift: Studien zur Hermeneutik des Evangeliums. FS O. Hofius* (BZNW 86; Berlin: W. de Gruyter, 1997), pp. 711–50, 737 (for the Matthean version).

[29] C. Heil, 'πάντες ἐργάται ἀδικίας', pp. 266–71.

[30] Contrary to J.J. O'Rourke, 'Possible Uses of the Old Testament in the Churches', in C.A. Evans and W.R. Stegner, eds, *The Gospels and the Scriptures of Israel* (JSNTSup 104; Sheffield: Sheffield Academic Press, 1994), pp. 15–25, 24 who asserts only a 'common sentiment'.

Q 13:24–27 refers to the eschatological judgement and reminds the audience that the end time has come and that it is difficult to enter through the narrow door. Moreover, there will be a time when the door is closed by the owner of the house and he will refuse entrance. The house owner is identified with Jesus and the motif of final judgement ascribes God's judgement to Jesus as the Son of Man. He will return with his followers to bring judgement (Q 22:28, 30), at which point, it will be too late to repent.

Ps. 6:9a stands at the end of a complaint (6:2–8), which changes into an expression of confidence (6:9b–11). The psalmist is sure that God has heard his words and therefore all his enemies 'shall be ashamed and struck with terror; they shall turn back, and in a moment be put to shame' (6:11). However, the fate of the enemies is due to God's help and the cry in Ps. 6:9a is not a word of judgement but a word of confidence in God's activity. In early Judaism, Psalm 6, like the whole book of Psalms, is attributed to David.[31] He sings the songs with the spirit of prophecy[32] and so his words can be read as words which will evoke a deeper meaning during the end-time. As narrated, Jesus takes up the words of David's prophecy, perhaps because the author knows that God has saved him from death (cf. Ps. 6:5) and not left him in the underworld (v. 6). According to early Christian thinking, Jesus is to be God's agent of judgement and is therefore able to carry out judgement himself, in contrast to the singer of Psalm 6.

Q 13:35b and Psalm 118:26a

Q 13:35b may be taken as a quotation of Ps. 118:26a, indicated by verbal identity between the source text and Q. Jesus threatens his hearers by announcing that they will not see him before they utter the words, 'Blessed is the one who comes in the name of the Lord'. There are a few small differences between Matthew and Luke but not in the quotation itself.[33] The Q text agrees exactly with the LXX, which is itself an accurate rendering of the Hebrew. One cannot therefore decide whether Q is dependent on a Greek or Hebrew source.

In Q 13:34–35, Jerusalem, the centre of Israel's hope, has a negative connotation: it is the place where the prophets and the envoys were killed (Q 13:34a). But Jerusalem is not a completely negative category in Q. It is also the place where the speaker has tried to gather his people at various times (13:34b). In the context, there is no indication of a speaker other than Jesus. However, gathering his people is typically the work of God himself and his selected envoys. The narrator of Q thus characterizes Jesus in this role.

---

[31] M. Daly-Denton, *David in the Fourth Gospel: The Johannine Reception of the Psalms* (AGJU 47; Leiden: Brill, 2000), pp. 59–102.

[32] 11QPs^a col. 27:11; see also Acts 2:30–31; 4:25; cf. C.A. Evans, 'The Dead Sea Scrolls and the Canon of Scripture in the Time of Jesus', in P.W. Flint, ed., *The Bible at Qumran: Text, Shape, and Interpretation* (Studies in the Dead Sea Scrolls and Related Literature; Grand Rapids: Eerdmans, 2001), pp. 67–79.

[33] On the reconstruction of the Q text, see U. Luz, *Das Evangelium nach Matthäus 3. Mt 18–25* (EKKNT, I/3; Zürich: Benzinger: Neukirchen-Vluyn: Neukirchener Verlag, 1997), pp. 377–78.

Because this meets with rejection, his endeavour is left until such time as the people acclaim, 'Blessed is the one who comes in the name of the Lord'. The reason for the interruption is not mentioned; it may well be assumed that the measure of opposition against God's mission in killing the prophets and envoys, including the killing of Jesus,[34] is responsible for the obstruction. Israel's blame is not a matter of the past[35] but a matter of the narrator's present. It is carried forward by refusal of the recent generation against the proclamation of the Q-group (Q 11:49–51; cf. 7:31–35; 11:29–32). With the help of the scheme of killing the prophets in Israel's past, Jesus' fate and the fate of the Q-group are taken together and interpreted alongside each other.

The gathering of the people is halted until the blessing of Ps. 118:26a is proclaimed. The community behind Q may represent a group proclaiming this blessing. However, Q 13:35b seems to have an eschatological outlook.[36] Confessing Jesus and following Jesus by taking up one's own individual cross (Q 14:27) will build up a community which will proclaim the Old Testament blessing at the time of the return of the Son of Man. The universal future realization of the expectations of Q by the returning Son of Man will bring the Q-community into their inheritance (Q 22:28, 30).[37]

Allusions and Echoes

Q 3:22 and Psalm 2:7

Whether this first reference to the book of Psalms should be included depends on the reconstruction of the document Q. In contrast to the proposal of the International Q Project, the CEQ claims with more emphasis that Jesus' baptism was part of Q.[38] Q 3:22 may have read something like this: '. . . my Son, the Beloved; with whom I am well pleased'.[39] The first allusion to the book of Psalms in Q was part of the designation of Jesus as Son of God by a heavenly voice. There is only a small verbal agreement between Q 3:22 and Ps. 2:7 in the words 'my son'. There is no hint at an act of procreation ('I have begotten you') from Ps. 2:7 in Q 3:22. One may perhaps speak of it as an

---

[34] A. Sand, *Das Evangelium nach Matthäus* (RNT; Regensburg: Pustet, 1986), p. 475; Tuckett, *Q and the History of Early Christianity*, p. 220.

[35] The scheme with which present time is presented according to Israel's guilt is taken from the Deuteronomistic historical view; cf. O.H. Steck, *Israel und das gewaltsame Geschick der Propheten: Untersuchungen zur Überlieferung des deuteronomistischen Geschichtsbildes im Alten Testament, Spätjudentum und Urchristentum* (WMANT 23; Neukirchen-Vluyn: Neukirchener Verlag, 1967).

[36] J. Gnilka, *Das Matthäusevangelium II*, (HTKNT I/2; Freiburg: Herder, 1988), pp. 304–305.

[37] The Son of Man will be welcomed at his arrival (*1 En.* 61:7; 62:6) and will execute judgment (*1 En.* 55:4; 61:9).

[38] U. Luz, *Das Evangelium nach Matthäus 1. Mt 1–7* (EKK I/1; Zürich: Benziger; Neukirchen-Vluyn: Neukirchener Verlag, 1985), pp. 150–51; U.B. Müller, ' "Sohn Gottes" – ein messianischer Hoheitstitel Jesu', *ZNW* 87 (1996), pp. 1–32, 27; H. Polag, *Christologie*, p. 151.

[39] Cf. the reconstruction of Q 3:22 according to CEQ: [[καὶ ... τὸ πνεῦμα ... ἐπ' αὐτόν ... υἱ ... .]]. This is a careful way to admit a Q-text. I have tried to fill the gap recognizing the hypothetical character of the reconstruction.

'echo' or faint allusion. One may also assume that there was a reference to a voice from heaven in Q. This voice directed the reader to God who is the 'author' of the quotation from Ps. 2:7 (the king quotes from God's decree) in Q 3:22. If God was the speaker of 'my son ...', this reference may be an example of a 're-used author'.[40] By the term 'my son', God addresses an individual with the words of the very famous text, Psalm 2. Here, the king of Israel is acclaimed as the beloved Son of God but without using the political terms from Psalm 2. Bearing in mind the frequent and varied uses of Psalm 2 in early Christianity, it seems probable that Ps. 2:7 forms the background of Q 3:22, expressing the close relationship between God and Jesus and proclaiming his messianic role.

Q 4:6–8 and Psalm 2:8

If document Q makes use of Psalm 2 in Q 3:22, this may strengthen the possibility of an allusion to Ps. 2:8 in Q 4:6–8.[41] Allison has tested the evidence and come to a negative conclusion.[42] His argument is not compelling, however, for he limits the biblical background of Q 4:5–7 mainly to the Mosaic tradition, especially to Deuteronomy 32. The intertextual paradigm points to different forms and signals of reception which have less verbal affinity but may nonetheless be present. The debated reference to Ps. 2:8 needs to be considered in the light of the undisputed reference to the book of Psalms in Q 4:10–11 (Ps. 91:11–12). Contrary to Q 4:10 ('it is written'), there is no place for a quotation formula in Q 4:6–8, for there is no full quotation. Further, the reference to Ps. 2:8 could not be used as a quotation for there are different speakers in both texts. In Psalm 2, God is the speaker but in the Q-document, it is the devil and, according to Q, the devil is not to be worshipped like God and cannot call the word of God his own. In contrast to Q 4:10, the devil is talking about his own activity in 4:6, to which the activity of God in Psalm 2 is a strong contrast. This may be the key for the interpretation of the allusion to Ps. 2:8.

Ps. 2:8	Q 4:5–8
Condition	
Ask (αἴτησαι) of me	*if you bow down* (προσκυνήσῃς) *before me*
Promise	
and I will make	*all these I will give you*
Content of the promise	
the nations your heritage, and the ends of	*all the kingdoms of the world*
the earth your possession	*and their splendor*

---

[40] For this intertextual phenomenon cf. J. Helbig, *Intertextualität und Markierung: Untersuchungen zur Systematik und Funktion der Signalisierung von Intertextualität* (Beiträge zur neueren Literaturgeschichte, III/141; Heidelberg: Winter, 1996), pp. 115–17.

[41] Catchpole, *The Quest for Q* (Edinburgh: T and T Clark, 1993), p. 230.

[42] Allison, *The Intertextual Jesus*, p. 238.

Although it should not be overlooked that there is little verbal agreement between the texts, there is nevertheless some significant agreement in structure. In both texts God should be adored by someone. Αἴτησαι means more than 'requesting' or even 'begging'. In Psalm 2 it shows the king's acceptance regarding the source of his political power. A basic question of Israel's kingship throughout the years of monarchy is, 'From whom does the king expect help and assurance in times of political struggle?' By addressing God as the source of his own political power, the king praises the Lord and thus performs an act of worship. An analogous semantics may be found in προσκυνήσῃς as well. If Jesus would fulfil the request of the devil he would be accepting him as the source of his (political) power. The use of the verb προσκυνέω fits with Q 4:8 (in contrast to LXX Deut. 6:13) and has its roots in biblical language. It may well have been influenced by political language (cf. Suetonius *Leg.* 2; Philo *Legat.* 116–7; Cass. *Gai.* 59, 24, 4).[43] However, venerating the devil is an act of illegitimate worship, since all power stems from God (Ps. 2:8). The promise given with the act of worship in both texts is the giving of power over the whole world to someone.

The faint allusion to Ps. 2:8 shows nearly the same use of irony as is found in Q 4:10–11. The devil offers something truly belonging to the Son of God (cf Psalm 2 as a whole). In Q 4:10–11, it is the protection by God through his angels, in Q 4:6–8 it is the power which belongs to the Son of God. The devil now places himself in the role of God. He not only asks for worship to be directed to him rather than God, he also claims the right to distribute empires and their splendour. Though this role is sometimes ascribed to the devil, it considerably differs from the distribution of power envisaged in Ps. 2:8.

On the mountain, probably Mount Sion, where the Jewish people expected the final judgement of God's adversaries to take place (cf. *4 Ezra* 13: 34–37; *Syr.Bar.* 40), God's enemy par exellence, the devil, offers Jesus a power which he will finally carry out as God's agent when he returns as the Son of Man (Q 22:28, 30). Again, in using scripture, the devil characterizes Jesus correctly, because the content of scripture is true. However, he fails with his offer because Jesus is obedient toward God and acts as his beloved Son. Jesus is the one who will obtain universal power, though according to Q, he already shows signs of that power in his earthly life.

Q 11:4 and Psalm 25:18

That the Lord's prayer is filled with traditional language is not to be doubted, though it is difficult to isolate any one specific source text. One possibility is in the petition for forgiveness of sins. There are some well-known differences

---

[43] G. Theissen, *Lokalkolorit*, pp. 218ff.; cf. the critical remarks by M. Myllykoski, 'The Social History of Q and the Jewish War', in R. Uro, ed., *Symbols and Strata: Essays on the Sayings Gospel Q* (Publications of the Finnish Exegetical Society 65; Göttingen: Vandenhoeck & Ruprecht, 1996), pp. 143–99, 157ff.

between the Matthean and Lukan version of the petition. The differences can be retraced to the Lukan redaction so that Matthew represents the Q-version: '*and cancel* our *debts* for us, as we have cancelled for those in debt to us.' In Ps. 25:18, God is asked to forgive all the sins of the petitioners. The words are very close to Lk. 11:4, for he uses ἁμαρτίας for 'sins' and includes the word 'all' later in v. 4. It is, however, more complicated in the Q-version. Here, we find a different Greek word for 'sins' (ὀφειλήματα) and there is no 'all'. In fact, ὀφείλημα is never used in the LXX as equivalent for the Hebrew חטא, so that it is rather unusual and may indicate that Q, contrary to Luke, is *not* referring to Ps. 25:18. However, it seems unlikely that a reader familiar with the Psalms would not remember David's cry for help and the repentance mentioned in Psalm 25, when he/she follows Jesus in addressing the Lord.

Q 13:19 and Psalm 104:12

There is a small collection of two parables in Q 13:18–21 about the growth of the kingdom of God. The first one compares the kingdom of God with a mustard seed. After being thrown in the garden the seed grows into a big tree in whose branches the birds of the sky will dwell. In Matthew and Luke, this is then followed by the parable of the leaven. In Luke the parable is in a different context to that of Mark 4 and suggests an alternative version was in existence. The Matthean version of the parable combines material from Q and from Mark, so that the Lukan version is closer to the original version of Q.

One could question whether a scriptural reference can be detected behind the words of Q 13:19 ('it grew and became a tree, and the birds of the air made nests in its branches').[44] After all, the phrase 'birds of the air' occurs nearly 40 times in the Old Testament. Allison[45] suggests Dan. 4:10, 12 (LXX), Dan. 4:11, 12, 21 (Theodotion) or Ezekiel 17, 31 as the most likely sources. However, the metaphor of 'birds nesting in the branches' in Q is more than just an image for the greatness of the kingdom. It is also a picture of God's welfare as the kingdom arrives, and this suggests Ps. 104:12 that also praises God's welfare in his creation is the key text, possibly combined with Daniel 4 or even with Ezekiel 17.[46] Since the LXX is close to the Hebrew, no decision about the original version can be made.

Q 13:29, 28 and Psalm 107:3; 112:10(?)

Intertextual links to the psalms may also be present in Q 13:24–14:23, the passage concerning the critique of Israel. The coming of a multitude from the

---

[44] J.D. Crossan, *In Parables: The Challenge of the Historical Jesus* (New York: Harper & Row, 1973), p. 47.

[45] Allison, *The Intertextual Jesus*, pp. 134–7, does not mention Ps. 104:12 at all.

[46] For the technique of combination of different passages from scripture in ancient Jewish and early Christian exegesis cf. M.J.J. Menken, *Old Testament Quotations in the Fourth Gospel: Studies in Textual Form* (CBET 15; Kampen: Kok Pharos, 1996), pp. 52–3.

east and the west (Q 13:29, 28) is placed in a different context in Matthew, where it is part of the healing of the centurion's son/slave. There are also a few important differences in the text itself. First of all, there is the matter of the sequence of the two verses. The Matthean sequence is more natural and may represent the original order of Q:

> (Q 13:29) And many shall come *from east and west* and recline (13:28) with Abraham and Isaac and Jacob in the kingdom of God, but you will be thrown out into the outer darkness, where there will be *wailing and grinding of teeth*.

Luke has added 'from north and south'. Matthew may have preserved the original introduction 'I tell you'.

Ps. 107:1–3 invites the exiles to give thanks to the Lord. Although the Lukan version is closer to the psalm, Q also resembles Ps. 107:3 ('gathered in from the lands, from the east and from the west, from the north and from the south') in the motif of gathering people from all over the world and in the terms used to describe the places they come from. However, the gathering is expressed differently. According to Q 13:29, people are coming themselves, whereas according to Ps. 107:3 God gathers the Diaspora. Gathering the Diaspora is a motif which also occurs in, for example, *Pss Sol.* 11:2; Zech. 8:7; Isa. 43:5; Bar. 5:5, so that it is not certain that Q 13:29 refers to Ps. 107:3. However, any reader who bears Psalm 107 in mind will find an allusion. The gathering of people coming also from the Gentile world is painted with the colours of the gathering of the Diaspora.

The proclamation of their arrival is followed by a direct address to the hearers: they will become outsiders, and they will react with 'wailing and grinding of teeth'. It is a puzzling question whether these words constitute an allusion to Ps. 112:10. If there is a reference to the book of Psalms in Q 13:29, the reader may expect another reference in the immediate context. Further, there is no real difference between 'they gnash their teeth' (Ps. 112:10) and 'gnashing of teeth' (Q 13:28). Nevertheless, 'gnashing of teeth' is an eschatological topos which can be found in the *Sibylline Oracles*:[47] 2:305–6; 8:104–5, 231, 350.

Ps. 112:10 addresses impious people who are opposed to the righteous ones. There is also an opposition in Q 13:29, 28 between the people from east and west and those addressed by Jesus' words. In Q, it seems likely that 'this generation' refers to those who refused the preaching of Jesus, which may at this point represent the teaching of the Q-group. In Q's view, 'this generation' is not willing to convert to the preaching of the Q-group. The designation of the outsiders as impious may come from Ps. 112:10. However, the first group mentioned in Q 13:28 is to be read with Q 14:16–23 in mind; it is not a group

---

[47] Allison, *The Intertextual Jesus*, pp. 169–70.

of pious people but they are people from 'on the roads, and whomever you find' (Q 14:23).

Concluding Remarks

At the time of Jesus and of his earliest followers, the psalms were widely used in personal piety, both for instruction and edification.[48] For example, we have discovered more copies of the book of Psalms at Qumran than of any other biblical book.[49] It is thus not surprising that Q contains a number of references to the psalms. This chapter discussed marked and unmarked quotations (Pss 6:9; 91:11–12; 104:12; 118:26). A number of less clearly indicated allusions or echoes (Pss 2:7, 8; 25:18; 107:3; 112:10[?]), which may nevertheless be important have also been discussed. In addition, there are biblical motifs and language, which could not be mentioned in this chapter, but form part of the ethical instruction of the document, as well as descriptions of the activity of God and Jesus.

The citations discussed above are in accordance with the LXX. However, this does not necessarily mean they are taken directly from the LXX, for they are almost all in exact agreement with the Hebrew text. Thus the detection of LXX references to the psalms cannot be used as a criterion to reconstruct the pre-history of the document.

As to the importance of the psalms for Q, it should be noted that this is not decided simply by the quantity of quotations and allusions. It is also important to ask about their function. Hieke has tried to show that the use of scripture in Q 4:1–13 indicates the fundamental validity of the Torah for Q.[50] Bearing in mind that all of the psalms were read in the light of Psalm 1 and thus as a resource for one's obedience to the Torah,[51] the above could be used to strengthen Hieke's thesis. On the other hand, it seems more likely that the quotations both from the Psalms and from Deuteronomy are intended to characterize Jesus and the Son of Man,[52] who is in Q a teacher, an agent of salvation. One main reason for using the psalms to characterize Jesus in this way is because David, whom ancient Judaism widely assumed was the author and singer of the psalms, was considered to be a prophet. In summary then, by quotation and allusion to selected psalms, Q describes Jesus as God's beloved

---

[48] N. Füglister, 'Die Verwendung des Psalters zur Zeit Jesu: Der Psalter als Lehr- und Lebensbuch', *Bibel und Kirche* 47 (1992), pp. 201–8.

[49] P.W. Flint, *The Dead Sea Scrolls and the Book of Psalms* (STDJ, 17; Leiden: Brill, 1997), pp. 27–49 (a survey of the scrolls, their editions and their extent).

[50] T. Hieke, 'Schriftgelehrsamkeit in der Logienquelle: Die alttestamentlichen Zitate in der Versuchungsgeschichte Q 4,1–13', in J.M. Asgeirsson, K. de Troyer and M.W. Meyer, eds, *From Quest to Q: FS J.M. Robinson* (BETL 146; Leuven: Leuven University Press Peeters, 2000), pp. 43–71, 69f.

[51] Füglister, 'Verwendung', p. 205.

[52] M. Labahn, 'The Significance of Eschatological Signs in Luke 7:22–23, in Comparison with Isaiah 61 and Qumran's 4Q521', in C.A. Evans, ed., *From Prophecy to Testament: The Function of the Old Testament in the New* (Peabody: Hendrickson, 2004), forthcoming.

and obedient son. He is completely on God's side, under the protection of his angels and obedient unto death. He wished to gather together the people of Israel and will finally carry out God's judgement when he returns as Son of Man. It can safely be concluded that the psalms were an important source for the Q community.[53]

---

[53] I am grateful to Steve Moyise for the revision of my English manuscript and to Maarten Menken for further remarks and hints.

4

The Psalms in Matthew's Gospel

Maarten J.J. Menken

Introduction

Together with Isaiah, the book of Psalms was the most widely used part of scripture among the first Christians. Matthew is no exception in this regard: we find in his Gospel many quotations from and allusions to the Psalms. A factor promoting this general interest in the Psalms (an interest which early Christianity inherited from Judaism) was no doubt the important place of these songs in both public and private worship.

In describing Matthew's use of the Old Testament, and thus his use of the book of Psalms, a distinction should be made between marked quotations, unmarked quotations and allusions. Marked quotations are more or less verbatim and thus easily recognizable renderings of a clause or a series of clauses from scripture, which are introduced or concluded by a formula that makes clear that the words in question come from scripture. Unmarked quotations are verbatim derivations without an introductory or concluding formula. Under allusions I subsume all other, vaguer ways of making use of the Old Testament, varying from an evident but not verbal reference to a biblical text to a faint echo. Unmarked quotations and allusions can have various reasons: from the conscious wish to give an Old Testament phrasing to unconscious influence of the cultural ambient. Marked quotations have a function in the argument, either directly, when Matthew himself quotes, or indirectly, when a person put on the stage by him, quotes. Here, scripture is mostly an authoritative instance that demonstrates or corroborates certain positions or shows certain events to be according to God's plan. In determining the role and function of the Psalms in Matthew, such explicit use is decisive.

If we try to make an inventory of the psalm quotations in Matthew, we are faced with a difficulty: it is sometimes difficult to establish whether we are dealing with an unmarked quotation or with an allusion. Consultation of editions of the Greek New Testament or of modern Bible translations quickly shows that one and the same fragment from Matthew is sometimes considered as a quotation and sometimes not. I have simply adopted as quotations those portions of Matthew's Gospel that are printed as Old Testament quotations in at least one of two widely used editions of the Greek New Testament: in NA[27] (shown in italics there) and/or UBS[4] (in bold there).[1] Any determination in this field has a certain amount of arbitrariness, and this procedure cannot be influenced by a possibly arbitrary selection on my part.

The Gospel of Matthew contains five marked quotations from the Psalms: 4:6 (= Ps. 91:11–12); 13:35 (= Ps. 78:2); 21:16 (= Ps. 8:3), 42 (= Ps. 118:22–23); 22:44 (= Ps. 110:1). There are ten unmarked quotations: 7:23 (= Ps. 6:9); 13:32 (= Ps. 104:12); 16:27 (= Ps. 62:13); 21:9 (= Ps. 118:25–26); 23:39 (= Ps. 118:26); 26:38 (= Pss 42:6, 12; 43:5), 64 (= Ps. 110:1); 27:35 (= Ps. 22:19), 43 (= Ps. 22:9), 46 (= Ps. 22:2). If I were to consider all other references to the Psalms in the margin of NA[27] as indicating allusions, there are 44 verses in Matthew that contain allusions to the book of Psalms.

In discussing Matthew's use of the Psalms, we should not only distinguish marked quotations, unmarked quotations and allusions; we should also make distinctions according to the sources from which the quotations came to the evangelist. In composing his narrative, Matthew used the Gospel of Mark, Q and some miscellaneous other materials (indicated as M).[2] Mark's Gospel, Q and M contained Old Testament quotations, and Matthew adopted most of these along with their context. Some of these quotations were copied by him without any changes, in others he made modifications. In the process of editing his sources, Matthew also added some Old Testament quotations of his own accord. Best known among these are the so-called 'fulfilment quotations' (1:22–23; 2:15, 17–18, 23; 4:14–16; 8:17; 12:17–21; 13:35; 21:4–5; 27:9–10).

Matthew borrowed seven psalm quotations from Mark: 21:9 (= Ps. 118:25–26, from Mk 11:9), 42 (= Ps. 118:22–23, from Mk 12:10–11); 22:44 (= Ps. 110:1, from Mk 12:36); 26:38 (= Pss 42:6, 12; 43:5, from Mk 14:34), 64 (= Ps. 110:1, from Mk 14:62); 27:35 (= Ps. 22:19, from Mk 15:24), 46 (= Ps. 22:2, from Mk 15:34). He took four psalm quotations from Q: 4:6 (= Ps. 91:11–12, cf. Lk. 4:10–11); 7:23 (= Ps. 6:9, cf. Lk. 13:27); 13:32 (= Ps. 104:12, cf. Lk. 13:19); 23:39 (= Ps. 118:26, cf. Lk. 13:35). He derived one psalm quotation from M: 21:16 (= Ps. 8:3). Three psalm quotations were evidently added by Matthew himself: 13:35 (= Ps. 78:2; cf. Matt. 13:34–35 with Mk 4:33–34); 16:27 (= Ps. 62:13; cf. Matt. 16:24–28 with Mk 8:34–9:1); 27:43 (= Ps. 22:9; cf. Matt. 27:39–44 with Mk 15:29–32).

In what follows, I shall discuss all 15 psalm quotations in Matthew. I shall do so according to the sequence in which the quotations occur in the Gospel, taking into account the distinctions made above. In each case, two questions will be asked: (1) In what textual form does Matthew present the quotation? Did he make use of the LXX, of another Greek translation, of his own

---

[1] With one exception: in NA[27], the words 'in the highest heaven' in Matt. 21:9 are considered to be a quotation from Ps. 148:1; Job 16:19; in reality, the phrase is just one with an OT colour.

[2] I follow the broadly accepted Two-Document Hypothesis. For a recent reconstruction of Q, see J.M. Robinson, P. Hoffmann, J.S. Kloppenborg and M.C. Moreland, eds, *The Critical Edition of Q* (Leuven: Peeters, 2000).

translation of the Hebrew original, or did he just copy the quotation from his source (Mark, Q, M)? (2) What does the quotation mean in its Matthean context? Finally, I shall summarize the results and make some general remarks on Matthew's use of the Psalms. Some of the allusions will be mentioned in passing.

The two questions in the preceding paragraph deserve some elucidation. We have to establish as well as we can the textual form in which Matthew found the quotation, because only then we can see what changes (if any) he made to it and how he interpreted it. This research may also contribute to our knowledge of the history of the Old Testament text in the first century. In this connection, Matthew's treatment of quotations which he found in his sources merits special notice, because it is sometimes assumed that he adapted their textual form to the LXX.[3] The second question, concerning the meaning of the quotation in the Matthean context, presupposes that the interpretation Matthew gives to a quotation, may differ from the meaning this quotation had in its original Old Testament context. In investigating the use of the Old Testament in the New Testament, we should always keep in mind that the New Testament authors read the Old Testament as interpreted in first-century Judaism.

Quotations from the Psalms in Matthew: Textual Form and Meaning

Matthew 4:6 = Psalm 91:11–12

In the temptation story, the devil challenges Jesus to throw himself down from the pinnacle of the temple, and he lends force to his provocation by appealing to Ps. 91:11–12:

> He [God] will command his angels concerning you,
> and on their hands they will bear you up,
> so that you will not dash your foot against a stone.[4]

Matthew's temptation story (4:1–11) has a parallel in Luke (4:1–13), and must come from Q. The wording of the quotation agrees completely in both Gospels (see Lk. 4:10–11), and it also agrees completely with Ps. 90:11–12 LXX. Does this mean that Q already contained the quotation in the textual form of the LXX? One could argue that the LXX is here a correct translation of the Hebrew original, and that any translation of the Hebrew might lead to the same result. However, the exact agreement extends over no less than three

---

[3] So, e.g., G.D. Kilpatrick, *The Origins of the Gospel according to St. Matthew* (Oxford: Clarendon, 1946), pp. 56–57; G. Strecker, *Der Weg der Gerechtigkeit: Untersuchung zur Theologie des Matthäus* (FRLANT 82; Göttingen: Vandenhoeck & Ruprecht, 1962, 2nd edn, 1966), pp. 21–29; U. Luz, *Das Evangelium nach Matthäus 1: Mt 1–7* (EKKNT 1/1; Zürich: Benziger; Neukirchen-Vluyn: Neukirchener Verlag, 1985, 3rd edn, 1992), p. 138.

[4] Translations of biblical passages have been taken from the NRSV, unless otherwise indicated.

lines of poetry. Besides, the two psalm verses have also been preserved in the later Greek translations of Aquila and Symmachus, and these renderings show that at least in v. 12 of the psalm alternative translations were quite possible. So we have to conclude that Q contained the quotation in its LXX form, and Matthew copied it from Q.

The extent of the quotation differs slightly between Matthew and Luke. After the first line, Luke has the words 'to protect you', which are missing in Matthew (the psalm text is in fact even longer). Did Matthew shorten the Q text or did Luke expand it? If Matthew had found the words in Q, he would not have had reason to omit them; for Luke, on the other hand, they were an appropriate expansion strengthening the effect of the quotation. So Matthew exactly copied not only the wording but also the extent of the quotation from Q.

In the temptation story, the devil makes three efforts to dissuade Jesus from being the obedient Son of God (cf. Matt. 4:3, 6): he challenges him to make loaves of bread out of stones, to throw himself from the temple roof, and to occupy the place of God himself. Three times, Jesus answers with quotations from words that Moses addressed to Israel in the book of Deuteronomy (4:4, = Deut. 8:3; 4:7, = Deut. 6:16; 4:10, = Deut. 6:13). Apparently, Jesus succeeds where Israel failed. In this connection, the devil supports his second challenge with Ps. 91:11–12. The words are originally part of a didactic poem on God's protection, but the devil now perverts them into an invitation to reckless behaviour. He abuses scripture for his own purposes, inviting Jesus to be some kind of Messianic stunt man instead of the obedient Son of God. The same theme will return in another psalm quotation (27:43, = Ps. 22:9), to be discussed later.

Matthew 7:23 = Psalm 6:9

At the end of the Sermon on the Mount, the Matthean Jesus warns his followers that to those who will not do the will of his Father in heaven, he will say when judging them:[5] 'Go away from me, you who work lawlessness.' Matt. 7:22–23 has a parallel in Lk. 13:26–27 and must come from Q. In Lk. 13:27, the same command reads: 'Depart from me, all you doers of injustice'. The words are an unmarked quotation from Ps. 6:9. In the LXX, they read: 'Depart from me, all you who work lawlessness'. Apart from the absence of 'all' in Matthew's text, all three Greek versions (Matthew, Luke, LXX) are adequate renderings of the Hebrew.

We are again confronted with the question of what the quotation looked like in Q, and this time it is not easy to answer. To reconstruct the text of Q, the basic procedure is to compare Matthew and Luke and to ask at every point of difference who of the two evangelists may have had reason to alter the text,

---

[5] I give literal translations of the quotation, its synoptic parallel, and its OT source.

who has the more common and thus probably secondary wording, what may have fitted in best with the interests of Q, etc. In the present case, this procedure leads to the result that 'go away' has a better chance to have been in Q than 'depart', that 'all' was probably missing in Q, and that 'who work lawlessness' has slightly better odds to represent Q's original wording than 'doers of injustice'. This means that, just as in the preceding case, Matthew has preserved the original text of Q, and Luke has modified it.[6]

At first sight, Matthew (following Q) seems to do no more here than put Old Testament language in the mouth of Jesus, who speaks of his role of eschatological judge. However, the latter part of Psalm 6 is about the vindication by God of someone who previously felt rejected and abandoned by God. Such language was easily applied to Jesus in early Christianity: Jesus' appearance 'on that day' (Matt. 7:22) as the one who will pronounce God's final verdict is considered as the moment of his ultimate vindication over against all those who do not do 'the will of my Father in heaven' (7:21). Factors advancing this interpretation may well have been that David was considered to be the author of the psalms, and that Psalm 6 was one of the psalms explicitly ascribed to him (see v. 1).[7] Many psalms were read in early Christianity as dealing with the passion and vindication of Jesus, the Son of David.

Matthew 13:32 = Psalm 104:12

According to Matthew's version of the parable of the mustard seed (13:31–32), the small seed becomes a tree, 'so that the birds of the air come and make nests in its branches'. These words constitute an unmarked quotation from Ps. 104:12. Just as Mark does (4:30–32), Matthew has Jesus narrate the parable of the mustard seed in the course of the parable chapter, but unlike in Mark, the parable is followed in Matthew by the parable of the leaven (13:33), a parable that is similar to the preceding one from the point of view of both structure and contents. Luke has the two parables in the same sequence, but not in the context of the parable discourse (see Lk. 13:18–19, 20–21), and in Luke the parallelism between the two parables is very close. The verbal similarity between the Markan and the Lukan version is very limited; at the same time there are several agreements in wording between Luke and Matthew against Mark (e.g., 'in its branches'). On the other hand, Matthew shares several details with Mark but not with Luke (e.g., 'so that'). All this clearly indicates that the parable was not only in Mark but in Q as well, and that Luke has used the Q version while Matthew has mixed the versions of Mark and Q.

[6] See C. Heil, "'Πάντες ἐργάται ἀδικίας'" Revisited: The Reception of Ps 6,9a LXX in Q and in Luke', in R. Hoppe and U. Busse, eds, *Von Jesus zum Christus: Christologische Studien* (FS P. Hoffmann; BZNW 93; Berlin: W. de Gruyter, 1998), pp. 261–76, esp. pp. 264–71.
[7] See M. Daly-Denton, *David in the Fourth Gospel: The Johannine Reception of the Psalms* (AGJU 47; Leiden: Brill, 2000), pp. 59–113.

Ps. 103:12 LXX reads in a literal translation: 'By them (i.e. the waters) the birds of the air will make nests'; these words are a correct translation of the Hebrew. The words 'in its branches' suggest that apart from the psalm verse, Dan. 4:12 or 4:21 has exerted influence. The psalm verse and the Daniel verses can be considered as analogous Old Testament passages, that is, they have at least one word in common and have a similar content. In early Jewish and early Christian exegesis and transmission of the Old Testament, it was considered legitimate to introduce into an Old Testament passage a word or words from an analogous one, either as a substitute or as an addition,[8] and this is what has happened here. In any case, it is not possible to precisely retrace the unmarked quotation to an extant version of the Old Testament text (Hebrew text, LXX etc.). As said above, Luke is probably close to the original Q version of the parable. If we assume that Luke's text of the final clause of the parable coincides with the text of Q (and there are no reasons to doubt this), then Matthew's final clause is perfectly explicable as Matthean redaction (by means of the insertion of 'come and') of the wording of Q ('the birds of the air ... make nests in its branches') combined with the Markan syntactical construction ('so that').

In the case of this quotation, Matthew (following Q) has borrowed an image from a psalm, to flesh out the contrast drawn in the parable between the inconspicuous beginning and the grand end of the mustard plant. In this respect, God's kingdom resembles the mustard plant.

Matthew 13:35 = Psalm 78:2[9]

In 13:34–35, Matthew concludes a series of parables addressed to the crowds with a summary to the effect that Jesus spoke to them in parables only. The evangelist continues (I translate literally): 'so that might be fulfilled what was spoken by the prophet Isaiah, when he said', and then follows Ps. 78:2:

 I will open my mouth in parables,
 I will utter things hidden since the foundation.

It is necessary to start with a textual problem. In the formula that introduces the quotation, the name 'Isaiah' is lacking in the large majority of textual witnesses, but found in an important and early segment of the textual tradition. The longer reading is the more difficult one and it has, therefore, a better chance of being the original text: it is much more probable that copyists, knowing that the quotation came in fact not from Isaiah but from a psalm,

---

[8] See M.J.J. Menken, *Old Testament Quotations in the Fourth Gospel: Studies in Textual Form* (CBET 15; Kampen: Kok Pharos, 1996), pp. 52–53 (with the lit. mentioned there).

[9] For a detailed study of this quotation, see M.J.J. Menken, 'Isaiah and the "Hidden Things": The Quotation from Psalm 78:2 in Matthew 13:35', in L.V. Rutgers et al., eds, *The Use of Sacred Books in the Ancient World* (CBET 22; Leuven: Peeters, 1998), pp. 61–77.

deleted the prophet's name, than that they wrongly inserted it.[10] So Matthew ascribes a psalm quotation to the prophet Isaiah – a point to which I shall return.[11]

The quotation under discussion belongs to Matthew's fulfilment quotations.[12] These quotations occur not in the words of one of the actors in the story, but in reflective commentaries of the evangelist. This already suggests that they belong to the editorial level of Matthew's Gospel. This suggestion is strengthened by the observations, that they are sometimes added by Matthew to materials that stem from Mark (Matt. 4:14–16; 8:17; 12:17–21; 13:35; 21:4–5), and that they often can be missed without a perceptible loss of flow of the narrative. Matthew introduces them with a stereotyped formula, which basically runs as follows: 'so that might be fulfilled what was spoken by the prophet, when he said'. The wording of this formula must also be due to Matthew.[13]

Scholars have intensively discussed the type of Greek Old Testament text used by Matthew for these fulfilment quotations. To my mind, the most plausible solution is that the evangelist made use of a LXX text that had been revised, mainly to make it agree more closely with the Hebrew text and to improve the quality of the Greek; there are no reasons to assume that Matthew himself was the reviser.[14] In the present case, the LXX basis is evident in the first line of the quotation in that the Hebrew singular משל, 'parable', has been translated by the Greek plural παραβολαί, 'parables'. The revision is perceptible in the second line in that the Hebrew verb נבע hiphil has been rendered by the Greek verb ἐρεύγεσθαι. Both the Hebrew and the Greek verb can be translated as 'to utter'; they share the basic meaning of 'making gush', a basic meaning which is absent from the LXX's φθέγγεσθαι, 'to speak'. Likewise, to translate קדם, 'primeval time', the LXX's ἀρχή, 'beginning', was replaced by καταβολή, 'foundation'. However, one element of the quotation

---

[10] For a similar scribal correction, see Matt. 27:9 ('Jeremiah' changed into 'Zechariah', in the introduction to a quotation from Zechariah).

[11] At the end of the quotation, the shorter reading 'since the foundation' should be preferred to the longer one 'since the foundation of the world': the longer one is an adaptation to prevalent usage (see, e.g., Matt. 25:34; Lk. 11:50).

[12] See K. Stendahl, *The School of St. Matthew and its Use of the Old Testament* (Philadelphia: Fortress Press, 2nd edn, 1968, orig. 1954); Strecker, *Weg der Gerechtigkeit*, pp. 49–85; R.H. Gundry, *The Use of the Old Testament in St. Matthew's Gospel, with Special Reference to the Messianic Hope* (NovTSup 18; Leiden: Brill, 1967, 2nd edn, 1975); W. Rothfuchs, *Die Erfüllungszitate des Matthäus-Evangeliums: Eine biblisch-theologische Untersuchung* (BWANT 88; Stuttgart: Kohlhammer, 1969); G.M. Soares Prabhu, *The Formula Quotations in the Infancy Narrative of Matthew: An Enquiry into the Tradition History of Mt 1–2* (AnBib 63; Rome: Biblical Institute Press, 1976); J. Miler, *Les citations d'accomplissement dans l'Évangile de Matthieu: Quand Dieu se rend présent en toute humanité* (AnBib 140; Rome: Biblical Institute Press, 1999).

[13] For details, see M.J.J. Menken, 'The References to Jeremiah in the Gospel according to Matthew (Mt 2,17; 16,14; 27,9)', *ETL* 60 (1984), pp. 5–24, esp. pp. 6–9.

[14] See M.J.J. Menken, 'The Old Testament Quotation in Matthew 27,9–10: Textual Form and Context', *Bib* 83 (2002), pp. 305–28; my other publications in this field are mentioned in n. 10 on pp. 309–10.

cannot possibly be considered as an adequate translation of the Hebrew: the word κεκρυμμένα, 'hidden things', which must be the equivalent of חירות, 'riddles'. How do we explain this peculiar rendering?

To answer this question, we first have to establish the meaning of the quotation in its Matthean context. When we compare Matthew to Mark, it becomes clear that Matthew in ch. 13 consistently makes Jesus' disciples into those who understand the true purport of the parables, 'the secrets of the kingdom of heaven' (13:11), and the crowds into those to whom these secrets remain hidden (see Matt. 13:10–17, to be compared with Mk 4:10–12). When Matthew perceives the fulfilment of Ps. 78:2 in Jesus' speaking in parables to the crowds, he obviously connects the first line of the quotation ('I will open my mouth in parables') with the fact that Jesus spoke in parables, and the second line ('I will utter things hidden since the foundation') with the fact that these parables contained a message concerning the kingdom of heaven that remained hidden from the uncomprehending crowds. The second line does not refer to revelation of secrets, but *to their being hidden* ('to utter' is not 'to make known').

Jesus' saying in Matt. 11:25, derived from Q (cf. Lk. 10:21), can put us further on the track: 'I thank you, Father, Lord of heaven and earth, because you have hidden these things from the wise and the intelligent and have revealed them to infants'. In the context of Matthew, the tenor of this logion is close to the idea about the function of the parables in Matthew 13: the revelation Jesus brings is destined for the elect, and remains hidden from the others. Now this logion clearly alludes to Isa. 29:14: 'The wisdom of their wise shall perish, and the discernment of the discerning shall be hidden'. In Matt. 11:25 (as already in Q), this verse from Isaiah, which constitutes a small unit with the preceding v. 13, must have been read as saying that God shall hide his revelation of true wisdom and discernment from those who seem to be wise and discerning. That *their* wisdom perishes and *their* discernment is hidden, implies that *true* wisdom and *true* discernment are hidden from them.[15] Isa. 29:13–14 can easily be considered as analogous to Ps. 78:1–2: the two passages share the words 'people' and 'mouth', and have a comparable content, at least if one reads them as Matthew or the early Christian tradition before him read them: God's secrets, the true wisdom and discernment, are hidden. Because of this analogy, it was permitted to replace 'riddles' by 'hidden things'.

We can now explain the seemingly wrong ascription of the quotation: by ascribing it to Isaiah, Matthew draws attention to the element in it that comes from Isaiah. This element, that would otherwise easily escape the reader or

---

[15] Matthew and other early Christians were clearly interested in Isa. 29:13–14; see, e.g., Mk 7:6–7 // Matt. 15:8–9; 1 Cor. 1:19; Col. 2:22.

listener, precisely makes the psalm verse applicable to Matthew's idea that Jesus' parables conceal the secrets of the kingdom from the crowds.[16]

Matthew 16:27 = Psalm 62:13

Matt. 16:24–28 is a series of logia on the consequences of discipleship, climaxing in a view of the eschatological future. Matthew borrowed the series from Mk 8:34–9:1. One of his modifications is that after the words on the future glorious coming of the Son of Man, he has added an unmarked Old Testament quotation:[17] 'And then he will repay everyone according to his doing.' That the small clause is a Matthean insertion is obvious, not only from its absence in Mark, but also from the typically Matthean introductory 'then' and from the circumstance that the theme of judgement according to what one has done is prominent in Matthew's Gospel (see esp. ch. 25).

There are two possible sources of the quotation: Ps. 62:13 and Prov. 24:12. The Hebrew of the psalm verse reads: 'For you repay a man according to his deed'; the LXX has: 'For you will repay everyone according to his works'. The Hebrew of Prov. 24:12 reads: 'And he will repay a person according to his work'; the LXX: 'Who repays everyone according to his works'. If we take into account that Matthew had to adapt person or tense of the verbal form to the new context, we can consider both parallels in their LXX version as possible sources of the quotation, apart from the final words ('his doing'). In both cases, the translation 'everyone' points to the LXX.

The difference between Matthew's quotation and the LXX is that the quotation has 'doing' (πρᾶξις) where the LXX has 'works' (ἔργα). The Greek word πρᾶξις is sometimes used by the later Greek translators of the OT, especially Symmachus. It may well have collective meaning and refer to human activity, and it is precisely in this sense that it functions in Matt. 16:27b. Taking into account the use of πρᾶξις among the later Greek translators, I would consider the Old Testament translation offered here in Matthew as a revision of the LXX. Matthew's vocabulary makes it improbable that he is responsible for this revision.

If Matthew is consciously quoting here, he applies an Old Testament statement about God as judge to Jesus. This has to be understood against a double background:

(a) In the ancient Greek translations of the Old Testament, the divine name יהוה is ususally translated as κύριος, 'Lord'. Because early Christians considered Jesus as κύριος, they easily applied Old Testament statements about God as 'Lord' to him (see, e.g., Isa. 40:3 in Matt. 3:3 and parallels).

---

[16] In a similar way, Matthew has ascribed in 27:9–10 a quotation from Zech. 11:13 to Jeremiah, because the word 'field' derives from Jer. 32:6–15. See R.H. Gundry, *Matthew: A Commentary on his Handbook for a Mixed Church under Persecution* (Grand Rapids: Eerdmans, 2nd edn, 1994), p. 557.

[17] Quotation and OT sources are literally translated.

(b) Early Christians assumed that God had delegated the execution of eschatological judgement to Jesus.[18]

Matthew 21:9 = Psalm 118:25–26

When Jesus enters into Jerusalem, the crowds acclaim him, according to Matthew, with the words:

> Hosanna to the Son of David!
> Blessed is the one who comes in the name of the Lord!
> Hosanna in the highest heaven!

Matthew's entry narrative (21:1–11) derives from Mark (11:1–11). Apart from 'to the Son of David', the words just quoted have been taken over verbatim from Mk 11:9 (cf. Lk. 19:38). The word 'Hosanna' comes from Ps. 118:25: ὡσαννά is a Greek transliteration of הרשיעה נא, 'save now', correctly rendered in the ancient Greek translations of the Old Testament as σῶσον δή. It seems that already in pre-Christian Judaism, the shout had developed from a prayer for help into a liturgical praise.[19] The clause 'Blessed is the one who comes in the name of the Lord!' comes from Ps. 118:26. Mark's version of it, and thus Matthew's as well, agrees with the LXX, but this fact is not very telling, because the LXX here offers a correct translation of the Hebrew and alternative translations are hardly possible. Psalm 118 is part of the *Hallel* (113–118), sung in Jewish liturgy, both in the time of the temple and afterwards, at various occasions, among them the festivals of Passover and Tabernacles.

Ps. 118:26 must originally have been a blessing of a person approaching the temple on a festive occasion. Early Christians read it as being about God's eschatological envoy, whom they identified with Jesus of Nazareth. Matthew contrasts, in his entry narrative, the positive answer to Jesus on the part of 'the crowds' with the negative reaction of 'the whole city', later concentrated into 'the chief priests and the scribes' (see 21:10–11, 15; cf. 2:3–4: 'all Jerusalem' concentrated into 'the chief priests and the scribes'). The application of Ps. 118:26 to Jesus is part of the positive answer of the crowds: the qualification 'the one who comes in the name of the Lord' is on a par with the titles 'king' (21:5), 'Son of David' (21:9), 'prophet' (21:11). Jesus is 'the coming one' (3:11; 11:3) in whom God is going to realize salvation for Israel and for the world, acclaimed by the crowds, rejected by the authorities.[20]

Matthew 21:16 = Psalm 8:3

Following on the cleansing of the temple, Matthew relates a small scene that

---

[18] See Acts 10:42; 17:31, and cf. Matt. 13:41–43; 25:31–46.

[19] See E. Lohse, 'ὡσαννά', *TWNT* 9:682–84.

[20] See J. Nieuviarts, *L'entrée de Jésus à Jérusalem (Mt 21, 1–17): Messianisme et accomplissement des Écritures en Matthieu* (LD 176; Paris: Cerf, 1999), pp. 107–13.

has no parallel in Mark or Luke (21:14–16). In the temple, blind and lame come to Jesus, and he heals them. The chief priests and the scribes, seeing his miracles and the children who acclaim him, become angry and ask Jesus whether he hears what they say. He answers, in v. 16, by asking if they have never read the words from Ps. 8:3:

> Out of the mouths of infants and nursing babies
> you have prepared praise for yourself.

The textual form of Matthew's quotation is that of the LXX. The Hebrew text is different; it reads in a literal English translation: 'Out of the mouths of infants and nursing babies you have founded strength'. The uncommon, even unique translations of יסד, 'to found', by καταρτίζειν, 'to prepare', and of עז, 'strength', by αἶνος, 'praise', show beyond doubt that the LXX is indeed the source of the quotation, and it is evident that only the LXX translation with its peculiar traits can serve in the present context: Jesus defends the song of the children in his honour by referring to words from scripture about infants and sucklings singing God's praise.

In the introduction, I have put this quotation in the category of quotations derived from M. This point requires demonstration: did Matthew indeed make use here of M, that is, of traditional material in which the quotation already occurred? The question is important, because in studying Matt. 13:35 and 16:27, we saw that when Matthew himself inserts quotations, he makes use of a revised LXX, and in such a revision the deviations from the Hebrew just noted would almost certainly have been corrected. I start with a series of observations:

(a) Matt. 21:14–16 is made up of two units, each belonging to a different genre. Verse 14 is a very brief and general report on Jesus' healings in the temple; vv. 15–16 is a controversy story. There is no intrinsic relationship between the two units: Jesus' answer refers only to the praise of the children, not to the healings, and their praise is not caused by the healings but simply mentioned next to them. So it seems that the connection between the summary of v. 14 and the controversy of vv. 15–16 is secondary.

(b) The summary of v. 14 probably stems from Matthew. The vocabulary betrays it ('to come to', 'blind' and 'lame', 'to heal'), and the brief scene has clear parallels in other summaries of Jesus' healing ministry in Matthew, most of which are almost entirely products of Matthean redaction.[21] Especially 15:30 is important in this respect, because almost all of the words of 21:14 are found there. If v. 14 indeed constitutes a Matthean summary, the artificial link with vv. 15–16 suggests that these verses belong, at least in their core, to Matthew's traditional material.

---

[21] See Matt. 4:23, 24; 8:16; 9:35; 12:15; 14:14; 15:30–31; 19:2.

(c) The controversy belongs together with the entry into Jerusalem, not with the cleansing of the temple: when he enters the city, Jesus is hailed by people shouting 'Hosanna'. In the present setting of Matt. 21:15–16, the children who acclaim Jesus appear (so to speak) out of the blue. If the controversy originally belonged with the entry, the children are part of the crowd accompanying Jesus.

(d) The controversy story has a parallel in Lk. 19:39–40: people sing Jesus' praise in Jerusalem after his entry, Jewish authorities take offence, and Jesus gives them a sharp retort. Although Matt. 21:15–16 and Lk. 19:39–40 differ in wording and in many details, their basic contents and pattern agree, so that they can be considered as two variants of a tradition which was immediately connected to Jesus' entry into Jerusalem.

So Matt. 21:15–16 stems, at least in its core, from a pre-Matthean tradition of Jesus' entry into Jerusalem. Matthew may have rewritten it in some respects, mainly to adjust it to its context, but the 'children' who acclaim Jesus must have belonged to the core, because they appear so unexpectedly in the present context. If the children acclaiming Jesus belong to the core, the quotation will also come from this pre-Matthean tradition, because the presence of the children and the contents of Jesus' answer presuppose one another. So Matthew did not himself make use of the LXX, but he found the LXX quotation in the materials which he used.

Matthew probably interpreted the quotation in connection with Jesus' saying in 11:25, that 'infants', not the wise and discerning, receive God's revelation in Jesus. He thus applied the quotation to his community: they are the 'infants', who have accepted God's revelation in Jesus and therefore praise Jesus.[22] Originally, the 'you' of the psalm verse is God; in the interpretation given in Matthew, it is Jesus. We observed the same shift in the interpretation of Ps. 62:13 in Matt. 16:27. The addressee of the praise of Psalm 8 is God. At the beginning and the end of the psalm, the psalmist sings to him: 'O Lord, our Sovereign, how majestic is your name in all the earth!' (vv. 2, 10). Early Christians had no difficulty in identifying the Lord of the psalm with their Lord, Jesus: as 'the one who comes in the name of the Lord', he was entitled to the same honour as the one who sent him (see for Matthew: 11:27; 28:18; outside Matthew, see especially the early Christian hymns in Eph. 1:20–22; Phil. 2:6–11).

Matthew 21:42 = Psalm 118:22–23

Jesus' action in the temple is followed, in both Mark and Matthew, by a series of confrontations between Jesus and the Jewish authorities. The parable of the

---

[22] See Nieuviarts, *L'entrée de Jésus*, pp. 196, 270–71, 287.

wicked husbandmen is the centre of one of these. At the end of the parable, Jesus asks his audience (the chief priests and the Pharisees, 21:45) if they have never read the words of Ps. 118:22–23:

The stone that the builders rejected
has become the cornerstone;
this was the Lord's doing,
and it is amazing in our eyes.

Matthew has derived this parable and the closing scene from Mark: Matt. 21:33–46 parallels Mk 12:1–12. Mark has the same quotation, in exactly the same form, in vv. 10–11 (cf. Lk. 20:17); so Matthew copied it from Mark without modifying anything. Mark's text of the psalm agrees completely with the LXX, and must come from there: at several points alternative translations were possible, and complete agreement over four lines of poetry is an unmistakable mark of literary dependence.

The story of the landowner whose slaves and son are maltreated and killed by wicked tenants refusing to hand over the produce, clearly has allegorical traits: it is a retelling of Israel's history in images derived from Isaiah 5. Israel's leaders did not fulfil their obligations to God, but instead maltreated or killed the prophets sent by him. He finally sends his Son Jesus, whom they kill; punishment awaits them, and God will end his relationship with them.

Jesus then quotes the verses from Psalm 118. The quotation gives another interpretation of his fate, adding the element of his vindication. 'The stone that the builders rejected' must be Jesus, who will be rejected by those whom he is addressing; that this rejected stone now occupies the important position of 'the cornerstone', must refer to his resurrection as his vindication by God. With the second part of the quotation, Jesus clearly states that this miraculous reversal is indeed God's work. The pattern of rejection and vindication that the psalmist draws with the metaphor of the stone, is found in overt language in Jesus' announcements of his passion and resurrection in Matt. 16:21; 17:22–23; 20:18–19. The scriptural word about the rejected stone is realized in what happens to Jesus. In fact, early Christians could easily read the entire thanksgiving for deliverance from distress of Psalm 118 as having been realized in Jesus' death and resurrection. In any case, the use of the psalm presupposes the Christian belief in Jesus' resurrection.

Matthew 22:44 = Psalm 110:1

The final confrontation between Jesus and the authorities (here the Pharisees) is a scene in which Jesus asks them whose son they think the Messiah is. They answer that the Messiah is the Son of David. He says: 'How is it then that David by the Spirit calls him Lord, saying,

> The Lord said to my Lord,
> Sit at my right hand,
> until I put your enemies
> under your feet?

If David thus calls him Lord, how can he be his Son?' Matt. 22:41–45 has a parallel in Mk 12:35–37; Matthew apparently borrowed the scene from Mark, enlivening it by making a monologue into a dialogue. In the quotation from Ps. 110:1, he did not make any modification: Matthew and Mark agree here completely (cf. Lk. 20:42–43). Mark's text is all but identical with the LXX, and must come from that translation: the Hebrew could have been rendered differently at some points, and the agreement over four lines of poetry is significant. There is, however, one substantial point of difference: instead of 'under your feet' (ὑποκάτω τῶν ποδῶν σου) in the final line, the LXX has 'a footstool for your feet' (ὑποπόδιον τῶν ποδῶν σου), which is a correct translation of the Hebrew. The change in the biblical text offered here by Mark, and in his wake by Matthew, is probably due to the influence of the analogous passage Ps. 8:7, where the psalmist says to God about human beings: 'You have put all things under their feet (ὑποκάτω τῶν ποδῶν αὐτοῦ)'. The combination of these two psalm verses, applied to the universal rule of Christ, is found elsewhere in the New Testament as well (see 1 Cor. 15:25–27; Eph. 1:20–22).

The interpretation of the psalm verse in Matthew presupposes its Davidic authorship (see Ps. 110:1). David spoke 'by the Spirit' (22:43), that is, as a prophet (cf. Acts 2:30), and in this quality, he reports a divine oracle. 'The Lord', who utters the oracle, is God (the LXX's κύριος renders the divine name יהוה. 'My Lord' (τῷ κυρίῳ μου), whom God invites to sit at his right hand, is the Messiah, traditionally considered as the Son of David, on the basis of Old Testament passages such as 2 Sam. 7:12; Jer. 23:5. So the question arises (22:45): how can the Messiah be at the same time David's Lord and his Son? An answer is not given here; Matthew even observes that 'no one was able to give him an answer' (22:46). From Matthew's perspective, the problem has been solved right from the beginning of his gospel. The genealogy of Jesus in 1:1–17 shows that Joseph is a descendant of David; the birth narrative in 1:18–25 shows that Mary's child is from the Holy Spirit. By Joseph taking Mary as his wife, Jesus is so to speak Son of David by adoption and Son of God by nature, and he can be addressed as 'Lord' (cf. Rom. 1:3–4).

Matthew 23:39 = Psalm 118:26

In Matthew 23, Jesus delivers a long discourse against the scribes and the Pharisees. It ends with a lament over Jerusalem (23:37–39), which has a parallel in Lk. 13:34–35 and must come from Q. Jerusalem has thwarted Jesus' wish to gather her children; their house will be left desolate to them (an allusion to the fall of Jerusalem and the temple), and they will not see Jesus again until they say: 'Blessed is the one who comes in the name of the Lord'. This is another unmarked quotation from Ps. 118:26. The textual form is the same as in 21:9. There, Matthew copied the quotation from Mark; here, he has borrowed it from Q.

The point in time at which Jerusalem will speak the words from the psalm, must be the eschaton: then Jesus will appear again, they will see him, and they will recognize him as 'the one who comes in the name of the Lord'. The preceding discourse against the Jewish authorities and the ensuing eschatological discourse (see esp. 24:30) suggest that Matthew's Jesus here speaks of judgement rather than salvation.[23]

Matthew 26:38 = Psalm 42:6, 12; 43:5

In Gethsemane, Jesus takes Peter and the two sons of Zebedee with him, and begins to be distressed. He then says to them (I translate literally): 'My soul is deeply grieved'. Matthew's passion narrative has almost in its entirety been derived from Mark; the clause just quoted also occurs, in precisely the same form, in Mk 14:34, and must come from there. It is an unmarked quotation from the book of Psalms. Psalms 42 and 43 constitute together one lament: the psalmist is in deep distress and is longing for God's presence. Three times (42:6, 12; 43:5), there is a refrain that starts with the question: 'Why are you cast down, O my soul?' The LXX translates, somewhat freely: 'Why are you deeply grieved, O soul?' In Mark and Matthew, 'deeply grieved' points, in combination with 'soul', indeed to this refrain in its LXX version as the source of the unmarked quotation.

We see here another example of language from psalms of lament put in Jesus' mouth; more examples will follow. Early Christians recognized Jesus in the suffering righteous one who feels abandoned by God as depicted in several psalms. It is quite possible that they hereby continued Jesus' own recognition of himself in these psalms.

Matthew 26:64 = Psalm 110:1

When Jesus is interrogated by the high priest, he finally seems to admit that he is the Messiah, the Son of God (26:64). Woven into an unmarked quotation from Dan. 7:13, there is an unmarked quotation from Ps. 110:1. About the Son of Man who will come on the clouds of heaven, Jesus says that he will be 'seated at the right hand of Power'. Matthew derived the words from Mk 14:62, where they are identical, except for word order. Mark has, in an extremely literal translation: 'at the right hand seated of Power'. In this respect, Matthew's text is closer to the LXX (and to the

---

[23] See U. Luz, *Das Evangelium nach Matthäus 3: Mt 18–25* (EKKNT 1/3; Zürich: Benziger; Neukirchen-Vluyn: Neukirchener Verlag, 1997), pp. 382–85.

Hebrew text; see above, on Matt. 22:44). Does this mean that Matthew adapted to the LXX? To my mind, there are simpler explanations. Matthew may have adapted this quotation to the marked one in 22:44 (which was copied verbatim from Mk 12:36). Besides, the change of word order is in line with Matthew's normal use of Greek verbs meaning 'to sit' and the like: if they are accompanied by an adjunct, the verb precedes and the adjunct follows.

With the words of the psalm, Jesus refers to the position at the right hand of God he will occupy after his resurrection. Those addressed will see him coming on the clouds of heaven at his parousia (cf. Matt. 24:30), and then it will become clear to them that God already vindicated him after his death.

Matthew 27:35 = Psalm 22:19

An unmarked quotation from Ps. 22:19 (cf. Lk. 23:34) is found in the crucifixion scene in Matthew's passion narrative:[24] 'They divided his garments by casting lots'. Matthew found the quotation in Mk 15:24: 'They divide his garments by casting lots over them'. The verse reads in the LXX, which is here an adequate translation of the Hebrew: 'They divided my garments among them, and over my clothing they cast lots'. Matthew has changed Mark's historic present ('they divide') into an aorist ('they divided'), and omitted the final words 'over them'. The former intervention enhances the similarity to the LXX, the latter diminishes it because the preposition 'over' disappears. Matthew clearly tends towards eliminating Mark's historic present; he largely restricts its use to verbs of speaking.[25] So the former change is adequately explained by Matthew's usual editing of Mark; there is no need to appeal to the LXX. Such an appeal would also make the omission of Mark's final words difficult to explain. This omission (and also that of the following words 'what each should take') is easily explained by Matthew's tendency to omit from Mark's narrative pieces of information which he deems superfluous.

Psalm 22 is a 'psalm of the suffering righteous one' (just as, e.g., Psalm 69), and one of the details of his suffering is that his opponents cast lots to divide his clothes. To describe what happened when Jesus was crucified, Mark uses the words of Ps. 21:19 LXX, and Matthew follows him. Just as in the case of the quotation from Ps. 6:9 in Matt. 7:23, it may well be relevant to this quotation that it comes from a psalm ascribed to David (see Ps. 22:1). We have already seen that David could be considered as a prophet of what would happen to the Messiah. We find an interesting example of this view in Acts 2:25–31 and 13:35–37: from the fact that things said by David about himself in Ps. 16:8–11

---

[24] I give quotation, synoptic parallel and OT sources in a literal translation.
[25] See F. Neirynck, with Th. Hansen and F. Van Segbroeck, *The Minor Agreements of Matthew and Luke against Mark, with a Cumulative List* (BETL 37; Leuven: Leuven University Press, 1974), pp. 223–29.

were not fulfilled in his life, Luke has Peter and Paul argue that David spoke about his offspring, the Messiah. Early Christians probably saw the sufferings depicted in Psalm 22 in the same light: David prophesied about the passion of the Messiah, and what happened to Jesus, was the fulfilment of David's words.

Matthew 27:43 = Psalm 22:9

Comparing Matt. 27:39–44 with Mk 15:29–32, we see that Matthew has prolonged the scoffing by the members of the Sanhedrin with the words:[26] 'He trusts in God, let him deliver now, if he wishes him'. This is an unmarked quotation of Ps. 22:9. The LXX differs somewhat: 'He has hoped in the Lord, let him deliver him; let him save him, for he wishes him'. This is for the most part an acceptable translation of the Hebrew. The problematic point is at the beginning of the verse. The Hebrew has there an imperative: 'roll away'. The LXX translator apparently vocalized the verbal form differently and read a perfect, and interpreted the metaphor of rolling away one's distress to God by the theological language of hoping in God. He must have felt legitimated to do so by the analogous v. 5 of the same psalm: 'They trusted, and you delivered them'. The Hebrew verb בטח, 'to trust', is rendered here in the LXX by ἐλπίζειν, 'to hope', and the translator has used the same verb in v. 9.

It is fairly obvious that Matthew as editor of Mark inserted the verse 27:43, and that it does not come from another source. First of all, the evangelist has the members of the Sanhedrin explain their quotation from the psalm with the words: 'For he said, I am the Son of God'. That Jesus dies as 'the Son of God', is a theme that Matthew derives from Mark (see 26:63 // Mk 14:61; 27:54 // Mk 15:39), but that he also expands (see 27:40 diff. Mk 15:30). Secondly, Matthew has not only borrowed but also expanded the Markan references to Psalms 22 and 69 in the context of our quotation.[27] The contents of 27:43 fit in well with clear Matthean interests; the verse must therefore be considered as due to Matthean redaction.

Some minor deviations from the text of the psalm in the quotation are easily explained as adaptations to the Matthean context, such as 'God' instead of 'the Lord' (Jesus dies in Matthew's view as 'the Son of God', cf. also the quotation from Ps. 22:2 in 27:46), and the addition of 'now' (to adapt to 'now' in the preceding verse). Without the editorial modifications, the quotation reads: 'He trusts in the Lord, let him deliver ... if he wishes him'.

What type of text do we have here? There is a LXX layer in it: in the case of the words translated as 'in' (ἐπί + acc.), 'deliver' (ῥυσάσθω) and 'wishes' (θέλει + acc.), the Hebrew could have been translated into Greek in various

---

[26] Quotation and OT sources are given in a literal translation.

[27] For borrowings from Mark, see Matt. 27:35, 39, 46, 48; for expansions, see Matt. 27:29 (mocking, Ps. 22:8), 34 (gall, Ps. 69:22), 49 (saving, Ps. 22:6, 9, 22), 50 (crying, Ps. 22:3, 25).

ways, but in all three instances, Matthew's quotation agrees with the LXX. On the other hand, 'he trusts' (πέποιθεν) and 'if' (εἰ) differ from the LXX. The latter word is an alternative translation of the Hebrew: the conjunction כִּי can mean both 'if' and 'for'. 'If' suits the context just as well as 'for', maybe even slightly better. In meaning, 'he trusts' does not differ very much from 'he hoped', so the translation 'he trusts' is based on the same interpretation of the Hebrew as the LXX. However, 'to trust' is a more adequate translation of the Hebrew verb בָּטַח; the later Greek translators of the Old Testament often prefer 'to trust' to 'to hope'. We have to conclude that the translation of Ps. 22:9 in Matt. 27:43 has the characteristics of a revised LXX: we see an obvious LXX basis, and corrections intended to render the Hebrew more adequately.

That Matthew translated the Hebrew himself is improbable on account of the LXX layer in the quotation. That he revised the LXX is also improbable: in the quotation from Isa. 42:1–4 in Matt. 12:18–21, Matthew left the verb 'to hope' in his Greek text unchanged (v. 21). This suggests that, had he found it in his Greek text of Ps. 22:9, he would have retained it. We have to asssume then that 'he trusts' was already in the text used by Matthew. So a good case can be made for the position that Matthew, in quoting from Ps. 22:9 in 27:43, made use of an existing revised LXX text.

The insertion of the unmarked quotation serves Matthew's aim of showing that Jesus is the righteous sufferer of Psalm 22. We have seen that he found this identification in Mark, and further elaborated it. Here, words of those who mock the psalmist and shake their heads (see Ps. 22:8, to be compared with Matt. 27:39), are put in the mouth of those who mock Jesus. Very much like the devil in the temptation narrative, they challenge Jesus to avoid passion and death; such things do not fit in well with their view of the Son of God. Jesus, on the other hand, accepts passion and death as the obedient Son of God.

Matthew 27:46 = Psalm 22:2

According to Matt. 27:46, Jesus utters, just before he dies, words from Ps. 22:2 in Aramaic: 'Eli, Eli, lema sabachthani?' The evangelist adds a Greek translation:[28] 'My God, my God, to what end have you forsaken me?' In Mk 15:34, which was Matthew's source here, Jesus' words read: 'Eloi, Eloi, lema sabachthani?' The translation is here: 'My God, my God, for what purpose have you forsaken me?' Ps. 21:2 LXX has: 'My God, my God, give heed to me; to what end have you forsaken me?' This is a reasonable translation of the Hebrew text, except for 'give heed to me', which has no equivalent there.

Matthew has changed the Aramaic part in one respect: 'Eloi' has become 'Eli'. This modification was probably motivated by the wish to make the intervention of the bystanders ('This man is calling for Elijah', 27:47) better

---

[28] Once more, it is necessary to give literal English translations of quotation, synoptic parallel and OT source.

understood. It requires no more than some elementary knowledge of Hebrew or Aramaic. The Greek translation has undergone three modifications (only the second one of these can be made visible in English):

(a) In Mark, 'my God' translates a Greek nominative; Matthew has quite correctly changed this into a vocative.
(b) The change of 'for what purpose' into 'to what end' also serves the goal of stylistic improvement (cf. Matt. 9:4 diff. Mk 2:8).
(c) Matthew has inverted the sequence of verb and object. This is a question of creating better Greek as well.

The second change assimilates the quotation to Ps. 21:2 LXX; the other changes make quotation and LXX more different. If Matthew intended to assimilate, it is inconceivable why he did not eliminate the other points of difference as well.

This time, Jesus identifies himself with the suffering righteous one by making words of Ps. 22:2 into his own words. It is remarkable that they are first given in Aramaic. This is not yet in itself an indication of historicity, but it points at least to ancient tradition. That Jesus felt abandoned by God, his Father, is a datum that has the earmark of historicity: it is at odds with the development of early Christian tradition, in which Jesus' closeness to God, even in his passion, is emphasized more and more. In Luke, Jesus' final saying is: 'Father, into your hands I commend my spirit' (23:46, = Ps. 31:6). In John, it is: 'It is finished' (19:30), and in this gospel Jesus says immediately before his passion: 'Yet I am not alone because the Father is with me' (16:32). Mark and Matthew have preserved that Jesus felt forsaken by God, and it is plausible that Jesus expressed this feeling by means of psalm words.

Conclusion

It has been established that Matthew's quotations from the book of Psalms do not agree with one single version of the Old Testament text. If the evangelist finds psalm quotations in his sources (Mark, Q, M), he simply copies them in the textual form they already have in the source (mostly the LXX). He sometimes makes small changes, but these belong to his normal treatment of his sources. There was no evidence that Matthew adapted quotations found in his sources to the LXX. A few quotations in which a small modification led to agreement with the LXX were found, but in such quotations other changes diminished the agreement, so that on the whole, Matthew's own usual editorial activity constitutes the best explanation for all changes made by him in quotations found in Mark, Q, or M.[29]

---

[29] See Soares Prabhu, *Formula Quotations*, pp. 77–84; G. Stanton, 'Matthew', in D.A. Carson and H.C.M. Williamson, eds, *It is Written: Scripture Citing Scripture* (FS B. Lindars; Cambridge: Cambridge University Press, 1988), pp. 205–19, esp. pp. 210–13.

There are also a few psalm quotations which Matthew as an editor inserted into his sources. Their textual form is best explained as a LXX that had undergone some correction, mainly to enhance its agreement with the Hebrew text and to improve the quality of its Greek. This textual form was encountered in the only Matthean fulfilment quotation coming from a psalm (13:35), and in the other psalm quotations that were inserted at the editorial level (16:27; 27:43). As I have said, use of this revised LXX accounts in my view for the peculiar textual form of Matthew's fulfilment quotations. This revised LXX probably was the evangelist's own biblical text, 'Matthew's bible', at least as far as the book of Psalms and the latter prophets are concerned.

Matthew's selection of psalm quotations is largely governed by tradition. For most of his psalm quotations, this is already evident from the fact that Matthew borrowed them from Mark, Q, or M. Very soon in the development of early Christianity, certain parts of the Old Testament and thus also certain psalms must have acquired special popularity because of their applicability to the Jesus event and its effects in the life of the church: they are referred to, by means of quotations and allusions, several times in the New Testament, and in various documents.[30] Limiting ourselves to marked and unmarked quotations from the psalms, we can draw up the following list (synoptic parallels have already been mentioned and are omitted here):

Ps. 6:9 in Matt. 7:23	Ps. 6:4–5 in Jn 12:27
Ps. 8:3 in Matt. 21:16	Ps. 8:5–7 in Heb. 2:6–8 Ps. 8:7 in 1 Cor. 15:27; Eph. 1:22
Ps. 22:2 in Matt. 27:46 Ps. 22:9 in Matt. 27:43 Ps. 22:19 in Matt. 27:35	Ps. 22:14 in 1 Pet. 5:8 Ps. 22:19 in Jn 19:24 Ps. 22:23 in Heb. 2:12
Ps. 78:2 in Matt. 13:35	Ps. 78:24 in Jn 6:31
Ps. 110:1 in Matt. 22:44; 26:64	Ps. 110:1 in Acts 2:34–35; 1 Cor. 15:25; Heb. 1:13 Ps. 110:4 in Heb. 5:6; 7:17, 21
Ps. 118:22–23 in Matt. 21:42 Ps. 118:25–26 in Matt. 21:9 Ps. 118:26 in Matt. 23:39	Ps. 118:6 in Heb. 13:6 Ps. 118:22 in 1 Pet. 2:7[31] Ps. 118:25–26 in Jn 12:13

It is evident that several early Christian authors were interested in Psalms 8, 22, 110, and 118. From a very early stage, these psalms have been influential in articulating ideas about the significance of Jesus: he has come in the name of God and is entitled to divine honour; he is the suffering righteous one, rejected by the authorities but vindicated by God; he now occupies the place of honour

---

[30] See C.H. Dodd, *According to the Scriptures: The Substructure of New Testament Theology* (London: Nisbet, 1952); B. Lindars, *New Testament Apologetic: The Doctrinal Significance of the Old Testament Quotations* (London: SCM Press 1961).

[31] One should add here the important allusion in Acts 4:11.

at God's right hand, is exercising universal rule and will return as the eschatological judge.

Matthew himself added three psalm quotations. One of these reinforces the traditional identification of Jesus as the suffering righteous one (Ps. 22:9 in Matt. 27:43), another one emphasizes a favourite Matthean theological theme: that Jesus will judge all according to their works (Ps. 62:13 in Matt. 16:27). The third one is the fulfilment quotation from Ps. 78:2 in Matt. 13:35: Matthew shows that in Jesus' parabolic discourse and its effects words from scripture are fulfilled. Again, a favourite Matthean theme is stressed by means of a psalm quotation.[32]

The hermeneutical point of view on which Matthew's interpretation of the psalms is based, is by and large that of fulfilment.[33] This point of view is of course not limited to the psalms; it concerns the rest of the Old Testament as well. Speaking of 'fulfilling' verbal utterances, either oral or written, is an evidently metaphorical way of speaking. The idea at the basis of the metaphor is that words can be 'empty', that is, without a referent in reality corresponding to them, and that they have to be 'filled' with reality. Before the coming of Jesus, scripture remains, so to speak, empty; Jesus is the reality that fills the words of scripture.[34] The point of view of fulfilment was generally accepted in early Christian mission, apologetics and theology, and it had an eschatological connotation: the fulfilment in Jesus marked the time of the end. Matthew found the idea of fulfilment of the scriptures in Mark (see Mk 14:49 // Matt. 26:56), but developed it on a much larger scale than his predecessor in his series of fulfilment quotations. The stereotyped formula with which he introduces these quotations, betrays that to his mind, the words of the prophets are the primary object of fulfilment. The only psalm quotation in this group (13:35) is also introduced as a prophetic quotation (which it partially is, as we have seen).

However, many of Matthew's psalm quotations are based on the concept of fulfilment without the terminology of fulfilment being used (and this already concerns Matthew's sources as well). It is evidently the case in the marked quotations from Psalms 8, 110 and 118 in 21:16, 42; 22:44: psalm words are realized in Jesus' entry into Jerusalem, his rejection and vindication, and his present position with God. Even in the mocking use of Psalm 91 by the devil in the temptation story (4:6), the idea of fulfilment could be in the background: the Christian reader of the story knows that God will protect his Son, but in a way that differs considerably from what the devil imagines here! For unmarked quotations, it is not always easy to tell whether the idea of

---

[32] See Matt. 5:25–26; 7:24–27; 11:16–19; 12:43–45; 13:1–52; 18:12–14, 23–35; 20:1–16; 21:28–22:14; 24:25–25:46.

[33] See R. Schnackenburg, *Die Person Jesu Christi im Spiegel der vier Evangelien* (HTKNTSup 4; Freiburg: Herder, 1993), pp. 127–34.

[34] See G. Delling, 'πλήρη, κτλ πλήρης.', *TWNT* 6:283–309, esp. 293–5.

fulfilment is behind them. The idea is no doubt present in the references to Psalms 110 and 118 in Matt. 21:9; 26:64. In the references to psalms of the suffering righteous one in Matt. 26:38; 27:35, 43, 46, it may also be in view, certainly insofar as this figure is identified with the Davidic Messiah. In a few cases, a future fulfilment of the psalm word is in view (possibly in Matt. 7:23; 16:27; clearly in 23:39). This may even be the case in the unmarked quotation from Ps. 104:12 in 13:32 (which is at first sight simply pictorial), if the birds of heaven stand for the Gentiles who will enter into God's kingdom.[35]

Matthew's view of the significance of the psalms is probably best perceptible in the way his Jesus introduces the quotation from Ps. 110:1 in 22:44: in the psalms, David spoke 'by the Spirit' about the son of David, who is at the same time the Son of God.

---

[35] See W.D. Davies and D.C. Allison, *A Critical and Exegetical Commentary on the Gospel according to Saint Matthew 2: Commentary on Matthew VIII–XVIII* (ICC; Edinburgh: T & T Clark, 1991), pp. 419–21.

Chapter 5

The Psalms in Luke-Acts

Peter Doble

Introduction

When Luke retold Jesus' story for Theophilus he prepared an 'orderly narrative' in two parts (Lk. 1:1–4; Acts 1:1). While his first part resembles other 'gospels', the second is unique in the New Testament. Continuing Jesus' story beyond his resurrection, Acts pictures 'apostolic' witnesses arguing from scripture that God had raised the crucified Jesus, making him both 'Lord' and 'Christ'. In this two-volume, systematic narrative, constituting nearly one-third of the New Testament, Luke made much of Jesus' story as *the fulfilling of scripture*, focusing especially on Psalms.

In Luke's narrative,[1] readers encounter fourteen quotations, or near-quotations, from Psalms,[2] six in Luke and eight in Acts (see Table 1).

Table 1   Psalm quotations in Luke-Acts

(a)	Lk. 4:10–11	(Dual Tradition)	Ps. 90:11–12
(b)	Lk. 13:35	(Dual Tradition)	Ps. 117:26
	(cf. (c) below)		
(c)	Lk. 19:38	(Triple Tradition)	Ps. 117:26
	(cf. (b) above)		
(d)	Lk. 20:17	(Triple Tradition)	Ps. 117:22
	(cf. (k) below)		
(e)	Lk. 20:42–43	(Triple Tradition)	Ps. 109:1
	(cf. (j) below)		
(f)	Lk. 23:46		Ps. 30:6
(g)	Acts 1:20		Ps. 68:26
			Ps. 108:8
(h)	Acts 2:25–28		Ps. 15:8–11
	(cf. Acts 2:31, adapted)		
(i)	Acts 2:30		Ps. 131:11

---

[1]   A διήγησις (Lk. 1:1–4).

[2]   References are to Rahlfs' *Septuaginta* (Stuttgart: Deutsche Bibelgesellschaft, 1979). Since Luke's references to scripture are exclusively from the LXX, the LXX numbering rather than the Hebrew will be used. For a modern English translation of the LXX Psalms, see A. Pietersma (trans.), *A New English Translation of the Septuagint and Other Greek Translations Traditionally Included under That Title: The Psalms* (Oxford: Oxford University Press, 2000).

Table 1 *continued*

(j)	Acts 2:34–35	Ps. 109:1
	(cf. (e) above)	
(k)	Acts 4:11	Ps. 117:22
	(cf. (d) above)	
(l)	Acts 4:25–26	Ps. 2:1–2
(m)	Acts 13:33	Ps. 2:7b
(n)	Acts 13:35	Ps. 15:10
	(cf. (h) above)	

2 'Using' Psalms

2.1 Introduction

Luke, however, makes more use of allusions than of quotations. To discover *how* Luke uses psalms it helps to plot their frequency and density in his narrative. A list of Luke's references to psalms was compiled from indexes in NA[27] and UBS[3], then cross-checked against margin or apparatus. A schema, whose base represents Luke-Acts' 52 chapters, then 'plots' these references on to Luke's narrative-structure, demonstrating their *frequency* and *density* in his two volumes. From Lk. 3:1–20:44 Luke's psalm-references are drawn from traditions shared with other synoptists, but he makes them distinctively his own. This schema in Figure 1 highlights Luke's sequencing of psalms *in blocks* from Lk. 20:17 to Acts 17:27.

Five of Luke's six psalm-quotations in his gospel (Table 1, a–e) are shared with Triple or Dual Traditions, leaving only his use of Ps. 30:6 – Jesus' word from the cross – as strictly 'Lukan'. Of these five shared quotations three (b–d) are drawn from Psalm 117 and two (b–c) of these are of one verse (117:26). The remaining shared quotations are from Pss 90:11–12 (a) and 109 (e). Psalm 90 is omitted here because its Lukan use differs little from that in Matthew; (b–e) are discussed in this section but, because (f) belongs to a pressing Lukan problem – *does* scripture tell of the Messiah's necessary suffering? – it is explored in Section 6, following examination of Luke's exposition of *how* apostles used psalms in their preaching (Sections 3–5.5 below).

One important feature of Luke's narrative emerges in his 'two-ness' of psalm-quotation: (b) is taken up at (c), highlighting Luke's journey narrative (Lk. 9:51–18:14); (d) is taken up at (k) and (e) at (j), linking gospel and Acts; (h) is taken up in (n). Ps. 117:26 appears at both Lk. 13:35 (b) and 19:38 (c); its use in these contexts demonstrates Luke's use of psalms.

Luke 13:35

Luke's quotation here accords exactly with the LXX and has become the focus of a prophecy to be fulfilled on Jesus' approach to Jerusalem. While he shares this first quotation and much of its setting (13:34–35) with Matthew (23:37–39),

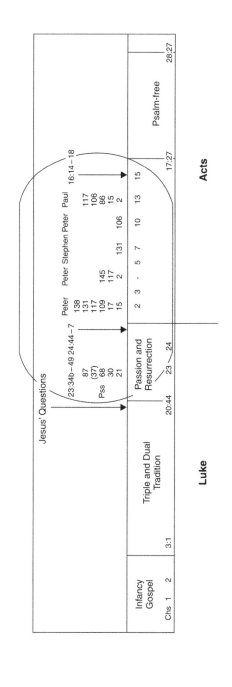

Figure 1   A Lukan schema

Luke has radically recontextualized it, making it an element of his journey narrative. Lk. 13:31–35 continues a thread linking Jerusalem with Jesus' death, focusing on that city as the place where this prophet *must* die. Luke's scene makes plain that Jesus' journey from Galilee to Jerusalem is not flight from Herod but fulfilment of his destiny, his *exodos* announced in Lk. 9:31. Jesus' journey continues outside Jerusalem until the moment of his 'Entry'.

Luke 19:38

Luke's account of Jesus' entry into Jerusalem (19:28–44) has much in common with its parallels, though two features reveal Luke's narrative thrust. First, his quoting of Ps. 117:26 is modified to 'Blessed is *the king* who comes in the Lord's name'; from Annunciation (Lk. 1:32–35) to Paul's dialogues (Acts 28:23–24) Luke's work is founded on Jesus' being the long-awaited Davidic king. Luke's systematic development of this theme throughout Luke-Acts means his '*the king*' (Lk. 19:38) encapsulates all that is intended by its parallels; further, Luke will significantly develop the notion of Jesus as David's son (see Lk. 20:42 below). Second, Luke's 'Entry' includes 19:39–44 which, as in Luke 13, links Jerusalem and its fate with this psalm. Consequently, in Luke's use, Ps. 117:26 has tightly linked Jesus' journey, his 'kingship', his destiny in Jerusalem and the city's fate. This 'two-ness' sets a pattern by which the second occurrence of a quotation fulfils or explains the first.

Luke 20:17

Psalm 117:22, quoted exactly from the LXX, appears also at Acts 4:11, there adapted to its context, explaining or fulfilling its presence in the gospel. This stone-saying, the culmination of Jesus' parable of the vineyard's wicked tenants, is part of the Triple Tradition, but Luke's quotation is shorter, more focused, than in its parallels; one possible reason for this lies in Luke's developing his story over two volumes so that Ps. 117:23 (Mk 12:11 // Matt. 21:42b) is alluded to in Paul's sermon at Pisidian Antioch (Acts 13:41).[3]

Luke's distinctive retelling of Jesus' parable and its stone-saying coheres with his using Psalm 117 in relation to Jerusalem. Here his version focuses on the scribes[4] and chief priests' perception that Jesus' parable, reporting that only 'the son' was killed, was told against them (20:19); Luke's reworking this parable prepares readers for his handling of Ps. 117:22 at Acts 4:11 while echoing Lk. 13:33–34.

Further, while the other synoptists extend their quotation into Ps. 117:23, Luke offers a two-fold proverb (20:18) which links 'stone' with other scriptural passages.[5] Here is almost certainly a thread from Lk. 19:44, echoing Isa. 8:11–15 and extending Luke's account of Jesus' entry, so that the one who

---

[3] See Section 5 below.
[4] *Diff.* Matthew's 'Pharisees' (21:45).
[5] E.g., Isa. 8:14 (cf 1 Pet. 2:7–8; Lk. 2:34) and Dan. 2:34–35, 44–45.

comes in the Lord's name (Ps. 117:26) warns the city of impending disaster in which not one stone will be left upon another.

But a key difference at Lk. 20:17 lies in the *form* of Jesus' question about this stone-saying; for Luke, Jesus' question is – 'what does this scripture mean?'

Luke 20:42–43

Luke's concern with scripture is evident in his formulating this Triple Tradition story. Addressed to Sadducees who had probed Jesus about 'resurrection', this brief, important passage cites Ps. 109:1 in a form nearer the LXX than that in its parallels.[6] While all synoptists attribute the psalm to David, Luke alone places it in 'the Book of Psalms'. His overt references to this Book (Lk. 20:42; Acts 1:20), to 'Psalms' (Lk. 24:44) and to 'psalm' (Acts 13:33, 35) signal his unique use of psalms. This quotation reappears at Acts 2:34–35 as the final term in Peter's argument developed throughout his Pentecost speech which uses psalms to contrast the biographies of Jesus and David.

In Luke-Acts psalms and David belong together. Luke's infancy prologue gives readers a lens through which to view his unfolding narrative: Jesus

> will be great, and will be called the Son of the Most High, and the Lord God will give to him the *throne* of his *ancestor David*. He will *reign* over the house of Jacob forever, and of his *kingdom* there will be no end (Lk. 1:32–33, my italics).

Another 'annunciation', anticipating Peter's affirmation that God had made Jesus both *Lord* and *Christ* (Acts 2:36), puts Jesus' birth in David's city: 'to you is born this day in the city of David a Saviour, who is the *Christ*, the *Lord*' (Lk. 2:11).

Luke's theme of God's kingdom in relation to Jesus underlies his narrative from its opening to its enigmatic ending (Acts 28:23). It is in Acts that readers see most clearly Luke's integrating of psalms with his 'David' theme and the ways in which David's psalms have been 'fulfilled' in Jesus' biography. References to David appear in blocks, as do those to psalms, in apostolic speeches.[7] In the final reference to David in Acts, James summarizes Luke's theological substructure:

> This agrees with the words of the prophets, as it is written, 'After this I will return, and *I will rebuild the dwelling of David*, which has fallen; from its ruins I will rebuild it, and I will set it up, *so that all other peoples may seek the Lord* – even all the Gentiles over whom my name has been called. Thus says the Lord, who has been making these things known from long ago' (Acts 15:15–18 quoting Amos 9:11–12, my italics).

---

[6] Luke has 'footstool' (ὑποπόδιον) rather than 'beneath' (ὑποκάτω).

[7] E.g., Acts 1:16; in Peter's speeches (2:25, 29, 31, 34; 4:25); in Stephen's speech (7:45); in Paul's sermon (13:22 [x2], 34, 36) and, climactically, at the 'Jerusalem Council' in James's summary (15:16).

Amos's oracle anticipates the restoration of David's kingdom; to this point Luke's narrative has been undergirded by a substructure comprising psalms and David's biography. Luke's narrative strategy is that David's fallen booth should *first* be rebuilt *so that* the rest of humankind might seek the Lord. James here exemplifies Luke's portrayal of apostles as those empowered by the risen Jesus both *to understand* and *to interpret* scripture, a major focus in Luke-Acts. He announced this focus in his preface (Lk. 1:1–4) and his work is characterized by a sense of necessity[8] that the scriptures should be fulfilled.

'While he opened the scriptures to us . . .' (Luke 24:32)

At the hinge of his narrative, in his account of Jesus' 'great commission' and linking his two volumes, Luke's readers encounter his unique statement of the role of scripture in his work:

> Then he said to them, 'These are my words that I spoke to you while I was still with you – that everything written about me in the law of Moses, the prophets, *and the psalms* must be fulfilled.' Then he opened their minds to understand the scriptures, and he said to them, 'Thus it is written, that the Messiah is to suffer and to rise from the dead on the third day, and that repentance and forgiveness of sins is to be proclaimed in his name to all nations, beginning from Jerusalem' (Lk. 24:44–47; italics added).

Jesus' apostles are validated and empowered as his witnesses (24:48) for a programme (24:47) taken up and amplified in Acts 1:8, a programme crystallized in James's summary speech (Acts 15). Apostles are equipped for their task by Jesus' opening 'their minds to understand the scriptures' (24:45). Thereafter, their business was arguing from scripture to prove that 'Jesus is the Christ': both Peter (Acts 2:16–36; 3:18–21) and Apollos (Acts 18:24–28) are portrayed quarrying scriptural material for this task.

More particularly, Peter and John are shown arguing their answers to Jesus' two questions about interpreting psalms: his question about Ps. 117:22 ('what does this scripture mean?', Lk. 20:17) is taken up at Acts 4:11; his question about David's son (Lk. 20:41–42) is definitively answered in Acts 2:14–36 which demonstrates from scripture how God has made Jesus both Lord and Christ (Acts 2:36). The focal texts of the first speeches in Acts are the only psalms which synoptic tradition reports Jesus using; Psalms 109 and 117[9] thus play a unique role in Luke-Acts, offering a definitive hermeneutical core to Luke's writing. *Jesus' questions are now given answers by his witnesses equipped with his own hermeneutic to relate his life and work to scripture.* Paul is shown fulfilling the same task (e.g., Acts 13), primarily proving from scripture that Jesus is the Christ.

Examination of these blocks of material, principally apostolic speeches, shows

---

[8] E.g., Lk. 9:22; 13:33; 17:25; 22:37; 24:6–7, 26–27, 44; Acts 1:16; 4:12; 5:29; 17:3.
[9] Hereafter called 'core' psalms.

apostles appealing to a succession of psalms whose surface appearance may seem 'tentative' but whose presence as a substructure throughout Luke-Acts becomes increasingly clear. Jesus' commission, however, opened his apostles' minds to grasp that 'it is written that the Messiah is to suffer and to rise from the dead on the third day' (Lk. 24:46, cf. Acts 17:2–3). While successive commentators have professed themselves puzzled by this *logion*, examination of Luke's Passion Narrative – using insights gained from exploring apostolic speeches – reveals that a key to their puzzle lies in his using psalms to build a comparative biography of David and Jesus; this is basic to grasping what Luke is about. It is written in the psalms that the Messiah must suffer.[10]

Consequently, we begin by exploring Luke's blocks of material, speeches first (to uncover their substructure), Passion Narrative (including Acts 1:16–20) next. The following table indicates Luke's range of psalms in these blocks; their 'texturing' is teased out in Sections 3–6 below.

Section	Psalms					
3	15	17	109	117	131	138
4	2	117	145			
5	2	15	88	106	117	
6	21	30	68	[37]	87	108

The schema in Figure 1 shows references to psalms 'bunched' (as above) within speeches and Luke's Passion Narrative. That Luke's speeches are *summaries* has long been recognized and cannot be reasonably doubted. Because these speeches are condensed, are their allusions to and echoes from psalms similarly condensed? What, precisely, is the intertextual[11] force of Luke's quotations and allusions? Answers to these questions, affecting the overall picture of preaching via psalms in Acts, are developed below.

Texturing and Intertextuality

Luke's condensing of psalms often 'conceals' the way in which he *uses* those psalms signalled by allusion. Reading psalms as 'wholes' reveals how they stand in complex relation one to another and to the 'events' of each narrative. This complexity may be thought of as 'texturing', an image of Luke's speeches as woven fabric rather than as a 'chain'. 'Texturing' allows readers to hear Luke's presentation of Jesus' biography compared with David's – distilled from 'his' psalms. Through psalms rich in his response to experience, the *psalmist* David allows readers to share in his personal, spiritual odyssey; *King* David appeals to God's promise, covenant, that his (David's) kingdom will be eternal, a promise at the heart of Luke's narrative. Yet Book III (Pss 72–88) ends with a psalm celebrating God's covenant with David but bitterly lamenting its failure in his own time (Ps. 88:39–46), pleading,

---

[10] And in the same psalms Acts 1:16–20 finds its roots.
[11] 'Intertextual' one with another and with Luke's traditional material.

> How long, O Lord? Will you turn away completely? Will your wrath burn like fire? Remember what my substance is. For, surely, you did not create all mortals in vain? What is humankind, that it shall live and not see death, shall rescue its soul from the power of Hades? (Ps. 88:47–49).

Death frustrated what God promised – until, Luke reports, God raised Jesus from the dead and exalted him. Luke's textured use of psalms, *developing this contrast between David and Jesus*, is the heart of apostolic preaching in Acts. For Luke, references to psalms are not 'proof texts' but signals of his narrative's theological *substructure*, the essential body of scripture revealing God's plan now fulfilled in Jesus.

These 'signalled' psalms *together* contribute to David's biography; readers need to 'hear' this biography. In Luke-Acts these psalms are interconnected thematically and verbally so that it proves helpful to think of their warp (thematic, vertical threads) and weft (horizontal threads linking themes to David's biography). This 'texturing' is explored in Sections 3–6.

3 Peter's Speech: Acts 2:14–36

Introduction

Even a cursory reading of Peter's[12] speech makes clear that its thrust is towards its concluding announcement (2:36):

> Therefore let the entire house of Israel know with certainty that God has made him both Lord and Christ, this Jesus whom you crucified.

Peter's proclamation to Israel's House is Luke's first report of apostles' witnessing in accord with Jesus' commission (Lk. 24:48–49, cf. Acts 1:4–6). Because Peter's concluding quotation is a *core* psalm (109:1), his speech may be understood as his answer to Jesus' question about how the Christ could be both David's son and Lord. For this task, Peter, the apostle, had been educated by his risen Lord in distinctive ways of interpreting scripture (Lk. 24:44–45). This speech is, however, part of a longer Lukan narrative development.

Peter's Speech's Narrative Context (2:1–47)

Luke's combination of event, speech and conclusion itself 'fulfils' Jesus' commission to his apostles (Lk. 24:48–49; Acts 1:4–6). Apostles, waiting in Jerusalem, had now been clothed with power from on high, baptized with the Holy Spirit (Acts 2:1–13). Peter's speech 'unpacked' Pentecost's events and uncovered longer narrative trajectories.

For example, the Christ now exalted at God's right hand, Jesus, has received the promise of Holy Spirit (*sic*) and poured it out (2:33). Readers may have recognized other elements in this trajectory, beginning with Jesus' question

---

[12] Peter's in that Luke attributes the speech to 'Peter'; questions of authorship belong elsewhere.

(Lk. 20:42) about 'the Lord at the right hand' (Ps. 109:1) and taking in Jesus' own combining of this psalm with Dan. 7:13 to produce: 'But from now on the Son of Man will be seated at the right hand of the power of God' (Lk. 22:69). This trajectory reaches its end in Acts 7:56 – ' "Look," [Stephen] said, "I see the heavens opened and the Son of Man standing at the right hand of God!" '

Peter's speech also initiates a trajectory from Acts 2:21, quoting Joel 3:5a – 'Then *everyone who calls on the name of the Lord* shall be saved'. This trajectory is part of a broader sweep from Simeon's canticle (Lk. 2:29–32) through Luke's appropriation (Lk. 3:6) of Isaiah's vision that 'all flesh shall see the salvation of God', taking in James's programmatic engagement with Amos 9 (Acts 15:16–18).

These two trajectories, the Lord at the right hand and the Lord whose name those seeking salvation should invoke, are the heart of Peter's speech; Joel and Psalms here symbolize Luke's deep engagement with scripture.

Three Quotations from Scripture[13]

Peter's speech offers a high density of scripture, indicative of Luke's approach. Of this speech's 23 verses, five derive from Joel, four are quoted from Psalm 15 and one from Psalm 109. These two quotations from psalms, one extended, agree *verbatim* with the LXX text. Luke occasionally omits an element from a quotation's conclusion, which ultimately figures significantly in his argument. For example, he omits the ending of the final verse from both Joel 3:1–5 and Ps. 15:8–11. There are, however, thematic and verbal connectors reaching from each of these two 'missing' elements to Luke's narrative or argument. This practice is, apparently, a sort of literary aposiopesis attributed to speakers.

Four Allusions to Psalms

There are, additionally, clear allusions to at least three psalms here: Acts 2:24 ('the pangs of death', Ps. 17:5); Acts 2:30 ('sworn . . . throne', Ps. 131:11); Acts 2:33 ('exalted . . . right hand', Ps. 117:16).

These allusions are participial constructions, giving them an 'incidental' feel, as though Theophilus might be expected to understand immediately these psalms' uses in apostolic preaching. Ps. 17:5 safely appears here because, although it offers only two common words in sequence, it both derives from a psalm of David's biography and belongs to a group of psalms sharing Luke's concern with 'death and Hades', a distinctive group. Because Ps. 131:11 has been adapted to Peter's speech, its allusion to David's descendant on his (David's) throne mixes thematic and verbal links. There are enough common words in sequence to convince most readers, and Luke returns to this psalm for his Stephen speech (Acts 7:46), so this key allusion may be thought secure.

---

[13] See Table 1 (h) and (i).

The third allusion 'works' only from a LXX text: Ps. 117:16 reads 'the right hand of the Lord *exalted me*' rather than the Hebrew Psalter's 'the right hand of the Lord *is exalted*' (118:16 MT). Luke's allusion is ambiguous, deploying a passive in which the dative is almost certainly instrumental ('by God's right hand') but offering also a locative sense ('to, at God's right hand'). Significantly, this is yet another *incidental* allusion to this core psalm, much used in Luke-Acts.

At Acts 2:34 one further allusion ('For David ... ascend into heaven', cf. Ps. 138:8), problematic for commentators, also makes a significant contribution to Peter's argument. Because most commentators look elsewhere for scriptural warrant that 'David did not ascend into heaven', this fourth allusion – a new proposal – needs justification. Psalm 138 'pertains to' David,[14] affirms his confidence in God's presence, a presence experienced as being held by God's 'right hand' (138:10; cf. 15:11b). This psalm entered this list *both* because it shares a focal Lukan theme in Peter's speech ('death and Hades') *and* is a psalm about David. Verse 8, a couplet about 'Hades', is also about 'heaven': [David speaks] 'If I should ascend into heaven...'[15] which bears a close verbal resemblance to Acts 2:34a, 'For David did not ascend into heaven...'[16] Given that Luke's allusion is adapted to the primacy of 'event', as at Acts 2:31, this shared verb 'ascend' (ἀναβαίνω) and 'into' (εἰς) followed by 'heavens' (psalm) (τοὺς οὐρανούς) or 'heaven' (Luke) (τὸν οὐρανόν) point far more securely to Ps. 138:8 as the source of Luke's allusion than the frequently proposed Ps. 67:19.[17] Thematic coherence, biographical contrast and verbal closeness point convincingly to Luke's alluding to Psalm 138 at Acts 2:34a.

Consequently, if these four allusions point to knowledge, shared by Luke and Theophilus, of a substructure of psalms encapsulating David's biography, then the psalms' role in Luke's unfolding Christology demands exploration. Together, Peter's quotations and allusions make up about 43 per cent of his speech.

Shape in Peter's Speech
How does Luke carry readers to his conclusion at 2:36 via these six quotations and allusions? Specifically, what force should readers give to Luke's 'therefore' in his formal announcement to Israel? This conjunction follows immediately on Peter's quoting Ps. 109:1, a core psalm here focused on the ambiguities of

---

[14] As its LXX title urges.
[15] ἐὰν ἀναβῶ εἰς τὸν οὐρανόν.
[16] οὐ γὰρ Δαυὶδ ἀνέβη εἰς τοὺς οὐρανούς.
[17] See especially A.W. Zwiep, *The Ascension of the Messiah in Lukan Christology* (Nov TSup 87; Leiden: Brill, 1997), p. 156.

the word 'Lord'. Through a dialogue between events and 'David' psalms, Luke shows that there is an apostolic answer to Jesus' question (Lk. 20:41–44); to grasp Luke's argument, readers need to track its themes (Lord, Christ, right hand, descent from David) throughout Peter's speech; this is done below.

One key pointer to this dialogue is found at Acts 2:31, a narrative hinge in Peter's speech, which shows Luke appropriating to Jesus a passage from a psalm which properly belongs to David's autobiography. This appropriation is made through a dialogue between two *facts* (or events) and two *promises* (in scripture). The facts are, first, while David remained dead (2:29), Jesus, *per contra*, had been raised from the dead (2:24, 32) even though 'you' crucified him (2:22–24). The two promises both initially related to David: first, because he was prophet as well as psalmist, David knew that God would put on (David's) throne one of his descendants (2:30; cf. Ps. 131:11); this is Luke's summary of a messianic hope traceable elsewhere in psalms to which he appeals. Second, David's trust in God was that *his flesh* would continue to live in hope: 'for you will not abandon my soul to Hades, or let your devout one see corruption' (Ps. 15:10). But this promise had failed – David remained dead and one could only imagine the state of his flesh. Yet, says Luke, David the prophet foresaw not his own but his descendant's, the Christ's, resurrection. This is why, at Acts 2:31b, David's words have been appropriated to Jesus, for they describe his 'event'.

That being so, it becomes possible to see another feature of Luke's appropriation of Psalm 15 to Jesus. Jesus' resurrection was affirmed by witnesses (2:32) who had also seen his exaltation (1:6–11) to God's right hand (2:33; cf. 7:55–56; Ps. 117:16). Careful readers would have noted that a key clause (italicized) did not appear at the end of Luke's quotation from Ps. 15:10–11:

> for you will not abandon my soul to Hades, or let your devout one see corruption. You made known to me ways of life. You will fill me with gladness along with your presence; *in (or 'at') your right hand are delights, completely.*

'God's right hand' was a significant element in David's hope, a basic element in Luke's understanding of Jesus as Christ, the Lord at the right hand, as Ps. 109:1 had said. Clearly, in this speech a dialogue, focused on Peter's themes, is in progress among Psalms 15, 109 and 117.

Through this dialogue it becomes possible to see how earliest readers might have heard clear echoes from the briefest of Lukan allusions, just as present readers can amplify for themselves Luke's brief summary of Jesus' biography. Readers need to remain aware that, at the end of his first volume, Luke reported that psalms, not only *Torah* and Prophets, were to shed light on Jesus' life and exaltation. What, then, of this dialogue?

(a) This is a Petrine speech about *Jesus*; readers cannot fail to notice Luke's emphasis. This speech's basic structure is found in Acts 2:22–24, 32–33 and 36, a structure which helps readers to identify Joel's 'Lord' of Acts 2:21 with the Jesus 'whom you crucified'.

(b) Into this summary Luke wove David's brief biography. Validating Luke's account of Jesus, David appears in two roles: primarily as *author* of psalms to which Luke will appeal, then as *subject* of those psalms. At 2:25, 30–31 David is identified as author of Psalm 15 and at 2:34 of Psalm 109. David appears as subject on one level at 2:30, where he is a prophet, knowing of God's promise to him of the continuity of his house and throne, and at 2:31 as one who foresaw the Christ's resurrection. Further, on another level, two unambiguous Lukan statements remove David from centre stage, 2:29 and 2:34; this is effectively done at 2:31 by Luke's crucially appropriating to Jesus the contents of Ps. 15:8–11.

(c) This process of appropriation is located in Luke's 'texturing' of Peter's speech, examined below in its warp and weft, its texturing *of psalms*. Themes important to Peter's argument establish the vertical columns (the warp) of Table 2.

Table 2.   A table of warp and weft in Acts 2:22–36.

Themes/ Psalm	Death and Hades	Right Hand		Christ	Lord
		Location	Help	Lamp	
17	17:5–6 (Acts 2:24)	17:49	17:36	17:50–51 (Acts 2:31) 17:29 'my lamp'	17:4, 7, 47, 50
15	15:10 (Acts 2:27, 31)	15:11b			15:8 (15:1)
131				131:10–12 (Acts 2:31) 131:17 'lamp for my anointed'	
117	117:17–18	117:16a (Acts 2:33)	117:15, 16b, 36	[117:29?] 117:5 cf. 117:10–14	
138	138:8b	138:8a (Acts 2:34 ἀνέβη)	138:10	[138:5]	
109		109:1 (Acts 2:34–35)	109:5 (cf. Lk. 20: 41–44)		109:1 (Acts 2:34–35)

Texturing in Peter's Speech

Of the six psalms discernible in Peter's speech, two (15, 17) belong to books traditionally recognized as David's (Pss 1–71). Two others (109, 138) are ascribed to David by their headings. One other (131) is a psalm focused sharply on David's person and on God's promise. The remaining psalm (117) is nowhere overtly ascribed to David, but is a core psalm, pervasive in Luke-Acts and closely associated with Jesus' life, death and resurrection.

These 'Lukan' psalms are about David's biography and covenant, a selection cohering with the narrative shape of Peter's speech, a comparative biography of David and Jesus. This biography focuses on two main issues, death and covenant, both now reviewed in the light of Jesus' resurrection from among the dead. When Luke signals a psalm, readers need to have that psalm to hand to discern how rich Luke's scriptural allusions really are. Table 2 indicates ways in which, for Luke, these psalms-in-dialogue, not isolated proof texts, carried God's plan revealed in scripture.

This appeal to Table 2 needs to be briefly demonstrated through its *weft* across the speech's thematic *warp*.

Death and Hades

While David was vividly conscious of the threat and finality of death and Hades (Ps. 17:5, 6), he nonetheless hoped for life (Ps. 15:9–10); his hope was that even if he descended into Hades, his Lord would be there (138:8). Psalm 117, of which Luke made so much, celebrating the reversal epitomized in its stone-saying (117:22),[18] expressed Psalm 138's *post-mortem* reversal in a different way (117:17–18):

> I shall not die, but I shall live ...
> The Lord disciplined me ... but he did not give me over to death.

Of Peter's six psalms, four have death or Hades as a significant element, so Luke was not dependent on only Psalm 15 which played its significant role because it focused *three* of Peter's speech's major themes.

Lord

Similarly, taking his cue from Joel's oracle (3:5a) at Acts 2:21, that everyone calling on the Lord's name will be saved, Luke set out to show that 'the Lord' referred to in that text was 'the Lord (Jesus)' now seated at God's right hand, the son whom David called 'Lord' (Ps. 109:1). Peter's first, brief allusion (Acts 2:24) to a psalm is to 17:5, 6, an allusion itself tightly sandwiched between two Davidic affirmations: first, 'I will call upon the Lord' (17:4); second, 'I called upon the Lord' (17:7). These are both thematic and verbal echoes of Peter's text (Acts 2:21); the probability that this is coincidence approaches vanishing

---

[18] Discussed in Section 4.

point. Peter's speech's subtext tells readers that David has been called in witness as one who called on the Lord's name, and if that brief allusion, though unquoted, is not clearly heard, then there can be no ambiguity at 2:25 where Peter reports, 'For David says concerning him, "I saw the Lord always before me, for he is at my right hand so that I will not be shaken..." ' But if Jesus assuredly 'is' both Christ and 'Lord' (2:36), then might not a retro-reading of psalms in the light of Peter's proclamation have thrown up the puzzling Ps. 15:2 – 'I said to the Lord, "You are my Lord..." ' – with its verbal echoes of the core Ps. 109:1? Such retro-reading then brings into focus 117:5 with its echoes of Joel 3:5a and Ps. 17:4, 7. What should a reader now make of 117:10–14, or even of 138:5?

Christ (χριστός)

Peter's confident proclamation (Acts 2:36) was that Jesus was not only Lord, but also 'Christ', a word absent from these psalms' signals in Peter's speech. Readers know, however, that this is a basic theme in Luke's two volumes. First, that Jesus is David's descendant who is to sit on David's throne for ever appears clearly in Gabriel's announcement to Mary (Lk. 1:32). In narrative terms, Gabriel's voice is 'from heaven', indicating to readers where Luke's narrative will be going. Then, as noted above, two of the active psalms in Peter's speech take up the theme of reversal with the result that however bad things seem for David or his descendant, in the end God's care will ensure David's triumph and that of God's anointed (χριστός; Pss 17:50–51; 131:10–12). It is because the whole of Psalm 131 is active beneath Peter's allusion to it at Acts 2:30 that the word 'Christ' emerges naturally at 2:31, echoing Ps. 131:17. To this subtextual activity should be added the fact that Luke's *climactic* psalm (109:1) *is a core psalm* – because it was focused by Jesus *in the context of the Christ's being David's son.* In sum, because the concept 'Christ' is subtextually active in three of Peter's six psalms, Israel may be confident that the one raised from the dead (2:31) and shown to be 'Lord' is also 'Christ' (2:36).

Sit at my right hand

Luke's focal core psalm (109:1) had to do not only with the Christ's being David's 'Lord', but also with God's invitation, 'Sit at my right hand.' This image is associated with 'exaltation'; the one whom God had raised from the dead had been 'exalted' to God's right hand. Two of Peter's six psalms speak of David's being exalted by God out of the reach of his enemies (17:49; 117:16a); one, a suppressed quotation, strongly implies the psalmist's presence at God's right hand (15:11b). But this image of the vindicated Lord's being at God's right hand had earlier been announced in Luke's trial scene (Lk. 22:69) where a creative meld of Ps. 109:1 with Dan. 7:13 opened a trajectory completed in Stephen's vision (Acts 7:55–56). Peter's speech shows how the *group* of psalms about David, not simply 109:1, had prepared readers for the Lord at the right hand.[19]

The common concerns of these six psalms centred on David's death and covenant; their accounting for an 'inexplicable' appearance of 'Christ' at Acts 2:31; their focusing newly on Psalm 138 as the scriptural source of 2:34, all strongly suggest their subtextual presence as wholes, *texturing* Peter's argument rather than offering proof texts.

4 The Stone-Saying and Community Prayer: Acts 4:1–31

Beneath Luke's narrative (4:1–31) lies a dialogue among three psalms, shaping both its language and structure. This narrative is a long development of which the community prayer is but a part, given meaning by, while itself giving meaning to, the whole. Consequently, while focusing on the shorter 4:1–31, we shall keep in view its place in the themes and developments of Luke's longer narrative (Acts 3:1–5:42). Examining this prayer quickly showed that both its psalm references are in dialogue with Luke's use of Psalm 117 in Peter's defence (Acts 4:11).

Together, defence and prayer offer clear *allusions* at 4:11 to Ps. 117:22, to Ps. 145:6 at 4:24 and a *quotation* of Ps. 2:1–2 at 4:25b–6. Only Psalm 2 is directly quoted with introductory formula; its wording is that of the LXX. Both Psalms 117 and 145 are allusive yet so woven into the fabric of Luke's narrative that their presence in the text *entails* their variation from an 'original'. Luke's allusion to Ps. 117:22 probably reflects his own well-targeted variation[20] on a LXX-like version known to him (see Lk. 20:17). These psalms work together to shape the language and 'meaning' of the Lukan unit within its context; their dialogue reflects Luke's previous use of them; this dialogical function of the psalms leaves traces of its presence in the language through which Luke tells his story. For convenience, we divide 4:1–31 into two distinct parts.

4.1 Psalms in Peter's Defence Speech

Luke's complex use of psalms effectively accounts for much of this speech's narrative.

Luke's longer narrative (3:1–5:42)

This is a two-fold conflict story featuring on-one hand two apostles (representing Jesus) and their fellow-travellers; on the other, authorities

---

[19] See P. Doble, *The Paradox of Salvation* (SNTSMS 87; Cambridge: Cambridge University Press, 1996), pp. 127–45.

[20] This variant allusion is shaped as much by its function in Luke's narrative as by its origin in the LXX. Luke's ὁ ἐξουθενηθεὶς ὑφ' ὑμῶν τῶν οἰκοδόμων is directed against 'the rulers' who are key characters in 3:1–5:42 and directed especially to Herod who is named at 4:27 and at Lk. 23:11 where it is said ἐξουθενήσας δὲ αὐτὸν ὁ Ἡρῴδης.

(ἄρχοντες) who intervene in the apostles' public witnessing to what they have seen and heard. The narrative's dynamic is that the authorities twice order the apostles to desist from witnessing 'in Jesus' name' (4:17–18; 5:28, 40), while, in memorable words, the apostles twice refuse to obey them (4:19; 5:29). This unit ends (5:42) by highlighting both the failure of the authorities' intervening and the faithful discharge of their task by the apostles who 'every day in the Temple and at home ... did not cease to teach and proclaim that the Christ is Jesus' (5:42).

Peter's defence 'speech' (4:8–12) and 'response' to the authorities' order to desist from witnessing (4:19–20) offer a model of the apostles' focused message: their action is in Jesus of Nazareth's name, 'whom you crucified, whom God raised from the dead'. Here readers encounter Peter's first allusion to a psalm, and that in striking format: 'This Jesus is

> the stone that was rejected by you, the builders;
> it has become the cornerstone'.

Two routes lead to Peter's stone-saying: the first traces references to Psalm 117 in Luke-Acts; the second explores the stone-*logion* as a proverb summarizing Psalm 117 – an example of *pars pro toto* (the part represents the whole).

Psalm 117 in Luke-Acts

We find in Luke-Acts *two* distinct references to Ps. 117:26 (Lk. 13:35 and 19:38), the first a quotation from the LXX, the second differing from it only in Luke's programmatic addition of 'the king'. Further, there are *two* distinct references to Ps. 117:22 (Lk. 20:17; Acts 4:11): the first is a quotation from the LXX while the second is adapted to Luke's narrative. So, at two indisputable places in Psalm 117 we find Luke *first* quoting accurately from the LXX before adapting that quotation to his own narrative. There are also two *probable* references to Ps. 117:16 (Acts 2:33 and 5:31), neither of which is a quotation from the LXX but both of which allusions could be derived only from the LXX.[21] At Acts 13:41 there is a probable use of Ps. 117:17, the verse following that just discussed.[22]

Consequently, at Acts 4:11 we should probably, first, think of Peter's identifying the stone-saying with Jesus as Peter's answer to Jesus' question (Lk. 20:17); then, second, understand this allusion as Jesus' representative's definitive statement to the authorities that this ancient, well-known proverb encapsulates Jesus' significance for them. Because Luke uses Psalm 117 at widely separated places in Luke-Acts, it is reasonable to infer his insight into this psalm's christological significance, making more likely a *pars pro toto* principle in its appearances; so Psalm 117 requires exploration.

---

[21] τῇ δεξιᾷ οὖν τοῦ θεοῦ ὑψωθείς (Acts 2:33); τοῦτον ὁ θεὸς ... ὕψωσεν τῇ δεξιᾷ αὐτοῦ (Acts 5:31); δεξιὰ κυρίου ὕψωσέν (Ps. 117:16).

[22] Examined in Section 5 below.

The stone-proverb as an epitome of Psalm 117

This proverb summarizes the psalm – from discard to key position, from rejection to exaltation.[23] Psalm 117 falls into five 'movements':

1. *(vv. 1–4)*, the psalmist invites Israel, Aaron and godfearers to affirm God's steadfast love (cf. v. 29).
2. *(vv. 5–9)*, distress leads the psalmist to a significant theological statement (vv. 8–9):

   It is better to trust in the Lord than to trust in mortals.
   It is better to hope in the Lord than to hope in rulers.

3. *(vv. 10–14)*, the psalmist exemplifies the 'distress' of v. 5, a potential military disaster averted by the kind of trust urged in vv. 8–9. He was pressed so hard as to be near falling, but God became his salvation (v. 14).
4. *(vv. 15–18)* the battle so unexpectedly won, the victorious army hymns its Lord in a song of salvation,

   The right hand of the Lord did valiantly;
   the right hand of the Lord exalted me ...
   while the psalmist reflects that for him it had been a close-run thing:

   I shall not die, but I shall live,
   and unpack the works of the Lord.
   The Lord disciplined me with discipline,
   but he did not give me over to death (117:17–18).

5. *(vv. 19–29)*, the victor approaches the Temple, contemplating the reversal of his fortune; an architectural proverb (117:22) epitomizes his experience of salvation, leading to exhortation to thanksgiving *because God can be trusted.*

From disaster to victory, from rejection to exaltation is here understood as 'salvation' (117:14, 15, 21, 28); this is a psalm of thanksgiving for 'salvation', with deep roots in Jewish thinking and in earliest Christian interpretation. Because the stone-saying encapsulates all this,where the proverb appears this whole psalm resonates.

Psalm 117 in dialogue with Psalm 145 in Acts 4

Ps. 117:8–9 affirm that trust in God is fundamental, and that without it there is no reversal of fortune. These verses evoke a distinct memory of the apostles' strong refusals to obey the rulers, refusals noted earlier as central to Luke's long narrative (Acts 4:19; 5:29). Similarity is not connection, but, apart from the

---

[23] After H.-J. Kraus, *Theology of the Psalms* (Minneapolis: Augsburg Press, 1986), pp. 193–94.

presence of this allusion to Psalm 117 at Acts 4:11, two further facts need to be taken into account.

First, Luke already knew of another psalm expressing the conviction affirmed in 117:8–9:

> Do not put your *trust in rulers*,
> And in *mortals* in whom there is no *salvation*.
> His breath will depart, and he will return to his earth;
> On that very day all their designs will perish.
> Happy is he whose helper is the God of Jacob ... (145:3–5a)

Connections with Psalm 117 are clear: 'salvation', 'trust', 'rulers' are verbal connectors; the sentiment is emphatically similar. Now, lest it should seem that Psalm 145 has been plucked from thin air, we add its vv. 5b–6a:

> whose hope is in the Lord their God,
> who made heaven and earth,
> the sea and all that is in them ...

and recognize them as the source of an allusion to Psalm 145 in the community prayer (Acts 4:24). In this prayer, this descriptor of God reflects Luke's associating two psalms (117 and 145) with the community's mapping of its own experience on to that pool of scripture which had been fulfilled among them (e.g., Ps. 2). This sounds like the beginnings of a scriptural substructure to Luke's defence and prayer.

The second, more important, factor takes up both psalms. Psalm 117 celebrates *salvation* as a gift from God to those who trust in God rather than in *rulers*; Psalm 145 is quite clear that one should not expect *salvation* from *rulers* because they are mortal. A conjunction of Psalm 117 with 145 appears to have helped Luke to the climax of Peter's defence. Immediately following his allusion to the stone-saying readers find the problematic 4:12:

> There is salvation in no one else, for there is no other name under heaven given among mortals by which we must be saved.

Luke probably associated 'there is salvation in no one else' with the stone-saying simply because both belonged to his psalms-substructure which looked to God for salvation, not to mortals.[24] Peter's is not an *intruded* claim to Jesus' uniqueness, but a summary of what both Pss 117:8–9 and 145:3–4 had said. This is the more likely when one recognizes that 'salvation'[25] makes its first appearance here in Acts, a verbal signal of a sub-textual dialogue between two psalms.

---

[24] And God had 'raised' Jesus from mortality.
[25] σωτηρία.

Luke and the rulers

There is another connection between these two psalms and Luke's narrative – the word 'rulers'.[26] Peter's defence speech is addressed directly to 'Rulers of the people . . .' (4:8), which is not simply reminiscent of Ps. 145:3 but also part of Luke's narrative strategy involving the word 'ruler'. While Luke explicitly identifies the stone proverb with Jesus, by varying its detail ('that was rejected by you, *the builders*') he has appropriated the proverb, to identify the 'rulers' whom he is addressing with those who rejected Jesus.

Within Peter's defence speech and the community prayer readers meet a high proportion of references to 'rulers'.[27] This heightened frequency highlights Luke's dramatic, stylized opening of the authorities' intervention against the apostles' preaching (Acts 4:5–6):

> The next day *their rulers*, elders, and scribes *gathered together* in Jerusalem, with Annas the high priest, Caiaphas, John, and Alexander, and all who were of the high-priestly family . . .

which leads almost seamlessly, 19 verses later (4:26), to Luke's quotation from Ps. 2:1–2, now appropriated to the apostles' and Jesus' situation:

> For in this city, in fact, *both Herod and Pontius Pilate*, with the Gentiles and the peoples of Israel, *gathered together* against your holy servant Jesus, whom you anointed . . .

But this is within God's plan revealed in scripture (Acts 4:28) – here revealed through Psalm 2. Luke's narrative thus already offers evidence of dialogue among three psalms, a substructure for the 'scripturized history' *both* of Peter's defence before the rulers *and* of the community's prayer. However, on the *pars pro toto* principle we need first to examine Psalm 2's 'biography' in Luke-Acts, then, to explore its 'shape'.

4.2 A Community Prayer

Psalm 2 probably appears at Lk. 3:22[28] and 9:35.[29] There are two undisputed appearances of this psalm in Acts: at 4:25b–26 (Ps. 2:1–2) and at 13:33 (Ps. 2:7). In the first instance, the whole psalm is evoked by its opening verses; in the second, the quotation is strongly linked with God's promise to David.

In Acts 4:1–31, Ps. 2 reflects the interests of its new home. The psalm's final macarism (2:12) coheres with Luke's use of two other psalms sharing Psalm 2's perspective on 'trusting the Lord' (Pss 117 and 145), and with the relevance of all three psalms to the apostolic community's conflict with Jerusalem authorities. Psalm 2's inner logic leads naturally to this macarism, for the

---

[26] ἄρχοντες.

[27] About ten times its frequency in Luke-Acts.

[28] Internal evidence suggests that the reading of manuscript D is to be preferred.

[29] Melding allusions to Ps. 2:7 and Deut. 18:15, 18.

psalm celebrates a reversal, contrasting the rebellious rulers' foolish action against God, and his anointed, with David's kingly status affirmed by God.[30] The psalm's concluding macarism epitomizes David's message to the nations: 'blessed are all those who trust in him'.

In this prayer of thanksgiving for Peter and John's release, Luke's introduction to (Acts 4:25a) and quotation of Ps. 2:1–2 emphasizes David's role in Luke's retelling Jesus' story. Again, a David psalm has been appropriated to events in Jesus' life, influencing Luke's narrative's language: the rulers 'gathered together' are plainly identified with those present at Jesus' trial.[31] Acts 4:25a is a notorious textual *crux* which impossibly mixes Davidic elements already established by his previous history in Luke.[32] It affirms that: David was the psalmist of Psalm 2 (although lacking that ascription in the LXX); its writing is attributable to God, whose Holy Spirit spoke through David (cf. Acts 1:16); David was Israel's father and God's servant (παῖς). Used of David, παῖς may either take up the title of Psalm 17 or echo Ps. 68:18; it possibly reflects both. Clearly, this way of speaking of David was current, though rare, in the psalms, occurring in one (68) which Luke had already used in both his first (Lk. 23:36) and second (Acts 1:20) volumes. That God had anointed Jesus makes him, like David whose heir he is, servant (παῖς) also.[33]

Psalms and the community's prayer

That this prayer is organically linked with Peter's speech and with Luke's longer narrative unit (3:1–5:42) is signalled by its introductory words (4:23), 'when they were released', a reference back to Peter and John's conflict with the rulers. The apostles reported what the principal priests and the elders said; readers are intended to 'hear' in this sentence the authorities' strict instruction to the apostles neither to speak nor to teach in Jesus' name. Luke has thus strongly linked this community's prayer with his longer unit's major theme. Their prayer falls naturally into three parts[34] leading to a conclusion identifying *this* community with Peter and John's witness.[35]

The first part, 4:24b–25a, reads:

> Master, who made the heaven and the earth, the sea, and everything in them, it is you who said by the Holy Spirit through our ancestor David, your servant …

The first word, 'Master',[36] is a Wisdom word for God, accenting that One to whom loyalty is due. It belongs to the same semantic range as 'ruler', but this

---

[30] There are clear links among Ps. 2, 2 Sam. 7:14–15 and Ps. 88:27–28.
[31] See the discussion in J.M. Harrington, *The Lukan Passion Narrative* (New Testament Tools and Studies 30, Leiden: Brill, 2000), pp. 691–804, 929–82.
[32] The difficult Alexandrian text is probably to be preferred.
[33] Making reference to Isa. 52:13 unnecessary.
[34] Two parts only are examined below.
[35] cf. 4:8, 13, 19–20; 5:29, 42.
[36] Δέσποτα cf. Lk. 2:29.

community knows the difference between the two. Their Master is characterized by two qualifying clauses. First, '[you] who made the heaven and the earth, the sea, and everything in them' is a clear allusion to Ps. 145:6[37] which earlier led us to the macarism of which it is a part (145:3–7), a macarism echoed as the epitome of Psalm 2 and paralleled in Ps. 117:8–9. Characterizing their Master as 'Creator' also makes it clear that he alone is to be trusted. The aptness of *this* psalm to *this* thanksgiving becomes clearer when readers recall that this Creator-Master also sets prisoners free (see 145:7b). Second, by his Holy Spirit, their Master also spoke through David the psalmist (4:25). This prayer's address is shaped to make David an agent in God's plan of salvation, a relation characterized by the word 'servant'. All that follows is to be 'heard' in the context of God's plan of salvation as it relates to David.

The second part, vv. 25b–28, is:

'Why did the Gentiles rage,
and the peoples imagine vain things?
The kings of the earth took their stand,
and *the rulers have gathered together*
against the Lord and against his Anointed (*Christos*).'
For in this city, in fact, both Herod and Pontius Pilate, with the Gentiles and the peoples of Israel, *gathered together* against your holy servant Jesus, whom you anointed, to do whatever your hand and your plan had predestined to take place.[38]

In NA[27] the text of Ps. 2:1–2 is identical with that in the LXX where it is a distinct unit marked off by a *diapsalma*[39] immediately following the words 'against his *Christos*'. Luke has directly linked David with this psalm. That the rest of Psalm 2 is in Luke's mind is suggested by his linking Jesus to David in two ways: first, the community's initial reference to Jesus is qualified by 'whom you anointed'; second, they appropriated to Jesus the 'servant' used of David (4:25, cf. 27, 30).

'... *whom you anointed* ...' (ὃν ἔχρισας, e*chris*as). Because Luke focuses in Acts on proving from scripture that the Christ (χριστός) is Jesus, Luke's qualifier echoes the psalm's words, 'against his Christ'; verb and noun share a common root, *chri*. This praying community has appropriated to Jesus the same Davidic position as that described in the psalm, a *christos* confronting a conspiracy against him. Here, in this prayer, Jesus' history is retold as *fulfilled* scripture. Where in Luke-Acts may readers find an account of Jesus' anointing? This prayer's 'whom you anointed' probably draws on vv. 6–7 of the recently quoted Psalm 2:

---

[37] See also Acts 14:15; 17:24.

[38] For discussion of Lk. 23:6–16 and Acts 4:25–27 see Harrington, *Lukan Passion Narrative*, pp. 710–804, 929–82.

[39] Pietersma, *New English Translation of the Septuagint*, understands this to be 'an interlude on strings', a definite break.

> But I was established king by him,
> on Sion, his holy mountain,
> by proclaiming the decree of the Lord:
> The Lord said to me, 'You are my son;
> today I have begotten you ....'

These verses plainly identify David as that 'anointed' against whom the rulers assembled together. Given this identity, then Luke's 'whom you anointed' points back to Jesus' baptism,[40] implying strong support for the Western text of Lk. 3:22. Luke's substructure also implies that Ps. 2:7 was understood *both* of Jesus' baptism *and* of his resurrection (Acts 13:32–36), the first expressing God's choice of Jesus as χριστός, the second confirming it.

Servant (παῖς, 4:27, 30) was in Luke's vocabulary from the beginning of his work (Lk. 1:69), part of his 'biography' of David. At Acts 4:25 'servant' carries with it overtones of David's struggle against nations and enemies (Pss 68, 17), a struggle focused and particularized in the prayer's quotation from Psalm 2. As David's heir, Jesus also is 'servant', a term used of him only[41] in this narrative unit (Acts 3:1–5:42), particularly in two clusters (3:13, 26; 4:27, 30). First, Jesus is twice called παῖς in Peter's explanation to 'the people' of how a lame man came to be healed (Acts 3:12–26). This speech's statement that the *christos* is Jesus (3:20) works together with its two-fold use of 'servant' to signal to a reader that within a broader theological framework Luke is still developing his Davidic thread.[42] Second, Jesus is twice called Παῖς in this community's prayer where references to David (4:25), to 'anointed' (χριστός, 4:26, 27), to 'servant' (παῖς, 4:27, 30) and the quotation of David's psalm all conspire to root this prayer in Luke's concern with God's fulfilment of his covenant with David. In sum, Luke's readers were expected to 'hear' this prayer through a basic 'theology' of David at each reference to him, and the whole of Psalm 2 at each reference to it.

4.3 Psalms in Dialogue: Acts 4:1–31

All three psalms share a common concern which is also the major theme of Luke's long narrative: whom to trust, God or the rulers? Psalms 145 and 2 share a macarism on this theme (145:5–9; 2:12).

In a conflict context, and immediately following Peter's allusion to the stone-proverb, interplay between Psalms 145 and 117 led the apostles to affirm that salvation is found in none other than Jesus (Acts 4:12) – implicitly excluding the rulers. Psalms 2 and 117, celebrations of 'reversals' attributable to God's acts, are both reversals in which the psalmist overcomes threats by 'the nations'. The stone-proverb about reversal (Ps. 117:22) is itself paralleled by

---

[40] See Acts 10:38; cf. Lk. 4:16–19.
[41] Lk. 2:43 may just be a prefiguring of what is to follow.
[42] Although at Acts 3:13 Luke's combination of 'glorify' and 'servant' *may* echo Isa. 52:13.

Ps. 2:6–7, which is followed by, 'Ask of me, and I will give you nations as your heritage....'.[43] There is a clear thematic reference back to Ps. 2:2, suggesting a background to Luke's 'whom you anointed' at Acts 4:27.

Because their compressed presence in Luke's text is extended by each psalm's unexpressed influence,[44] their interacting in this way strongly suggests an established scriptural base *antecedent to* Luke-Acts. That together these psalms make possible this community's answer to Jesus' question (Lk. 20:17), and do so in a parallel conflict context, reveals one of the ways in which they 'scripturized' history.

5 Paul's Sermon: Acts 13:16–41

5.1 Introduction

Like Peter's speeches, Paul's[45] sermon is essentially comparative biography interwoven with, and building on earlier exploration of, psalms. Unlike them, it is 'sermonic' in construction. In so condensed a report of Paul's address at Pisidian Antioch its density of reference to scripture is remarkable, confirming readers' impression of the intensely scripture-based nature of apostolic activity in the community's earliest years.

Two quotations are drawn from psalms explored earlier. At 13:33b, Luke cites Ps. 2:7; at 13:35b, Ps. 15:10b. With one minor exception, both quotations follow the LXX text. Although his authorship is implied, neither psalm is formally attributed to David, for this sermon's introductory formulae emphasize God's role in speaking through scripture.

Two allusions contribute to Paul's argument. At 13:22 are two words unique to Ps. 88:21, εὗρον Δαυὶδ (I have found David). The following verse (13:23) relates Jesus to God's *promise* to give Israel a Saviour from among David's descendants. Psalm 88 is a psalmist's passionate reflection on God's *promise* to David, detailed in vv. 2–5, 29–30, 36–38. *Together*, Acts 13:22–23 strongly suggest that Psalm 88 is in view, so these two words, uniquely combined, do not stand alone. It would be hard to find a more radical reflection on David's story than Psalm 88, a psalm *available* to Luke, *central* to his major theme – rebuilding David's house – and the *concluding* psalm of Book III of a Greek Psalter. At 13:26 is an allusion to Ps. 106:20, which is not a rhetorical flourish but, as shown below, an integral step in the logic of Paul's argument.

One intertextual echo completes this sermon's texturing. At 13:41, Paul ends by quoting from Hab. 1:5. Although slightly abbreviated and with its word 'work' repeated, this quotation is 'Septuagintal'. As a congregation might expect from a concluding prophetic quotation, this verse ties together the

---

[43] See James's programme (Acts 15:15–18).

[44] E.g., the presence of 'salvation' (σωτηρία), 'whom you anointed' (ὃν ἔχρισας), 'who made heaven and earth...'.

[45] 'Paul' signifies 'the speaker in Luke's text'.

sermon's threads – while interacting with Psalm 117, *one of Luke's core psalms*. Once this sermon's dialogue with a core psalm has been established, its argument through texturing becomes clearer.

Paul's Sermon's Contexts

Paul's sermon (Acts 13:16b–41), the first of a two-part unit (13:14–52), reports to synagogue congregants God's rebuilding of David's house (13:32–33), while linked events on the following Sabbath initiate Paul and Barnabas's 'turning to the Gentiles' (13:46–47). Luke thus portrayed Paul fulfilling God's programme (13:14b–52) later located by James in Amos's words (15:13–31).

Paul's sermon also falls within a longer narrative (13:1–14:28) culminating in Paul and Barnabas's relating 'all that God had done with them and how he had opened a door of faith for the Gentiles' (14:27). While his longer unit describes Paul's and Barnabas's circular mission, commissioned by the Syrian Antioch Church (13:1–3),[46] Luke reports events only in Pisidian Antioch and Lystra; Paul's Antioch sermon is probably 'typical'.

Luke's longer narrative stands at the threshold of, and is essential to, the 'Jerusalem Council' (15:1–35) and James's programmatic exegesis of Amos's words.[47] Yet Luke's narrative brought to the Council *two* threads of witness to God's dealings with the Gentiles: Peter's testimony (15:7–11) is added to that of Paul and Barnabas (15:12, cf. 14:27–15:4). Each of these threads *first* showed its witness in a Jewish context arguing from scripture, essentially the psalms, that 'the Christ is Jesus'; events then ensured that each witness widened his ministry to include Gentiles and found warrant for doing so.[48] More importantly, Luke had long prepared readers for the programme articulated at its end by James.[49] These two threads meet, and end, in James's decision in Jerusalem. It is from this larger context that Paul's synagogue sermon derives its two-fold significance.

'Texturing' in Paul's Sermon

Whatever his sources may have been, Luke has so reworked this condensed material that it is safer to explore it as part of his developing narrative than to

---

[46] 'The 'work' (Acts 13:2, 41(*bis*); 14:26).

[47] See Section 5.2 above.

[48] Saul (Paul) is portrayed proclaiming Jesus in synagogues: Acts 9:19b–22, 29(?); 11:26(?); 13:4–12. Paul's scriptural base for turning to Gentiles (13:47) is drawn from Isa. 49:6, an oracle embedded by Luke in Simeon's acknowledgement of Jesus' saving significance (Lk. 2:29–32) and echoed in accounts of Paul's conversion (e.g., Acts 9:15). Peter's earlier ministry in Jerusalem has shown readers *how* it is that Jesus is both Christ and Lord and *what* the stone-saying (Ps. 117:22) means for his Jewish hearers. Luke's long and multiple retelling of the Godfearer Cornelius's meeting with Peter (10:1–48) is also resumed in a Jerusalem setting (11:1–18). Peter's warrant for baptizing this Gentile and his companions is the gift of the Spirit (10:44–48, cf. 11:16–18).

[49] E.g., *first* to Israel (Lk. 1:16–17, 31–33), *then* to others (Lk. 2:28–32); see also Lk. 24:47; Acts 1:8; 2:21. This 'programme' is reflected in the structure of Acts.

attempt to retrieve a sermon preached by Paul.[50] The immediate context for Paul's sermon is set by 13:14–16, echoing Luke's reporting of Jesus' sermon at Nazareth (Lk. 4:16–30).[51] On the Sabbath, Paul and Barnabas attended synagogue where, after readings from *Torah* and the *Nebi'im*, the president asked them to address the people if they had a word of encouragement (cf. Acts 4:36).

Shape in Paul's Sermon

Paul's sermon falls into three parts signalled by its preacher's direct address to his congregants. The first part (13:16–25) surveys Israel's history focused on David, of whose posterity God, as promised, brought to Israel a Saviour, Jesus. The second (26–37) focuses on Jesus: by raising Jesus God had fulfilled for the congregants his promise made to their forefathers. Jesus' story[52] is of one who died, but was raised from the dead, no longer to return to corruption (13:34).

Paul's peroration (13:38–41), introduced by Luke's formulaic 'Let it be known to you brothers', highlights Jesus' significance for the congregants who are bidden beware that they do not fall foul of the prophet's warning (13:41, italics added):

> Look, you scoffers!
> Be amazed and perish,
> for *in your days* I am doing a *work*,
> a *work* that you will never believe,
> even if someone '*unpacks*' it for you.

Paul's Suppressed Allusion

Acts 13:41 is a near-quotation: it has no word not found in Hab. 1:5; it lacks some words from the Greek version; 'work' is emphasized by repetition.[53]

Paul's repeated 'work' encapsulates the narrative thrust of the apostles' circular mission (13:1–14:28), for 13:2 and 14:26 form an *inclusio*, characterizing the whole. Paul's accenting God's 'work' (13:41) poses questions about this *work's* nature – Gentile mission? Jesus' resurrection? James's programme implied in the two-fold (Acts 15:13–18), 13:13–52?

---

[50] See, e.g., J.W. Bowker, 'Speeches in Acts: A Study in Proem and Yelammadenu Form', *NTS* 14.1 (1967), pp. 96–111. See B. Witherington, *The Acts of the Apostles* (Grand Rapids: Eerdmans / Paternoster, 1998), p. 408.

[51] Parallels between the two synagogue sermons are noted by many writers. See L.T. Johnson, *The Acts of the Apostles* (Sacra Pagina 5; Collegeville: The Liturgical Press, 1992), p. 230; R.C. Tannehill, *The Narrative Unity of Luke-Acts* (Minneapolis: Fortress Press, 1986), pp. 164–6.

[52] There are close verbal links between Acts 13:27–31 and Luke's Passion narrative; Acts 13:34–37 echoes Acts 2:25–32 (see Section 3 above).

[53] See J.A. Fitzmyer, *To Advance the Gospel* (Grand Rapids: Eerdmans, 1998), p. 306. *Contra* Fitzmyer, Luke's text discloses no more than that he used a Greek Bible.

But this is a work 'which you will not believe even if someone unpacks[54] it for you' (ἐκδιηγῆται ὑμῖν). Paul's warning to Antioch's congregants (13:40–41) forms another *inclusio*, with 13:15, and is further amplified by his pointing to Jerusalem's people and rulers who, though hearing the prophets weekly, failed to grasp their message (13:27). These congregants had themselves been listening to Paul's exposition of what David and Isaiah had to say about Jesus' story as God's fulfilling his ancient promises.

There is another important dimension to Paul's uncharacteristic quotation. In relation to God's 'work' the prophet's closing words are, 'even if someone unpacks it for you'. Its final position stresses this clause: what I have translated as 'unpack', ἐκδιηγέομαι, appears only twice in the New Testament, here and at Acts 15:3 where Paul and Barnabas 'unpack' the Gentiles' conversion. Nor is this a common LXX word, found mostly in Sirach, but also in Job, Ezekiel and two psalms. Examination of its occurrences uncovers close similarity between Habakkuk's clause and Ps. 117:17–18, a likeness unmatched elsewhere:

> I shall not die, but I shall live, and *unpack the works of the Lord* ....

The presence here of the unusual 'unpack' in close association with Paul's emphasized 'work' is remarkable enough, but if one recalls that Luke has twice before 'unpacked' news of Jesus' suffering and resurrection through the stone-proverb (Ps. 117:22), then it becomes wise to look at the proverb's context whose italicized words are shared with Habakkuk (117:22–24):

> This was the Lord's doing; and it is *marvellous* in our eyes.
> *This is the day* that the Lord made; let us rejoice and be glad in it.[55]

Because this core psalm encapsulates Luke's story of Jesus' great reversal, the prophet's 'someone' doing the unpacking was thus not only Paul, but Jesus. Similarly, this Habakkuk extract is not 'Paul', but Luke once more evoking Psalm 117 – towards which his other allusions move.

Psalm 88:21 (Acts 13:22)

UBS[3] and NA[27] agree in attributing 'I have found David' (εὗρον Δαυὶδ) to Ps. 88:21. This sermon's dynamic is rooted in God's promise of an heir to David; in Acts 2 and 7,[56] Psalm 131 performed the task fulfilled in Antioch by Psalm 88. It would be difficult to find in scripture a stronger statement of God's covenant with David (88:4–5, 29–30, 36–38), or stronger dismay that God had broken his promise (88:39–46). This is a bitter summary, inverting promise into disaster and ending with a complaint against God – 'you covered

---

[54] My translation.
[55] Precisely the verse used by Mark and Matthew but absent from Lk. 20:17.
[56] On Stephen's speech see P. Doble, 'Something Greater than Solomon', in S. Moyise, ed., *The Old Testament in the New Testament* (JSNTSup 189; Sheffield: Sheffield Academic Press, 2000), pp. 181–207.

[David] with shame'. Yet dismay was not despair, for this psalmist still demanded to know *when* God would keep his promise (88:47, 50–52).[57]

'Covenant' is not the only link between sermon and psalmist. As in other speeches, *mortality* figures large. This psalmist reminds God that, like all humans, he is mortal (88:48a); he generalizes his problem of mortality (88:48b–49), making it one of the group of 'Death and Hades' psalms from which 'Peter' chose four to texture his Pentecost speech.

Where this psalmist demanded to know *when* God would keep his promise, Paul announced that God *had* kept it (Acts 13:23, 32). Further, the psalmist's question at Ps. 88:49 is linked by Paul with God's ancient promise (Acts 13:32). Its internal logic points to Psalm 88 setting Paul's sermon's agenda; Ps. 117:17–18 actually 'answers' the question posed by 88:49. Paul took his 'hearers' from its first allusion to his sermon's final intertextuality through a carefully textured substructure (see Table 3). Two words signal a large intertextuality.

Table 3   Paul's sermon: Acts 13:16–41

Psalm	88:49b	88:27b–28	88:29b	88:49a
	Who is the man who will *rescue*?	*My Father* ... *Prototokos firstborn*	My *Covenant* with him will stand *firm*	... who shall live and not see *death* ... ... his life from *Hades'* hand ...
106:20 (Acts 13:26)	*Rescued* them from their *corruptions*			And they drew near to the gates of *death*, [Ps. 106:18b]
2:1–3, [6–9] (Acts 13:33)		*My son* ... I have *begotten* ...		
[Isaiah 55:3] (Acts 13:34)			... *covenant*, David's holy and *firm* things	
15:10 (Acts 13:35)	Neither will you give your holy one to see *corruption* ...			... my soul to *Hades* ...
[117:17–18] (Acts 13:41)				The Lord did not deliver me to *death* ... ... I shall not *die*, but I shall live and 'unpack' the works of the Lord.

---

[57] This psalm climaxes with 'your anointed'; 88:52, cf. 39.

Psalm 106:20 (Acts 13:26)

Paul's rhetorical address to his brothers echoes this great psalm of thanksgiving.[58] Psalm 106 belongs to the substructure of Acts: Luke used this allusion at Acts 10:36; for his Infancy Gospel he drew on Ps. 106:9b, 10 (Lk. 1:53a, 79); he took over the Dual Tradition's *logion* at Lk. 13:29 (106:3). Here, 106:20 is a middle term between Psalms 88 and 15, anticipating Psalm 117.

This 'message of salvation' at the opening of the sermon's second section both takes up the word 'saviour' from Paul's affirmation that God has now acted (13:23) and transforms the synagogue officials' invitation (13:15): for their 'message of encouragement' Paul offers a 'message of salvation'. Yet the significant, active part of 106:20 remains invisible: the God who 'sent out his message' (106:20a) was the same God who 'rescued them from their corruption' (106:20b).[59] One can hardly doubt that this is another example of 'active suppression' for it carries two words central to Paul's sermon: 'rescued' (ἐρρύσατο) and 'corruption' (διαφθορῶν). 'Corruption' appears four times at the heart of Paul's argument (13:34–37), an emphasis which, focused on Ps. 15:10, echoes Peter's Pentecost Speech. This missing element (Ps. 106:20b) anticipates Ps. 15:10's appearance at Acts 13:35. Readers would also have recognized that when Ps. 88:49 asked who might 'rescue' (ῥύσεται) his life from Hades' hand, it was first answered by Ps. 106:20's affirmation that *God rescues* – from 'corruption'. So Paul's 'message of salvation' *included* the news that God had rescued Jesus from corruption.

In this compressed sermon, Luke's brief signal has focused on the wider context in Ps. 106:18–21, revealing ways in which Luke's subtext amplifies his narrative.

Psalm 2:7 (Acts 13:33)

This verse is a notorious *crux*: commentators divide over whether 'today' refers to Jesus' resurrection[60] or whether it points back to Jesus' baptism.[61] This difficulty results from atomistic readings of Acts 13:33. When read as part of Luke's substructure, this surfacing of Ps. 2:7 can be seen as part of a development that began in Acts 4:25–27.[62] Within the Jerusalem community's prayer, Ps. 2:1–2 was appropriated to Jesus both historically (4:25–27) and textually in that 'whom you anointed' (ὃν ἔχρισας, links to the 'anointed' (χριστός, '*Chr*ist') of Ps. 2:2. This appropriation to Jesus of *Christos* indicated the active presence of Ps. 2:7 in Luke's subtext. So at Acts 13:33 Theophilus, bringing with him previous experience of Psalm 2, extended his own

---

[58] An echo recognized by NA[27].
[59] *Diff.* Pietersma, *New English Translation of the Septuagint.*
[60] E.g., J.A. Fitzmyer, *The Acts of the Apostles* (AB 31; New York: Doubleday, 1998), pp. 516–17.
[61] E.g., C.K. Barrett, *The Acts of the Apostles* (ICC; Edinburgh: T & T Clark, 1994), pp. 645-7.
[62] See the discussion in Section 4.2 above.

understanding of this psalm as Luke approached the end of his narrative-thread about God's rebuilding David's house.

Paul's 'good news' to Antioch's congregants is repeatedly that God has fulfilled his promise to their forefathers:[63] David's throne is now occupied by Jesus. This fulfilment was possible only because God raised from the dead this Jesus whom the rulers crucified. Consequently, 'today' is not to be pressed, for it refers to David's experience of being king. The *crux* is further eased when we render 13:32–33 as 'And we bring you the good news that, by raising Jesus, God has fulfilled for us, their children, this [promise] made to our forefathers, as it is written in the second psalm, "You are my son; today I have begotten you".'

Did this quotation emerge into Paul's sermon because it evoked not only its fuller context in Ps. 2:6–9,[64] but also 'answered' Ps. 88:27–29? The terrible questions in Ps. 88:47–50 climax in 'Lord, where is your steadfast love of old, which by your truth you swore to David?' Paul's good news is that God has fulfilled this promise so that 'You are my son...' was now appropriated to Jesus – and Jesus fitted this promise (88:27–28):

> He shall call upon me, 'You are my Father,
> my God, and the supporter of my salvation!'
> I will make him the firstborn (πρωτότοκόν),
> high among the kings of the earth.

That Jesus called on God as 'Father' needs no exploration here. That Luke thought of Jesus as 'son' is evidenced in, e.g., Lk. 1:32–35; 10:21–22; 20:9–19; at Lk. 2:7 he reports Jesus' birth as that of Mary's 'firstborn' (πρωτότοκός).[65] What is more significant is that these connectors stand immediately before a strong form of the Davidic covenant (88:29–30):

> Forever I will keep my steadfast love for him,
> and my covenant with him will stand firm.
> I will establish his seed forever and ever,
> and his throne as long as heaven endures.

Beneath the text of Paul's compressed sermon, Luke has brought Psalms 2 and 88 into active dialogue. He now (re)turns to Psalm 15.[66]

Psalm 15:10b (Acts 13:35)

Here again, Theophilus could bring his previous experience of Psalm 15 from Peter's Pentecost address (Acts 2:14–36).[67] In Paul's compressed sermon we

[63] Acts 13:23, [26], 32, [38], [41].
[64] Linking it with Acts 4:25–27.
[65] *Hapax legomenon* in Gospels and Acts.
[66] Via Isa. 55:3 which is not discussed here; its links with Luke's substructure are noted in Table 3.
[67] See Section 3 above.

also hear not an isolated quotation but an evocation of Christian understanding of Psalm 15; this one phrase recalls its first, unquoted clause (15:10a), for they belong together (cf. Acts 2:31). Just as Ps. 106:20's unquoted element is central to Paul's sermon, so 15:10a reaches back to, and answers Ps. 88:49 with its persistent question about Hades.

This sermon's 'good news' is that God has fulfilled his promise. That promise, hinted at in its allusion (13:22–23) to Psalm 88 remained threatened by death: 'What is humankind, that it shall *live* and *not see death*,[68] shall *rescue* its soul from the power of *Hades*?' (88:49).

Luke knew that it was God who *rescued* from corruption – Ps. 106:20 had made that confidence part of his message of salvation. He also knew that for Jesus Hades had no power – Ps. 15:10a affirmed to David that God would not abandon his soul to Hades. Further, beneath the deceptively 'Pauline' choice of this sermon's prophetic conclusion lay another affirmation: 'I *shall not die*, but *I shall live*, and unpack the works of the Lord' (Ps. 117:17–18; cf. 88:49). In Paul's sermon's substructure, hidden in a quotation from Habakkuk (Acts 13:41), there is thus yet another link, between Psalms 88 and 117. And Ps. 117:22 also undergirds Luke's Passion Narrative.

6 Luke's Passion Narrative: Luke 23:34–49

The story of Jesus' suffering and death was known to Luke's readers, for his two volumes were designed to confirm Theophilus in the things in which he had *already* been instructed (Lk. 1:1–4). By its sequence of predictions that *the Son of Man* would suffer and be killed[69] Luke's first volume prepared readers for Jesus' death. Travelling to Emmaus, two of Jesus' followers heard from the risen Jesus, 'Was it not necessary that *the Christ* should suffer these things and then enter into his glory?' (24:26). Readers had probably met the kind of apostolic preaching (pictured in Acts) where Jesus' suffering and death were intertwined with scripture. Above all, they would recall that the risen Jesus was reported to have educated his apostles in his own hermeneutic for reading scripture, helping them grasp that *the Christ* should suffer and rise from the dead (24:44–47). Commentators[70] note that scripture knew nothing of a suffering Christ; this section suggests Luke's probable source.

Luke's Distinctive Passion Narrative

Conventionally, scholars have treated Luke 22–23 as Luke's Passion Narrative, subjecting it to such intense scrutiny that the literature on these chapters is

---

[68] Answered by Ps. 117:17–18.
[69] E.g., Lk. 9:22, 44; 18:31.
[70] E.g., J.A. Fitzmyer, *The Gospel According to Luke* (AB 20-20A; New York: Doubleday, Vol I 1981, Vol II 1985), p. 1581; cf. F.F. Bruce, *The Acts of the Apostles* (London: Tyndale Press, 1952), p. 111.

immense.[71] Luke's *plot* is distinctive in that his portrayal of Jesus differs from that in its parallels;[72] his *approach* is distinctive in two ways. First, in his portrayal of Jesus' death (23:34–49) Luke uses psalms eight times more frequently than in Luke 22–23, a density demanding exploration.[73] Second, because Luke's *choice* of psalms for this brief narrative is 'Davidic', readers 'hear' David's voice. This is important for a reading of the Passion Narrative, for we saw in earlier sections that Luke characteristically appropriates to Jesus psalms of David's autobiography.

Allusion and Text

Luke's narrative *alludes* to Psalms 21, 68 and 87, which are so woven into his text that it is unsafe to comment on their text type. There is, however, a near-quotation at Lk. 23:46 where Luke's report of Jesus' last word closely resembles Ps. 30:6. Adapting this verse to event, Luke changed its verb's tense: 'Father, into your hands I *commit* my spirit'; in all other respects, this is a quotation from 30:6 in a Greek Psalter.

Luke's unique 'word' here bears heavily on one's understanding of his using psalms. He knew, and used, Mark's tradition; he knew, and used, Psalm 21; he clearly knew *and did not use* Mark's tradition about Jesus' last word from the cross – a Hebraized Aramaic form of Ps. 21:2 (22:1 MT).[74] In this, Luke's non-usage coheres with his avoidance of Hebrew and Aramaic terms; yet he also avoided a Greek form of Mark's 'word'. One sound reason for Luke's refusal of Ps. 21:2 lies in its using 'abandon' or 'forsake' (ἐγκαταλείπω). Apostolic speeches emphasize the significance of Ps. 15:10 with its strong affirmation: 'you will not abandon my soul to Hades'. Further, psalms witness that a 'righteous one' (δίκαιος) is *not* abandoned, so Luke's subtext precluded a 'Markan' last word.[75] David's biography was emphatic that he trusted God, knowing that he would not be abandoned. If Jesus' life, death and resurrection appropriated David's psalms, then Ps. 30:6 is an appropriate last word, which Ps. 21:2 is not.

Psalms of David's Suffering

Luke's dense narrative reveals that he transformed tradition's use of Psalms 21 and 68 while focusing on Psalms 30 and 87. These psalms' presence here as subtext requires that modern readers acquaint themselves with all four as a biography of suffering, for these psalms vividly picture David's sufferings as

---

[71] See, e.g., the (limited) bibliographical survey in Harrington, *Lukan Passion Narrative*.

[72] See, e.g., Doble, *Paradox of Salvation*.

[73] An instance of *gezerah shewa* at Lk. 22:69, melding Ps. 109:1 with Dan. 7:13, belongs to a Lukan trajectory ending at Acts 7:55–56; its significance cannot be pursued here.

[74] See R.E. Brown, *The Death of the Messiah* (AB Reference Library; New York: Doubleday, 1994), pp. 1078–88; V. Taylor, *The Gospel According to St Mark* (London: Macmillan, 1952), pp. 592–4.

[75] See Doble, *Paradox of Salvation*, pp. 161–83.

attributable to enemies whose hatred became violent (Pss 21, 30, 68). Although physical suffering figures in these psalms, its 'spiritual' dimension feels more oppressive: David is surrounded, observed and mocked. His hope, however, is that God would neither forsake nor abandon him; yet his plight brought David so near to death and Hades (Pss 21:16; 37:21; 87:5–6) that he wondered whether God could work wonders for the dead (87:11–13). Here is a psalmist's depiction of *post-mortem* 'existence' marked by its sense of utter separation from God – and from friends, for 'I passed out of mind like one who is dead' (30:13).

One psalm from this group makes a clear, unambiguous statement of David's unconditional trust in God: Psalm 30 is epitomized by its sixth verse, 'Into your hands I will commit my spirit . . .' A pulsing 'sense of God' pervades this psalm by someone suffering yet looking to God for salvation, reversal of the way things now are. For the heart of this word from the cross is that it is God who saves. Reflection on these psalms' characteristic features discloses how significantly Psalm 30 figures in them, yet as a whole it resonates with a deep sense of trust in God. This is *the* psalm which in large measure encapsulates David's 'passion', the 'anointed' (χριστός) and 'righteous one' (δίκαιος).

Jesus' death scene is reported by a variety of *narrators*: Luke, the rulers, soldiers and the first criminal largely speak in their own voices. The second criminal's rebuttal of his fellow's taunting of Jesus is reported in direct speech, as is the centurion's response to Jesus' end. At the scene's heart, after Luke's reporting solemn events, Jesus himself speaks. Significantly, in this narrative distinctive 'David' psalms also address its reader, their subtextual presence shaping and colouring Luke's scene by their interrelatedness and their witness to its significance: *here is David's voice, appropriated to Luke's Jesus to recount his sufferings and dying.*[76]

Psalms in Dialogue (Luke 23:34b–49)

As in the apostolic speeches of Acts, here also warp and weft weave their texture, more descriptive than polemical.

Warp

This vertical interconnectedness of psalms opens with a 'traditional' allusion: at 23:34b Luke shares Ps. 21:19 with Mark and Matthew (Mk 15:24 *et par*). Within 23:35–43 readers find an ordered Lukan rewriting of Mk 15:29–32, crafted around a shared allusion to Ps. 21:8–9 with its picture of mockery and taunting:

> All who saw me mocked at me;
> they talked with their lips, they moved their heads:
> 'He *hoped* in the Lord, let him *deliver* him
> let him *save* him, because he wanted him!'

---

[76] This perspective is developed below in *Weft*.

From here on Luke parted company with Mark, rewriting this death scene without further allusion to Psalm 21.[77]

At 23:46 Luke portrays a Jesus dying with confident trust in the Father. Because Ps. 21:4–9 ends with taunting around the word *save*, its accenting of *hope* is often missed. But the sufferer's *hope* is a trigger for his opponents' taunts and Psalm 30 is quintessentially a psalm of *hope* (see 30:2, 7, 15, 25) in the face of great suffering (30:10–14). It cannot be accidental that this psalm, from which the Lukan Jesus' last words are drawn, embodies the *unexpressed element* of Ps. 21:9 – 'He hoped in the Lord, let him deliver him . . .' Another unexpressed element echoes from Jesus' last word: 'Into your hands . . . *you redeemed me, O Lord, God of truth'*. This decompressed last word highlights the taunting of those mocking him as a travesty of this sufferer's hope in God.

Yet his suffering is real (30:10–14); insulted by enemies, an object of fear to his acquaintances (30:12), he 'passed out of mind like one dead' (30:13). Because Luke knew another psalm about both 'fearful acquaintances' and 'like one dead', by analogy with Psalm 87, at 23:49 he transformed Mk 15:40–41.

Weft

Such linkage, by keyword and analogy, misses Luke's achievement in these verses so densely intertextualized with psalms, for his signalled allusions echo David's voice, now appropriated to Jesus' situation, adding content and colour to Luke's taut narration. The 'signal' is often, though not always, the final line only of a block of text. We noted earlier how at Lk. 23:34b Luke transformed a shared allusion to Ps. 21:19; 21:13–19 amplifies Luke's brief 23:33–34, voicing Jesus' experience, often in painful detail.

In 23:35–43 Luke surveyed 'the company of evildoers' surrounding Jesus (Ps. 21:17), transforming Mk 15:29–32 into both a distant echo of the temptation narrative (Lk. 4:1–12) and a reflection on Ps. 21:8–9. Replacing Mark's allusive 'they shook their heads' (21:8b), Luke focused on 'all who saw me mocked me' (Ps. 21:8a), dividing 'who saw me' from 'mocked' and giving them respectively to 'the People', 'the rulers', about whom he has much to say,[78] 'the soldiers' and 'one of those crucified with him'.

Echoing Ps. 21:9 (and Luke's temptation narrative), each group frames its conditional (*if* you are God's Anointed, King of Israel, Christ) before taunting Jesus with 'save yourself'. These 'rulers' belong to the subtext from Psalms 2, 117 and 145 explored in Acts 3–5. Luke's soldiers have been imported from Mk 15:16–20 and given the task (Lk. 23:36) of 'fulfilling' Ps. 68:22; if this echo signals the last line of Ps. 68:14–22, then the appositeness of David's lament to Jesus' situation is clear. Taunts, not comforters, surrounded him (Ps. 68:21).[79]

---

[77] *Diff.* Mk 15:34. See Brown, *Death of the Messiah*, pp. 1455–67.
[78] See Section 4.
[79] A key psalm taken up at Acts 1:20.

At Lk. 23:46, embedded in nature's lament over these events, Jesus' dying word expresses the trust affirmed in Ps. 30:2–6. Here, prefaced by 'Father', is a last word whose context crystallizes all the gentleness and forbearance characteristic of Luke's Jesus. His suffering, however, was real (Ps. 30:10–14); insulted by enemies, a horror to his acquaintances (Ps. 30:12), Jesus was near to passing out of mind, like one dead (Ps. 30:13). This is the voice of a failing life, but the analogous Psalm 87, echoed at Lk. 23:49, has become a *post-mortem* voice.

Although Psalm 87 is not 'Davidic', it belongs to a first-person 'death and Hades' group, and vv. 4–13 provide a vision of the pit, the grave, Hades to which, according to Ps. 15:10, God would not abandon his 'anointed' and from which, the apostles testified, God had raised Jesus. Read against its signal allusion in Lk. 23:49, this long passage (Ps. 87:4–9) is descriptive; its focal question (Ps. 87:11–13) echoes that at Ps. 88:49 which immediately precedes the psalmist's plea that God would act to fulfil his promise to David.

'It is written ...'

At its heart, Luke's Passion Narrative has a brief, *distinctive* account of Jesus' death (Lk. 23:34b–49) with a high density of allusion to psalms of David's suffering. When a reader 'hears' each allusion as a signal to recall its context, the sequencing of these 'decompressed files' works intertextually with Luke's story of Jesus' death; *this sequence becomes the suffering one's voice from the cross.*

Further, this sequence of psalms, mostly by David, God's anointed (*christos*), has been appropriated to the Jesus proclaimed as Christ (*Christos*, Acts 2:36) by Peter and John. *This sequence is, consequently, scripture in which 'it is written' that the Christ should suffer* (Lk. 24:46, cf. v. 26). According to Peter, while Jerusalem's rulers had crucified Jesus, God had raised him from the dead, a twofold event interpreted as 'this Jesus is the stone that was rejected by you, the builders; it has become the cornerstone' (Acts 4:11). Luke's Passion Narrative is also his account of Jesus' rejection by rulers (LK. 23:13, 35); in Luke, Psalm 117 is ever near.[80]

Acts 1:20 quotes Pss 68:26 and 108:8. While Judas' place in Jesus' story[81] is too complex to explore here, we note that at Acts 1:20 Peter has linked Psalm 68's malediction on David's enemies (vv. 22–29) with Judas' death; Ps. 108:8 probably emerged by analogy with it. Substructurally, Acts 1:15–20 extends Luke's Passion Narrative, because not only is Judas the guide for Jesus' captors, but Psalm 68 is a traditional element in the Passion story.

---

[80] *Contra* W. Weren, 'Psalm 2 in Luke-Acts: An Intertextual Study', in S. Draisma, ed., *Intertextuality in Biblical Writings* (Kampen: Kok, 1989), pp. 189–203.

[81] See, e.g., Lk. 6:16; 22:3–6, 21–23, 47–48. See further W. Klassen, *Judas: Betrayer or Friend of Jesus?* (London; SCM Press, 1996).

7 Conclusions

(1) Luke's quotations, and details of some allusions, confirm that his Psalm-book was a Greek version like that of Rahlfs' *Septuaginta*, a conclusion consistent with his using no words of Hebrew or Aramaic origin.[82]

(2) Through his distinctive use of psalms Luke retold Jesus' story as the fulfilling of scripture, particularly that relating to David's place in God's 'plan'.

(3) Sections 2–6 examined psalms working in clusters as a substructure of Luke-Acts, shaping its distinctive narrative. Luke 'textures' psalms one with another and with traditional material about Jesus; atomistic readings miss the character of his engagement with this 'christianized hymnbook'.

(4) Luke's textured appeal to this psalms-substructure implies his readers' familiarity with at least those psalms examined in this chapter.

(5) In condensed 'speeches', Luke's Peter and Paul sound alike, largely because they voice *his* basic 'Christ-talk' rooted in David's psalm-[auto]biography. Since this christology also shapes his Passion Narrative it probably represents Luke's own understanding of Jesus' story[83] and informs his writing to assure Theophilus of the *reliability* of what he was taught about 'the things fulfilled among us' (Lk. 1:1–4).[84]

(6) In sum, *Psalms are a precondition of, rather than additional to, Luke's narrative*, confirming that through Jesus God fulfilled his promise to David of a kingdom without end, that the Christ is Jesus.[85]

---

[82] Except 'Hakeldama' (Acts 1:19) and 'amen' (ἀμήν) used with verbs of saying (Lk. 4:42; 12:37; 18:17, 29; 21:32; 23:43), and only on Jesus' lips. But see Fitzmyer, *Luke*, pp. 114–27.

[83] Rather than an anachronistic account of primitive preaching.

[84] Here we 'arrive where we started, and know the place for the first time'.

[85] Long after this chapter was submitted, I finally decided that, on internal grounds, the D reading at Lk 3:22 should probably be preferred to the text of NA27. Ps. 2:7 should therefore be added to the list on p. 83 and linking it to the same quotation at Acts 13:33.

Chapter 6

The Psalms in John's Gospel

Margaret Daly-Denton

A Profile of Johannine Psalm Usage

To answer an apparently straightforward question like, 'How many times does the fourth evangelist refer to the psalms?' is not a simple matter. Yet this seems to be a reasonable point at which to begin. It is possible to identify six clear quotations from the psalms in the fourth gospel:

> Zeal for your house will consume me (Jn 2:17, from Ps. 69:10).
> I said, 'You are gods' (Jn 10:34, citing Ps. 82:6).
> Blessed is he who comes in the name of the Lord (Jn 12:13, from Ps. 118:26).
> He who ate my bread has lifted his heel against me (Jn 13:18, from Ps. 41:10).
> They hated me without a cause (Jn 15:25, from Ps. 69:5).
> They parted my garments among them and for my clothing they cast lots (Jn 19:24, from Ps. 22:19).

A seventh refers to the Exodus story in words drawn from one of the historical recitals of Israel's history found in the Psalter:

> He gave them bread from heaven to eat (Jn 6:31, from Ps. 78:24).

In three other passages where 'the Scripture' introduced by John is not a *verbatim* quotation of any biblical passage, the Psalter appears to be the stronger 'contender' of two (or perhaps more) potential scriptural sources:

> From within him shall flow rivers of living water (Jn 7:38, cf. Ps. 78:16, 20).
> I thirst (Jn 19:28, cf. Ps. 69:22).
> Not a bone of him shall be broken (Jn 19:36, cf. Ps. 34:21).

In this chapter, these 'composite' quotations will be discussed more briefly, without excluding the other biblical sources that may have also contributed to the Johannine 'scriptures'.

Before proceeding, a few methodological points should be clarified. A quotation will be regarded as any reference to the psalms which the author 'signposts' by means of an introductory phrase such as, 'to fulfil the Scriptures' or 'as it is written'. The narrative itself may sometimes indicate a quotation, as in Jn 12:13 or 19:28. An author can, of course, refer to an existing work in a more informal way such as an allusion. This would be a less obvious appearance of the precursor text where, instead of providing a verbal 'signpost', the author calls on knowledge held in common with the audience, referring to this 'presupposition pool' either verbally or thematically. An even less distinct form of reference to a precursor text might be called an echo. While quotations are clearly made intentionally, echoes are spontaneous evocations of existing texts. While an allusion usually has fairly substantial volume (a phrase or at least several words in common with the precursor text), an echo may be quite fleeting, often not more than one word. To recognize an echo is not necessarily to claim that the author intended it. It is rather to recognize that no writing is entirely original but is a tissue of references to pre-existing works. Attentiveness to echo can enable us to hear some of the resonances with which a work such as the fourth gospel resounded for its original audience. We will find that an ear attuned to echoes can discern layers of intertextual reference that greatly enhance our appreciation of John's Gospel.

While the gospels were written in Greek, the psalms were originally composed in Hebrew. They were known to the New Testament authors, however, in a Greek translation. Sometimes the actual wording (verbal form) of a quotation in John's Gospel does not completely match any version of this Greek translation known to us. Several explanations suggest themselves. Perhaps the evangelist is quoting from memory. Perhaps his knowledge of a Hebrew or Aramaic version of the psalm has coloured the quotation. It may be that other scriptural sources have contributed to what is, in effect, a composite citation. It could even be that John has adapted the wording in order to enhance the quotation's effectiveness in supporting his argument.

A final methodological point concerns the belief, universal in the Judaism contemporary with early Christianity, that King David was the 'author' of the psalms and that many of them tell of events in his career. We find this honorific attribution most clearly articulated by Luke (e.g., Acts 2:25, 29, 34; 4:25) but it is the unspoken presupposition that underlies the early Christian penchant for reading the psalms as prophetic of Jesus. The Jesus that emerges from the pages of the gospels is reminiscent not only of the David of the 'historical' narratives, but also of the imagined David the psalmist. He is also suggestive of the expected 'new' David, as, for example, an echo of Ezek. 37:22–25 in Jn 10:16 clearly shows. It is important to state that this is true, even of the fourth gospel where there is no mention of a Davidic ancestry for Jesus and where Jesus is never referred to as 'Son of David'. It is precisely as psalmist, rather than as ancestor of the Messiah, that 'David' figures in the Johannine portrayal of Jesus.

Comparing Johannine with Synoptic Psalm Usage

If we were to accept that there are ten psalm quotations in the fourth gospel, how would this compare with synoptic psalm usage? In order to answer this question adequately, we need to ensure that we are comparing like with like. When referring explicitly to the scriptures, John shows a preference for explicit citation with a formula of quotation such as, 'This happened to fulfil the scripture . . .' or 'It was written . . .'. Such formulae correspond to our inverted commas or quotation marks. The synoptics generally prefer what might be called quotations without inverted commas. In these instances, the authors apparently intend that knowledgeable readers will pick up the reference to a psalm, for example, to Ps. 22:18 in the account of the soldiers sharing out Jesus' clothes among themselves (Mk 15:24). If we allow for what is simply a different narrative technique, we will find that synoptic allusions are frequently comparable to Johannine quotations in terms of volume and function.

The following list shows what proportion of explicit 'scriptures' in the four gospels comes from the psalms:

3 out of 14 in Mark,   i.e. 21%
7 out of 38 in Matthew, i.e. 18%
5 out of 16 in Luke,   i.e. 31%
10 out of 16 in John,   i.e. 62%

Even allowing for some distortion in these figures, it is evident that the fourth evangelist favours the Psalter as a scriptural source.

In the course of this chapter, we will also discover that John is noticeably independent in his choice of psalm passages, avoiding some of the passages quite extensively quoted in the synoptics and choosing other psalm passages that are found neither in the synoptics, nor anywhere else in the New Testament. His preference for formal citation over against verbal allusion makes his psalm usage more emphatic. Moreover, psalm reference is spread throughout the whole gospel, rather than mainly concentrated in the passion sequence, as in the synoptics.

'Zeal for your house will consume me' (John 2:17, from Psalm 69:10)

The first psalm quotation in the gospel occurs in a story that John would have received as part of the tradition about the final days of Jesus' ministry. Even though he has moved this story to the early part of his narrative, he still preserves the memory that Jesus' angry disruption of the trading in the temple precipitated the escalation of the hostility that would eventually lead to his death. The quotation is introduced as a line of scripture that the disciples spontaneously thought of when they witnessed Jesus' action in the Temple:

ὁ ζῆλος τοῦ οἴκου σου καταφάγεταί με.
Zeal for your house will consume me.

The quotation is accurate, except for the verb 'consume'. The Greek verb καταφαγεῖν, 'to consume', 'to devour', is an intensive form of the verb φαγεῖν, 'to eat'. In the psalm, this verb is in the past (Greek: aorist) tense. John, however, uses the future tense (Greek: future middle voice), adapting the wording, as Jewish scholars of the period regularly would, in order to enhance its effectiveness. He thus makes of it a programmatic scripture pointing forward to its fulfilment in Jesus' death.

In recalling this 'scripture', the disciples comment, perhaps with a certain amount of foreboding, on Jesus' uncompromising zeal for God's house and all that it stands for. Later in this scene, we encounter another level of remembering, that of the Paraclete-inspired community of disciples looking back on this event in the light of their Easter experience (Jn 16:13). According to John, 'When therefore he was raised from the dead, the disciples remembered that he had said this; and they believed the scripture and the word of Jesus' (2:22). What did Jesus say in this scene? 'Destroy this temple and in three days I will rebuild it.' This motif belongs to the judicial trial of Jesus in the synoptic gospels (Mk 14:58). John is bringing the trial of Jesus 'forward' so that, in effect, it is already in progress at the very outset of Jesus' ministry. What was the scripture? It could be the sacred writings of Israel in general (as, probably, in Jn 20:9) but it could equally be the scripture quoted earlier in this scene, 'Zeal for your house will devour me'. The author instructs his audience to take the word 'temple' metaphorically as a reference to Jesus' body, destroyed in death but rebuilt through his resurrection. The scripture too must be heard figuratively. There is a hint in the verb 'consume' that this burning zeal may well devour Jesus himself. There are faint but unmistakeable echoes of Elijah's costly zeal (1 Kgs 19:10; Sir. 48:2) and of the flames that consume a victim acceptable to God and thereby manifest God's presence (Lev. 9:14; 2 Chron. 7:1; 1 Kgs 18:38). Both of these motifs, the Elijah-likeness of Jesus and the sacrificial-theophanic character of Jesus' death, will be developed further as the gospel unfolds.

Fundamental to the Easter experience of the disciples is their conviction that Jesus' death fulfilled the scriptures. We know that Psalm 69 was familiar to the early Christians because other motifs from it are woven into their telling of the story of Jesus' crucifixion – in particular the vinegary drink (Ps. 69:22), but also, the idea that in his death Jesus bore the reproaches of those who insulted God (Ps. 69:10b, as developed by Paul in Rom. 15:3). In the previous line to 'Zeal for your house has devoured me', the psalmist laments that he has become a stranger to his brothers. John has just told his readers that Jesus had been with his mother and brothers in Capernaum (2:12), thereby encouraging his audience to draw the conclusion that he left them to go to Jerusalem. Later the evangelist will comment that even Jesus' brothers did not believe in him (7:5), suggesting perhaps that Jesus' devotion to God's cause has made him, like the psalmist, a stranger to his brothers. So it is quite possible that the author wants his audience to keep the whole psalm in mind, especially since in 15:25 he will use another motif from it to show that the opposition of those who hated Jesus without cause has been prophetically foretold in scripture.

Psalm 69 comes from book 2 of the Psalter, a collection entitled 'The Prayers

(Hebrew: *Tefilloth*; Greek: ὕμνοι) of David the Son of Jesse' (see Ps. 72:20). John's temple scene follows an inaugural sequence of scenes in which characters refer to Jesus as 'Messiah' (1:41), 'Son of God' and 'King of Israel' (1:49). These titles cast him in a 'Davidic' role, so it is logical, in terms of John's plot, that David's words in Ps. 69:10 would occur to the disciples as appropriate to Jesus. In this context, it is important to remember that our familiarity with later christological developments makes it difficult for us to hear 'Son of God' as a messianic title, but this is the original sense of the title (see 2 Sam. 7:14; Ps. 2:7; cf. Ps. 89:27–30). At issue here, therefore, is Jesus' kingship, and for John, the word 'King' can be used of Jesus only in a profoundly figurative sense, to be articulated much later in the narrative. From our knowledge of messianic expectations current in first-century Judaism, we know that the purging and re-founding of the Temple is part of the scenario for the expected King.[1] In view of the emphasis that John places on the traders, it may well be that he expects his readers to understand Jesus as inaugurating the great 'Day of the Lord' when, according to the final lines of the prophecy of Zechariah, 'there shall no longer be a trader in the house of the Lord of Hosts'. Because of Jesus, John would say, special ritual arrangements for accessing the holiness associated with the Temple are no longer necessary. That holiness is available to all in the new 'temple of his body' (Jn 2:21).[2]

'I said, "You are gods"' (John 10:34, from Psalm 82:6)

This quotation occurs in a scene which exemplifies John's tendency to present Jesus as already on trial even during the ministry, Jn 10:22–39. In fact, there is a decidedly forensic character about this scene. Two 'rounds' of prosecution and defence, complete with witness statements, end in failed attempts to execute judgement. The first round of the debate centres on Jesus as the Christ, the second on his status as 'Son of God'. No doubt this structure corresponds to the two-pronged question of the High Priest in the synoptic tradition, 'Are you the Christ, the Son of the Blessed One?' (Mk 14:62).[3]

---

[1] See *Ps. Sol.* 17:21–22, 36. Cf. Mk 14:61 where a report that Jesus claimed to be able to destroy and rebuild the temple prompts the High Priest to ask him if he is the Christ.

[2] See F.J. Moloney, 'Reading John 2:13–22: The Purification of the Temple', *RB* 97 (1990), pp. 432–51; B.G. Schuchard, *Scripture within Scripture: The Interrelationship of Form and Function in the Explicit Old Testament Citations in the Gospel of John* (SBLDS 133; Atlanta: Scholars Press, 1992), pp. 17–32; M.J.J. Menken, *Old Testament Quotations in the Fourth Gospel: Studies in Textual Form* (CBET 15; Kampen: Kok Pharos, 1996), pp. 37–46; A. Obermann, *Die christologische Erfüllung der Schrift im Johannesevangelium: Eine Untersuchung zur johanneischen Hermeneutik anhand der Schriftzitate* (WUNT 2/83; Tübingen: Mohr Siebeck, 1996), pp. 114–28; J.D.M. Derrett, 'The Zeal of the House and the Cleansing of the Temple', *DRev* 95 (1997), pp. 79–94; M. Daly-Denton, *David in the Fourth Gospel: The Johannine Reception of the Psalms* (AGJU 47; Leiden: Brill, 2000), pp. 118–31.

[3] In Lk. 22:67, 70 there are two separate challenges to Jesus – as the Christ and as Son of God – indicating a similar narrative expansion of the more concise tradition reflected in Mk 14:62. The Lukan Jesus replies to the challenges in words similar to Jn 10:25.

The quotation from Psalm 82 occurs in Jesus' second 'defence' speech dealing with his status as 'Son of God'. The psalm is quoted accurately from the Septuagint:

ἐγὼ εἶπα· θεοί ἐστε.
I said, 'You are gods'.

This is Jesus' riposte to the charge of blasphemy. In the synoptics, Jesus' reply to the accusation of blasphemy alludes to Ps. 110:1: 'The Lord said to my Lord, sit at my right, until I make your enemies a footstool for your feet' (Mk 14:62; Matt. 26:64; Lk. 22:69). Although this is the psalm passage most frequently referred to in the New Testament, the fourth evangelist avoids it. This is probably because its two-stage application to Jesus in early Christianity (e.g. Rom. 1:3–4) and its suggestion of elevation from a higher to a lower status do not resonate with his particular christological stance. Instead, in this scene, with characteristic independence, John adduces another psalm to furnish scriptural testimony in support of Jesus' claim to be 'Son of God'. This psalm will also serve to convey the Johannine conviction that the judgement is not a future event when Jesus will come on the clouds of heaven (as in the synoptics), but a present reality as people choose either to accept or reject his revelatory self-disclosure (Jn 3:19). With consummate irony, the author will create a reversal situation where accused and accusers change roles. By the end of the scene, the would-be judges will themselves have been judged.

This is the only reference to Psalm 82 in the whole New Testament. Are we to think that John took v. 6 in isolation from its context (a common technique in Jewish exegesis), or should we look at the whole psalm? The fact that 'the gods' appear also in v. 1 of the psalm suggests that the whole psalm might be relevant. The textual history of this psalm reflects the problems that Jewish copyists, translators and commentators had with its apparently pre-monotheistic portrayal of a heavenly court where God stands and delivers judgement in the midst of an assembly of gods (cf. Job 1:6). Some of these scholars took the Hebrew word for these 'gods', *elohim*, to mean 'angels' or 'heavenly beings'. Translators of the psalm into Greek had various devices at their disposal. The LXX translator adapted the text slightly so that the God of Israel would deliver judgement on (not 'in the midst of') lesser gods. Another translated the line, 'God stands in the assembly of God'. Another solved the problem by translating *elohim* as 'strong ones'. Then there was always the possibility of reading the word 'gods' figuratively. The psalm identifies 'the gods' as 'sons of the Most High' in v. 6. Are these the same gods as those mentioned in v. 1? Who are they anyway? Some ancient interpreters said they were the Israelites after their reception of the Law. Others saw them as angels appointed to guard each nation or as judges appointed to pronounce just verdicts in the name of God.[4]

---

[4] For a convenient survey of these interpretations, see Schuchard, *Scripture within Scripture*, pp. 62–63.

Our concern is with the evangelist's reading. Have we any way of knowing who he thought the 'gods' of Psalm 82 were?

The forensic character of the scene in Jn 10:22–39 may suggest an answer. A first clue is that Jesus identifies 'the gods' as 'those to whom the word of God came' (10:35). This phrase alludes to the common biblical commissioning formula, 'The word of the Lord came to . . .', used for judges, kings like David and Solomon, prophets.[5] To hear Psalm 82 as a 'pre-text' to this Johannine scene is to draw a comparison between the Jewish leadership, claiming the authority to judge Jesus as guilty of blasphemy, and Jesus himself, uniquely commissioned by God to provoke the judgement (Greek: κρίσις) that actually condemns his opponents.

The backdrop to this scene is the Feast of Dedication (*Hannukka*) commemorating the re-consecration of the second temple in 164 BCE. The location is the portico named for David's son Solomon who dedicated the first temple. The quotation comes from David's psalms, as sung in the temple liturgy. The scene follows the 'Shepherd Discourse' with Jesus continuing to speak in shepherd/king mode in vv. 26–29. Allusions to the one flock and one shepherd of Ezek. 34:11, 22–23 earlier in John 10 have already signalled that Jesus is the 'David' through whom God will shepherd Israel. Israelite kings bore the title 'Son of God' because they were believed to embody God's rule. The king is even called 'god' in Ps. 45:7 and 'mighty god' in Isa. 9:6. David's royal line is 'like God' according to the Hebrew of Zech. 12:8. There are, therefore strong biblical precedents for the Johannine modification of the messianic title, 'Son of God'. John can claim, therefore, that 'Son of God', must be understood in the full Johannine sense, if it is to be an adequate title for Jesus.

Jesus introduces the quotation with the rhetorical question, 'Is it not written in your law?' The word 'your' has an argumentative function, to be encountered again in Jn 15:25. The term 'Law', though strictly speaking a reference to the Pentateuch, covers the whole of Scripture.[6] Jesus uses a form of argumentation 'from lesser to greater' that we know from the 'rules' (*middoth*) for scripture interpretation attributed to the late first-century BCE sage, Hillel. No doubt, the use of this technique tells us something about the style of debate employed by the Johannine circle, as it is quite different to what we know of Jesus' own more poetic and evocative style of scripture reference. The logic of the argument seems to be that if there is a sense in which leaders, shepherds, judges in Israel could be called 'gods', then how much more appropriately can Jesus be called Son of God and this, not just in a Jewish messianic sense (as a royal title) but in a unique sense. The complete psalm verse provides a warrant for this fuller understanding:

---

[5] 1 Kgs 6:11; 1 Chron. 22:8; Isa. 2:1; Jer. 1:2, Mic. 1:1; Zeph. 1:1; etc.
[6] See 1 Cor. 14:21, Rom. 3:19, Jn 12:34.

I said, you are gods
and all of you sons of the Most High.

In Hebrew poetics, parallel pairs of lines express the same idea in two ways for literary effect. The second line can certainly be glimpsed behind Jesus' words in v. 36, 'I am the Son of God'. The psalm itself makes 'Son of God' an equivalent designation to 'god'. This equivalence points not only to Jesus' status, but to the status of those who accept him and are reborn as children of God (Jn 1:12–13). In Ps. 82:6, therefore, the Law itself vindicates Johannine Christology on two important grounds. First, there is no blasphemy in Jesus' statement, 'I am the Son of God'. Secondly, to take the title 'Son of God' in the full Johannine sense is not to repudiate Jesus' messianic role, as some fellow believers in Jesus, dubious about Johannine Christology, might think. It is to understand it more profoundly.[7]

'Blessed is he who comes in the name of the Lord' (John 12:13, from Psalm 118:26)

This is the only psalm quotation found *verbatim* in all four gospels. All four evangelists depend on their audience's capacity to recognize this as a line from Psalm 118:

εὐλογημένος ὁ ἐρχόμενος ἐν ὀνόματι κυρίου.
Blessed is he who comes in the name of the Lord.

Psalm 118 was actually a familiar psalm in late Second Temple Judaism, especially through its association with the Feast of Tabernacles and as the final psalm of the Egyptian Hallel, sung at the annual Passover Meal. No doubt, the gospel writers could also depend on their audience's prior familiarity with the story of Jesus' solemn entry into Jerusalem.

John is particularly independent in his account. His Jesus is walking towards Jerusalem when the crowds begin to wave palm branches and to sing out, 'Hosanna! Blessed is he who comes in the name of the Lord, even the King of Israel!' The palm branches, unique to John's version of events, probably indicate a nationalistic understanding of Jesus' messiahship.[8] The Johannine Jesus' reaction is to find a donkey and ride it into Jerusalem as an enactment of Zechariah's prophecy concerning the expected king (Zech. 9:9). He thereby both affirms and critiques the crowd's enthusiastic reception of him. Yes, he is

---

[7] N.A. Dahl, 'The Johannine Church and History', in J. Ashton, ed., *The Interpretation of John* (Philadelphia: Fortress Press; London: SPCK, 1986), pp. 122–40; Jerome Neyrey, 'Jesus the Judge: Forensic Process in John 8:21–29', *Bib* 68 (1987), pp. 509–42; Schuchard, *Scripture within Scripture*, pp. 59–70; Obermann, *Erfüllung*, pp. 168–85; M.J.J. Menken, 'The Use of the Septuagint in Three Quotations in John: Jn 10,34; 12,38; 19,24', in C.M. Tuckett, ed., *The Scriptures in the Gospels* (BETL 131; Leuven: Leuven University Press – Peeters, 1997), pp. 367–93, esp. 370–82; Daly-Denton, *David*, pp. 164–76.

[8] Cf. 1 Macc. 13:51; 2 Macc. 10:7. Coins minted during the Jewish revolts of 66–70 and 135 CE bore the image of a palm tree.

indeed 'the one who comes in the name of the Lord, even the King of Israel', but not quite the kind of king they had in mind. The waving of the branches, also unique to John, is evocative of the liturgy for the Feast of Tabernacles. It may be that John wants his readers to think of Zechariah's 'Day of the Lord', a great Feast of Tabernacles, when living waters will flow out from Jerusalem and the Lord will be king over all the earth (Zech. 13:1; 14:8–9:16). As we have seen, Jesus has already inaugurated that Day by ensuring that there are no longer traders in the House of the Lord (Zech. 14:21; cf. Jn 2:16).

'Hosanna' is a Greek transliteration of the Hebrew and Aramaic imperative addressed to God, 'Save!' from the preceding verse of the psalm. In New Testament times, 'Hosanna' was a popular liturgical refrain, acclamatory rather than supplicatory in character. Like Luke, John adds an interpretative 'gloss' to the psalm quotation, 'The King of Israel'. This forms an inclusion with Nathanael's declaration at the outset of the ministry where it is clearly a messianic title (1:49). By this stage of the gospel, however, the term 'king' as a designation for Jesus is being progressively deconstructed and reworked so that it can only be used in an ironic sense as part of a particular 'Johannine-speak'. Eventually Jesus' kingship will be defined as bearing witness to the truth (18:37).

Some Jewish interpretations of Psalm 118 focus on a verse that the synoptic evangelists and the author of 1 Peter see as fulfilled in Jesus:

> The stone which the builders rejected
> has become the cornerstone (Ps. 118:22).[9]

The Jewish readings apply this verse to the young David of 1 Sam. 16:1–13, rejected by his elders, but chosen by God for kingship.[10] This story is the background to the first scene in the fourth gospel (Jn 1:19–34) where the role of Samuel, rather than that of Elijah (as in the synoptics) is clearly John's 'model' for his portrayal of John the Baptist. For those of the original audience, knowledgeable enough to recognize the source of the quotation, the speaker is David whose experience of distress, of being surrounded by enemies, and of being lifted up by God (as 'documented' in 'his' psalms) will figure prominently in the fourth gospel account of Jesus'death.

As we have seen, Jesus' finding of the donkey and sitting on it enacts the 'correct' Johannine reading of the psalm verse, 'Blessed is he who comes in the name of the Lord'. In any literature, a quotation, even a 'word for word' repetition, is a rereading and a radical reinterpretation of the precursor text that generates new meaning. This is particularly so of Ps. 118:26, as quoted in Jn

---

[9] Even the verb 'rejected' occurring in the synoptic passion predictions (e.g. Mk 8:31; Lk. 9:22) may be an echo of this passage.

[10] See the *Targum* to Ps. 118 and the *Midrash* on Ps. 118:21. Although these sources possibly did not reach written form until the ninth century, the NT can demonstrate that they contain elements of interpretative traditions belonging to much earlier periods.

12:13. For John, Jesus is 'the one who comes' (ὁ ἐρχόμενος) and his coming is 'in the name of the Lord' (ἐν ὀνόματι κυρίου). In the Judaism of the time, 'the one who comes' or 'the one who is to come' was a kind of technical term for the expected Messiah or end time prophet.[11] Several Johannine characters use it in this way, expressing varying levels of comprehension of Jesus (Jn 1:15; 4:25; 6:14; 7:25–31). In applying it to Jesus, the fourth evangelist draws his readers towards a more profound identification of Jesus. True, he is 'the one who comes', but the important thing is to know where he comes from. Jesus comes 'from above' (8:23), from the heavenly realm 'into the world' (1:1–16; 3:16; 6:38). To recognize Jesus as coming 'in the name of the Lord' is to acknowledge his divine origins (3:31; 5:43; 7:29) and to see his coming 'in the name of the Lord' as what Bultmann called 'the inbreaking of the beyond into this life'.[12] The psalm quotation is thus a vehicle for John's 'emissary Christology', based on the ancient laws of agency in which the one who is sent is treated with the respect owed to his sender.[13] The fourth evangelist thus exploits to the full the potential of a 'scripture' from the tradition to convey his understanding of Jesus' identity. Appropriately, the crowd in his version of the story address their singing of 'Hosanna!' to Jesus, thereby invoking him as 'Saviour of the world' (cf. Jn 4:42). As we found with the first psalm quotation, the evangelist adds a note making the point that the deeper meaning of the chant the people had sung to Jesus did not register fully with the disciples until after the resurrection (Jn 12:16).[14]

'He who ate my bread has lifted his heel against me' (John 13:18, from Psalm 41:10)

The 'scripture' here is universally recognized as Ps. 41:10 in spite of discrepancies between John's version and all Greek versions known to us. The Johannine citation corresponds to the verbal allusions of varying volume in the synoptics (Mk 14:18; Matt. 26:23; Lk. 22:21). We should, first of all, compare John's quotation with the LXX version:

Jn 13:18
ὁ τρώγων μου τὸν ἄρτον ἐπῆρεν ἐπ' ἐμὲ τὴν πτέρναν αὐτου.
The one eating my bread has lifted his heel against me.

---

[11] Dan. 7:13; Mal. 3:1; Hab. 2:3.

[12] R. Bultmann, *The Gospel of John: A Commentary* (Oxford: Blackwell, 1971), p. 404.

[13] P. Borgen, 'God's Agent in the Fourth Gospel', in Ashton, ed., *The Interpretation of John*, pp. 67–78.

[14] E.D. Freed, 'The Entry into Jerusalem in the Gospel of John', *JBL* 80 (1961), pp. 329–38; Obermann, *Erfüllung*, pp. 185–203; Daly-Denton, *David*, pp. 176–87. The following authors' discussions of the quotation of Zech. 9:9 in Jn 12:15 are also relevant: Schuchard, *Scripture within Scripture*, pp. 71–84; Menken, *Old Testament Quotations*, pp. 79–98; Obermann, *Erfüllung*, pp. 203–15.

LXX Ps. 40:10

ὁ ἐσθίων ἄρτους μου ἐμεγάλυνεν ἐπ' ἐμὲ πτερνισμόν.

The one eating of my breads has magnified craftiness against me.

John uses a different verb 'to eat'. He uses 'bread' in the singular. His main verb and its direct object are quite different. The position of the possessive pronoun μου is also different. John's version is actually closer to the Hebrew of Ps. 41:10 – '(the one) who ate of my bread has made great the heel against me'. A possible recollection of this or of the Aramaic would not, however, explain the use of the verb 'lift'.

The apparent discrepancies are well within normal practice among Jewish exegetes of the time. First, the LXX version, with its reference to trickery perpetrated on an unsuspecting victim would be entirely at variance with Johannine Christology. In order to insist on Jesus' omniscience and sovereign control over the events of 'the hour', the fourth evangelist adjusts the psalm quotation slightly. The means of doing this lay readily to hand in a technique commonly used at the time. An analogous passage of scripture would be adduced to clarify or strengthen the particular point being made. We know of this technique, called *gezerah shawah* (identical category), from the rules for exegesis (*Middoth*) attributed to Hillel. Even without intentionally setting out to use this technique, the fourth evangelist would have been operating out of a consciousness of the Psalter as David's composition. Ps. 41:10 was not the only occasion when David lamented the treachery of a table companion. In Psalm 54 he was even more explicit:

> It is not an adversary who deals insolently with me . . .
> but it is you, my equal, my companion, my familiar friend.

The Hebrew continues, 'We held sweet converse together . . .' (Ps. 55:15). The corresponding line, as John would have known it in the LXX version, is even more appropriate to the 'last supper' scene. It refers to the intimate friend as sweetening food in companionship with the psalmist (ὃς ἐπὶ τὸ αὐτὸ μιο ἐγλύκανας ἐδέσματα). Menken suggests that the supposed Davidic authorship of the psalms would have allowed for a further analogous text to be influential – 2 Sam. 18:28 where the opponents of David at the time of Absalom's revolt are described as those who 'raised their hand' against their king. He thinks that this idiom may explain the verb 'lift' in John's quotation.[15] While this could well be the case, it is, perhaps, an unnecessarily convoluted solution. The connection between Ps. 41:10 and Ps. 55:13–14 is probably sufficient explanation for two reasons. First, the Hebrew of both psalm passages uses the verb *higdil* (lift). Second, later Jewish readings of Psalm 55, which most probably contain interpretative traditions going back to New Testament times,

---

[15] Menken, *Old Testament Quotations*, pp. 133–4.

envisage it as David's prayer when he realized that Achitophel was a co-conspirator of Absalom (see 2 Sam. 15:31).[16]

In all three synoptics, Jesus' reference to the disloyal table companion, couched in allusion to Ps. 41:10, is followed by a statement that scripture is being fulfilled (Mk 14:21; Matt. 26:24; Lk. 22:22). The Johannine Jesus actually sets this particular 'scripture' in motion there and then, engaging Judas in an enactment of Ps. 41:10. Several features of this throw light on the precise verbal form of John's quotation. Jesus takes the initiative, by no means the victim of a traitor's 'craftiness'. The food that Jesus hands to Judas is definitely bread. John's word ψωμίον is a diminutive of ψωμός, 'a piece of bread'. This provides a link to the bread (singular) in the quotation, which in turn recalls Jesus' giving of the bread at the miraculous feeding (Jn 6:11), an action performed in that scene by Jesus himself, not by the disciples (as in the synoptics). The reference to bread, also echoes the quotation about the manna in Jn 6:31, 'He gave them bread from heaven to eat'. Thus we find our attention drawn back to ch. 6 where, significantly, the first reference to Judas as betrayer occurs (Jn 6:64, 70–71). It is there that the verb 'to eat', τρώγειν, used in John's quotation of Ps. 41:10 occurs four times (Jn 6:54, 56, 57, 58). Even the non-LXX word order in John's psalm quotation, 'he who eats of me the bread...' has its counterpart in the Bread of Life Discourse (Jn 6:54, 56).

The precise verbal form of John's quotation from Ps. 41:9, therefore, seems to be the product first of the evangelist's perception of Judas as an Achitophel figure, a dramatic foil to Jesus, the 'David' on whose lips the psalms find fulfilment. Secondly, the psalm quotation with its echoes of John 6, suggests that Judas might stand for former Johannine believers who partook of Jesus' 'bread' (his revelatory self-disclosure primarily, but also the eucharist), subsequently defected from the community of believers and denounced disciples of Jesus to hostile elements within the Jewish leadership. As received in late Second Temple Judaism, the psalm depicts David confronted with Achitophel's disloyalty. As reread by the fourth evangelist, it shows Jesus confronted with Judas' betrayal. At a third level, it speaks of Johannine Christians and their experience of the denials, denunciations and betrayals through which they share in Jesus' triumphant death.[17]

'They hated me without a cause' (John 15:25, from Psalm 69:5, etc.)

There is no passage in the Scriptures with exactly the wording of John's 'scripture':

---

[16] M. *'Abot.* 6:3; *Targ. Ps.* 55:14; *Midr. Teh.* 3,4; 55,1.

[17] T.F. Glasson, 'Davidic Links with the Betrayal of Jesus', *Exp* 85 (1973–74), pp. 118–19; F.J. Moloney, 'A Sacramental Reading of John 13:1–38', *CBQ* 53 (1991), pp. 237–56; Schuchard, *Scripture within Scripture*, pp. 107–17; Menken, *Old Testament Quotations*, pp. 123–38; Obermann, *Erfüllung*, pp. 255–71; Daly-Denton, *David*, pp. 191–201.

ἐμίσησάν με δωρεάν.
They hated me without cause.

The most frequently proposed sources for the quotation are Ps. 69:5 or Ps. 35:19 where the psalmist refers to opponents as 'those hating me without cause' – οἱ μισοῦντές με δωρεάν. The motif of groundless hatred also occurs in Ps. 109:3 and Ps. 119:161, although not in exactly these words. Since all of these possible sources are in the Psalter, we are dealing here with what we might call a familiar phrase from the psalms of David that, in the evangelist's view, finds its full significance on Jesus' lips. The formula with which John introduces the quotation is the longest in the gospel, 'But in order that the word that is written in their law might be fulfilled...' It could even be more effectively translated as an exasperated imperative, 'Let what is written ... be fulfilled!'[18] As we found at Jn 10:34, the term 'Law' is not confined to the Pentateuch. The pronoun 'their' has a similar argumentative function to that of the 'your' in Jn 10:34. In the narrative setting of the quotation, five references to hatred of both Jesus and his disciples create the effect of a crescendo building up to 'They hated me without a cause'. Within narrative time, Jesus is speaking of the future for his 'own' when the world's hatred will bear down on them, but, of course, for the author and his audience, this is a present reality. As we gather from elsewhere in the gospel, at the time of writing, believers in Jesus are being expelled from the synagogue and even killed (Jn 9:22; 16:2).

Appropriately for this part of the gospel (chs 13–17) where the focus is on the community of Jesus' 'own', the quotation encourages hard-pressed disciples, but not without a touch of that polemical harshness which frequently appears in the fourth gospel. If we were to imagine how this quotation 'worked' for its intended audience, as we did with Ps. 41:10, we might discern what the author implies. David the psalmist had reason to lament that he bore the brunt of the hatred of those opposed to God. Jesus, coming in God's name was hated by those opposed to his Father (Jn 15:23). Now Johannine Christians, sent in Jesus' name, experience the same hatred. The fact that this fulfils the scripture is reason to have confidence. This and the previous quotation that we have discussed should be seen against the background of the Johannine circle's sectarian mentality. The author is anxious to provide his audience with a frame of reference in which they can make sense of what is happening to them. As a beleaguered smaller group on the point of expulsion from the larger group, they comfort each other with the claim that they have a superior insight into the true meaning of scripture. This

---

[18] M. Zerwick, *Graecitas Biblica: Novi Testamenti Exemplis Illustrata* (Rome: Pontifical Biblical Institute, 1966), p. 141.

reassures them that they are actually insiders while those wanting to expel them are in fact the real outsiders.[19]

'They parted my garments among them . . .' (John 19:24, from Psalm 22:19)

With this quotation, John is on common ground with the synoptics. Before discussing the actual quotation, we should pause to note John's selectivity with regard to his use of Psalm 22 in his crucifixion scene. Mark and Matthew both put the opening line of the psalm on Jesus' lips. All three synoptics allude to Psalm 22 in their accounts of the mockery by the bystanders. The fourth evangelist seems intent on correcting these applications of the psalm to Jesus. Far from experiencing forsakenness, the Johannine Jesus remains assured that the Father is with him (Jn 8:29; 16:32). There is an unmistakable serenity about John's description of the 'lifting up' of Jesus on the cross. His selectivity with regard to Psalm 22 is a hint that the one verse that he does decide to use will accord with his view that Jesus' death was actually a royal enthronement and the most complete manifestation of his glory.

In contrast with the synoptic allusions to Ps. 22:19, the psalm verse appears in the fourth gospel first by way of enactment and then in a formal quotation of the full verse:

διεμερίσαντο τὰ ἱμάτιά μου ἑαυτοῖς
καὶ ἐπὶ τὸν ἱματισμόν μου ἔβαλον κλῆρον
They divided my clothing among them;
and for my robe (i.e. raiment) they cast lots.

As frequently happens in Hebrew poetry, the second line of a parallel pair repeats the same information in different words. For John, though, this is an opportunity for *midrash*. He presents the two parallel lines of the psalm verse as enacted by the soldiers. The feature that has teased and fascinated exegetes ever since is that the robe was not torn. Some have suggested High Priestly symbolism; others, the unity of the Church.[20] To see the untorn robe as an indication of God's protection and vindication of Jesus would seem to point in a fruitful direction as this would be in keeping with the Johannine project: to show that Jesus' death was actually his glorification.

The approach to Ps. 22:19 that would be most consonant with the exegetical methods to which the fourth evangelist was clearly an heir would be to search the scriptures for other torn or untorn robes. In 1 Kgs 11:29–31 the prophet Ahija tears his valuable new garment into twelve pieces, gives away ten to Jeroboam and keeps only two, symbolizing the division of the kingdom and the consequent diminishment of Solomon's sovereignty. This scene carries

---

[19] Schuchard, *Scripture within Scripture*, pp. 119–23; Menken, *Old Testament Quotations*, pp. 139–46; Obermann, *Erfüllung*, pp. 271–82; Daly-Denton, *David*, pp. 201–208.

[20] For a survey of opinions, see I. de la Potterie, *The Hour of Jesus: The Passion and Resurrection of Jesus According to John* (New York: Alba House, 1989), pp. 100–104.

echoes of the tearing of Saul's cloak by David at En-Gedi (1 Sam. 24:1–22), a portent of Saul's impending loss of the kingship and of David's superiority. Another fragment of biblical lore referring to robe-tearing is 1 Sam. 15:27–28:

> As Samuel turned to go away, he (Saul) laid hold upon the skirt of his (Samuel's) robe, and it tore. And Samuel said to him, 'The Lord has torn the kingdom of Israel from you this day, and has given it to a neighbour of yours, who is better than you'.

Without the names in brackets, it is not clear who is tearing whose robe. The versions of the Septuagint that have come down to us clarify the sense by adding in 'Saul', as we have done here, and as the RSV and many other modern versions also do. It is conceivable though, that the fourth evangelist had an ambiguous version of this passage before him, as the Hebrew still is. He might then have understood it as the Jewish scholars responsible for the *Midrash on Psalms* several centuries later would – that Samuel tore Saul's robe to signify that God was tearing the kingdom from his hand and giving it to the young man who had already prophetically torn Saul's robe in the cave at En-Gedi.[21] If it is possible that such a reading might have influenced the fourth evangelist, then the tunic of Jesus that is not torn may refer to his royal status, as inscribed with pointed intentionality by Pilate in the immediately preceding scene. The tunic without seam is a costly garment, another hint, perhaps, that it is actually a royal robe. The Johannine view of Jesus lifted up on the cross and drawing all people to himself is inspired by the prophetic vision of the ingathering of the tribes into the restored kingdom of David. Understood in this way, the tunic is also a symbol of unity, of the gathering into one of all the scattered children of God (Jn 11:51–52). Thus, in an entirely unexpected way, God fulfils the promise to David, 'I will establish the throne of his kingdom for ever'. Jesus robe is not torn. Nathan's oracle explains why. 'I will not take my steadfast love from him as I took it from Saul' (2 Sam. 7:15).[22]

Quotations Where the Psalter Is One of Two or More Possible Sources

The quotation in Jn 6:31:

ἄρτον ἐκ τοῦ οὐρανοῦ ἔδωκεν αὐτοῖς φαγεῖν
He gave them bread from heaven to eat,

exemplifies the irony of which the fourth evangelist is a past master. It occurs in the direct speech of people who have no idea of the aptness of its application to Jesus. Their challenge is tantamount to saying, 'Surely you are not greater

---

[21] *Midr. Teh.* 57:3.
[22] Schuchard, *Scripture within Scripture*, pp. 125–32; Obermann, *Erfüllung*, pp. 282–97; Menken, 'Septuagint', pp. 386–92; Daly-Denton, *David*, pp. 208–14.

than Moses, who gave our fathers the bread of heaven to eat?' The quotation most probably comes from Ps. 78:24 (LXX Ps. 77:24):

καὶ ἔβρεξεν αὐτοῖς μαννα φαγεῖν
καὶ ἄρτον οὐρανοῦ ἔδωκεν αὐτοῖς.
And he rained down manna for them to eat
and gave them bread from heaven.

If Psalm 78 is the source of the quotation, John seems to have taken φαγεῖν (to eat) from the first line of the parallel pair. It is quite possible that other texts about the manna such as Exod. 16:4, 15 or Neh. 9:15 could also have been influential, notably Exod. 16:15 where φαγεῖν occurs. The word ἐκ (from) in Jn 6:31 seems to be the result of Johannine redaction. This has enabled the 'scripture' to speak of the bread of heaven in personified and dynamic terms, as 'that which comes down out of heaven' (Jn 6:33; cf. 8:23, 42), and thus make an important christological statement.[23]

The quotation in Jn 7:38 is notoriously difficult to identify:

ποταμοὶ ἐκ τῆς κοιλίας αὐτοῦ ῥεύσουσιν ὕδατος ζῶντος
From within him shall flow rivers of living water.

Ps. 78:16, 20 has been cogently suggested as its source. There is great uncertainty about how John's text should be punctuated at this point and, consequently, whether the 'him' in the quotation refers to Jesus or to the believer. In the history of the interpretation of this passage, this has affected the ascription of the quotation, with sources as diverse as Exod. 17:6, Isa. 48:21–22, Isa. 55:1, Isa. 58:11, Jer. 2:13, Jer. 17:13, Prov. 18:4, and Cant. 4:15 being suggested, to name but a few. Raymond Brown and Maarten Menken concur that the citation straddles vv. 16 and 20 of Psalm 78.[24] Both verses refer to the water from the rock of Exodus 17. The psalm source leaves unexplained the word ζῶντος (living). The most likely influence here is Zech. 14:8 with resonances of Ezekiel 47, in view of John's conviction that the true temple is Jesus' body. Menken suggests a further contribution, from Ps. 114:8 which also deals with the water-flowing rock.[25] An awareness of the layers of interpretation which Jewish tradition piled upon this rock can throw light on this quotation. In particular, the belief attested in 1 Cor. 10:4 that the rock followed the people of Israel on their desert journey and was eventually identified as the 'Rock of Sion', the foundation of the Temple seems to have influenced the fourth gospel.[26]

---

[23] Schuchard, *Scripture within Scripture*, pp. 33–46; Menken, *Old Testament Quotations*, pp. 47–66; Obermann, *Erfüllung*, pp. 132–50; Daly-Denton, *David*, pp. 131–44.

[24] R.E. Brown, *The Gospel According to John, I – XII* (AB 29; Garden City, NY: Doubleday, 1966), p. 322; Menken, *Old Testament Quotations*, p. 189.

[25] Menken, *Old Testament Quotations*, pp. 200–1.

[26] Menken, *Old Testament Quotations*, pp. 187–206; Daly-Denton, *David*, pp. 144–63.

When the Johannine Jesus cries out, διψῶ, 'I thirst' (Jn 19:28), we tend, on the analogy of the synoptics, to see an allusion to Ps. 69:22:

> For food they gave me poison;
> in my thirst they gave me vinegar to drink.

As in so many other instances, however, the fourth evangelist has his unique 'take' on this element of the passion tradition. Jesus takes the initiative. He gives the cue, as it were, for the fulfilment of the scriptures to be enacted. A major question concerns the introductory formula. Does Jesus say, 'I thirst' in order to fulfil the scripture? Or is it a matter of Jesus, knowing that all was now finished in order to fulfil the scripture, then going on to cry out, 'I thirst'? The Greek allows either reading. The word that John has used up to this point for 'fulfilled' (πληρωθῇ) is not used here. Instead we find a word meaning 'fulfilled' in the sense of 'completed' (τελειωθῇ). The actual word, διψῶ, does not occur in Ps. 69:22, but perhaps the real evocation of the psalm is the narrative account of Jesus' cry, the giving of the drink and Jesus' drinking. Some have suggested that the precise verbal form of the quotation may be explained by Ps. 42:3 or Ps. 63:2 where the psalmist expresses his longing for God in terms of thirst. At this more figurative level, Jesus would be expressing his longing to return to the Father. This reading would not exclude a reference to the tradition of Jesus' physical thirst, but it would bring the thirst motif to a level of interpretation more in keeping with John's theological schema. This would make sense of John's insistence that Jesus accepts the bitter drink (cf. Jn 18:11). It is precisely the lightness of the one-word evocation of Ps. 69:22 that suggests to the reader a deeper thirst of Jesus, thereby hinting at the profound significance of 'the Hour'.[27]

Another 'scripture' which, at least partially, quotes the psalms occurs in Jn 19:36:

> ὀστοῦν οὐ συντριβήσεται αὐτοῦ.
> Not a bone of him shall be broken.

This is one of two 'scriptures' introduced by the evangelist under a single introductory formula in which he defends his eyewitness testimony to the death of Jesus. Most commentators see here a reference to the prescriptions concerning the paschal lamb:

> ...and you shall not break a bone of it (Exod. 12:10, 46).
> ...and they shall not break a bone of it (Num. 9:12).

In terms of verbal form, however, the quotation is quite close to Ps. 34:21:

---

[27] G. Bampfylde, 'John XIX 28: A Case for a Different Translation', *NovT* 11 (1969), pp. 247–60; Obermann, *Erfüllung*, pp. 350–64; Daly-Denton, *David*, pp. 219–28.

κύριος φυλάσσει πάντα τὰ ὀστᾶ αὐτῶν,
ἓν ἐξ αὐτῶν οὐ συντριβήσεται.
The Lord will guard all their bones;
not one of them will be broken.

The paschal lamb symbolism resonates well with the Passover references in the Johannine account of Jesus' hour (13:1; 18:28) and with John the Baptist's identification of Jesus as 'the Lamb of God' (1:29, 36). A cogent case can, however, be made for Ps. 34:21 as source for this quotation. In view of current Jewish beliefs about the resurrection of the dead based on Ezek. 37:1–14, it is possible that the preservation of Jesus' bones was seen as a pledge of his resurrection.[28] In fact, according to *Jub.* 49:13, the intact bones of the paschal lamb symbolized Israel's hope of a glorious future, 'because no bone of the children of Israel will be broken'. Both possible sources can therefore illuminate this Johannine 'scripture'.[29]

Echoes of the Psalms

To read a gospel so rich in biblical symbolism with an ear, not only for explicit quotations but also for fleeting echoes of the psalms can be a most rewarding approach. One might hear, for example, Ps. 89:5, 37 'behind' the discussions of the populace about Jesus in Jn 7:42 and 12:34. Jesus' insistence that no one will snatch his sheep out of his hand might recall Psalm 95 where, as in the shepherd discourse (Jn 10:3–4) the sheep of God's hand listen to God's voice and see God's works (Jn 10:37–38). The incident where those coming to arrest Jesus fall backwards (Jn 18:6) might recall Ps. 27:2. Thomas's profession of faith, 'My Lord and my God' (Jn 20:28) might be recognized as an important Johannine borrowing of the language of the psalms. The psalmist addresses God in exactly these words in Ps. 35:23, even if in a slightly different order. Clearly the Johannine circle's conviction that for Jesus, to be 'Son of God' means to be so completely one with the Father allows that he can be appropriately identified with the 'Lord and God' addressed in the psalms.

Conclusion

We have seen that the precise verbal form of John's psalm quotations could be the result of intentional redaction or of spontaneous recollection. Similarly, psalm allusions and echoes could be intentional hints at Jesus' true identity, or inadvertent recourse to a familiar religious culture which provides the symbolic categories within which it is possible to attempt some account of the

---

[28] D. Daube, *The New Testament and Rabbinic Judaism* (London: Athlone Press, 1956), p. 309.
[29] Schuchard, *Scripture within Scripture*, pp. 133–40; Menken, *Old Testament Quotations*, pp. 147–66; Obermann, *Erfüllung*, pp. 298–310; Daly-Denton, *David*, pp. 229–40.

significance of Jesus. It is not necessary to decide between the two. This presentation has shown that the voice of 'David' the psalmist is both overtly quoted and subliminally influential in the fourth gospel portrayal of Jesus. There is no doubt that the book of 'the scriptures' that the fourth evangelist favours most as a witness to Jesus has exerted a profound influence on his composition. The study of the Johannine reception of the psalms has much to contribute to the search for the origins of Johannine Christology.

7

The Psalms in Romans and Galatians

Sylvia C. Keesmaat

Romans: Introduction

My exploration of the psalms in the book of Romans will build on recent work on Romans that interprets Paul's letter as a discussion of the question of God's faithfulness to Israel, or, as Richard Hays puts it, a discussion of the question of theodicy.[1] This discussion of theodicy will be further shaped by my use of recent scholarship that places this epistle firmly in the context of Rome, the heart of the empire.[2] Where does the world meet righteousness and faith? In the imperial narrative of Caesar or in the story of Israel as reinterpreted in the light of the story of Jesus? As Israel's faith was always formed and lived in the shadow of empire, so also is the faith that Paul commends to the Christian community in Rome at the heart of the empire. In order to heighten both the parallels and the tensions between imperial justice and the justice of God that Paul proclaims in this letter, I will translate δικαιοσύνη as *justice* throughout this chapter.[3]

From Disorientation to Reorientation: The Narrative Shape of the Psalms in Romans

Disorientation: 'I am not ashamed of the Gospel'

Paul's programmatic statement in Rom. 1:16–17 is rooted in a challenge to the

---

[1] Richard B. Hays, *Echoes of Scripture in the Letters of Paul* (New Haven: Yale University Press, 1989), p. 38. Although the question of theodicy in Israel's scriptures is deeply rooted in the question of God's faithfulness to Israel, it is also overwhelmingly concerned with why idolatrous pagans who practise injustice appear to be triumphant. I would like to suggest that this is true for the letter of the Romans as well.

[2] For more detail on the imperial context of Romans see the essays in Richard A. Horsley, ed., *Paul and Politics: Ekklesia, Israel, Imperium, Interpretation: Essays in Honour of Krister Stendahl* (Harrisburg: Trinity Press International, 2000).

[3] It was the goddess Iustitia (justice; the Latin equivalent of the Greek δικαιοσύνη) who was so closely identified with the reign of Augustus. See N.T. Wright, *The Letter to the Romans* (The New Interpreter's Bible Volume X; Nashville: Abingdon, 2002), p. 404. On *Iustitia*, the Roman equivalent of δίκη, Wright refers to Ovid, *Letters from the Black Sea* 3.6.25 and the *Acts of Augustus* ch. 34. The translation of δικαιοσύνη as *justice* rather than *righteousness* also moves this term beyond the realm of biblical studies and theology, which is virtually the only context in which the word righteousness is used in English (with the exception of the phrase self-righteous), and places it once again firmly in the realm of social, political and cultural life, to which it referred in the first century. The translation of δικαιοσύνη as *justice* also puts the question of justice at the centre of this important epistle, just as it was firmly at the centre of Israel's scriptures.

gospel of the empire, for it was the imperial assertion that Caesar was the one who bought 'good news' through military victory.[4] This challenge is deepened by allusions to a number of psalms which resonate with his programmatic statement of Rom. 1:16–17. He begins to explain his eagerness to proclaim the gospel in Rome in this way: 'For I am not ashamed (ἐπαισχύνομαι) of the gospel'. As Hays has indicated '*aischynein* and its near relatives *kataischynein* and *epaischynesthai* appear repeatedly in the very prophecies and lament psalms from which Paul's righteousness terminology is drawn'.[5] Most notable of these is Ps. 71:1–2:[6]

> O Lord, in you I hope (ἤλπισα),
> never let me be put to shame (καταισχυνθείην).
> In your justice (δικαιοσύνῃ) deliver me and have mercy on me,
> Turn your ear to me, and save (σῶσόν) me.

The psalmist continues with a plea for God's rescue from the unjust (ἀδικοῦ ντος, v. 4; cf. Rom. 1:18,29), and roots his hope (ἐλπίς) in God's justice (τὴν δικαιοσύνην) and salvation (τὴν σωτηρίαν) (vv. 14–15). It is clear that such justice will not only rescue the psalmist, but will also result in defeat of the enemies, who will be disgraced and put to shame (αἰσχυνθῶσιν; v. 24).[7]

In order that the psalmist or the nation is not put to shame, God needs to act with justice and salvation. As Wright puts it: ' "Shame" in such a context is what God's people feel when their enemies are triumphing; it is what Israel (and many other peoples) felt in Paul's day suffering at the hands of Rome'.[8] To the Romans, at the heart of an empire that lauded '*fides*' (the Latin equivalent of the Greek *pistis*, faith or faithfulness) as an appropriate response to the salvation of Caesar, Paul asserts in Rom. 1:16 that this gospel is the power of salvation (σωτηρίαν) to everyone who has faith.[9] In asserting that he is not ashamed of the gospel, echoing this psalm of lament with its plea for justice and

---

[4] See N. Elliott, 'Paul and the Politics of Empire' in Horsley, ed., *Paul and Politics*, p. 24.

[5] Hays, *Echoes*, p. 38. Hays also refers specifically to Ps. 44:10; Ps. 24:2; Isa. 28:16 LXX (to which Paul appeals directly in Rom. 9:33); and Isa. 50:7–8.

[6] This psalm is also discussed in Wright, *Romans*, p. 424. For discussion of the language of Paul's source text, see C.D. Stanley, *Paul and the Language of Scripture: Citation Technique in the Pauline Epistles and Contemporary Literature* (SNTSMS 74; Cambridge: Cambridge University Press, 1992); J. Ross Wagner, *Heralds of the Good News: Isaiah and Paul 'In Concert' in the Letter to the Romans* (NovTSup 101; Leiden: Brill: 2002).

[7] Walter Brueggemann describes how lament mobilizes God not to religious succour, but to juridical action that rescues and judges, 'The Costly Loss of Lament', in P.D. Miller, ed., *The Psalms and the Life of Faith* (Minneapolis: Fortress Press, 1995), p. 107.

[8] Wright, *Romans*, p. 424.

[9] On *fides* as a virtue of the empire, Dieter Georgi refers to the *Acts of Augustus*, chs 31–33, in 'God Turned Upside Down', in R.A. Horsley, ed., *Paul and Empire: Religion and Power in Roman Imperial Society* (Harrisburg: Trinity Press International, 1997), p. 149.

salvation, Paul evokes for his hearers the fulfilment of this plea. God has not shamed his people, God has brought salvation and justice.[10]

However, in Ps. 44:10 the rhetoric is turned up a notch. In this communal lament, the psalmist recalls God's mighty deeds of old, wherein God drove out the nations (v. 3) and gave victory to his people (vv. 2–9). In v. 10, however, there is a turn: 'But now you have rejected us and shamed (κατῇσχυνας) us'. Not only does this verse reverse the shame attributed to the enemies in v. 8, the theme of shame reappears again at the end of this section (v. 16) in which the psalmist describes the way God has abandoned the people. After a striking assertion of innocence (part of which is quoted in Rom. 8:36; cf. Ps. 44:23 which we will discuss below), the psalmist calls on God to arise (vv. 24, 29) and help his people.[11]

In echoing the language of these psalms, Paul is evoking a context where God's justice and steadfast love are appealed to for salvation. And in asserting that he is *not* ashamed, Paul is thereby suggesting to his readers (hearers) that God *has* arisen, that God *has* acted according to his justice, that God *has* acted to save, that God *has* judged those who practise injustice, that God *has* vindicated his people, and that *this* is the gospel, the good news that challenges the so-called 'good news' of Rome.

But Paul has also evoked the world of the lament, where the question of God's faithfulness and justice is up for grabs, where the psalmist insistently petitions God to do something about the injustice and rejection that he has faced. This is a world where 'the old worldview, old faith presuppositions, and old language are no longer adequate'.[12] In evoking this world, where the experience is one of radical dissonance, even in the midst of *asserting* God's justice and faithfulness, the *question* of God's justice whispers around the edges of Paul's language, setting up the ethos of much of the rest of the letter, but particularly chs 9–11. In spite of Paul's confident assertions, the uncertainty of disorientation reverberates behind his language: But have you put your people to shame?[13]

---

[10] A similar plea is found in Ps. 25:1–3, which also calls for God to reverse the tables and put to shame those who are pointlessly lawless.

[11] The word used in the call for God to 'rise up' (ἀνάστηθι ἀνάστα) in Ps. 44:24, 27 is the same as that used for Jesus' resurrection from the dead (ἀναστάσεως νεκρῶν) in Rom. 1:4, suggesting that God has vindicated his people in Jesus' resurrection.

[12] W. Brueggemann, 'The Psalms and the Life of Faith', in Miller, ed., *The Psalms and the Life of Faith*, p. 19.

[13] Throughout this chapter I will employ Brueggemann's distinction between psalms of orientation, disorientation and reorientation, but especially the latter two categories. Laments describe an experience of disorientation by complaining that reality is not as it should be. When the wicked prosper and the righteous are oppressed, something is awry in covenantal life. Psalms of thanksgiving, and sometimes psalms of recital, give voice to a reorientation that has come through a time of confusion and trouble to a new place of hope and resolution. See W. Brueggemann, *The Message of the Psalms* (Minneapolis: Augsburg, 1984), and 'Psalms and the Life of Faith', pp. 3–32.

Reorientation: The Justice of God Is Revealed

For the moment, however, such echoes are swallowed up in the confident assertion of the rest of vv. 16–17:

> For I am not ashamed of the gospel; it is the power of God for salvation (σωτηρίαν) to everyone who has faith, to the Jew first and also to the Greek. For in it the justice (δικαιοσύνη) of God is revealed (ἀποκαλύπτεται) through faith for faith as it is written, 'The one who is just (δίκαιος) will live by faith'.

The confidence of Paul's assertion is reinforced by the echo of Ps. 98:2–3 in this verse.[14]

> The Lord has made known his salvation (σωτήριον),
> in the presence of the nations (ἐθνῶν)
> he has revealed (ἀπεκάλυπσεν) his justice (δικαιοσύνην).
> He has remembered his mercy to Jacob,
> and his truthfulness (ἀληθείας) to the house of Israel:
> All the ends of the earth have seen
> the salvation (σωτήριον) of our God.

This echo not only reaffirms the continuity of Paul's Gospel with the justice of God revealed through the ages to Israel, it also asserts the continuity of Paul's Gospel with the hope of the psalmist that God's justice will be revealed in the presence of the nations. Furthermore, the psalmist's conviction that the ends of the earth have seen the salvation of our God foreshadows the theme of Gentile and Jew praising God together that is the climax of Paul's argument in chs 9–11.[15]

This psalm, moreover, is a psalm of thanksgiving, which celebrates not only the salvation of God in the past (vv. 1–2), but also the coming of God to judge the earth in justice (δικαιοσύνη). It is, therefore, a psalm of reorientation, a psalm that has come through lament, that has come through the plea for salvation, to a place of thanksgiving for that salvation. This is a psalm sung by those for whom the world has been created anew, by those who have experienced a new reality emerging around their God, in the face of what seemed to be a historical ending.

Paul's allusions in these two verses, therefore, to psalms of lament and a psalm of reorientation respectively, not only thematically set the stage for the rest of the letter, but also anticipate the dynamic of the letter as a whole, a dynamic that moves from lament to thanksgiving and praise.[16]

---

[14] Hays, *Echoes*, pp. 36–7.

[15] Hays, *Echoes*, p. 36.

[16] This dynamic is consistent with the dynamic of Israel's conversation with God in the psalms, which begins in hurt, rage, need, indignation and isolation and moves to celebration and praise; see W. Brueggemann, 'Praise and the Psalms: A Politics of Glad Abandonment', in Miller, ed., *The Psalms and the Life of Faith*, p. 115.

A Justice Revealed in Judgement?

Before we move on to the rest of the letter, have one more connection arising out of Psalm 98 needs to be noted. The psalm ends with the assertion that God is coming to 'judge the world in justice (δικαιοσύνη) and the peoples with equity' (Ps. 98:9).

God's justice, or righteousness, is not only shown in salvation, but also in judgement.[17] The lament psalms call for this judgement upon the unjust and the psalms of thankfulness celebrate it. And the unveiling of such judgement against the Gentiles who oppress God's people seems to be a part of the justice of God in Romans as well. Paul's argument unfolds with a series of clauses all linked by γάρ. 'I am eager to proclaim the gospel...*for* I am not ashamed of the gospel, *for* it is the power of God for salvation...*for* in it the justice of God is revealed...*for* the wrath of God is revealed (vv. 15–18). Just as in Psalm 98, in Romans God's justice is contrasted with injustice (ἀδικίαν) and ungodliness, an injustice moreover, which suppresses the truth (ἀλήθειαν; Rom. 1:18).

Such a claim, which exalts the justice of God, would have had strong resonance with the community in Rome. Roman justice, as I indicated above, was one of the chief virtues of the empire. Such a challenge to the justice of Rome is not just found in the claims of the God whose gospel is now salvation, it is also found in the subsequent indictment of Gentile society, characterized by ἀδικία, injustice.

Thus Paul's argument moves into an indictment of sinfulness that will continue until 3:20. At this point, however with Psalm 98 still reverberating in the background, and with standard Jewish polemic against paganism and more widespread polemic against the morality of the empire ringing in our ears, the indictment seems to fall heavily on ungodly and unjust Gentiles.[18] But when Paul continues the indictment in 1:23 by saying, 'They exchanged the glory (ἤλλαξαν τὴν δόξαν) of the immortal God for images (ἐν ὁμοιώματι) resembling a mortal human being or birds or four-footed animals or reptiles', he is alluding to Ps. 106:20: 'They exchanged their glory (ἤλλάξαντο τήν δόξαν), for the image (ἐν ὁμοιώματι) of an ox that eats grass'. In Psalm 106, however, these verses refer to the incident of the golden calf in the exodus narrative and hence to *Israel* exchanging their glory. As a result, already here there are hints of the turn that is coming in 2:1: Israel, too, is part of this indictment.[19]

---

[17] Hays, *Echoes*, p. 41.

[18] Elliott argues that Romans is a defiant indictment of the rampant injustice and impiety of the Roman 'golden age', 'Paul and the Politics of Empire', p. 37.

[19] Wright, *Romans*, p. 433, also discerns echoes to Ps. 81:13 in the language of 'God gave them up' in Rom. 1:24, 26, 28. The lack of any similarity between the Greek of Rom. 1:24, 25, 28, and the Greek of Ps. 81:13 makes me hesitant to make the identification.

A Just Judgement: Romans 2:5–10

However, even when Paul begins to make the case explicitly against Israel as complicit in the injustice that is typical of Gentiles and the empire, his echoes of the psalms create resonances which whisper around the edges of his argument, affirming God's faithfulness in the midst of judgement.

As Paul continues, God's just judgement is elaborated in this refrain from Ps. 62:13, quoted in Rom. 2:6): 'For he will repay each one according to his deeds.' The repeated appeal to God as Saviour in Ps. 62:2, 3, 7, 8 and to God's compassion (v. 12) reveal the overwhelming hope that the psalmist has in God in spite of the falsehood, extortion and robbery that surround him (vv. 5, 11).

This psalm, however, also reinforces Paul's contrast admirably. The psalmist contrasts those who hope in God at all times (v. 9), with those who hope in injustice (ἀδικίαν; v. 11). According to the psalmist, God's salvation and compassion are manifest in God's judgement over injustice. Precisely Paul's point. Hence he continues his argument by contrasting those who obey the truth with those who obey injustice (ἀδικί:α, Rom. 2:8), and by further describing such injustice in terms of robbery and a heart set on riches (Rom. 2:10).

As if to ensure that the overtones that he has evoked earlier in contrasting God's justice with the (in)justice of the empire are caught by his audience, Paul outlines a reward for those whose works are judged to be good by God's 'just judgment': glory and honour and peace (2:10). The importance of honour and glory in status-worshipping Rome cannot be overemphasized, nor can its links with extortion and setting one's heart on riches.[20] The echoes of the psalm add overtones that reinforce Paul's language here. And in promising peace, Paul is promising that God's justice will result in the one thing that the empire prided itself upon more that anything else: the Pax Romana, a peace brutally enforced to bring glory and honour to Rome.[21]

Paul's echo of Psalm 62, therefore, reinforces the contrast between the justice of God and the injustice of the empire that he has been tracing through these verses, but does so in such a way that the dividing line between Jew and Greek wavers and is redrawn; it now runs between the just and the unjust, Jew and Greek alike.

Lament and the Depths of Disorientation

The Indictment Builds: Romans 3:4

Such a redrawing of the boundaries continues in Paul's use of psalms in Romans 3. And the struggle which such a redrawing posed for Paul is evident

---

[20] Klaus Wengst, *Pax Romana and the Peace of Jesus Christ*, trans. John Bowden (London: SCM Press, 1987), pp. 33–6.

[21] On imperial peace see Wengst, *Pax Romana*, pp. 8–11.

in his continued use of psalms of lament in this chapter. Paul's apparently reasoned argument notwithstanding, there is an ethos of disorientation throughout these verses.

In the midst of contrasting God's faithfulness, truth and justice with human unfaithfulness, falsehood and injustice at the beginning of Romans 3, Paul evocatively echoes the penitential Psalm 51. This psalm is attributed to David after Nathan had confronted him about his sin with Bathsheba. As Hays points out, 'Psalm 51, like Paul's argument in Roman 3:1–20 pivots on the contrast between God's blamelessness and human guilt'.[22] Such a contrast reinforces the justice of God in carrying out judgement, as reflected in the verse Paul quotes from Ps. 51:5: 'so that you might be justified (δικαιωθῆς) in your words and triumph when you are judged'. Paul uses this psalm to proclaim God's justice in judgement in the context of a plea for mercy. Such a tone of repentance and the plea for forgiveness indicate that God's justice and salvation are found not only in God's judgement but also in God's deliverance.

Not One Is Just: Romans 3:10–20

Such an emphasis continues in the cluster of texts cited in Rom. 3:10–18. In this passage, Paul juxtaposes verses from five psalms, all of which can be described as psalms of lament.

> [10]As it is written,
>   No one is just (δίκαιος), no, not one; (= Eccl. 7:20)
> [11]there is no one who has understanding
>   no one who seeks for God.
> [12]All have turned aside, together they have become worthless;
>   there is no one who does good,
>   there is not even one. (= Pss 14:1–3; 53:3–4)
> [13]Their throats are opened graves,
>   they use their tongues to deceive. (= Ps. 5:10)
>   The venom of vipers is under their lips. (= Ps. 140:4)
> [14]Their mouths are full of cursing and bitterness. (= Ps. 10:7)
> [15]Their feet are swift to shed blood, (= Isa. 59:7; Prov. 1:16)
> [16]ruin and misery are in their paths,
> [17]and the way of peace they have not known.
> [18]There is no fear of God before their eyes. (= Ps. 36:2)

Although it is clear from the context of the quotations in this letter that Paul is appealing to these verses to illustrate how both Jews and Greeks are under the power of sin (Rom. 3:9) so that the whole world will be held accountable to God, the problem, as Steve Moyise points out, is that in their original contexts these verses do not refer to all people, but rather to the wicked.[23]

---

[22] Hays, *Echoes*, p. 50.
[23] Steve Moyise, 'The Catena of Romans 3.10–18', *ExpT* 106 (1995), p. 368.

Perhaps most striking is the overwhelming identification of the wicked ones with the other nations, whom God will punish when he delivers his people (Pss 14; 9:6, 12, 16, 20–21; 10:16). In contrast to the wicked, these psalms describe the just (δίκαιος) as those who hope in God (Pss 5:13; 140:14), the poor and the oppressed (Pss 9:9, 12, 18; 10:12, 14, 18; 14:6; 140:12), for whom God will act.

None of these psalms, however, would describe Gentiles and Jews as being in some way united in sinfulness. For the psalmists the contrast between the wicked and the righteous clearly parallels the Gentile/Jew divide. But Paul's psalmic collage engages in the same kind of interpretative move that the prophets made when, after proclaiming judgement on the nations, they then turned and applied the same judgements to Israel.[24] This is by no means a new move in the scriptures of Israel; it is, however, a move which led to much of the anguish of those same prophets over Israel, and which gave rise to the exilic reinterpretation of the psalms of lament as anguished cries of the nation before God.

But even if Paul is extending the judgement of these psalms beyond the Gentiles to Israel, the fundamental distinctions that the psalms set still whisper through his words: God is a God who will act on behalf of the righteous, on behalf of the poor and the orphan, on behalf of those who seek him. And the volume of such an assurance swells as the indictment swells. The quotation in v. 18: 'there is no fear of God before their eyes', is from Psalm 36, which itself has strong resonances with Paul's assertion of God's faithfulness at the start of Romans 3. So perhaps these verses whisper through Paul's language of indictment:

> Lord, your mercy (ἔλεός) is in the heavens,
> and your truth (ἀλήθειά) to the clouds;
> your justice (δικαιοσύνη) is like the mountain of God,
> your judgements like the great deep;
> you save (σώσεις) humankind and creatures, O Lord (Ps. 36:6–7).

Already at the end of this indictment, the echoes that Paul's quotations create anticipate God's just salvation proclaimed in Rom. 3:21–26.

In these verses however, God's judgement remains necessary for God's salvation of humankind and, indeed, all creatures. Just as the context of the psalms of lament is one where in a situation of overwhelming unfaithfulness, the just, the poor and the oppressed are waiting for God's righteous judgement to save them, so in this passage of Romans, the heightening of the injustice,

---

[24] E.g., Ezekiel 28–36; cf. Amos 1–2.

unfaithfulness and duplicity of the present context creates the circumstances in which God will act.[25]

The overwhelming condemnation of Rom. 3:10–18 comes to a climax in two other quotations. First, in Rom. 3:19, Paul asserts that the law speaks these words 'so that every mouth may be stopped', an echo of Ps. 63:12. The effect of such scriptural witness is that there is no more to say, it has been established 'beyond any possible doubt' that 'God is just in his judgment of the world'.[26] The underlying question of God's justice, raised by Paul in Rom. 3:5–6, appears, on the surface at least, to be answered definitively here, in the face of the overwhelming evidence of human injustice. However, the deep overtones of God's just judgement on behalf of the needy, found throughout these verses still resonates both in this quotation from Psalm 63, and, even more powerfully, in Paul's second allusion, to Ps. 143:2 in Rom. 3:20.

As Hays has argued at some length, Paul's echo of Ps. 143:2 functions as a bridge to Rom. 3:21 and following, demonstrating how God's justice is the ground of hope for the psalmist.[27] As in the other psalms quoted in Rom. 3:10–18, the psalmist in Psalm 143 appeals to God's truth and justice as the basis for deliverance (vv. 1, 11). Unlike the previous psalms, however, which draw a strong contrast between the wicked and the just, or the oppressed, this psalm contains a more universal confession: 'no living being will be justified before you' (ὅτι οὐ δικαιωθήσεται ἐνώπιόν σου πᾶς ζῶν, v. 2). This does not mean, however, that the psalmist is not experiencing oppression from enemies. The psalm ends with this appeal:

> By your justice (ἐν τῇ δικαιοσύνῃ σου) you will lead me out of the oppression (θλίψεως) of my life; /And in your mercy you will obliterate my enemies, /And you will destroy all those who oppress (θλίβοντας) my life, /because I am your servant (Ps. 143:11–12).[28]

The language of oppression (θλῖψις) is picked up by Paul in Rom. 8.35, the first trial in the list after his rhetorical question: 'What, then, shall separate us from the love of Christ?' Paul's echo of Psalm 143 here, therefore, not only maintains the volume of the voices that affirm God's saving justice, but also allows the voices of those who hope in that justice in the face of oppression to be heard.[29]

---

[25] Contra J.D.G. Dunn, *Romans 1–8*, (WBC 28A; Dallas: Word, 1988), p. 149, who asserts that the catena works because Paul has undermined the clear distinction between the unrighteous and the righteous. I am here in fundamental agreement with Moyise, 'The Catena of Romans 3.10–18', p. 368, who points out that rather than being undermined, such a distinction continues to function throughout Romans.

[26] Hays, *Echoes*, p. 50.

[27] Hays, *Echoes*, pp. 51–2. See also his 'Psalm 143 and the Logic of Romans 3', *JBL* 99 (1980), pp. 107–15.

[28] This translation from Hays, *Echoes*, p. 51.

[29] The language of hope is also found in Ps. 143:8: 'Let me hear of your steadfast love in the morning, for in you I will hope' (ἤλπισα); as well as in Rom. 8:24–25.

The use of these psalms of lament throughout Romans 3, then, evokes both judgement and promise. Such an intermingling of voices creates a tension in this text: a tension between acknowledging that all have sinned and fall short of the glory of God, and acknowledging that while God's justice has been revealed through the faithfulness of Jesus Christ, such a revelation doesn't seem to have stopped the suffering of the innocent, or the apparent abandonment of (at least some of) Israel by God. As we shall see, that tension is heightened as the letter continues.

A Moment of Peace: Romans 4:7–8

Before we get to the heightening of that tension, however, Paul takes us through the story of Abraham. Within that story, he invokes David to speak of those 'to whom God reckons justice apart from works' (Rom. 4:6):

> Blessed are those whose iniquities are forgiven/and whose sins are covered/blessed is the one against whom the Lord will not reckon sin (Ps. 32:1–2; quoted in Rom. 4:7–8).

This is a psalm of reorientation and as such demonstrates the deep roots of the thankfulness of those who now view lament from the other side. The bulk of Psalm 32 recounts the anguish and crying (κράζειν) of the psalmist and the way in which God delivered him from oppression (θλίψεας). The rejoicing to which the just (δίκαιοι) are called, therefore, is deeply rooted in a memory of redemption from oppression. Even though Paul is describing here a moment of reorientation – the turn in his argument from the irrefutable sinfulness of humanity to God's justification of such sinners by faith – his quotation of Psalm 32 keeps the tension alive that underlies his argument: lament always precedes thankfulness and even in the midst of faithfulness, unfaithfulness is lurking.

A Return to Lament

The echoes of the psalms of lament in Rom. 2:6, 3:4, and 3:10–20 all form part of the indictment that Paul is building against Gentile and Jew alike. And while the overall intertextual effect of drawing on these psalms is to increase the volume of the whispers of God's love and faithfulness to Israel, they also contribute to the underlying question that moves just below the surface of the text: is God just? And both in his overt argumentation, and in his echoes from the psalms, Paul's answer to this question is, ' yes, based on human sin, and on the witness of scripture, God is just'.

However, whereas the psalms witness to an expectation that God's justice would be manifest always *for* Israel and *against* the Gentiles, Paul uses these verses to show how the injustice of the Gentiles is matched by the injustice of Israel, raising the question of how God will then work to save God's people. Hence, I suggest, Paul's deep resonance with the psalms of lament, the psalms of disorientation. If Israel is also unfaithful and unjust, if Israel seems to be suffering the judgement of the nations, then the world is in disarray. This is, for Paul, a moment of deep cognitive dissonance, a moment of deep disorientation. And such dissonance can only be adequately described using the language of lament. Throughout the twists and turns of Paul's argument, such dissonance surfaces briefly here and there, until in Romans 8, it comes to expression in one of Israel's most poignant communal psalms of lament: Psalm 44.

The Suffering of this Present Age: Romans 8:31–39

I have argued elsewhere that three models of subversive speech shape Rom. 8:14–39: credo recital, lament and thanksgiving. These are models of subversive speech that Brueggemann has argued are constitutive to Israel's language as she protested in her praise the ideology and idolatry of the empire.[30] For the purposes of this chapter, I would like to briefly explore the second of these: lament.

The psalms of lament contain Israel's most insistent language before the face of God. They articulate the groans of those living in the shadow of empire, the cry of those protesting the injustice of empire, and the plea of those who expect redemption from the violence of empire. It is no surprise, therefore, to find that Romans 8 describes precisely these groans, this cry, and such a plea.

Like those who protest the injustice of empire in the psalms, Paul portrays Christian believers as those who cry 'Abba, Father' (Rom. 8:15). In the story of Israel, this cry to God as father is a cry for redemption out of suffering.[31] The Greek word that Paul uses for this cry, κράζειν, is the word that is overwhelmingly found in psalms of lament to describe those crying out to God in the midst of their oppression. Most notably, it occurs in a number of those psalms that are explicitly quoted by Paul in Romans.[32]

Similarly, the groans of those living in the shadow of empire are reflected in Romans 8 in the groaning of creation (v. 22), believers (v. 23), and God's very Spirit (v. 26). This language of groaning originated in Israel's first experience of empire, and was repeatedly used when Israel found herself suffering under imperial control during her history.[33]

But besides the language of crying out and groaning, which describe a community engaged in lament, there are a number of other clues in this passage that suggest that the suffering which the Roman community faced was suffering that originated at the hands of empire.

In the first instance, the context for the intercession of the Spirit is described

---

[30] See Sylvia C. Keesmaat, *Paul and his Story: (Re)Interpreting the Exodus Tradition* (JSNTSup 181; Sheffield: Sheffield Academic Press, 1999), pp. 124–33.

[31] See Keesmaat, *Paul and his Story*, pp. 74–7.

[32] Pss 18:7, 42; 32:3; 69:4.

[33] See, e.g., Exod. 2:23–24; Judg. 2:18; Pss 31:11; 38:10–11; Isa. 24:7; 30:15; Lam. 1:18, 21–22; Ezek. 21:11–12; 1 Macc. 1:26; 3 Macc. 1:18. Further on the background for the language of groaning in Israel's scriptures see Keesmaat, *Paul and his Story*, pp. 107–10.

thus by Paul: 'The Spirit helps us in our persecutions' (v. 26).[34] This, along with references to 'oppression (θλῖψις), distress, persecution (διωγμός), peril and sword (μάχαιρα)' (v. 35), as well as to 'death, rulers and powers' (v. 38), suggests that the suffering that Paul is referring to had something to do with the rulers who have the power to wield the sword in Rome, and who have already introduced oppression, distress, persecution, peril and sword into the Jewish community there.[35]

It is in this context that Paul introduces in Rom. 8:36 a quotation from Ps. 44:23:

> For your sake we are being killed all day long;
> we are accounted as sheep to be slaughtered.

This psalm has extensive parallels with Romans 8. The psalm begins with a credo recital, the remembrance of God's defeat of the nations in the conquest (vv. 2–9). God is the one who saved them from their oppressors (τῶν θλιβόντων; cf. θλῖψις in Rom. 8:35). But, in spite of their praise of God, the psalmist cries out: yet have you abandoned us! (vv. 10–17). God has rejected and shamed (κατήσχυνας) them (44:10), and shame (ἡ αἰσχύνη) now covers the face of the psalmist (44:16). Then in v. 18, there is a turn once again. In the face of God's apparent rejection, the psalmist asserts that Israel has not been false to the covenant. The contrast is striking between the allegations of God's neglect and the faithfulness of the people.

In spite of all that has happened, the psalmist asserts that Israel has remained faithful and has not been false. These overtones resonate in the back of the verses that Paul then quotes from Psalm 44, and they are the more striking because this was the contrast that Paul drew in Romans 3, but in the inverse. There *God's* faithfulness, truthfulness and justice is contrasted with the unfaithfulness, untruthfulness and injustice of Israel and humanity as a whole. In Psalm 44 that contrast is inverted, raising overtly this time the question that is at the heart of Romans: is God just?

Immediately following the assertion that it is precisely because of their faithfulness to God that they are suffering, the psalm calls out to God to rouse himself, to rise up and not cast them off until the end.[36] Sandwiched between

---

[34] As Michael Barré has convincingly argued, based on the Septuagint and intertestamental usage, Paul uses ἀσθένεια to refer to persecutions, which are interpreted as being part of the eschatological ordeal, 'Paul as "Eschatalogic Person": A New Look at 2 Cor 11:29', *CBQ* 37 (1975), pp. 510–12.

[35] On μάχαιρα as execution, see Ernst Käsemann, *Commentary on Romans* trans. and ed. (Geoffrey Bromiley; Grand Rapids: Eerdmans, 1980), p. 249. While it is not at all clear that all of the Jews were expelled from Rome in 49 AD, the fact still remains that the Jews were the subject of an edict at that time, and hence the target of the imperial authorities. For a recent discussion which questions the historical plausibility of a wholesale expulsion of the Jews from Rome, see Mark D. Nanos, *The Mystery of Romans: The Jewish Context of Paul's Letter* (Minneapolis: Fortress Press, 1996), pp. 372–89.

[36] Hays, *Echoes*, p. 60.

this plea and another for God to rise up is a further question to God: why do you forget our poverty and oppression (θλῖψως)?

Aside from the quotation itself, the number of echoes between Psalm 44 and Romans 8 are quite high.[37] The background of the psalm, too, with its context of oppression raises the question of God's faithfulness and presence in the midst of such suffering. The plea for God not to cast his people off forever is answered overtly in Rom. 11:1.[38] However, a more subversive answer is given at the end of Romans 8, with the assertion that we are more than conquerors through him who loved us. The language of the conqueror has, of course, run as a subtext throughout the psalms of lament, more overtly in those psalms where Israel calls for God to release her from the nations that have conquered her, and even more prominently in those psalms where Israel has called on God to conquer her enemies as a sign of faithfulness. For both oppressor and oppressed alike, the question of who has conquered whom is a vital one.

For the Christians in Rome the phrase was even more fraught. What else was Rome than the conqueror of the whole world, the victor over the pagan hordes, whose status as conqueror was celebrated on coin and portal where subjugated peoples were depicted in positions of subservience to victorious Roman conquerors?[39] For a small beleaguered community in Rome, the power of such conquerors was all pervasive. Hence the whole discussion of Rom. 8:17–39: what is the meaning of this suffering in which the believing community and, indeed, the whole creation finds itself? Does such suffering mean that a successful charge has been brought against those whom God called (v. 33)? Does it mean that they have been condemned (v. 34)? Does it mean that God's love has been withdrawn (v. 35)? Does it mean that the oppressor is victorious?

And, a related question is this: How does the Christian community respond to such suffering? How does the Christian community respond to the violence of the empire? Does it take up the cry of the psalms of lament and demand that God grind the nations into dust, defeat the evildoer and enable his people to oppress their foes?[40]

Paul's answer, along with his quotations from Ps. 118:6, Ps. 110:1 and Ps. 44:23, weave together various themes from Israel's scriptures into an entirely new cloth. With the psalmist he asserts, 'If God is for us, then who is against us?' (Rom. 8:31; cf. Ps. 118:6), but, unlike the psalmist, who has already been

---

[37] One parallel that I have not discussed here is that between God who searches the heart in Rom. 8:27 and the God who searches the heart in Ps. 44:22.

[38] Hays, *Echoes*, p. 59.

[39] Rome's depictions of their subjugation of other peoples is described in P. Zanker, *The Power of Images in the Age of Augustas* (trans. Alan Shapiro; Ann Arbor: The University of Michigan Press, 1990), pp. 185–7.

[40] See, for example, Pss 10:15–16; 94:23; 140:10–12; cf. Pss 18:30; 34:17; 69:23–29.

rescued from his oppression, Paul is asserting God's presence in the midst of such oppression. His confession in 8:34 that Jesus is seated at the right hand of God alludes to Ps. 110:1; but unlike the ruler of that psalm, whose enemies become his footstool, the messiah called Jesus intercedes even for those who have killed him. And Paul's echo of Ps. 44:23 answers the plea of the psalmist for God to arise and redeem this defeated and suffering people, with the paradoxical assertion that those who suffer are not the defeated, but are more than conquerors.

The whole dynamic of this passage rejects the traditional categories about who is victor and who is conquered. The messiah who died and was raised is the one in the position of authority at the right hand of God, and those who suffer are the ones who are – not conquered – but more than, indeed above, the conquerors. Paul is rejecting the imperial categories here of victory, categories beloved by both Israel and Rome, and is replacing them with the category of suffering love. The way to respond to the violence of the empire is to bear it; and in that bearing to reveal that one is part of the family of Jesus (Rom. 8:17, 29) and therefore one of those who cannot be separated from God's love. It is such love, such 'relentless solidarity', that enables the Roman Christians to bear the suffering that they experience at the hands of their persecutors. And, paradoxically, such love is what gives the community the context in which to voice their complaint and insist, again and again, that God be called to account. Brueggemann describes the dynamic in this way: because the one we address 'has promised to be in the darkness with us, we find the darkness strangely transformed, not by the power of easy light, but by the power of relentless solidarity'.[41]

This is, also, I submit, the same relentless solidarity that enables God to bear with the suffering caused by his people in Romans 9–11. Paul's assertions of the presence of God in the midst of a suffering community, therefore, sets up the context for a lament of his own in Romans 9–11. In the power of God's relentless solidarity Paul is empowered to face the darkness of his own people's disbelief.

The Lament over Israel

Richard Hays has argued that the overall structure of Romans 9–11 is broadly analogous to the structure of a lament psalm.[42] Given such an overall structure, it is not surprising that Paul's quotations of the psalms continue to draw on the lament tradition. The first such allusion is actually a quotation of Isa. 28:16, and is found in Rom. 10:11: 'As it is written: "no one who has faith in him will be put to shame".' As we saw above, this is language that also echoes a

---

[41] Brueggemann, *The Message of the Psalms*, p. 12.

[42] Hays, *Echoes*, p. 64.

number of the psalms of lament, including Psalm 44. These echoes move behind Paul's discussion throughout these verses, although now, in light of the magnificent assertion of Romans 8, the continued faithfulness of God to those who appear to have been shamed before the nations is affirmed. By the time Paul asserts that those with faith will not be put to shame in 10:11, the assertion of both Rom. 1:16, and the affirmation of Romans 8, with its echo of Psalm 44, whispers through this text, suggesting that even if by the standards of the nations God's people have been put to shame, this is in fact not the case.

Their Voice Has Gone Out: Romans 10:18

In spite of such an affirmation, however, Paul's argument continues to describe a people who have *not* had faith in Christ as Lord, even though they have heard (10:16–21). The quotation from Ps. 19:5 in Rom. 10:18 recalls Rom. 1:20. His echo of Psalm 19, however, suggests that it is the gospel of Christ that the heavens and earth declare to the ends of the world. Whereas in Romans 1 the evidence of God's power and divine nature meant that the Gentiles were without excuse, here the evocation of creation to assert the universal reach of the gospel means that *Israel* is without excuse.[43]

This quotation, along with the following quotations from Deut. 31:21 and Isa. 65:1–2, functions rhetorically like the catena of Rom. 3:18–20, firmly characterizing Israel in terms of disobedience. But here a rhetorical move is made beyond Romans 3: there Israel is identified with Gentile sinners; here, Paul's quotation functions to emphasize that the Gentiles are more obedient than Israel. As a result, Paul's only quotation from a psalm of orientation in Romans, a psalm that shows no evidence that suffering will ever be the lot of those who follow the law, functions rhetorically to deepen his anguish over Israel, now more disobedient than the Gentiles.[44] Such anguish leads, inevitably, to the unthinkable question of Rom. 11:1. If Israel has so clearly rejected the gospel, has God in turn rejected his people?

God Has Not Abandoned his Inheritance (Has He?): Romans 11:1–2

The question urgently needed to be asked, and, as far as Paul is concerned, it needed to be emphatically answered in the negative. In Rom. 11:1, all of the whispered affirmations that have swirled around Paul's quotations of the psalms of lament up until this point, affirmations of God's steadfast love and faithfulness to Israel, come to explicit expression in Paul's argument. The condemnation of the wicked and the lament over the rejection of God's people now fade into the background as Paul asks: 'God has not cast off his

---

[43] Contra Hays, *Echoes*, p. 175, who suggests that this echo is an example of Paul simply appropriating the language of a text without wrestling seriously with it.

[44] On the confidence in the status quo that undergirds the psalms of orientation see Brueggemann, *The Message of the Psalms*, pp. 25–49; and 'The Psalms and the Life of Faith'.

inheritance, has he?' (Rom. 11:1).[45] This question, along with its answer a verse later, 'God has not cast off his people, whom he foreknew' echoes Ps. 94:14: 'For the Lord will not cast off his people, and he will not leave his inheritance'. The psalm continues in this way, 'until justice (δικαιοσύνη) returns for judgement, and all the upright in heart will follow it' (Ps. 94:15).

Even though this psalm of lament is echoed in the arguments of Romans in ways similar to the psalms we have discussed so far, Paul's explicit echo of the promise of God's faithfulness here renders a different intertextual effect from Paul's previous quotations and allusions. Whereas in Romans 3, 4 and 8, Paul relied on the unstated correspondences to keep the subtext of God's faithfulness to Israel a strong thread running through his arguments concerning Jewish and Gentile unfaithfulness, here the urgency of Paul's argument requires that the subtext be made explicit through his echo. The subtext, then, that whispers through these verses, only to become the text again as Romans 11 progresses, is that of God's faithfulness in spite of Israel's unfaithfulness.[46]

One other subtext that is evoked by this psalm, one that does not become explicit until Romans 12 and 13, is that of the wicked rulers, who contrive mischief by statute, band together against the life of the just, and condemn the innocent to death (Ps. 94:20–21). Given the context of persecution highlighted at the end of Romans 8, these struggles are relevant to the struggles of this Christian community. In this light, it is not surprising that Paul uses the Elijah story (which was a story of persecution), in Rom. 11:2–4 and that his argument turns to how the Christian community responds to persecution and the state in Rom. 12:14–13:10. The cry for vengeance against the wicked with which Psalm 94 begins is also one that is picked up in Rom. 12:19 by Paul. In the light of the overwhelming calls for deliverance from the nations in the psalms of lament that we have described, as well as the explicit reference to such suffering in Romans 8, we need to acknowledge the link between the unfaithfulness of Israel with which Paul is struggling here, and the suffering that this community is undergoing at the hands of the empire. The psalms assert that such suffering means that God has not abandoned Israel; Paul affirms the same. The psalms pray for God to be faithful to his people and avenge their suffering. Paul also affirms God's faithfulness and calls for the community to leave vengeance to the Lord. These parallels suggest that the context of the empire and the suffering it creates raised for this community the question of God's faithfulness.

---

[45] While the majority of early texts read 'his people', other textual witnesses, including P[46], F G it[b,f,g,x], Ambrose, Ambrosiaster, Pelagius, and the Gothic, read 'his inheritance'. For a rationale for accepting this reading see Wagner, *Heralds*, p. 222.

[46] This theme is heightened when one realizes that an echo of 1 Sam. 12:22 is also present in Rom. 11:1. In the context of Israel demanding a king, Samuel charges that the people have rejected God, but that God will not cast away his people, for his name's sake. See also Wagner, *Heralds*, p. 229.

Their Eyes Are Darkened: Romans 11:9–10

A few verses later, the assertion that God has not rejected his people seems to pale. In Rom. 11:9–10, Paul once again draws on two psalms of lament, Psalms 69 and 35.[47] In both of these psalms, the psalmist calls upon God for deliverance in the face of treacherous enemies. In addition, both call down curses upon their oppressors. One of these contains the central theme of Israel's shame on account of her faithfulness to God (Ps. 69:7, 20); the other calls for such shame to be the lot of the wicked (Ps. 34:5, 27).

However, rather than drawing on the assertion of God's faithfulness, which was front and centre only a few verses ago, Paul applies to a part of Israel the curses that the psalmist applies to his oppressors (οἱ θλίβοντές in Ps. 69:19): 'And David says: "Let their table become a snare and a trap, a stumbling block and a retribution for them, let their eyes be darkened so they cannot see, and keep their back forever bent"' (Rom. 11:9–10), a mixed quotation from Ps. 69:23–24 and Ps. 35:8. We see, then, that Paul inverts the meaning of these psalms. The deep tension of his argument between God's faithfulness to Israel and Israel's own rejection of God's grace in Jesus is reflected in the deep tension of Paul's hermeneutical moves, which on the one hand affirm the faithfulness of God to God's inheritance, and, on the other, depict Israel in terms of the wicked.

Such a tension is not resolved, ultimately, until Romans 15. Although Paul's dense and scripturally allusive lament over Israel ends at the close of Romans 11, the issues that occasioned these chapters are preoccupied with the shape of this community in the face of oppression (θλίψει, Rom. 12:12) and persecution (v. 14) under a hostile empire. And the call to an ethic of suffering love is strongly reminiscent of Romans 8 (see especially 12:14–13:10). Similarly, the discussion of the strong and the weak culminates in ch. 15, where the unity of both strong and weak is designed to culminate in the unity of both Jew and Gentile praising God. Jewett argues that the emphasis on mutual love in the love-feasts (Rom. 13:10) of early house and tenement churches sets up Romans 14–16. These chapters deal 'with the question of inclusion of outsiders and other ethnic groups into the local love-feasts in Rome. A new empire of inclusion is here seen to be replacing the empire of privilege, power and domination.'[48] As Wright aptly sums up: 'If the church divides along lines related to ethnic or tribal loyalty, it is still living in the world of Caesar'.[49]

---

[47] On the textual argument for Psalm 35 in addition to Psalm 69 as the background to Rom. 11:9, see Wagner, *Heralds*, pp. 259–61.

[48] Jewett, 'Response: Exegetical Support from Romans and other Letters' in Horsley, ed., *Paul and Politics*, p. 68.

[49] Wright, *Romans*, p. 739. Wright also draws out the imperial overtones in Romans 14.

A Messianic Community: Rom. 15:3

Paul's quotation of Psalm 69 in Rom. 15:3 demonstrates yet again the varied ways in which scripture informed his thinking. Rather than using this psalm to speak of those within Israel who are blind to God's grace in Jesus, here Paul uses Ps. 69:10 to christologically describe the strong within the Christian community in Rome. In a double hermeneutical move, Paul applies the words of the psalmist, 'the insults of those who insulted you fell upon me', to the messiah and uses this as the basis for the ethic to which he is calling the Christians in Rome.

Such an echo also serves to reinforce Paul's argument in ch. 8 that suffering is not a sign of God's rejection, along with his call in ch. 12 to be patient under oppression, to bless those who persecute, and overcome evil with good. The effect of Paul's quotation is to evoke the righteous sufferer of Psalm 69 as an example for the Roman church. The result of such an identification of the righteous sufferer with the community in Rome results in the sort of welcome and service that Christ embodied, in a manner fully consistent with chs 12–14. Such service confirms God's truthfulness, thus confirming the promises to the patriarchs, and results in Gentiles glorifying God for his mercy (Rom. 15:7–9).

All Peoples Praising God: Reorientation at the Last

It is here, finally, in Rom. 15:7–13, that the underlying tensions of Paul's quotations of the psalms are finally resolved. The deep anguish of the psalms of lament, the sorrow over Israel's unfaithfulness, the agony of the suffering of God's people, all come to their conclusion in these verses. And, like the psalms of reorientation, Paul's concluding descriptions of doxology are not cheap descriptions of joy, but are rooted in the lament from which they arise. This is praise that has come through the anguish and seen that there is indeed hope (Rom. 15:13); this is praise in response to a messiah who became a servant, who suffered the insults that the community also bears.

This does not mean that there is no tension in the psalms that Paul quotes in these verses. The quotation of Ps. 18:50 in Rom. 15:9, uses a verse in which the psalmist promises to praise God before the Gentiles after God has given victory over those same Gentiles, whom the psalmist has ground into fine dust (vv. 38–49). 'Therefore I will praise you among the Gentiles, and sing to your name', is, for the purposes of the psalmist, praise that glorifies the victory of Israel over her enemies. And, although it is true, as Hays points out, that the verse that follows upon Paul's quotation speaks of 'magnifying the saving deeds of his king, and performing mercy for his messiah, for David and his seed forever' (Ps. 18:51),[50] it is also clear that these saving deeds involve the defeat of foreigners, and that God's mercy for his messiah means defeat for Israel's enemies.

[50] Hays, *Echoes*, p. 72.

This tension is also found in the quotation from Isa. 11:10, in which the hope of the Gentiles is closely aligned with the rule of Israel over them. As Robert Jewett points out, this tension is contextualized by Paul's references here to Deut. 32:43 in Rom. 15:10 and Ps. 117:1 in Rom. 15:11. Psalm 117, with its repeated uses of 'all' (Praise the Lord, all the nations [τὰ ἔθνη], Praise him, all peoples) 'stresses that no people is to be excluded from this common praise of God'.[51] In addition, the argument of chs 12–15 for mutual acceptance, love and service, culminates in Paul's description of the messiah as one who became the servant. This reinforces the character of the messiah, whom this community follows, as a messiah who does not violently subjugate his enemies, but who rather dies for them. We see, then, that by the end of the letter the nationalistic overtones of Psalm 18, and indeed of a number of the other psalms of lament have been completely recontextualized. Such recontextualizations serve to challenge both the empire that engages in violent oppression, and Israel's hope in similarly violent revenge. Thus, Paul's language of praise 'is at the same time and inevitably a *polemical act*'.[52] It is a polemical act not only because Paul extols a messiah who is fundamentally different to anything the empire has on offer, but also because this community, where strong and weak, Jew and Gentile praise God together, is a fundamental challenge to the empire, with its clear distinctions between ethnic groups and social sectors. This is a gospel which undermines all that the gospel of Caesar needs in order to maintain its violent control over the known world. By the end of the epistle to the Romans, Paul – both through his argument and psalmic allusion – has evoked another story, another set of symbols, and another praxis that stand in judgement over the story, symbols and praxis of the empire that surrounded on every side the house churches in Rome.

Lament and Allusion in Galatians

The letter to the Galatians is not as densely packed with scriptural allusion and citation as is the letter to the Romans. This may be because both subject matter and context are substantially different from Romans, even though the main issue under discussion is whether the Christians in Galatia should follow Jewish law, including circumcision.

However, there is some suggestion that the imperial context of Galatians is not that far removed from that of Romans. N.T. Wright has argued that the language of 'gospel' in Galatians itself contains an implicit challenge to the empire, both because of its roots in the Septuagint (where the gospel announced by Isaiah is that God is coming to overthrow the tyrants and

---

[51] Jewett, 'Response', p. 69.
[52] This is one of the characteristics of the act of praise, according to Brueggemann, 'Praise and the Psalms', p. 118.

oppressors and announce freedom to their victims), and because of its overtones for those who live in the empire, an empire whose ruler proclaims a gospel rooted in military might. He then reads Galatians as a word about a new messiah, who has come to establish a new people, Jew and Gentile, which challenges both imperial paganism and a Judaism that would be like paganism by holding to its nationalistic aspirations.[53] Paul's allusions to the psalms in Galatians support such a reading of the text. In addition, it is clear that this community, and Paul himself when he first came to them, has experienced some suffering, although it is more likely that such suffering came from Jewish rather than imperial sources.[54]

A Different Justice

The two most prominent allusions to the psalms in Galatians are both to psalms of lament.[55] Paul quotes Ps. 143:2 in Gal. 2:16: 'We ourselves are Jews by birth and not Gentile sinners; yet we know that a person is justified not by works of the law but through the faithfulness of Jesus Christ, so that we might be justified by the faithfulness of Christ, and not by doing the works of the law, because no one will be justified by the works of the law' (Gal. 2:15–16). The parallels with Romans 3 are obvious, yet the overtones that the allusion to Psalm 143 carries are unique to Galatians. Paul's modifications of the language of Ps. 143:2 serve to reinforce points made later in the letter. In Psalm 143, this verse reads, 'because no one living will be justified before him'. Paul adds 'by works of the law' to strengthen his point, and he changes the phrase 'no one living will be justified' to 'no flesh will be justified'. According to Hays, Paul 'is perhaps subtly anticipating the argument he will make later in the letter against "those who want to make a good showing *in the flesh*" by compelling the Galatians to be circumcised (6:12)'.[56]

This psalm appeals both at the start and the finish to God's justice as the basis for redemption (Ps. 143:1, 11). These overtones have the effect of affirming that we are heard in our suffering, that in spite of the fact that no one has acted justly, God will act for justice on our behalf. God will be faithful purely for the sake of God's truthfulness, and for the sake of God's name. Such a confession, of course, stands in stark opposition to the view that roots divine justice in obedience to the law. For the Galatian community, perhaps taking refuge in the law in order to avoid persecution of the churches from zealous

---

[53] N.T. Wright, 'Gospel and Theology in Galatians', in L. Ann Jervis and Peter Richardson, eds, *Gospel in Paul: Studies in Corinthians Galatians and Romans for Richard N. Longenecker* (Sheffield: Sheffield Academic Press, 1994), pp. 233–36.

[54] References to suffering in the letter include Gal. 3:4 ('Did you suffer so much for nothing?'); 6:2; 6:12. I have also argued that the cry 'Abba, Father' in 4:6 indicates a context of suffering. See Keesmaat, *Paul and his Story*, pp. 74–77; 179–81. On persecution see Robert Jewett, 'The Agitators and the Galatians Congregation' *NTS* (1970–71), pp. 198–212.

[55] Some have noticed the conceptual parallels between Gal. 4:26 and Ps. 86:6. This allusion seems to me to be very faint.

[56] R.B. Hays, *The Letter to the Galatians* (New Intepreter's Bible XI; Nashville: Abingdon, 2000), p. 241.

Jews who disapproved of close association with Gentiles, Paul's language makes clear that justice – the vindication of those who are suffering – is rooted not in any works of the law. The overtones of Psalm 143 flesh out his point and deepen it: justice is rooted in God's own justice, given only because of God's truthfulness, mercy and for the sake of God's name.

Are there also overtones that challenge the justice of the empire, rooted in the force of arms? Psalm 143, with its appeal for salvation from enemies and from oppression (θλίψεως; vv. 9–11) certainly presents a challenge to the pagan nations in its affirmation of God's continued justice that will cut those enemies off (v. 12). For the hearer of this epistle who was familiar with this psalm, the overtones would have helped to fill out the allusive context already set up by Paul's provocative use of the word 'gospel'. For those with ears to hear, the echoes are there: not the story of the law enforcers, nor the story of Rome, but only the story of Jesus establishes the just relationship once more.

A Different Messiah

The second allusion to the psalms in Galatians is also to a psalm of lament: Psalm 89 in Gal. 3:16. The parallels between this psalm and Galatians are extensive; just as Paul emphasizes God's faithfulness to the offspring of Abraham, so the psalmist outlines God's promises to the offspring of David, the anointed one.[57] Although Paul begins by talking about Abraham and his seed, he is moving within a story line where the promises made to the seed of Abraham are continued in the seed of David.[58] By using the language of both the anointed (the messiah), and the seed, Paul creates an echo with Psalm 89, an echo that increases in volume when one realizes that there are other points of parallel with Galatians.[59]

However, the most striking parallel is the most unexpected. Psalm 89 begins by recounting God's unconditional promise to David, the anointed, and to his seed for ever. The verses quoted above convey the tone of the first 38 verses. Then, suddenly, there is a turn. God is accused of rejecting his people and his messiah in v. 39 (χριστόν). In the midst of this rejection, the anguished cry goes up, 'How long?' (v. 47). And, in a striking parallel with Galatians, the psalmist ends this way:

> Remember, O Lord, how your servant is taunted,
> how I bear in my bosom the insults of the nations (ἐθνῶν),
> with which your enemies taunt, O Lord,
> with which they taunted the footsteps of your messiah (χριστοῦ) (Ps. 89:51–52)

---

[57] Ps. 89:4–5, 21, 30, 37.
[58] Hays, *Galatians*, p. 264.
[59] For instance, this is a messiah who will cry to God, 'You are my Father' (compare with Gal. 4:6: 'God has sent the spirit of his Son into our hearts crying, Abba, Father!').

This psalm describes the suffering of the messiah, a suffering which is central to Galatians (2:20; 3:1; 6:17).[60] The close identification of Paul with the suffering messiah in the letter (2:20; 6:17), and the assertion that those advocating circumcision were doing so in order to avoid persecution for the cross of the messiah (6:12) creates points of resonance with the text. Such echoes firmly place the messiah that Paul describes in Gal. 2:16 in the story line of the promise to Abraham and to David. Psalm 89 describes a messiah who suffers; Jesus is such a messiah. The intertextual matrix of this psalm, then, serves to support Paul's argument that it is the story of the suffering messiah, Jesus, who fulfils the promise for these Christians, not the law.[61]

Suffering and Lament in Paul and Beyond

At the end of our discussion of Paul's use of the psalms in Romans and Galatians, this question remains: what is the effect upon the believing community of Paul's use of the psalms? I have three suggested answers.

(1) For these communities, Paul's quotations from the psalms of lament serve to situate the suffering of the community as a whole in the context of the story of Israel. In that story, God comes in justice, to save, judge and restore those to whom he has pledged his troth, even in the face of their unfaithfulness. And, while a number of the psalms that Paul quotes are drawn on extensively elsewhere in the New Testament to apply to Jesus, Paul's use of these same psalms identifies the suffering of the messiah with the community. Since many of these psalms were applied to the suffering of Israel by first-century Jews, Paul's application of them to the church recalls them to their function as the scriptures of Israel.

(2) Paul's appropriation of the language of lament also serves to keep the question of God's justice open for the communities to which Paul writes. For those suffering at the heart of the empire, or for those suffering at the hands of zealous missionaries who insist on law observance, the question of God's justice in the midst of oppression needs to be present. The psalms of lament permit this kind of questioning. Walter Brueggemann describes the importance of lament for questions of justice because lament:

> redresses the distribution of power between the two parties, so that the petitionary party is taken seriously and the God who is addressed is newly engaged in the crisis in a way that puts God at risk.[62]

---

[60] It is tempting to suggest that Paul is echoing Ps. 89:51 (I bear in my bosom the insults of the people) in Gal. 6:17 (I bear on my body the marks of Jesus). On the one hand, the extensive echoes between Psalm 89 and Galatians make such an echo plausible; on the other hand, the lack of any similarity in vocabulary lessens the volume.

[61] Some discern echoes to Pss 125:5 and 128:6 in Gal. 6:16. These echoes are faint, and space does not permit an exploration of them here.

[62] Brueggemann, 'The Costly Loss of Lament', p. 102.

Was anything at stake in Paul's discussion of the justice of God in Romans? Yes, the status of Israel put God's justice at risk, and Paul plunged into the depth of the lament psalms to address the issue.

But lament also keeps the question of justice front and centre in the praxis of the community.[63] By drawing on the tradition of lament, by modelling such lament in the epistle to the Romans, by describing the life of the community as legitimately expressed in lament in Romans 8 and Gal. 3:4 and 4:6, and by using the hope implicit in the psalms of lament to challenge the claims of the empire, Paul is calling the Christian community to not let go of the questions of justice. He is calling them to keep the questions of justice front and centre in their communities, in the way that they eat (cf. Gal. 2:11–14; Rom. 14), in the way that they speak of one another (Gal. 5:15–26; Rom. 14:10–13; 16:17–18), and in the Lord that they model themselves after (Gal. 2:20; 6:2; Rom. 8:17; 15:7–8).

Paul uses the psalms of lament in Galatians and Romans, and the psalms of reorientation in Romans in ways which undermine a central part of the story of Israel. The psalms of reorientation quoted in Romans 15 celebrate God's defeat of the enemies of Israel. And the psalms of lament call for violent revenge upon the Gentiles. All of these are undermined by the story of a messiah who demonstrated God's justice by suffering, dying and rising up. The call of Romans to love and feed our enemies (Rom. 12:14–20) is a direct challenge not only to the empire that was the cause of so much oppression, but also to the story of Israel, who called for a violent response to such oppression. In the face of such suffering, Paul tells a story that results not in acting like the conqueror, but instead in groaning with a suffering world. Here Paul's echoes continue the story, and undermine it with the story of Jesus. And this is, in the end, what makes his use of the psalms truly radical, and truly life-giving.[64]

---

[63] Brueggemann, 'The Costly Loss of Lament', p. 107.
[64] My thanks to Brian Walsh, whose critical and constructive comments were invaluable in writing this chapter.

8

The Psalms in 1 and 2 Corinthians

H.H. Drake Williams, III

Introduction

During his second missionary journey, Paul founded the church at Corinth in 50 CE. His missionary efforts started first in the synagogue where he reasoned with many from the scriptures on the Sabbath. As a result of his teaching there, some Jews became Christians (Acts 18:4, 8). When he received resistance from many within the synagogue, however, Paul turned his attention to the Gentiles, and witnessed to them for a year and a half (Acts 18:6, 9–11). These Gentiles, who were largely from Greek and Roman descent, comprised the majority of the city and most likely the church in Corinth.[1] After leaving the city Paul wrote and visited with the Corinthians on a number of occasions. Some of these visits and letters were heated and quite painful (e.g., 1 Cor. 5:9–11; 2 Cor. 2:1; 12:14; 13:1–2). The records that we have of such interaction are the letters of 1 and 2 Corinthians.

In the midst of these letters, Paul uses a great deal of Old Testament scripture to support his challenges and encouragements to the Corinthian congregation. A number of scholars are noticing the citations, allusions and echoes to scripture that comprise a significant part of his composition.[2] These scripture references emerge from all parts of the Old Testament.

One book that has been influential upon Paul's writing is the book of

---

[1] Note the many scholars who find that Greek and Roman culture formed the backdrop to the Corinthian church. E.g., R.M. Grant, *Paul in the Roman World: The Conflict at Corinth* (Louisville: Westminster/John Knox, 2001); A.D. Clarke, *Secular and Christian Leadership in Corinth: A Socio-Historical and Exegetical Study of I Corinthians 1–6* (AGJU 18; Leiden: E.J. Brill, 1993); D. Litfin, *St. Paul's Theology of Proclamation: 1 Corinthians 1–4 and Greco-Roman Rhetoric* (SNTSMS 79; Cambridge: Cambridge University Press, 1994); B.W. Winter, *Philo and Paul among the Sophists: A Hellenistic-Jewish and a Christian Response* (SNTSMS 96; Cambridge: Cambridge University Press, 1996); A.C. Thiselton, *The First Epistle to the Corinthians: A Commentary on the Greek Text* (NIGTC; Grand Rapids/Cambridge: Eerdmans/Paternoster, 2000), pp. 1–22; G.D. Fee, *The First Epistle to the Corinthians* (Grand Rapids: Eerdmans, 1987), pp. 1–3.

[2] E.g., B.S. Rosner, *Paul, Scripture, and Ethics: A Study of I Corinthians 5–7* (AGJU 22; Leiden: E.J. Brill, 1994); P.J. Tomson, *Paul and the Jewish Law: Halakha in the Letters of the Apostle to the Gentiles* (CRINT 3.1; Assen: Van Gorcum, 1990); D.W. Kuck, *Judgment and Community Conflict: Paul's Use of Apocalyptic Judgment Language in 1 Corinthians 3:5–4:5* (NovTSup 66; Leiden: E.J. Brill, 1992); S.J. Hafemann, *Paul, Moses, and the History of Israel* (WUNT 81; Tübingen: J.C.B. Mohr [Paul Siebeck], 1995); H.H.D. Williams, *The Wisdom of the Wise: The Presence and Function of Scripture within 1 Cor. 1:18–3:23* (AGJU 49; Leiden: Brill, 2001).

Psalms.[3] Paul cites from it, alludes to it, and uses wording from it in many of his letters. The following is an examination of his use of the book of Psalms within the Corinthian correspondence. This study will consider the scripture citations of Ps. 94:11 in 1 Cor. 3:20, Ps. 8:7 in 1 Cor. 15:27, Ps. 116:10 in 2 Cor. 4:13, and Ps. 112:9 in 2 Cor. 9:9. It will also examine the significant allusions of Ps. 24:1 in 1 Cor. 10:26 and Ps. 110:1 in 1 Cor. 15:25. While others note the influence of other portions from the Psalms within the Corinthian correspondence, their influence is less certain than these citations and allusions.[4] This study will consider these well agreed upon citations and allusions and then will draw conclusions regarding the presence and function of the Psalms within 1 and 2 Corinthians.

Psalm 94:11 in 1 Corinthians 3:20

The first clear appearance of the Psalms in the Corinthian correspondence is found in 1 Cor. 3:20, at the conclusion of Paul's discourse against human wisdom. Paul's argument against such wisdom began in 1 Cor. 1:17 when he stated that he must preach the gospel message of the crucified Christ rather than speak in human wisdom. Human wisdom empties the power of the cross of Christ. It is also due to be destroyed and rendered useless by the Lord in the future, and even currently it is foolishness and powerless in God's sight (1 Cor. 1:18–25). Since human wisdom detracts from the cross of Christ and diverts attention away from the eternal realities of the gospel message, Paul chooses not to approach the Corinthians with such human wisdom. He would rather proclaim God's foolish but powerful message of the crucified Christ (1 Cor. 2:4–5).

After describing the wisdom that he does preach, warning the Corinthians of their immature conduct, and stating the true conduct of a Christian worker, Paul returns to his argument against human wisdom in 1 Cor. 3:18–3:23.[5] In 1 Cor. 3:18 he warns the Corinthians not to deceive themselves. If someone

---

[3] For a broad overview of Paul's use of the Psalms see R.A. Harrisville, 'Paul and the Psalms: A Formal Study', *Word and World* 5 (1985), pp. 168–79.

[4] E.g., NA[27] suggests the possible influence of these texts from the Psalms within the Corinthian epistles: Ps. 2:11 (2 Cor. 7:15); Ps. 31:24 (1 Cor. 16:13); Ps. 33:10 (1 Cor. 1:19); Ps. 38:1 (1 Cor. 11:24); Ps. 50:12 (1 Cor. 10:26); Ps. 53:5 (2 Cor. 11:20); Ps. 66:5 (1 Cor. 3:17); Ps. 70:1 (1 Cor. 11:24); Ps. 73:28 (1 Cor. 6:17); Ps. 78:15 (1 Cor. 10:4); Ps. 78:18 (1 Cor. 10:9); Ps. 78:24 (1 Cor. 10:3); Ps. 78:31 (1 Cor. 10:5); Ps. 79:1 (1 Cor. 3:17); Ps. 89:12 (1 Cor. 10:26); Ps. 99:6 (1 Cor. 1:2); Ps. 105:39 (1 Cor. 10:1); Ps. 106:14 (1 Cor. 10:6); Ps. 106:37 (1 Cor. 10:20); Ps. 109:28 (1 Cor. 4:12); Ps. 112:4 (2 Cor. 4:6); Ps. 115:5 (1 Cor. 12:2); Ps. 118:17 (2 Cor. 6:9); Ps. 119:32 (2 Cor. 6:11); Ps. 136:2 (1 Cor. 8:5); Ps. 138:1 (1 Cor. 11:10); Ps. 145:13 (1 Cor. 10:13); Ps. 150:5 (1 Cor. 13:1).

[5] Cf. E.E. Ellis, *Prophecy and Hermeneutic in Early Christianity: New Testament Essays* (WUNT 18; Tübingen: J.C.B. Mohr [Paul Siebeck], 1978), pp. 216f; D.A. Koch, *Die Schrift als Zeuge des Evangeliums: Untersuchungen zur Verwendung und zum Verständnis der Schrift bei Paulus* (BHT 69; Tübingen: J.C.B. Mohr [Paul Siebeck], 1986), pp. 273–77.

thinks that they are wise in this age, Paul exhorts them to become fools so that they may become wise since the wisdom of this world is foolishness in God's sight. He then supports his argument with two scripture citations, one from Job 5:13 in 1 Cor. 3:19 and then the citation of Ps. 94:11 in 1 Cor. 3:20. From these two citations, he then draws the conclusion that nobody ought to boast in human leaders for all things belong to them in Christ (1 Cor. 3:20–22).

Ps. 94:11 (LXX 93:11)	1 Cor. 3:20
The LORD knows our thoughts,	and again, 'The Lord knows the thoughts
that they are but an empty breath.	of the wise, that they are futile.'
κύριος γινώσκει τοὺς διαλογισμοὺς	κύριος γινώσκει τοὺς διαλογισμοὺς
τῶν ἀνθρώπων ὅτι εἰσὶν μάταιοι	τῶν σοφῶν ὅτι εἰσὶν μάταιοι

The presence of these two scripture citations is clear in 1 Cor. 3:19–20. Paul introduces the Job citation in 1 Cor. 3:19 with a strong introductory formula γέγραπται γάρ ('for it is written'). This introductory formula would be readily recognized for use in introducing Old Testament texts because Jewish writers regularly employ it when a scripture text is cited.[6] It is also easily recognizable for a Gentile reader who may be less familiar with the recognition of scriptural language.[7]

Paul then connects the Job citation in 1 Cor. 3:19 to the citation from Ps. 94:11 in 1 Cor. 3:20 with the words καὶ πάλιν ('and again'). These two words clearly associate the citation from the psalm with the strong introductory formula used earlier in 1 Cor. 3:19, and thus indicates that what follows in 1 Cor. 3:20 is also taken from scripture. The close agreement between Ps. 94:11 and 1 Cor. 3:20 confirms this and many scholars acknowledge the presence of Ps. 94:11 in 1 Cor. 3:20.[8]

The one difference in wording between Ps. 94:11 and 1 Cor. 3:20 is that the word σοφός ('wise') is substituted for ἄνθρωπος ('men'). This, however, is a minor difference in wording and has not deterred scholars from declaring this to be a scripture citation. Many consider this alteration as a Pauline adaptation.[9] Paul has been rebuking human wisdom within 1 Corinthians 1–3, and thus it is likely that he is substituting this word here.

[6] E.E. Ellis, *Paul's Use of the Old Testament* (Edinburgh: T & T Clark, 1957), pp. 23, 49. Cf. B.M. Metzger, 'The Formulas Introducing Quotations of Scripture in the New Testament and the Mishnah', *JBL* 70 (1951), pp. 297–307. In Paul's writing, see Rom. 1:17; 2:24; 12:19; 14:11; 15:3; 1 Cor. 1:19; 9:9, Gal. 3:10; 4:22, 27.

[7] See C.D. Stanley's study that addresses the recognition of scripture from a Gentile perspective: *Paul and the Language of Scripture: Citation Technique in the Pauline Epistles and Contemporary Literature* (SNTSMS 69; Cambridge: Cambridge University Press, 1992), pp. 33–37, pp. 186–88.

[8] E.g., W. Schrage, *Der erste Brief an die Korinther* (EKKNT 7; Zürich: Benziger, 1991), I,p.; F.G. Lang, *Die Briefe an die Korinther* (NTD 7; Göttingen: Vandenhoeck & Ruprecht, 1986), p. 57; Thiselton, *First Corinthians*, p. 323; Fee, *First Corinthians*, p. 152.

[9] O. Michel, *Paulus und seine Bibel* (Darmstadt: Wissenchaftliche Buchgesellschaft, 1972), pp. 78–79; Ellis, *Paul's Use of the Old Testament*, p. 15; Koch, *Die Schrift als Zeuge des Evangeliums*, pp. 152–53; Stanley, *Paul and the Language of Scripture*, pp. 194–95.

The citation from Ps. 94:11 has two functions within Paul's argument. First, it serves to support Paul's assertion that the wisdom of this world is foolishness and worthless in God's sight (1 Cor. 3:19; cf. 1 Cor. 1:18–25). It does so by declaring that the thoughts of the wise are 'futile' or 'empty breath' (μάταιος).[10] When this word is used in other places in Pauline literature, the word indicates the worthlessness of human abilities (1 Cor. 15:17; Tit. 3:9).[11] The meaning of 'empty breath' (μάταιος) in other places in the Psalms in the Septuagint also indicates the worthlessness of human wisdom.[12] The Hebrew equivalent for 'futile' or 'empty breath' in Ps. 94:11 (הבל) is also a word that portrays the ephemeral and worthless nature of human ideas as in other places within the Psalms.[13]

The context of this psalm and parallel ideas within early Jewish literature also support the claim that human wisdom is worthless. Ps. 94:11 contains many warnings for those who are wise in their own estimation. God is the one whose abilities are far greater than those who are in the world (Ps. 94:8–10). God is also the one who can avenge and judge the earth (Ps. 94:1–3, 13, 23). Such ideas are also found throughout many sections of contemporary Jewish literature.[14] Paul as a first-century Jewish writer would have likely been familiar with many of these texts or ideas.[15] Human wisdom, when seen against the Jewish backdrop of Ps. 94:11 is comparatively worthless in God's sight and worthy of God's judgement.

The citation from Ps. 94:11 performs a second function within 1 Corinthians 3, leading to Paul's next point that all things are theirs in Christ (1 Cor. 3:21–23). While this is not explicit from the words cited from Psalm 94, its context indicates that there is great reward for those within God's plan. In this psalm the Lord teaches his people, does not abandon his people, and aids his people in time of need (Ps. 94:12–23).[16] The righteous will ultimately be blessed in the future since they have God's promised loyal commitment (Ps. 94:12–15). The great blessing of the righteous both now and in the future is a central theme that is found in the broader context of Ps. 94:11. Blessing for

---

[10] Biblical quotations are taken from the NRSV. 1 Cor. 3:20 uses the word 'futile' while Ps. 94:11 uses the words 'empty breath'.

[11] Cf. Acts 14:15; Jas 1:26; 1 Pet. 1:18.

[12] Note the following LXX references: Pss 5:10; 11:3; 23:4; 59:13; 61:10; 107:13.

[13] Cf. Pss 31:7; 39:6, 7, 12; 62:10; 78:33; 144:4. M.E. Tate, *Psalms 51–100* (WBC 20; Dallas: Word Books, 1990), p. 484. A.A. Anderson, *The Book of Psalms* (NCB; London: Oliphants, 1972), II, p. 673.

[14] See texts like 4Q184 1–3, 8–11, 13–15; 1QS v 18b–20; 11QTgJob xxx 1–10 (Job 38:3–13); Wis. 9:13–18; 13:1–2; Bar. 3:29–37; *4 Ezra* 4:1–12; *LAB* 49; 1 Macc. 2:61–64; *Pss. Sol.* 14:6–10; Sus. 42–43; *Sib. Or.* 3:8–10, 24–35. Williams, *The Wisdom of the Wise*, pp. 315–24.

[15] For an explanation of Paul as a first-century Jewish writer, see Rosner, *Paul, Scripture, and Ethics*, pp. 15–17, 26–58; Williams, *The Wisdom of the Wise*, pp. 25–28.

[16] See also the citation of Ps. 94:14 in Rom. 11:2 where Paul proclaims the certainty of the Lord's commitment to the Jewish people even in spite of their sin. J.D.G. Dunn, *Romans 9–16* (WBC 38B; Dallas: Word Books, 1988), pp. 636–37; Harrisville, 'Paul and the Psalms', p. 177.

God's people despite the impending judgement and destruction on human wisdom is also an idea found within early Jewish literature.[17] As surely as human thinking is futile and demands his righteous judgement, trusting in God's ways brings blessings. The presence of this citation from Ps. 94:11 thus supports Paul's assertions that human thinking is futile and also leads to his next point that great blessings are found for those who follow his ways.

Psalm 24:1 in 1 Corinthians 10:26

The next clear reference to a text from the Psalms within the Corinthian correspondence is Ps. 24:1 in 1 Cor. 10:26. This reference is found in direct support of Paul's statement in 1 Cor. 10:25, where he encourages the Corinthians to eat whatever is sold in the marketplace without questioning one's conscience. It is also found in Paul's conclusion to his discussion regarding food sacrificed to idols and weak and strong brothers (1 Cor. 10:23–11:1). Since this section functions as a recapitulation of his argument from a few chapters earlier regarding weak and strong brothers,[18] the broader context of this passage deserves some explanation before commenting on the presence and function of Ps. 24:1 in 1 Cor. 10:26.

Paul's argument about food sacrificed to idols and weak and strong brothers began in 1 Corinthians 8. Food sacrificed to idols was a significant issue at Corinth for it was likely that 'scarcely any other meat would be for sale except for that supplied by the temple'.[19] This led the weak brothers to abstain from eating food and the strong brothers to believe that they could eat such food without sinning.

In 1 Cor. 8:1–13 Paul encourages love for Christian brothers to be the primary concern for weak and strong brothers. Within his argument he states clearly that an idol is of no account in this world for there is no God but one (1 Cor. 8:4–6). While stating this, though, he also notes that a weaker brother may be confused and may not have such knowledge, and thus, it is important for the strong to act in a way that demonstrates care for the weaker brother (1 Cor. 8:7–13). Paul then uses himself as an example as one who had knowledge and personal rights but laid them down for the benefit of others (1 Corinthians 9).

Now that he has described the proper conduct of the strong brother, he speaks about the dangers of idolatry. He warns them not to fall into the previous mistakes of God's people who fell into disobedience due to idolatry, sexual immorality, or grumbling (1 Cor. 10:6–10). He challenges the strong brothers to be careful that they do not fall, for God's people from the past serve

---

[17] Cf. Wis. 9:13–18; *LAB* 49; 1 Macc. 2:61–64; *Pss. Sol.* 14:6–10; Sus. 42–43. Williams, *The Wisdom of the Wise*, pp. 318–25.

[18] Thiselton, *First Corinthians*, pp. 779–80.

[19] J. Murphy-O'Connor, *St. Paul's Corinth: Texts and Archaeology* (Wilmington: Glazier, 1983), p. 33.

as examples to warn those who think that they are strong (1 Cor. 10:6, 11–12). From this point, Paul warns them all to flee from idolatry and stay true to the Christian faith (1 Cor. 10:14–22).

With the largest part of his argument on strong and weak brothers behind him, Paul now concludes his argument with some final statements. In 1 Cor. 10:23 he cites a Corinthian slogan, stating that everything is permissible but noting that not everything is beneficial or constructive. In 1 Cor. 10:24 Paul returns to encouraging selflessness, by stating that nobody should seek his own good, but the good of others (cf. 1 Cor. 8:1–13). He then states his conclusion about food offered to idols that is sold in the marketplace. He states that it can be eaten without raising any question of conscience (1 Cor. 10:25). Since this may be questionable to some who have followed his argument thus far,[20] Paul refers to Ps. 24:1 to support this assertion. From this point, Paul states that freedom extends to eating a meal at an unbeliever's house (1 Cor. 10:27) but not eating something that one knows to have been offered in sacrifice (1 Cor. 10:29–30). Freedom is still subject to other's self-awareness, and all should be done for the glory of God (1 Cor. 10:31–33).

The reference to Ps. 24:1 lends support to his argument. There is some debate, however, about how such a reference ought to be categorized. Some scholars see Ps. 24:1 as a citation, detectable because of the change of style in Paul's writing and the notable similarity between the two texts.[21] Others do not regard it as a citation. The only word that would set this reference apart from the rest of Paul's discussion in 1 Cor. 10 is the word γάρ ('for'), which is a common word in Paul's writing. A Gentile reader could simply pass over this passage without recognizing it as a reference to scripture.[22] With this consideration in mind, it is best to conclude that Ps. 24:1 is a Pauline allusion to this psalm rather than a citation from it, owing to the lack of a clear introductory formula.

Ps. 24:1 (LXX 23:1)	1 Cor. 10:26
The earth is the Lord's and all that is in it (τοῦ κυρίου ἡ γῆ καὶ τὸ πλήρωμα αὐτῆς), the world, and those who live in it;	for 'the earth and its fullness are the Lord's.' (τοῦ κυρίου γὰρ ἡ γῆ καὶ τὸ πλήρωμα αὐτῆς)

Like the use of Ps. 94:11 in 1 Cor. 3:20, the reference to Ps. 24:1 both supports and extends Paul's argument. First, it supports Paul's argument by causing the

---

[20] Note even some commentators' surprise. Fee, *First Corinthians*, p. 480; Thiselton, *First Corinthians*, pp. 783–84.

[21] Lang, *Die Briefe an die Korinther*, p. 130. Koch, *Die Schrift als Zeuge des Evangeliums*, pp. 21–24; Thiselton, *First Corinthians*, p. 785; Fee, *First Corinthians*, p. 482.

[22] Stanley, *Paul and the Language of Scripture*, pp. 37, 195. Cf. M. Fox, 'The Identification of Quotations in Biblical Literature', *ZAW* 92 (1980) p. 427. Fox states, 'If there is no marking at all, we must start with the assumption that there is no quotation, or at least that the quotation is an expression of the speaker's viewpoint and sentiments'.

Corinthians to remember that God created all things including the meat that they eat and the idols of this world. Since God rules over these, the Corinthians should not worry about their own consciences when they eat.[23] The entirety of what is in the world that was created by God is set forward in this allusion from Ps. 24:1 and is representative of a well-known idea within Paul's thinking and from Old Testament and contemporary Jewish writing.[24]

The allusion to Psalm 24 further emphasizes the great sovereignty of God. Indeed, God's rule over all creation can be seen from the context of Psalm 24 where God's greatness as the King of Glory is celebrated (Ps. 24:7–10). He is the one who subjugated the waters of chaos.[25] He is the one who is strong and mighty in battle in Ps. 24:8. He is also described as the Lord of hosts (Ps. 24:10), a term that is repeatedly used to indicate God's strength. Thus, when the context from Psalm 24 is considered, it further emphasizes the greatness of God over anything in creation.

The allusion to Ps. 24:1 also extends Paul's argument by implying that the Corinthians should be subject in all of their conduct to God. Since all of the earth is the Lord's, their conscience should be regulated in the Lord. Paul thus concludes in 1 Cor. 10:31, 'So, whether you eat or drink, or whatever you do, do everything for the glory of God'. The Corinthians should not feel as if they possess unrestrained freedom. Instead, they should conclude that they should do everything for God's glory since this is the logical outcome of the fact 'that the earth and its fullness are the Lord's'.

Other factors from the context and use of Ps. 24:1 support the idea that total liberty should not be found in the Corinthians' self-awareness. The context of Psalm 24 declares that the earth is the Lord's and then clearly states who can approach him. It is those who have pure hearts and clean hands and have not sworn deceitfully (Ps. 24:3–4). Reverence for the Lord rather than total liberty is found in the context of this psalm.

The uses of this psalm or similar ideas that stem from it in early Jewish literature also indicate that reverence for the Lord is envisioned rather than total liberty. Lang even suggests that Ps. 24:1 or ideas from it were used as a grace before meals.[26] Everything that one ate would be acknowledged and subject to God's ownership of the world. Thus in summary, freedom of conscience within the framework of reverence for the Lord is what is supported from the presence of Psalm 24 in 1 Cor. 10:25.

---

[23] For the debate on whether the self-awareness is the potential eater's or the weak Christian brother, see Thiselton, *First Corinthians*, pp. 640–4, 784–5.

[24] Cf. Gen. 1–2; Ps. 104:24; Isa. 40:28; 42:5; 45:12; Amos 4:13; Col. 2:16; 1 Tim. 4:4; Jdt. 9:12; 13:18; Wis. 1:14; Sir. 17:1; 38:4; 49:14; Bar. 3:32; Bel. 1:5; *4 Ezra* 6:38ff.

[25] P.C. Craigie, *Psalms 1–50* (WBC 19; Waco: Word Books, 1983), pp. 211–12.

[26] Lang, *Die Briefe an die Korinther*, p. 130. Cf. *Tos. Ber.* 4.1. Barrett suggests the emergence of thanksgiving at meals from Ps. 24:1. C. K. Barrett, 'Things Sacrificed to Idols' in *Essays on Paul* (London: SPCK, 1982), pp. 40–59.

Psalm 8:7 in 1 Corinthians 15:27 and Psalm 110:1 in 1 Corinthians 15:25

Paul's next citation from the Psalms occurs in 1 Cor. 15:27 in the midst of his affirmation that there will be a resurrection of the dead (1 Cor. 15:12–34). Some within the Corinthian congregation doubted whether there would be such a resurrection (1 Cor. 15:12). Paul addresses these doubts by considering the consequences of their lives without a resurrection. He states that if there is no resurrection of the dead, then Christ has not been raised (1 Cor. 15:13). Moreover, if there is no resurrection of the dead, then their faith is useless, they are still in their sins, those who have died are eternally lost, they are without hope, and Paul is guilty of being a false witness of God (1 Cor. 15:14–19). These consequences would be grave indeed.

Of course, there is no need to worry about these hypothetical consequences as Paul explains that Christ has been raised from the dead (1 Cor. 15:21). Christ's resurrection is the first fruits of those who have fallen asleep, and as a result all who are in Christ will be made alive (1 Cor. 15:22–23). The end will certainly come when all powers, dominions, and authorities are destroyed, and he hands over the kingdom to God the Father (1 Cor. 15:24–26). In support of Paul's claim that all powers and authorities will be placed under Christ's feet and thus be subjected to God, he refers to two texts from the Psalms. In 1 Cor. 15:25 he alludes to Ps. 110:1, and then he cites Ps. 8:7 in 1 Cor. 15:27.

The presence of these two texts from the Psalms is well recognized.[27] While there are a few who would consider it as a citation, it is best seen as an allusion. There is no overtly recognizable introductory formula like γέγραπται γάρ ('for it is written') or καθὼς γέγραπται ('just as it is written').[28] Moreover, only the words ἐχθρός (enemy) and πούς ('foot') directly correspond to Ps. 110:1. It is thus best seen as an allusion.[29]

Ps. 110:1 (LXX 109:1)	1 Cor. 15:25
The LORD says to my lord, 'Sit at my right hand until I make your enemies your footstool.' (ἕως ἂν θῶ τοὺς ἐχθρούς σου ὑποπόδιον τῶν ποδῶν σου)	For he must reign until he has put all his enemies under his feet (δεῖ γὰρ αὐτὸν βασιλεύειν ἄχρι οὗ θῇ πάντας τοὺς ἐχθροὺς ὑπὸ τοὺς πόδας αὐτοῦ.).

It is likely that Paul had Ps. 110:1 in mind since it is an often repeated text within early Jewish literature and within Christian writings.[30] There is a recognizable change in style and grammar from what surrounds this reference in 1 Corinthians 15. Furthermore, the reference to Ps. 110:1 is often

---

[27] R.B. Hays, *First Corinthians* (Interpretation; Louisville: John Knox Press, 1997), p. 265; Conzelmann, *1 Corinthians*, p. 272; Schrage, *Der erste Brief*, 3:176–77; A. Robertson and A. Plummer, *A Critical and Exegetical Commentary on the First Epistle of St. Paul to the Corinthians* (ICC; Edinburgh: T & T Clark, 1911) p. 356; Fee, *First Corinthians*, pp. 754–55.

[28] See Stanley, *Paul and the Language of Scripture*, p. 206.

[29] Cf. Thiselton, *First Corinthians*, p. 1234.

[30] See M. Hengel, *Studies in Early Christology* (Edinburgh: T & T Clark, 1995), pp. 185–214. Cf. D.M. Hay, *Glory at the Right Hand: Psalm 110 in Early Christianity* (Nashville: Abingdon, 1973). Consider these appearances of Ps. 110:1 in the New Testament: Matt. 22:44; 26:64; Mk 12:36; 14:62; 16:19; Lk. 20:42f; 22:69; Acts 2:33–34; 5:31; 7:55f; Rom. 8:34; 1 Cor. 15:25; Eph. 1:20; Col. 3:1; Heb. 1:3, 13; 8:1; 10:12f; 12:2; 1 Pet. 3:22.

combined with Ps. 8:7 in other passages of writing in the New Testament and early Christian literature (Eph. 1:20–22; 1 Pet. 3:22; Pol. *Phil.* 1:1f).[31] This citation from Ps. 8:7 appears clearly in 1 Cor. 15:27.

Ps. 8:7 is well recognized as a citation within 1 Cor. 15:27 as many have noticed.[32] There is an overlap between Paul's writing and a number of words within the text from Ps. 8:7. Furthermore, there is an interpretative comment immediately following the citation. This would distinguish Ps. 8:7 enough from what surrounds it in 1 Corinthians 15 and alert a Gentile reader to the presence of this scripture reference.[33]

Ps. 8:7 (LXX 8:7)	1 Cor. 15:27
You have given them dominion over the works of your hands; you have put all things under their feet (πάντα ὑπέταξας ὑποκάτω τῶν ποδῶν αὐτοῦ).	For 'God has put all things in subjection under his feet (πάντα γὰρ ὑπέταξεν ὑπὸ τοὺς πόδας αὐτοῦ).' But when it says, 'All things are put in subjection,' it is plain that this does not include the one who put all things in subjection under him.

There are a number of textual differences that ought to be noted in this citation, however. Paul has changed the verb ὑποτάσσω ('subjected') from the second person to the third person form. This makes the most sense within the context in which he is using the citation. He also has a different expression for 'under your feet'. This is most likely due to his preference for the preposition ὑπό in his writings. Paul never uses ὑποκάτω.[34] These variations in wording should be seen as Pauline adaptations.

Both Ps. 8:7 and 110:1 contribute to Paul's argument in 1 Corinthians 15. The destruction of every ruler, power and authority in 1 Cor. 15:24 immediately precedes the allusion to Ps. 110:1. Ps. 110:1 states how enemies will be subjected to God. The subjugation of all creation to Christ and ultimately to God can be seen from Ps. 8:7 in 1 Cor. 15:27. When both of these texts are considered together, they provide a double grounding for the total reign of Christ over every ruler, power and authority.

The context and parallels in Jewish interpretation of each of these texts contributes something to Paul's argument. The context of Psalm 110 speaks of

---

[31] Hengel, *Studies in Early Christology*, pp. 163–72.

[32] Fee, *First Corinthians*, p. 757; Thiselton, *First Corinthians*, p. 1235; Schrage, *Der erste Brief an die Korinther*, III, p. 181.

[33] Stanley, *Paul and the Language of Scripture*, pp. 106–107; Thiselton, *First Corinthians*, p. 1235.

[34] Stanley, *Paul and the Language of Scripture*, pp. 206–207; Koch, *Die Schrift als Zeuge des Evangeliums*, pp. 111, 140.

sitting at the right hand of God in two places (Ps. 110:1, 5). Throughout the psalm the ideas of rule and power are associated with the one who sits in that place (Ps. 110:2, 3, 6). Being seated at the right hand of God tells of the great power and authority that one has in that position. The right side is the side of honour, happiness and success.[35] The one at God's right hand is closely allied with him and in a seat of great privilege and authority (cf. Ps. 2:4).[36] As a result of the power and authority that are found at the right hand of God, enemies will be subjugated, people will volunteer to serve, kings will be shattered, and judgement will be pronounced upon the nations (Ps. 110:2–3, 5–6). The power and authority that is found at God's right hand is set forward clearly in early Jewish literature, too, much of which may have been influenced by Ps. 110:1.[37] The context and early Jewish parallels help to bolster Paul's claims that every dominion, power and authority, and even death itself will be subjected to Christ in the future.

The context of Psalm 8 and Jewish parallels also supports Paul's claim of the subjection of all things to Christ. Instead of considering power in relation to sitting at the right hand of God as in Psalm 110, authority and dominion are portrayed in relation to all of creation. Repeatedly, Psalm 8 speaks of the authority of God over all creation (8:3–5, 10). The majesty and dominion of God is repeated in the opening and closing of Psalm 8, suggesting that this is the main theme of the Psalm. In Ps. 8:4–5, the natural human response to God's acts of creation is awe and recognition. Ps. 8:5–8 describes how God will make humankind master over the works of his hands, and this leads to praise for God's creating ability (Ps. 8:10).[38] Similar references to creation in early Jewish literature also elicit respect for God's dominion, power and strength.[39]

Together Ps. 110:1 and Ps. 8:7 with their contexts and parallels within early Jewish literature establish strong support for Paul's argumentation in 1 Corinthians 15.[40] As the representative of humanity (1 Cor. 15:21–22), God will grant Christ dominion and set him over the work of all creation. As the reigning one who has ascended to the right hand of God (1 Cor. 15:25), all enemies including death will be subjected to him. Together these two texts with their contexts and early Jewish parallels also infer the end point of Paul's argument in 1 Cor. 15:28. Since Christ is at God's right hand and will be greater than all powers, dominions and authorities and have everything subjected to him, God who has the ultimate power within the universe will

[35] A. Soggin, 'ימין', ThWAT 3 (1982), pp. 660f. Cf. Gen. 35:18; 1 Kgs 2:19; Ps. 45:10; 80:18; Eccl. 10:2.

[36] Cf. M. Dahood, Psalms III: 101–150 (AB 17A; Garden City: Doubleday, 1970), pp. 113–14.

[37] Cf. 1 En. 51:3; 55:4; 61:8; 62:2; 4Q491. Hengel, Studies in Early Christology, pp. 185–212.

[38] Craigie, Psalms 1–50, pp. 107–10.

[39] Cf. Sir. 16:17–20; 4 Ezra 3:1–5; 6:38–59.

[40] For a christological idea in early Jewish interpretations of these two texts from the Psalms, see Koch, Die Schrift als Zeuge des Evangeliums, p. 245.

ultimately be all in all. Christ will be over all and God's dominion and power will be all in all (1 Cor. 15:28).

Psalm 116:10 in 2 Corinthians 4:13

The first clear reference to the Psalms in 2 Corinthians is the citation of Ps. 116:10 in 2 Cor. 4:13. The citation is found in the midst of Paul's discussion about his new covenant ministry (2 Cor. 2:12–7:4). Throughout many passages in 2 Corinthians, Paul is distinguishing himself from others who are competing for the Corinthians' allegiance. He must counter his opponents who appear in Corinth with letters of recommendation (2 Cor. 3:3), who claim a superior Jewish heritage (2 Cor. 11:22–23), and are boasting in their accomplishments (2 Cor. 10:8–18).[41]

In his argument that precedes 2 Cor. 4:13, Paul has explained his new covenant ministry. In 2 Cor. 2:12–3:3 he has explained this ministry in the Spirit and his suffering role within that ministry. He is the one who is being led unto death and suffers in Christ's triumphal procession (2 Cor. 2:14). As a result of his faithful suffering, however, the sweet fragrance of Christ is made manifest through him leading people from death into death and from life into life (2 Cor. 2:12–16). Paul and his gospel message are the turning points for people and their relationship with the Lord, since the Lord is making him sufficient for such service and using the gospel message to bring people to life or death (2 Cor. 2:12–17; cf. 1 Cor. 1:18).[42]

In 2 Cor. 3:1–4:6, Paul expresses the tremendous glories of his ministry in the Spirit. The Spirit mediated through Paul's new covenant ministry has written Christ himself upon the Corinthians' hearts (2 Cor. 3:1–3) and is producing life through Paul's ministry (2 Cor. 3:4–6). Continuing on through 2 Corinthians 3, there are other attributes that can be seen that are glorious about Paul's ministry in the Spirit. It brings righteousness (2 Cor. 3:9), is permanent (2 Cor. 3:11), produces freedom (2 Cor. 3:17), transforms into God's likeness (2 Cor. 3:18), and creates the new light of the glory of God (2 Cor. 4:6).[43] Paul's ministry is far superior to the old covenant ministry of Moses, which veils hearts (2 Cor. 3:7–18). If Moses' ministry was glorious, then Paul's new covenant ministry of the Spirit is even more so (2 Cor. 3:9).

In 2 Cor. 4:7–15, Paul now addresses the apparent discrepancies between this glorious new covenant ministry and his human condition that the

---

[41] For a further description of Paul's opponents see J. L. Sumney, *Identifying Paul's Opponents: The Question of Method in 2 Corinthians* (Sheffield: Sheffield Academic Press, 1990).

[42] See S.J. Hafemann, *Suffering in the Spirit: An Exegetical Study of II Cor. 2:14–3:3 within the Context of the Corinthian Correspondence* (WUNT 2.19; Tübingen: J.C.B. Mohr [Paul Siebeck], 1986), pp. 89–176.

[43] Note the new creation imagery with the new covenant idea (2 Cor. 3:6). Cf. 2 Cor. 1:20–22; 3:3; 5:15–17; 6:1–2.

Corinthians were concerned about. Unlike the glories of his ministry that he has stated, this section contains many statements of Paul's weakness. He feels 'afflicted in every way ... perplexed ... persecuted ... struck down ... always carrying in the body the death of Jesus' (2 Cor. 4:8–11). In 2 Cor. 4:7 he states that he has this treasure in clay jars and then later in 2 Cor. 4:12 that death is continually at work in him. Despite his declared weakness, Paul triumphantly states that he is not undone since the power of God is at work in his life and in the lives of others to whom he ministers (2 Cor. 4:7–10). Death is at work in him, but the life of Christ is at work among the Corinthians (2 Cor. 4:11–12).

It is into this context that Paul introduces his citation from Ps. 116:10. The citation is introduced with an introductory formula, κατὰ τὸ γεγραμμένον ('according to what is written') that alerts readers to a scripture citation. While the introductory formula is not used elsewhere in Paul's writing, it is not dissimilar to the standard introductory formula καθὼς γέγραπται ('just as it is written'), which he uses to introduce scripture citations in 2 Cor. 8:15; 9:9.[44] While the citation that follows this introductory formula is rather short, just three words in length, it is in full agreement with the LXX of Ps. 116:10.

A number of textual witnesses differ from the LXX version in that they add καὶ after διό.[45] While it is possible that the longer text is original, it is more likely that it is a scribal assimilation to the interpretative comment that follows, καὶ ἡμεῖς πιστεύομεν διὸ καὶ λαλοῦμεν ('we also believe, and so we speak'). In this case the second καί means 'also'. The strength of the external evidence, however, further substantiates that Paul faithfully reproduced the wording of the LXX in 2 Cor. 4:13.[46]

Ps. 116:10 (LXX 115:1)	2 Cor. 4:13
I kept my faith, even when I said, 'I am greatly afflicted' (ἐπίστευσα διὸ ἐλάλησα ἐγὼ δὲ ἐταπεινώθην σφόδρα).	But just as we have the same spirit of faith that is in accordance with scripture – 'I believed, and so I spoke' (ἐπίστευσα διὸ ἐλάλησα) – we also believe, and so we speak (καὶ ἡμεῖς πιστεύομεν, διὸ καὶ λαλοῦμεν).

The citation from Ps. 116:10 [115:1] functions within the argument to support Paul's argument thus far. It first explains why Paul continues to speak amid such adversity. Despite the suffering and hardship just described in 2 Corinthians 4, faith in God and the gospel inevitably demands its proclamation.[47] Those of faith speak from what they believe like the psalmist

---

[44] P. Barnett, *The Second Epistle to the Corinthians* (NICNT; Carlisle/Grand Rapids: Eerdmans, 1997), p. 240.

[45] The addition is found in ℵ F G 0186 1175 sy while the text without καὶ is witnessed by P⁴⁶ B Cᵛⁱᵈ ΔΨM latt.

[46] Stanley, *Paul and the Language of Scripture*, p. 216.

[47] M.E. Thrall, *The Second Epistle to the Corinthians* (ICC; Edinburgh: T & T Clark, 1994), p. 338. C.K. Barrett, *A Commentary on the Second Epistle to the Corinthians* (BNTC; London: A & C Black, 1973), p. 142.

did.[48] Paul has exhibited that he, too, will speak what he believes in other places in the epistle (2 Cor. 2:17; 12:19; cf. 4:2–6).[49] Both the psalmist and Paul continue to speak what they believe despite adversity. The citation from the psalm also suggests that Paul finds his faith to be similar to the psalmist. Both find themselves in the situation of death (Ps. 116:3–4; cf. 2 Cor. 4:11–12); both are rescued by the Lord and praise God for their deliverance (Ps. 116:1–2, 4–9; 2 Cor. 1:3, 11; 2:14; 4:8–10, 15);[50] and both find their faith able to conquer the suffering and life threatening situations that they encounter.

Since Paul cites Ps. 116:10 [115:1] in 2 Cor. 4:13, it also suggests that the character of Paul's life as an apostle that was portrayed in 2 Cor. 4:7–12 is not new. He stands in the line of the suffering righteous from the past as expressed from Ps. 116:10 who is most likely David.[51] There is a long tradition of the suffering righteous from the Old Testament and early Jewish literature.[52] Paul is likely well aware of the righteous suffering tradition since he refers to similar ideas in other places of his writing (Rom. 5:1–11; 8:18–39; 15:1–6; 1 Cor. 1–4; 2 Cor. 1:3–11; 6:1–10; 7:5–7; Phil. 1–3).[53]

Paul's awareness that his life and conduct are oriented to both God and humankind may also be indicated from the context of this citation. From the context of 2 Corinthians 4, some argue that when Paul and his companions 'speak the gospel, they speak only to human beings'.[54] In the surrounding context of Ps. 116:10, the speaker also speaks in the presence of God (Ps. 116:9, 13–17). When such an idea is heard within 2 Corinthians 4, it draws attention to God's presence when Paul preaches his message and connects 2 Corinthians 4 with other passages where he speaks before God (cf. 2 Cor. 2:17; 12:19; 13:3). Thus, when the context of the citation is considered, it suggests that Paul's suffering lifestyle and his gospel message are lived and spoken before both God and humankind.

Finally, the context of the citation from Psalm 116 also infers the idea of thanksgiving. Psalm 116 has been denoted as an individual song of

---

[48] Barrett, *2 Corinthians*, p. 143.

[49] Note the connection of speaking found between 2 Cor. 2:17 and 2 Cor. 4:13 which would strengthen the connection between these two texts. Barnett, *2 Corinthians*, p. 239.

[50] S. J. Hafemann, *2 Corinthians* (NIVAC; Grand Rapids: Zondervan, 2000), p. 187.

[51] Thrall, *2 Corinthians*, I, p. 340; Barnett, *2 Corinthians*, p. 241. Note that A.T. Hanson sees a christological reference in the psalm. Cf. A.T. Hanson, *The Paradox of the Cross in the Thought of St Paul* (JSNTSup 17; Sheffield: Sheffield Academic Press, 1987), pp. 51–53; A.T. Hanson, *Jesus Christ in the Old Testament* (London SPCK, 1965), p. 10–47.

[52] E.g., Ps. 23:4–5; 69:33–34; 71:20–21; 94:19; Jer. 16:7; Wis. 2:12–30; 5:1–7; *T. Ben.* 3–5; *T. Jos.* 1:3–7; *T. Jud.* 21–25; *1 En.* 66:6. For a listing of such traditions see K.T. Kleinknecht, *Der leidende Gerechtfertigte: Die alttestamentlich-jüdische Tradition vom 'leidenden Gerechten' und ihre Rezeption bei Paulus* (WUNT 2.13; Tübingen: Mohr [Siebeck], 1984), pp. 19–162.

[53] Kleinknecht, *Der leidende Gerechtfertigte*, pp. 194–365.

[54] Thrall, *2 Corinthians*, p. 341; Barnett, *2 Corinthians*, pp. 241–42.

thanksgiving.[55] Thanksgiving is also found in the response that the psalmist makes to his rescue from death and his vow of thanksgiving (Ps. 116:12–13, 17). Since Paul claims the same spirit of faith from the psalmist, it is logical for Paul to speak also of thanksgiving (2 Cor. 4:15). This he does in 2 Cor. 4:15 when he states 'everything is for your sake, so that grace, as it extends to more and more people, may increase thanksgiving, to the glory of God'.[56]

Psalm 112:9 in 2 Corinthians 9:9

The second citation of the Psalms in 2 Corinthians is in 2 Cor. 9:9.[57] It is found in the section where Paul is calling the Corinthians to complete the collection for the saints. Paul had established the collection in Corinth during Titus's visit (2 Cor. 8:6, 10; 9:2; cf. 1 Cor. 16:1–2), but the Corinthians had ceased sending their collection to the poor in Judea. In 2 Corinthians 8–9, Paul is going to encourage the Corinthians to continue contributing.

There are a number of viewpoints regarding the contextual unity of this section. Some scholars see 2 Corinthians 8 and 9 as being from separate letters since they are essentially covering the same ground.[58] Others see these chapters as being grouped together.[59] In either case, both chapters do encourage the Corinthians to contribute to the collection for believers in Jerusalem. Their cumulative appeal for funding is in mind whether these chapters were written together in one letter or separately.

Within 2 Corinthians 8–9, Paul uses a variety of appeals to encourage the Corinthians to contribute once again to the collection for the poor in Judaea. In 2 Cor. 8:1–7, he appeals to the example of the Macedonian churches that gave despite their severe trials and extreme poverty. They gave beyond their ability, and thus he encourages the Corinthians to follow their example. In 2 Cor. 8:10–11, he attempts to remind them of their generosity that initiated

---

[55] B.W. Anderson, *Out of the Depths: The Psalms Speak for Us Today* (Philadelphia: Westminster Press, 1983), p. 242.

[56] For an explanation that divine grace is what increases and thus the thanksgiving of God's people increases in 2 Cor. 4:15 see Thrall, *2 Corinthians*, pp. 345–47.

[57] Some note the presence of a citation of Ps. 119:32 in 2 Cor. 6:11. Harrisville, 'Paul and the Psalms', p. 175; NA[27]. Others see an influence of this text on 2 Cor. 6:11. Cf. Thrall, *2 Corinthians*, pp. 469–70; G.K. Beale, 'The Old Testament Background of Reconciliation in 2 Corinthians 5–7 and its Bearing on the Literary Problem of 2 Corinthians 6:14–7:1', *NTS* 35 (1989), pp. 569, 576–77. Due to the lack of an introductory formula, the verbal overlap of only a few words (καρδία, ἐγω and πλατύνω), the similarity to other scripture texts (cf. Deut. 11:16; Isa. 60:5), the absence of a clear stylistic change in composition, and the lack of frequency that Paul cites Ps. 119, it is best to consider that Paul has used scriptural language rather than allude to a specific passage. Cf. R.P. Martin, *2 Corinthians* (WBC 40; Waco: Word Books, 1986), pp. 185–6; Barnett, *2 Corinthians*, p. 335. Major studies on Paul's citations (i.e., Koch and Stanley) also omit this reference.

[58] See H.D. Betz, *2 Corinthians 8 and 9* (Philadelphia: Fortress Press, 1985); F.G. Lang, *Die Briefe an die Korinther* (NTD 7; Göttingen: Vandenhoeck & Ruprecht, 1986). For discussions of the integrity of 2 Corinthians see Thrall, *2 Corinthians*, pp. 1–77; Barnett, *2 Corinthians*, pp. 15–40.

[59] Cf. F.F. Bruce, *1 and 2 Corinthians* (London: Oliphants, 1971); V.P. Furnish, *2 Corinthians* (AB 32A; Garden City, NY: Doubleday, 1984); Martin, *2 Corinthians*.

the collection the previous year, and he exhorts them now to finish what they began. In 2 Cor. 8:16–24 he commends to the Corinthians Titus, his chief delegate, along with a brother renowned among the Macedonian churches, and a third Christian brother. These three will help to finalize the collection among the Corinthians prior to Paul's arrival (2 Cor. 9:1–5).

In 2 Cor. 9:6–15 he sets forth the many blessings of generous giving. In 2 Cor. 9:6 he refers to the principle of sowing and reaping, a principle well known in Jewish literature and used by Paul on other occasions (cf. Gal. 6:7), to encourage giving to those in need.[60] In 2 Cor. 9:7, Paul expresses the pleasure of God when a believer gives cheerfully to him. He encourages cheerful giving, not as those under compulsion or reluctantly. He notes that God is able to make all grace abound so that at all times they may have all that they need (2 Cor. 9:8). From thence, his argument proceeds to explain the many spiritual blessings that will result from their giving. These blessings will benefit not only those to whom they give, but also benefit themselves and result in thanksgiving to God (2 Cor. 9:10–14). Paul then concludes this section with praise to God for his indescribable gift (2 Cor. 9:15).

Ps. 112:9 (LXX 111:9)	2 Cor. 9:9
They have distributed freely, they have given to the poor; their righteousness endures forever;	As it is written, 'He scatters abroad, he gives to the poor; his righteousness endures forever'.
ἐσκόρπισεν ἔδωκεν τοῖς πένησιν ἡ δικαιοσύνη αὐτοῦ μένει εἰς τὸν αἰῶνα τοῦ αἰῶνος	καθὼς γέγραπται ἐσκόρπισεν ἔδωκεν τοῖς πένησιν ἡ δικαιοσύνη αὐτοῦ μένει εἰς τὸν αἰῶνα

In the midst of 2 Cor. 9:6–15 Paul cites Ps. 112:9. The textual affinity with the LXX of Ps. 112:9 is clear. The only notable omission is τοῦ αἰῶνος. There are a number of lesser manuscripts of 2 Corinthians that include it but the most significant manuscripts clearly favour its absence.[61] This omission is most likely a Pauline interpretation for Paul never uses the longer expression in his writings.[62] It is possible that Paul is using a variant text, for the longer and shorter expressions are frequent in the LXX.[63]

This quotation from Ps. 112:9 contains a number of ideas that Paul incorporates into his argument. First, it continues the idea from 2 Cor. 9:8 that God lavishly provides when people give offerings to him. This description is in agreement with the description of the righteous man of Psalm 112, which is a

---

[60] Cf. Job 4:8; Prov. 11:21, 24, 26, 30; 22:8; Jer. 34:17; Hos. 10:12, 13.

[61] The phrase is included in F G K 0243 0236 326 629 630 1241 1739 1881 al a vg^{cl} bo^{mss}. The other major witnesses (Χ A B et al.) omit it. See C.D. Stanley, Paul and the Language of Scripture, p. 233.

[62] Koch, Die Schrift als Zeuge des Evangeliums, p. 116.

[63] Cf. the variations listed in Hatch and Redpath on Ps. 9:18; 20:4, 6; 24:2; 36:27; 40:12; 44:6; 47:14; 60:8; 84:5; 103:31; 144:2 (E. Hatch and H.A. Redpath, A Concordance to the Septuagint and the other Greek Versions of the Old Testament [including the Apocryphal books] [Graz: Akademische Druck- u. Verlagsanstalt, 1975]).

wisdom psalm. In wisdom psalms actions and consequences are clearly displayed.[64] In Psalm 112 the righteous person fears the Lord, keeps his commandments, deals justly, and gives generously (Ps. 112:1, 5). As a result of his fear and obedience to the Lord, God has blessed him (Ps. 112:2–3, 7–9). So, too, Paul uses the example from this wisdom psalm to express how true righteous people give and as a result will be blessed. It fits well with Paul's statement from 2 Cor. 9:6 that 'the one who sows sparingly will also reap sparingly, and the one who sows bountifully will also reap bountifully'.

Secondly, the citation introduces the idea of righteousness into the discourse. Paul has used this idea in other portions of 2 Corinthians (3:9; 5:21; 6:7, 14; 11:15) but has not used it in reference to giving. With the reference to Ps. 112:9, he claims that the idea of God's righteousness is revealed in their giving to the poor.[65] This idea of righteousness from the citation of Ps. 112:9 [111:9] extends into 2 Cor. 9:10 where Paul states that God will 'increase the harvest of your righteousness'.

There is debate, however, as to what this righteousness refers. There are four current options: (1) The righteousness of the giver since the context of 2 Corinthians 9 is referring to those who give?[66] (2) God's righteousness, since God was the main subject from 2 Cor. 9:8?[67] (3) The Christian's righteousness as he is working jointly with God, noting how God is the main subject of 2 Cor. 9:8, 10 and that the righteous person is the main subject in Psalm 112?[68] (4) Righteousness as the expression of Christ at work in the Christian?[69]

It is best to see the righteousness granted as intimately connected with the God who provides the means to give. This would take into account the interconnectedness between God's provision and the Corinthians' ability to give that is found within 2 Cor. 9:8–10. In 2 Cor. 9:8, God provides the necessary resources so that the Corinthians can give and so that they may share in every good work of God. In 2 Cor. 9:10 God generously supplies the seed and will multiply it for the Corinthians so that they can give and also receive a harvest of righteousness.[70] In 2 Cor. 9:11 the Corinthians will be enriched in every way that will produce thanksgiving to God. The interrelation between God's provision for that giving and the Corinthians giving continues throughout 2 Cor. 9:11–14. This is also supported from the context of Psalm 112, in which the act of giving to God is a fruit of good works, which is itself

---

[64] Cf. other wisdom psalms such as Pss 36, 37, 49, 73, 78, 127, 128, 133. Anderson, *Out of the Depths*, pp. 223–27.

[65] Barnett, *2 Corinthians*, p. 439.

[66] Thrall, *2 Corinthians*, pp. 580–83.

[67] Barnett, *2 Corinthians*, p. 440.

[68] Furnish, *2 Corinthians*, pp. 448–49; Hafemann, *2 Corinthians*, p. 368.

[69] This is similar to God at work in the Christian, but it would involve reading the psalm contextually with christological glasses. A.T. Hanson, *Studies in Paul's Technique and Theology* (London, 1974), pp. 179–80.

[70] Barnett, *2 Corinthians*, p. 439.

based on the good works of the Lord (Ps. 112:1–3). Early Jewish literature also supports the idea that the righteous person is known for his almsgiving.[71]

This finds further support if the ideas of Psalm 111 are heard in 2 Cor. 9:8. While texts from Psalm 111 are not present as a citation or an allusion, some scholars believe that it has influenced Paul in 2 Cor. 9:8–9.[72] The psalmist thanks God for redemption and food, and this leads to his generosity. The righteousness of the one who gives to the poor endures forever (Ps. 112:9) since it has been created and sustained by the Lord's righteousness that also endures forever (Ps. 111:3).[73]

From his citation in 2 Cor. 9:9, Paul then moves on to 2 Cor. 9:10. This text restates 2 Cor. 9:8 and summarizes 2 Cor. 9:6–10.[74] The God who supplies both seed to the sower and bread for food will also supply and multiply their seed for sowing (2 Cor. 9:10). Once again, the context of Ps. 112:9 indicates the great abundance that is found among the ones who follow the Lord (Ps. 112:2–3, 7–9). It thus greatly supports Paul's encouragement for the Corinthians to give since the Lord is the one who will supply their needs and also develop their righteousness as God's people.

Conclusion

In the letters that we have from the Corinthian correspondence, Paul has referred clearly to the Psalms to support his argument in six places. He has cited the Psalms four times (Ps. 94:11 in 1 Cor. 3:20, Ps. 8:7 in 1 Cor. 15:27, Ps. 116:10 in 2 Cor. 4:13, and Ps. 112:9 in 2 Cor. 9:9). He has also alluded to the Psalms in two other places (Ps. 24:1 in 1 Cor. 10:26, Ps. 110:1 in 1 Cor. 15:25).

Paul seems to have paid strict attention to the types of psalms that he used. He has taken portions from two wisdom psalms (Ps. 94; 112), two hymns (Ps. 8; 24), a thanksgiving psalm (Ps. 116), and an enthronement psalm (Ps. 110). A text from a wisdom psalm (Ps. 94) was employed to counter ideas of wisdom at Corinth. Another text from a wisdom psalm (Ps. 112) was chosen to indicate that godly actions produce godly consequences. The hymn of Psalm 8 was used to display God's authority over all creation which is now seen in Christ. The hymn of Psalm 24 explained the greatness of God over food offered to idols and the reverence that all God's people must display for what they eat. The enthronement psalm (Ps. 110) was chosen to emphasize the

---

[71] Tob. 4:10–11; 12:8–9; 14:11; Sir. 3:30; 17:22; 29:12; 40:17, 24. See also *Lev. Rab.* 34; *Pes. Rab.* 25. H. Strack and P. Billerbeck, *Kommentar zum Neuen Testament aus Talmud und Midrasch* (Munich: C.H. Beck, 1926), III, p. 525.

[72] Barnett, *2 Corinthians*, p. 439; Hafemann, *2 Corinthians*, p. 368; Furnish, *2 Corinthians*, p. 448.

[73] Hafemann, *2 Corinthians*, p. 368.

[74] Furnish, *2 Corinthians*, p. 449.

reign of Christ as king. The thanksgiving psalm (Ps. 116) is used in support of Paul's integrity.[75]

Not all psalm-types are represented in Paul's quotations and allusions in 1 and 2 Corinthians. For example, he does not seem to have made use of covenantal psalms, psalms of Zion, liturgical psalms, songs of trust, or Torah psalms. Most notably, he has not referred to a lament psalm,[76] even though his distress about the chaos at Corinth and his poor treatment by the Corinthians is so evident.

Regarding the text that he reproduces in his citations, Paul feels free to adapt the text slightly for his own argument. While he does not alter the texts greatly, he does feel free to insert small connecting words like $\gamma\acute{\alpha}\rho$ in 1 Cor. 10:26 or interpret texts, such as substituting $\sigma o \phi \acute{o} \varsigma$ for $\ddot{\alpha}\nu\theta\rho\omega\pi o\varsigma$ in 1 Cor. 3:20. He also interprets and abbreviates citations such as Ps. 8:7 in 1 Cor. 15:27 and Ps. 116:10 in 2 Cor. 4:13. In his significant allusions to the Psalms in 1 and 2 Corinthians, he does maintain the wording from the LXX.

The context of each of the psalms also influences his writing. While context has been a debated issue with regards to Paul's use of scripture,[77] the context of the citations and allusions to these psalms appears to influence or, at the very least, displays significant overlapping with Paul's ideas. Parallels to these citations and allusions in early Jewish literature more often than not also support Paul's use of these psalms.[78]

In all cases, Paul's use of citations and significant allusions to the psalms in 1 and 2 Corinthians directly support the current argument, while also extending to what follows. In other words, they are not there just for rhetorical effect. The presence and function of these psalms influences notable discussions on Paul's rebuke of wisdom (1 Cor. 3), food sacrificed to idols (1 Cor. 10), the authoritative position of the risen Christ (1 Cor. 14), his glorious apostolic ministry of suffering (2 Cor. 4), and his encouragement to give to the saints in Judaea (2 Cor. 9). This indicates that Paul found the psalms an effective support for a whole host of situations in the Corinthian church. The fact that he refers to the psalms so often suggests that these predominantly Gentile Corinthians would have had some familiarity with the psalms, particularly books 1, 4 and 5 from the Psalter.

---

[75] Contra Harrisville, 'Paul and the Psalms', p. 169.

[76] Cf. Harrisville, 'Paul and the Psalms', p. 168.

[77] For the debate surrounding a New Testament author's respect for scripture context, see G.K. Beale, ed., *The Right Doctrine from the Wrong Texts? Essays on the Use of the Old Testament in the New* (Grand Rapids: Baker Books, 1994).

[78] This is in agreement with previous studies that have compared scripture with early Jewish literature within 1 Corinthians: Rosner, *Paul, Scripture, and Ethics*; Tomson, *Paul and the Jewish Law*; Williams, *The Wisdom of the Wise*.

9

The Psalms in Ephesians and Colossians

Thorsten Moritz

Introduction: Methodological Concerns and Possibilities

There isn't a major commentary on Ephesians that neglects to discuss the relationship between this letter and Colossians. The affinity is such that one probably has to concur with the majority conclusion that the relationship is literary in nature.[1] This makes the following observation particularly intriguing: Whereas Ephesians uses the Old Testament frequently (including the Psalms on three occasions)[2] and even expands Colossians frequently by adding Old Testament material, Colossians seems disinterested in appealing to the Old Testament,[3] with practically no references. This evidently needs to be accounted for by any proposed theory of the relationship between the two letters.[4]

There are some cases of the use of the Old Testament in Ephesians (and elsewhere in the New Testament!) which involve a quotation, but which are nonetheless indirect. This is not a contradiction in terms. When an Old Testament verse or fragment becomes so embedded in the exegetical tradition

---

[1] The clearest example of verbal overlap occurs in the concluding sections of the two letters (Eph. 6:18–22 and Col. 4:3–8).

[2] The major examples are: Eph. 1:20–23/Pss 110:1 and 8:7; Eph. 2:13–17/Isa. 52:7 and 57:19; Eph. 4:8/Ps. 68:19; Eph. 5:14/Isa. 26:19 and 60:1f; Eph. 5:31/Gen. 2:24; Eph. 6:2f/Exod. 20:12. There is also a cluster of more fragmentary examples in Eph. 4:25–30 and 5:18/Zech. 8:16, Ps. 4:6, Deut. 24:15, Lev. 19:11, Isa. 63:10 and possibly Prov. 23:31.

[3] It is technically possible to argue with P. O'Brien, *Colossians, Philemon* (Waco: Word Books, 1982), p. 191 that Col. 3:10 alludes to Gen. 1:26 (the overlapping words are κατ᾽ εἰκονα – 'according to the image'), though the well-known character of the latter makes the assumption of a direct allusion less likely and certainly not necessary. As far as the Psalms are concerned, the only possible use in Colossians is found in 3:1 (ἐν δεξιᾷ τοῦ θεοῦ καθήμενος – seated at God's right hand'). There is no doubt that the phrase ultimately goes back to Ps. 110:1 (κάθου ἐκ δεξιῶν μου). Given that this is the most frequently used OT fragment in the New Testament, the question may be raised to what extent the phrase in Col. 3:1 is actually a quotation, rather than being a reflection of common early Christian theology which, to be sure, was ultimately influenced by the wording of the Psalm. I argued in T. Moritz, *A Profound Mystery: The Use of the OT in Ephesians* (Leiden: Brill, 1996), p. 12, that the prominent 'hinge' location of Col. 3:1 makes a deliberate quotation more likely. On reflection I question the weight of that argument.

[4] My assumption is throughout that Ephesians was written after Colossians and with the benefit of the author's knowledge of Colossians (especially if both were written by Paul, something I continue to regard as plausible).

of the later believing community that people become virtually unaware of the original text and co-text, any subsequent use of that fragment may well be a reflection of such later reflection, rather than the original text itself. Needless to say, this needs to be tested and argued on a case by case basis. It is even conceivable that the fragment gradually undergoes transformation into something that is no longer verbally congruent with the original text. Where a subsequent author quotes such a version, it is imperative not to confuse this with an ordinary quotation of the original *Vorlage* or text basis, especially where no such direct quotation is announced in the text by introductory formula. In short, even where we find an actual quotation our alternatives are not limited to 'direct quotation' and 'deliberate or unwitting rewording by the quoting author'. We need to add the possibility of an author's deliberate reference (implied or explicit) to a third party exegetical or theological tradition which itself made use of the ultimate *Vorlage*.

There is a related issue that is worth mentioning. Reading scholarly discussions of assumed New Testament quotations from the Old Testament one sometimes gains the impression that such quotations necessarily imply an interpretative quality. The potential disconnect in making such an assumption emerges when one encounters an example (as we will do below) of a third party quotation, such as described in the previous paragraph. If a quotation has its proper reference not in the ultimate *Vorlage*, but in the mediating tradition that intervenes between the original text and the quotation, the objective behind the quotation (by which I mean the author's illocutionary intent) has to do with the mediating tradition, not the Old Testament text. A New Testament author may well on occasion wish to comment critically or complimentarily on the use of an Old Testament fragment before him, rather than interpreting the actual fragment itself. This possibility has not nearly received the attention it should have been accorded by New Testament interpreters. It is one of the aims of this chapter to demonstrate the feasibility and indeed necessity of pursuing this line of thinking in our quest to throw light on the use of the Old Testament in the New.

The Use and Neglect of the Old Testament in Ephesians and Colossians Respectively

The striking imbalance between Ephesians and Colossians when it comes to the use of the Old Testament has to my knowledge not adequately been accounted for by scholarship up to this point.[5] Table 1 illustrates the issue. The italicized portions in the fourth column indicate the verses that make use of the Psalms.

---

[5] My own attempt to solve the riddle is found in T. Moritz, 'Reasons for Ephesians', *Evangel* 14.1 (1996).

Table 1

Colossians		Ephesians	
(Parallel text unit)	*(Verse with OT material)*	*(Parallel text unit)*	*(Verse with OT material)*
1:13	–	1:15–23	*1:20.22*
1:3–27; 2:9–14	–	2:11–18	2:13.17
2:15	–	4:8–10	*4:8*
3:5–12	3:10(?)	4:25–5:2	*4:25f.*30; 5:2
3:16	–	5:13–20	5:14.18
3:18f	–	6:1–4	6:2
–	–		6:10.14f.17

Ephesians builds on Colossians not least by the addition of Old Testament material. That in itself is enough to caution against a quick identification of the audience of Colossians as Jews, whereas Ephesians is assumed to address Gentiles. The situation is more intricate. At the very least Table 9.1 makes a more Judaizing readership (or a Gentile-Jewish mix, or an audience of former God-fearers) more likely for Ephesians than for Colossians. How else could the preoccupation with the Old Testament in this letter, which rivals that of Galatians be explained? We certainly need to keep these possibilities (Judaizers; Jewish-Gentile mix, God-fearers) in mind as we approach the use of the Psalms in Ephesians.

Ephesians 4:26 and Psalm 4:5 as Test Case: Subtle Appropriation or Innocent Language Borrowing?

The wording of the first half of Eph. 4:26 clearly agrees with Ps. 4:5a (LXX) and it is only in the light of this agreement that the question of any influence of Ps. 4:5b (LXX) on Eph. 4:26 enters the frame. Deut. 24:15 is much closer in wording, although the word order is different, thus probably ruling out an intentional quotation. Ps. 4:5b (LXX) has at best a conceptual link with Eph. 4:26. It is of course possible that Paul, having quoted Ps. 4:5a (LXX) now proceeds to spell out the content of v. 5b in words reminiscent of Deut. 24:15. Perhaps it was the community preserving thrust of Deuteronomy 24 with its practical regulations to protect the weak that inspired Paul to apply the principle of same-day payment to the matter of same-day forgiveness. Ephesians 4 is at this point as community-centred as Deuteronomy 24 and the concern for the poor expressed in Deuteronomy 24 finds a clear parallel in Eph. 4:28. Any role Ps. 4:5b (LXX) may have played in Eph. 4:26b is at most a by-product of the use of Ps. 4:5a (LXX) in Eph. 4:26a. What is interesting hermeneutically is the possibility of a New Testament author glossing one Old Testament text (Deut 24) in the words of another (Ps. 4:5). Once more this would show that Old Testament wording can be borrowed by the New Testament for purposes other than straightforward interpretation.

Ephesians 1:20–23 and Psalms 110:1 and 8:7: Ascension and Dominion – The Lord Rules

A number of fundamental issues – both methodological as well as theological – are lurking behind any attempt to do justice to these texts. Chief among them are the following: (1) To what extent is Ephesians interested in the speech act of the actual Old Testament texts? (2) How prevalent was the combination of these two psalms in early Christianity? What is the history of effect of these psalm fragments? Is Ephesians a reflection of a more widespread appropriation of these texts or can we detect a degree of original exegetical work on the part of the author?

Textual Affinities

Commentators tend to be quick to point out that the phrase 'seated at his right hand' in Ephesians 1 derives from Ps. 110:1, whereas the phrase 'subjected under his feet' goes back to Ps. 8:7b. Though probably correct, the fact must not be ignored that Eph. 1:22 is only marginally closer to Psalm 8 than to Psalm 110. It is possible that Paul only thought of Psalm 110 at this point, but that his choice of wording was subconsciously influenced by the wording of Psalm 8. However, the fact that Paul in 1 Cor. 15:25, 27 appears to have combined fragments from the same two psalms – using the same wording in the case of Psalm 8(!) – may favour the assumption that in Ephesians we also have a combination of elements taken from both psalms.

The list of powers in Eph. 1:21 could well be an interpretation of 'your enemies' in Psalm 8.[6] Ephesians is particularly interested in the present subjugation of the 'powers', presumably because of the threat posed by them and through their societal agents to the Christian believers in the Western Asia Minor region. Later we will encounter a similar use of a psalm to highlight both the threat by the 'powers' and their subjugation in Eph. 4:8–10 (cf. Psalm 68).

Psalms 8 and 110 in the New Testament

This is one of very few occasions in the New Testament where resurrection and exaltation motifs are combined. This does not prevent scholars from arguing, though, that the use of these psalms here is likely mediated via earlier Christian exegetical traditions.[7] On closer inspection this is by no means

---

[6] The reasons behind the elaborate power language of Ephesians are ably discussed and illustrated in C. Arnold, *Ephesians: Power and Magic* (Cambridge: Cambridge University Press, 1989).

[7] See for instance W. Loader, 'Christ at the Right Hand: Ps. CX.1 in the New Testament', *NTS* 24 (1974), pp. 199–217 and A. Lincoln, 'The Use of the OT in Ephesians', *JSNT* 14 (1982), p. 41.

assured. The assumption is largely built on the observation that Ps. 110:1 plays a major role in early Christianity, as evidenced by its frequent use in the New Testament.[8] Elsewhere I have discussed the great variety of wording, grammar and word order represented in these texts.[9] I concluded then – and still do – that the only reasonably firm inference that can be drawn from these other texts is that the phrase 'on his [*or* God's] right hand' played a core role in early Christian confession. This is a far cry from concluding with any degree of confidence that Ephesians must have obtained its wording through early Christian mediation. The possibility of the author having consciously used the psalm itself is certainly worth entertaining.

With reference to the allegedly frequent combination of Psalms 110 and 8 in the New Testament we again have reason to be cautious. The only certain parallel in this regard is 1 Cor. 15:25–27. The selected words from Psalm 8 are identical to those in Ephesians 1 (ὑπέταξεν ὑπὸ τοὺς πόδας αὐτοῦ). 1 Corinthians 15 also takes over the reference to the enemies in Ps. 110:1, but other than Ephesians 1 it does not gloss it by way of piling up 'power' terminology. As mentioned above, the departure by Ephesians from the psalm is easily explained with Arnold by placing it against the canvas of the socio-religious challenges of the intended audience. In any case, the actual overlap between Ephesians and 1 Corinthians is minimal at this point. The argument for two other frequently cited cases of combining these two psalms is even weaker. One of these, Heb. 1:13–2:8, celebrates Christ's superiority over the angels by stringing together elements from various psalms. Psalms 8 and 110 are two of these psalms, but they are separated by appeals to Psalms 2 and 102 respectively. Both in terms of proximity and introductory formulae there is little reason to argue for a combination of Psalms 8 and 110 as such in Hebrews 1 and 2. If anything, Psalms 2 and 102 are, relatively speaking, stronger candidates for such a combination. The other text is 1 Pet. 3:22. It may well be that the appeal to Psalm 110 was coloured somewhat by the language of Psalm 8 (1 Pet. 3:22 has ὑποταγέντων. But in terms of postulating a common early Christian source behind Ephesians 1 and 1 Peter 3 the lack of precise verbal overlap between these two texts outweighs the possibility of terminological influence of Psalm 8 on 1 Peter 3. The commonly voiced assumption that early Christianity was fond of combining Psalms 8 and 110 owes much to scholars relying on each others' conclusions and is, in fact, hard to support.

Apart from the unwarranted claim just mentioned, there is a derivative assumption that tends to be made frequently, namely that Psalm 8 played a major role in early Christian, even pre-Pauline, Christology. Needless to say, the case for such influence can relatively easily be made for Psalm 110. But

[8] Prime contenders are Mk 12:36; Matt. 22:44; Lk. 20:42 and Acts 2:34. Part of the verse appears in Heb. 1:13 and 1 Cor. 15:25. Possible candidates for an allusion are Acts 5:31; 7:56; Rom. 8:34; Col. 3:10 and 1 Pet. 3:22.
[9] Moritz, *A Profound Mystery*, pp. 11f.

Psalm 8 is another matter and Dunn,[10] among others, fails to give reasons for this claim. It is true that the mention of a 'son of man' would have made Psalm 8 appealing for such purposes, but given the lack of evidence, the psalm was apparently not recognized across the early Christian board as inherently messianic. It is at least possible that Ephesians, or more generally the Pauline tradition, may have used Psalm 8 and combined it with Psalm 110, not because this was the done thing in early Christianity, but because Paul saw fit to make the connection between the two psalms and his own 'subjection of the evil powers' theme. Terminologically and conceptually the link can easily be made. The main elements that tie the psalms together are (1) the ruler/subjection motif and (2) the fact that God provides the 'power' necessary to defeat the enemy. But both 1 Corinthians 15 and Ephesians 1 seem especially interested in the one element (πάντα) where Psalm 8 goes beyond Psalm 110.

The Suitability of Psalms 8 and 110 for Ephesians

The conviction expressed in Ephesians 1 that all powers will be subjected implies that no-one other than God himself will be directly involved in the subjection. Psalm 110 proved emminently suitable for this purpose, given that it speaks in uncharacteristically high terms of Israel's king, even to the point of him being invited by God to share his throne. This by far exceeds what David himself had been promised. The christological potential of this psalm is therefore self-evident. In Ephesians 1 it is exploited not least to pave the way for the extension of the messianic enthronement privileges to those 'in Christ' (2:6). It is interesting to note the parallels between this psalm and Daniel 7,[11] another text which left its mark on Ephesians.[12] Both texts clearly envison a dramatic enthronement of the messiah in a way which transcends anything claimed in the Old Testament for any of Israel's earthly kings. Somewhat astonishingly the psalm does not appear to have a significant role in Qumran. One might speculate that this has a lot to do with the perceived misuse of the psalm by the Hasmonaeans.[13] By analogy the apparent lack of messianic use of this psalm in the rabbinic literature predating 260 AD could be explained as a reaction to the (perceived mis-)use of the psalm by the early Christians. Mk 12:35–37 and 14:61–64 may well indicate such a messianic understanding even for the time of Jesus, though neither text actually proves that.[14]

Psalm 8 also recognizes the all-pervasive quality of God's power (vv. 1, 4,

---

[10] J.D.G. Dunn, *Christology in the Making* (London: SCM Press, 1980), pp. 110f.

[11] Both texts combine the following elements: (1) Thrones in the heavenly court, with God sitting on one of them. (2) The son appearing before God to be invested with power and authority, in short, to be enthroned. (3) The enemies facing destruction. (4) A reference to the ensuing kingdom.

[12] For details see C. Caragounis, *The Ephesian Mysterion: Meaning and Content* (Lund: Gleerup, 1971), pp. 121ff.

[13] 1 Macc. 14:41; *Jub.* 32:1 and 36:16; *Test. Levi* 8:3; 18.

[14] R.T. France, *Jesus and the Old Testament* (Grand Rapids: Baker Books, 1982), p. 164.

10), though on balance its focus is more 'down to earth'. The crucial question here is the identity of the 'son of man' mentioned. The allusion in v. 5 to Gen. 1:26 may hold a key insofar as the psalm can be interpreted as a meditation on the biblical creation account(s). Humanity is only 'a little lower than God'[15] in the sense that God has delegated to us the management of his creation. Theologically Psalm 8 is close to the creation accounts of Genesis. Given the lack of reference to the Fall it may well be that the psalmist is primarily interested in the pre-Fall status of humanity.[16] Indirect confirmation comes from 1 QS 11:20–22 which poses the same question as Ps. 8:5 and proposes to answer it by relating the psalm to Gen. 2:17. If this understanding of the psalm holds water, we have here a case of a psalmist searching for an answer to present evil by looking back to humanity's pre-Fall status. It is hard to avoid the impression that he must have longed for a reinstatement of those conditions. It is not the case that those conditions are assumed by the psalmist to be a present reality.[17] But his look back generates a sense of real optimism, based particularly on God's 'majesty in all the earth'. In the final analysis the psalm is thoroughly compatible, therefore, with the much more explicit eschatology of Psalm 110. How, then, does Ephesians use these psalms to support its theological stance and pastoral implications?

Clearly 1:20–23 is a climactic celebration of the death, resurrection and enthronement of the 'Beloved' (v. 6). On the basis of what God has achieved in him there is reason to be optimistic in terms of the summing up of all things (v. 10). More immediately our text applies this eschatological framework to the religio-cultural situation of his audience.[18] The evil powers have truly been subjected under Christ (vv. 21f). It is here that Ephesians makes its unique contribution by applying the christological cluster of death-resurrection-enthronement to the needs and existential *Weltangst* of his addressees. It does so especially by employing the language of the psalms to the specific problem of evil powers.[19] The fundamental importance of this cluster is seen in its reapplication to Christ-followers as early as in 2:5f. As a brief comparison with the Colossian parallel (1:13) shows, we have here one of a number of passages where Ephesians goes well beyond Colossians in underpinning a major theological argument by appealing to a crucial Old Testament precedent. Can we be more specific? What is it that makes this implicit cross reference to the psalms so appealing?

---

[15] As discussed elsewhere, I regard this translation as superior to the alternatives ('for a little while', 'gods') – cf. Moritz, *A Profound Mystery*, pp. 17f.

[16] *Pace* H. Kraus, *Psalmen I* (Neukirchen: Neukirchner Verlag, 1978), p. 212.

[17] Again *pace* Kraus, *Psalmen I*, p. 212.

[18] For the most competent and helpful discussion of this see Arnold, *Ephesians*.

[19] This last aspect is paralleled in 1 Cor. 15:25–27, thus once again tying Ephesians and 1 Cor. 15 closely together.

Interpreting the Use of Psalms in Ephesians 1

I suggest that Ephesians here reflects the same clear appreciation of the relationship between protology (Gen. 1!) and eschatological potential in Psalm 8 as evidenced in 1 Cor. 15:25–27. In contrast to Ps. 110:1, which evidently played a major role in early Christianity, this use of Psalm 8 in the Pauline tradition is a unique contribution within early Christianity. By singularly combining these psalms in this fashion, Ephesians and 1 Corinthians 15 highlight the role of the messianic death-resurrection-enthronement cluster as a hinge between protology and eschatology. Christ is centrally engaged in the restoration of humanity, a point picked up more explicitly in 2:15 with reference to the role of the cross in the creation(!) of this renewed humanity. The application of Ps. 110:1, with its reference to enthronement to the subjection of the powers, is intensified in v. 22 precisely by appealing to the eschatological overcoming of evil longed for in Psalm 8. In so doing, Psalm 8 is accorded a role in the eschatological interpretation of the present which outpaces the explicit claims of the psalm itself. But this role is entirely compatible with the psalm's conceptual gap between protology and eschatology and the eschatological potential opened up thereby. It is particularly appropriate in the light of early Christian claims that the death-resurrection-enthronement cluster means nothing less than the fulfilment of the vision of Ps. 110:1. Crucially, and in fulfilment of the implied expectation of Psalm 8, the 'son of man' (= humanity) is no longer 'a little lower'. Insofar as people are found 'in Christ', they are now enthroned with him (Eph. 2:6). The reader can therefore have every confidence that the summing up of all things 'in him' will eventually also be effected powerfully (Eph. 1:10). It is no coincidence that when the fulfilment of this expectation is fleshed out in Eph. 4:8–10, once again it is done with the help of language from a psalm, this time Psalm 68.

Ephesians 4:8–10 and Psalm 68:19: Ascension and Gifts – The Lord Provides

Once again we encounter a psalm quotation in connection with the ascension theme. But this time there is a twist to the story. To quote Stoeckhardt's sarcastic remark: 'one may turn, stretch or לקחת as one will, one will never force it to mean "giving"'.[20] He is referring, of course, to the well-known conundrum that whereas the psalm speaks of 'receiving gifts' (לקחת), Ephesians quotes it as saying 'giving gifts' (ἔδωκεν).[21] Stoeckhardt's warning has not

---

[20] G. Stoeckhardt, *Commentary on St. Paul's Letter to the Ephesians* (St. Louis Concordia Publishing House: 1952), p. 191.

[21] Relatively minor differences between the quotation and the psalm include the following: (1) change of finite verb to participle (ἀναβὰς); (2) change of person from second singular to third singular (ἠχμαλώτευσεν, ἔδωκεν); (3) change from singular to plural (ἀνθρώποις); (4) omission of preposition; (5) addition of the article (τοῖς). Details in H. Hoehner, *Ephesians* (Grand Rapids: Baker Books, 2002), pp. 524f.

prevented scholars from either downplaying the discrepancy or explaining it half-heartedly as messianic exegesis or allegory.[22] Stoeckhardt himself made the intriguing comment that Ephesians may not be quoting the psalm at all.[23] How so? The wording is too close for us to walk away from seeing some kind of quotation at work. We will see, however, that Stoeckhardt's point could prove to be well taken, albeit not quite in the way imagined by him.

Ephesians and the Targum (Psalms): A Common Tradition?

One possible approach is to look for textually related versions and to postulate some literary or traditional link, such as with the Aramaic Targum.[24] Whether such a link would suffice to exonerate the writer of Ephesians is a matter of debate. The more fundamental difficulty with this view emerges when Gnilka, among others, argues that the quotation in Ephesians provides evidence of the significant age of the Targumic tradition.[25] Such classic circular reasoning, however implied, serves to illustrate the gravity of the exegetical problem at hand. To be sure, the Targum noticeably agrees with Ephesians in translating 'give' instead of 'receive'.[26] But apart from this agreement it is no closer to Ephesians than either the Masoretic text (MT) or the LXX. In fact, on grounds of verbal overlap Ephesians is closer to the MT and LXX than to the Targum. To make matters more difficult, the date of this particular Targum is probably at least half a millennium later than that of Ephesians.[27] In an age where we quite rightly exercise great caution in reading rabbinic sources even from the late second century back into the first, it seems dubious to ignore the issue of dating the Targum. It is *possible* that the Targum preserves a tradition that underlies the Ephesian version, but is it likely? And what is gained by postulating such a scenario? Not a great deal it would appear.[28]

The Targum may not give us a textual basis on which to explain Ephesians,

---

[22] For a convenient summary of some (but by no means all) of the more plausible approaches to this problem see P. O'Brien, *The Letter to the Ephesians* (Grand Rapids: Eerdmans, 1999), pp. 289–93. Hoehner, *Ephesians*, p. 526 has since added his view that Ephesians may be treating the psalm in a 'sound bite fashion' (my words) similar to the reporter who summarizes a longer speech in a couple of sentences. But it seems far from clear how such a 'sound bite' could work as a summary if it does not agree with the original at least in principle. It is doubtful that this suggestion helps explain the change in wording, which, after all, is introduced explicitly as a quotation.

[23] Stoeckhardt, *Commentary*, p. 191.

[24] The most sustained effort to underpin this approach by appealing to the Targum is that by W. Harris, *The Descent of Christ: Ephesians 4:7–11* (Leiden: Brill, 1996).

[25] J. Gnilka, *Der Epheserbrief* (Freiburg: Herder, 1971), p. 207.

[26] Cf. similarly the Syriac *Peshitta*, though its value as evidence is far from widely accepted, both on textual and dating grounds.

[27] For details see Moritz, *A Profound Mystery*, pp. 59f.

[28] One sometimes finds references to *T. Dan.* 5:10f as possible evidence for an early tradition behind the Targum (e.g. Hoehner, *Ephesians*, p. 526), but the differences in wording and concepts are such that a major leap of imagination would be required to see a connection.

but it is immensely instructive to trace the reasons for the change of wording reflected in the Targum. Our enquiry needs to start with the rabbinic uses of this psalm. The common ground shared by the pertinent texts is the application of this psalm to the giving of Torah. The difference between these traditions and the Targum is that the former emphasize the reception of the Torah by Moses (rather than the giving by God), thus not necessitating any adjustment of the verb from 'receive' to 'give'. These rabbinic sources do not, therefore, take us any closer to Ephesians in terms of underlying textual versions. They do, however, provide a conceptual missing link for us by testifying to a development in the psalm's history of effect of which the actual change in wording in the Targum may well have been the culmination.

The Psalm's Jewish History of Effect

An interesting feature of the Psalm's history of effect is its use in connection with the Jewish Pentecost festival. By the late second century BC this festival had in effect become a Torah commemoration. It appears from *Meg.* 31a that Psalm 68 was one of the main texts used in that context.[29] We can assume, therefore, that the psalm was widely known in first-century Jewish circles[30] and that any change in its wording such as that found in Ephesians 4 would almost certainly have been noticed. This raises the question whether – for whatever reason – the changed wording in Ephesians reflects the desire to make some sort of 'statement'. It was Knox who asked whether the author of Ephesians may have endeavoured to take away the psalm from Judaism.[31] Could it be that the psalm is now being claimed for the purposes of Christian Pentecost? The co-text of 4:8–10 concentrates precisely on the outworking of the Spirit in terms of the giving of gifts to Christ's body (vv. 11ff). The irony of claiming the psalm for this Christian purpose would lie in the fact that it is the Spirit's provision for the church which is being celebrated as God's greatest gift *per se*, rather than the gift of Torah. If so, we are here witnessing a Christocentric realignment of primary loyalties among God's people.

Returning briefly to the question of tradition history, it appears that Ephesians may have been more concerned with the way Psalm 68 was used in Judaism than with interpreting the psalm in its original textual setting. The lack of awareness of this possibility may well prove to be one of the main deficiencies of those approaches that seek a solution to the verbal discrepancy between Ephesians and the psalm in supposedly peculiar interpretative practices of the day. One way of testing the possibility explored in the present chapter is

---

[29] Cf. *Jub.* 6:17–19 and 1 QS 1:7–2:19.

[30] For the likelihood of Ps. 68 being operative behind Acts 2:33 see J. Dupont, 'Ascension du Christ et don de l'Esprit d'apres Actes 2:33' in B. Lindars and S. Smalley, eds, *Christ and Spirit in the New Testament* (Cambridge: Cambridge University Press, 1979), pp. 219ff.

[31] W. Knox, *St. Paul and the Church of the Gentiles* (Cambridge: Cambridge University Press, 1939), p. 223.

to compare the form and the original thrust of the psalm with its history of effect as outlined above. This will also help to put into perspective proposals such as that by Penner, who argues that Ephesians really is offering an interpretation of the original psalm, albeit the entire psalm, not just a verse or two.[32]

Ephesians 4:8 – A Summary of Psalm 68?

Penner's case depends in part on the assumption that the psalm is built around the centre of v. 19 and that this is the reason why this particular verse is being (mis-)quoted. The likeliest outline of the psalm, however, does not see v. 19 as its centre, but vv. 20f.[33] Quite apart from this observation, it is hard to see how v. 19 could have the summative function within Psalm 68 claimed by Penner. Finally, even if such a function could be established for the verse in question, this would not, in fact, solve the central problem of verbal discrepancy. It can hardly be claimed that the giving of gifts to God's people is the psalm's 'real' theme.

Elsewhere, in discussing possible candidates for the historical occasion of Psalm 68, I suggested that the most promising avenue is to give full weight to a number of allusions within this psalm to the text (and time!) of Judges 4 and 5.[34] If so, the ascension mentioned is to be taken literally, that is, as a reference to the celebratory ascent to the mountain top, following military victory. The psalm is far from interested in the giving of Torah to God's people. That kind of theological connection was, as we saw, made from the second century BC onwards, but it finds no place in the contextual or co-textual setting of Psalm 68. This in itself is not enough to rule out the possibility that Ephesians does in fact interpret the original psalm, but it hardly makes it a more likely proposition. I am equally unpersuaded by Merklein when he mentions the possibility that 'taking' could be interpreted as 'taking for, i.e. giving'.[35] This pushes the boundaries of plausibility too far. Even the classic 'rabbinic technique' defence, so often called upon in New Testament studies, will do little to cover up the commentator's desperation at this point. We need to explore fresh avenues.

The Introductory Formula

Ephesians 4:8 introduces the quotation with the relatively rare formula διὸ λέγει. Two of only four New Testament occurrences are found in Ephesians, the other being 5:14.[36] It would be unwise to over-construct the extent to

---

[32] E. Penner, 'The Enthronement Motif in Ephesians' (PhD Thesis, Fuller Theological Seminary, 1983), pp. 98f.

[33] Details in Moritz, *A Profound Mystery*, p. 66.

[34] Morits, *A Profound Mystery*, pp. 64f.

[35] H. Merklein, *Das kirchliche Amt nach dem Epheserbrief* (Munich: Kösel, 1973).

[36] C.f. Heb. 3:7 and Jas 4:6. According to *Thesaurus Linguae Graece* there are just three pre-Christian references in the entire corpus of available Greek literature.

which the formula may shed light on our understanding of the quotation. A few observations may be helpful, though. (1) διό itself tends to be used in Ephesians to advance an argument from the level of abstract theology to parenetic significance or vice versa.[37] Whatever the direction, it serves to connect what follows closely to what precedes. (2) The fact that διὸ λέγει undoubtedly introduces a quotation should not be interpreted precipitately to mean that we are entitled to supply 'scripture' as its subject. Eph. 5:14, for instance, while using some scriptural fragments, is not actually a quotation from scripture. (3) The author's excellent knowledge of scripture evidenced elsewhere further cautions against the assumption that the text quoted in 4:8 was meant as a direct reference to Old Testament scripture. The fact that this psalm was extremely well known in first-century Jewish (and God-fearer) circles makes a blatant misquotation or a simple *faux-pas* equally unlikely, especially given the exposition's apparent lack of interest in the changed wording. It would appear, therefore, that we need a more nuanced explanation of the author's use of Psalm 68 related material and the exposition that follows than simply to call it a midrash.

A Possible Setting for the Quotation

The combination of quotation formula and Old Testament material parallels Eph. 5:14. As I have attempted to show elsewhere,[38] Eph. 5:14 most likely quotes a well-known early Christian tradition. This kind of scenario ought to be tested for Eph. 4:8 as well. Whether the quoted material comes from an early Christian or Jewish source is unclear. But given the Jewish history of effect of Psalm 68, it may be best to surmise that v. 8 was the Christian answer to the perceived Jewish misuse of this psalm. Clearly this needs to be tested further, but if correct, it would mean that the exposition which follows in vv. 9f may well represent an original contribution insofar as it puts an early Christian response to the psalm's use in Jewish Torah celebrations within the context of a descent/ascent framework. If so, the irony of the exposition in vv. 9f would be that Eph. 4 pretends – by emulation of Jewish hermeneutics – to claim the psalm for christological and pneumatological purposes precisely in a way which was critical of those analogous Jewish efforts. We saw above that the evidence of the psalm's Jewish history of effect is consistent with this line of conjecture. Whether or not vv. 9f are properly classified as midrash, the main issue is that the text which is being interpreted looks more like a parody of the Jewish use of Psalm 68 than Psalm 68 itself. It is as if the writer had been saying, 'If you claim Psalm 68 for purposes of celebrating the giving of the Torah to Israel, even at the expense of the psalm's original wording, we, as Christ followers, reserve the right to emulate that. The difference is that we

---

[37] Eph. 2:11ff; 4:25ff; 5:14.
[38] Moritz, *A Profound Mystery*, pp. 97–116.

would apply the psalm to Christ's giving of spiritual gifts to his people, not the giving of the Law to Israel.'

Far from simply being a Christocentric reading of the psalm itself,[39] Eph. 4:8–10 more likely represents a deliberate broadside against Jewish Torah celebrations. In the light of Eph. 2:13–17 this would not be surprising. It was on the cross that Christ brought the Mosaic Torah to its goal and end. The strong language employed in ch. 2 leaves little to the imagination. The implied audience – whether God-fearing or Jewish Christian – needed reminding that the Mosaic Torah had no normative place in the Christ covenant which was sealed on the cross. Judaism (and Christian Judaizers!), the implied argument goes, may continue to celebrate Torah as God's great gift to his people. But, as emphasized in Ephesians, the gift that really matters is precisely not the Law of Moses, but Christ and the spiritual gifts which he poured out for the church at his 'descent' at Pentecost. Jewish Pentecost may have been turned into a Torah commemoration with the help of a necessarily radical rereading of Psalm 68, but the real story has decisively moved on to the point of Christ's pouring out of the Spirit. To emphasize this very point, at least some early Christians poignantly emulated the Jewish reinterpretation of the psalm. Ephesians, in turn, quotes this Christian parody of the Jewish use of Psalm 68 and appends an exposition which shows the benefits for God's people of the one who truly is God's greatest gift, his son Jesus Christ. He not only gave himself, he ascended to make available the spiritual gifts which his people needed. These gifts are listed and discussed in vv. 11–16 in ways which underline the implication that they truly are superior to what the Mosaic Law was able to achieve for God's people. After all, it was Christ who ascended above the heavens and who is seated next to the Father (1:20). And it is Christ in whom all wisdom is revealed (3:9), a claim reserved in Jewish circles for the Mosaic Law.[40]

The reasoning and method in Ephesians at this point is remarkably reminiscent of Rom. 10:4ff, including the ascension theme. It would take us too far afield to enter into the authorship debate surrounding Ephesians. Suffice to say that the use of Old Testament material, however indirectly mediated, in Eph. 4:8–10 is fairly close to that in Romans 10, even to the point of implied polemics against Torah observant Christian Judaizers.[41] Both cases involve appeals to Old Testament material – in the one case abbreviated by Paul, in the other mediated via early Christian polemics. Both appeals would have been found by many to depart from the original locution, but both were necessary if the author was going to make the case for Christ as the superior

---

[39] As G.B. Caird, 'The Descent of Christ in Eph. 4,7–11', *Studia Evangelica II* (1964), p. 543 would have us believe.

[40] Cf. *Shab.* 88b among numerous other texts.

[41] Note the deliberate and calculated omission of the phrase 'that you may observe it' from the quotation from Dent. 30:14 in Rom. 10:8.

gift. The underlying Old Testament texts are so well known that Paul must have expected that his departure from the Old Testament text would have been noticed. Indeed, that was a crucial ingredient in the intended speech act as described above. The rhetorical logic is not dissimilar to those parables which rely on surprise as a major hermeneutical factor. The added element here is that the polemic of Ephesians is achieved by emulating the perceived special pleading involved in the annual Jewish Pentecostal appropriations of Psalm 68.

The Exposition in 4:9f

What about the exposition in vv. 9f? There are three key elements. The first of these is the 'filling' theme. Since this fulfilment theme is not directly related to the use of the psalm, no further discussion is required at this point.

The second key notion is that of 'ascension'. This is a well-known feature from Jewish sources. Especially noteworthy are those texts where the theme is linked to the giving of Torah. Compared to these texts, the unique feature we find in Ephesians is the inference of the descent from the ascent. There are Jewish texts which similarly infer such a descent from the ascent mentioned in Psalm 68.[42] It is precisely this implication which makes possible any use of this psalm as part of the Jewish Pentecost festival. Ephesians seizes upon this implication and applies it to Christ's movement in incarnation and ascension. As elsewhere in early Christianity, the latter is undoubtedly not understood as departure, but as enthronement (Eph. 2:5f – cf. Dan. 7:13 and Ps. 110:1). Caird's proposal,[43] based on von Soden and Abbott, that the descent is a reference to Pentecost is attractive, but not ultimately convincing. If the descent followed the ascent, how can it necessarily be inferred from the latter? The question is not whether Ephesians 4 has Pentecost in mind – it undoubtedly does. But the pouring out of the spiritual gifts is a distinct step after the ascension, which in turn follows the initial descent. The point of 4:9f is to remind the implied Christian audience of their common descent-ascent Christology,[44] but to do so in a way which tacitly brings out Christ's superiority over the Law of Moses. This is done not by interpreting Psalm 68 itself, but by utilizing an early Christian tradition which polemically emulates the Jewish reinterpretation of Psalm 68 in the context of Jewish Pentecost. Christ's superiority is ultimately demonstrated by his pouring out of the Spirit from a position which only God himself could occupy. Pentecost became

---

[42] A noteworthy example is *Excd. R.* 28:1. Cf. A. Segal, 'Heavenly Ascent in Hellenistic Judaism, Early Christianity and their Environment', *ANRW* 23.2 (1980), pp. 1352–68. Lincoln's point that a prior descent has the advantage of following the order of YHWH's movement in the psalm ignores that it is the people's representatives' movement (ascent, presumably followed by descent) that inspired the Jewish use of this psalm as part of Pentecostal Torah celebrations. Cf. A. Lincoln, *Paradise Now and Not Yet* (Cambridge: Cambridge University Press, 1981), p. 160.

[43] Caird, 'Descent', pp. 537ff.

[44] Acts 2:23f; Jn 3:13, 6:33–62 and 20:17.

possible precisely because of the ascension which it validates.[45] The Mosaic Law, important as it was, descended with Moses from the mountain – a descent which was not followed by an ascension.

Thirdly and finally, 4:9f celebrate the subjection of the powers. Once again, the link with 1:21f is obvious. Noticeably both texts use motifs from the Psalms to express the subjugation of the evil powers under Christ. Like Psalms 110 and 8, Ps. 68:19–22 also expresses the defeat of the enemies. The difference is that in this particular psalm the subjection of the powers is not a matter of future expectation – it has already been achieved. This fits well with the more realized aspects of the eschatology of Ephesians. Having led captivity captive (v. 8), as evidenced in his ascension/enthronement (v. 9), Christ proceeds to 'fill all things' (v. 10) by giving gifts to his followers (v. 11). It is in this sense that the church proves to be 'His body, the fullness of him who fills all in all'. The two major passages in Ephesians which employ language from the Psalms are evidently closely connected and throw significant light onto each other.

---

[45] This is different from saying that Pentecost is a necessary consequence of the ascension, something Ephesians does not claim. Such a claim would be implicit if Caird's understanding of the movement sequence were correct.

10

The Psalms in Hebrews

Harold W. Attridge

Introduction

The Epistle to the Hebrews resonates with the Psalms.[1] The text, neither an epistle, nor to Hebrews,[2] is an elaborate early Christian homily, probably composed sometime in the last third of the first century, to encourage a community to remain faithful to its commitments. To achieve this aim, Hebrews paints an elaborate portrait of Christ as the true high priest, whose death had two significant consequences. As the antitype of the Yom Kippur ritual, it effected expiation of sins. It also fulfilled Jeremiah's prediction (Jeremiah 31) of a new covenant.[3] Despite the elaborate imagery that draws on Jewish apocalyptic traditions and conventional Platonism, the fundamental thrust of Hebrews is to sketch a Christian virtue ethic by focusing on the ultimate paradigm of commitment to God. Christ's willing acceptance of God's will earned him his seat at God's right hand and showed his followers what they must do as fellow heirs of the promised covenant.

The Structural Significance of Psalm 110

Citation of authoritative texts plays a vital role in the programme of Hebrews. The most important is undoubtedly Psalm 110, which appears, either explicitly or by allusion, some more than a dozen times in the text. The homily focuses on two verses. The first, Ps. 110:1, appears as a *Leitmotif* signalling the Son's exaltation. The climax of the exordium alludes to it ('he took a seat at the right hand of the Majesty on high', 1:3). It appears again as an explicit citation at the end of the scriptural catena in ch. 1 ('Sit at my right hand until I make your enemies a footstool for your feet', 1:13). Allusions appear again at 8:1, explicitly styled as a summary (κεφάλαιον) of what preceded, and at 10:12, another summary paragraph that recapitulates the

---

[1]   For earlier literature, see Simon J. Kistemaker, *The Psalm Citations in the Epistle to the Hebrews* (Amsterdam: Van Soest, 1961).

[2]   On the introductory issues, see Harold W. Attridge, *Hebrews: A Commentary on the Epistle to the Hebrews* (Hermeneia; Philadelphia: Fortress Press, 1989), pp. 1–13, and more recently, Craig Koester, *Hebrews* (AB 36; Garden City: Doubleday, 2001), pp. 41–53. For a 'socio-rhetorical' perspective, see David A. deSilva, *Perseverance in Gratitude: A Socio-Rhetorical Commentary* (Grand Rapids: Eerdmans, 2000).

[3]   The same prediction appears in the Dead Sea Scrolls: cf. 1QS i 8, v 8; CD iii 12–14.

exposition of the Yom Kippur and covenant motifs in chs 8–10. The allusion to Ps. 110:1 at 10:12 in fact serves as an *inclusio*, framing the discussion of the two crucial themes of atonement and covenant. The final allusion to Ps. 110:1 and the 'session' motif appears at 12:2 ('having endured the cross, despising its shame, he took a seat at the right hand of the throne of God'), part of the introduction to the final paraenetic section of the text, where the homilist draws practical implications for living in a covenant inaugurated by the atoning sacrifice of the great High Priest.

The prominence of Ps. 110:1 in these structurally significant positions is hardly surprising, given the extensive use of the psalm by early Christians to express their belief that the exalted Jesus had triumphed over death.[4] Hebrews stands squarely in that tradition but innovates by appealing to Ps. 110: 4, which promises an eternal priesthood 'after the order of Melchizedek'.

Uses of Ps. 110:4 are clustered in chs 5–7.[5] The first is an explicit citation at Heb. 5:6, in conjunction with Ps. 2:7 ('you are my son, today I have begotten you'), which had previously appeared in the scriptural catena at 1:5. By juxtaposing the two verses the homilist connects the major christological themes of sonship and priesthood.[6] The text will develop that connection through the exposition of the Yom Kippur typology. First, however, the homilist must ground his claim that Christ is indeed a 'high priest', Ps. 110:4 is the lynchpin to the argument. If Ps. 110:1 is generally understood to be a word of God addressed to the Son, then the continuation of that divine address in v. 4 must also address the Son. If so, then the Son is a 'priest', but a peculiar kind of priest, one 'according to the order of Melchizedek'.

Exploration of that theme is apparently an innovation by our homilist. The hortatory interlude of 5:11–6:20 delays the novel exegesis, while repeated allusions to Ps. 110:4 at 5:10 and 6:20 remind the audience that the claim of a 'priesthood after the order of Melchizedek' is at the centre of the argument.

Chapter 7 develops the claim. To liken the addressee of Psalm 110 to Melchizedek is in effect to attribute to him an eternal priesthood, superior to that of the descendants of Abraham and Levi. The admittedly playful (Heb. 7:9) details of the argument finally hinge on fundamental convictions about the ultimate significance of Christ. Much has been written on the chapter and on the significance of the comparison with Melchizedek.[7] The author studiously

---

[4]   In this sense, see Acts 2:34–35; Rom. 8:34; 1 Cor. 15:25; Eph. 1:20; Col. 3:1. A different use appears at Matt. 22:44; Mk 12:36; Lk. 20:42. See David Hay, *Glory at the Right Hand: Psalm 110 in Early Christianity* (SBLMS 18; Nashville: Abingdon, 1973).

[5]   Cf. 5:6, 10; 6:20; 7:3, 11, 15, 17, 21.

[6]   See William Loader, *Sohn und Hoherpriester: Eine traditionsgeschichtliche Untersuchung zur Christologie des Hebräerbriefes* (WMANT 53; Neukirchen: Neukirchener, 1981).

[7]   See Fred L. Horton, *The Melchizedek Tradition: A Critical Examination of the Sources to the Fifth Century A.D. and in the Epistle to the Hebrews* (SNTSMS 30; Cambridge: Cambridge University Press, 1976). See also Attridge, *Hebrews*, pp. 192–95; Koester, *Hebrews*, p. 345, n. 207.

avoids any direct claims about the mysterious figure of Psalm 110 and Genesis 14. How much he assumed from traditions about Melchizedek as a heavenly or eschatological figure[8] is unclear. What is important for his argument is the absence of information in scripture about Melchizedek's earthly connections and positive details about his relationship to Abraham.

Ps. 110:4 bears even more weight. The evidence of scripture enables the author to override, however archly, the problem of the non-priestly lineage of Jesus (Heb. 7:13). The claim, built on the verse, about the Son's heavenly and 'eternal' priesthood also establishes a foundation for the ironic play on the Platonic associations of what is 'heavenly' and 'eternal' that takes place in ch. 10.[9]

Psalm 110, therefore, is a critical text for Hebrews, providing elements of the surface structure of the homily and leverage for the conceptual claims that undergird the text's Christology.

The Psalms in Argument

A Scriptural Catena Celebrating the Eternal and Exalted Son

While Psalm 110 is crucial for the literary and conceptual structure of the homily, other psalms play significant roles in making the text's persuasive case. The text begins with a catena or florilegium of scriptural quotations, in which the Psalms play a major role. The role of Psalm 110 in introducing the catena and providing its climax has already been noted. Five other verses from the Psalms appear in the collection, scoring significant points about the Son. Ostensibly arguing, in good epideictic fashion, that the Son is greater than the angels, the homilist selects texts with care to depict the glorious status of the Son of God, now enthroned at God's right hand.

The first is Ps. 2:7 ('you are my beloved Son, today I have begotten you'), cited as the voice of God at Heb. 1:5. The verse is linked, with the logical πάλιν, 'again',[10] to 2 Sam. 7:14 (= 1 Chron. 17:13). The two verses appear in tandem in the Dead Sea Scrolls (4QFlor 1:10–19) and their association was probably a traditional bit of Messianic proof-texting.

In the psalm, the person of the king expresses confidence in Yahweh's protection. The nations may conspire and the peoples plot, but the one who sits in the heavens laughs at them and terrifies them with his wrath. In painting this reassuring picture of divine patronage, the psalmist cites the 'decree of the

---

[8] This image is particularly true of the Qumran fragment, especially 11QMelch. For that text, related fragments, and discussion see Paul Kobelski, *Melchizedek and Melchiresa* (CBQMS 10; Washington, DC: Catholic Biblical Association, 1981).

[9] Debates about the 'Platonism' of Hebrews continue, but usually miss the rhetorical playfulness with which Hebrews handles terms with philosophical connotations. See Attridge, *Hebrews*, pp. 267–67.

[10] Cf. 1:6, 2:13 and 4:5.

Lord' that elevated him to royal status. Like the prophecy of Nathan in 2 Sam. 7:14, the text reflects ancient royal ideology that the king was a 'son of God' made such by his royal installation, a metaphorical 'begetting'.

Early Christians used the verse widely to express their understanding of the significance of Jesus. The earliest allusion to the verse is Paul's solemn introduction of himself and his gospel in Rom. 1:1–7. The good news, says Paul, pre-announced by the prophets, was about God's son, a descendant of David according to the flesh, but one 'designated Son of God in power by the spirit of holiness from the resurrection of the dead' (Rom. 1:4). Paul's expression focuses on the eschatological event of Christ's exaltation as the defining moment of his sonship. Acts 13:33–34, depicting Paul in the synagogue of Pisidian Antioch, shares the Christology of Rom. 1:4. Invited to give a homily,[11] the apostle recounts salvation history culminating in the death and resurrection of Christ, an event promised by 'the second psalm'.

While Rom. 1:4 and Acts 13 both seem to understand Christ's exaltation as the inauguration of his divine sonship, other early Christians understand Christ's sonship as either inaugurated or manifested earlier in his career. The accounts of his baptism in the Synoptic Gospels all report a divine voice from heaven announcing the sonship of Jesus.[12] All probably allude to Ps. 2:7. Mark and Luke[13] make the allusion more transparent by having the divine voice address Jesus directly, while in Matthew the voice addresses the crowd and refers to Jesus in the third person. While the differences among the Synoptics reveal interesting christological nuances,[14] all point to an application of Ps. 2:7 to Jesus at a point prior to his resurrection. The Matthean and Lukan infancy narratives suggest that the divine sonship is not a metaphorical 'begetting' of the royal Son, but has to do with the virginal conception of Jesus,[15] although they do not explicitly cite the psalm.

Whether Hebrews shares the eschatological perspective of Paul and Acts or understands the divine sonship of Jesus in another context is a disputed point. The tradition of citing Ps. 2:7 in connection with Christ's exaltation points in one direction. The cosmic perspective of the prologue of Hebrews points in another direction. The problem will become clearer as the catena progresses.

Ps. 2:7 appears again at Heb. 5:5, linking the theme of Christ's sonship to the claim that he is a priest. However Hebrews understands the claim, it insists on the fundamental importance of Christ's sonship. The ambiguities in what

---

[11] The term used at Acts 13:15 is λόγος παρακλήσεως, 'word of encouragement', also used as a self-description at Heb. 13:22.

[12] Matt. 3:16–17; Mk 1:10–11; Lk. 3:21–22.

[13] The Western text (D) of Lk. 3:22 makes the allusion to Ps. 2:7 explicit by adding 'Today I have begotten you.' A few later cursives (1574 pc) bring the text into conformity to Matthew's third person form.

[14] In Mark, the revelation of Jesus' Messianic status seems to be a private affair, seen and heard by Jesus alone.

[15] Matt. 1:23, citing Isa. 7:14; and Lk. 1:30–33.

follows in the catena may be gestures to various ways of conceiving that status. What the homilist wants to add is his own reflection on the priestly character of the Son.

The catena continues in Heb. 1:6 with the citation of a verse that echoes Ps. 97:7, 'Worship Him, all His angels' (LXX: προσκυνήσατε αὐτῷ πάντες οἱ ἄγγελοι θεοῦ) and the Song of Moses at Deut. 32:43 (LXX) 'Let all the sons of God worship Him' (προσκυνησάτωσαν αὐτῷ πάντες υἱοὶ θεοῦ). Like the latter, Hebrews uses the third person imperative; like the former, it directs the address to 'angels' rather than 'sons' of God. The closest parallel to the citation in Hebrews is found in the psalter appended to Codex Alexandrinus (καὶ προσκυνησάτωσαν αὐτῷ πάντες οἱ ἄγγελοι θεου), suggesting a possible dependence of Hebrews on a Greek psalter.[16] The citation, in any case, clearly displays the tendency of the Greek translation of Ps. 97:7. The original psalm celebrated the majesty of the divine kingship and describes a terrifying theophany (Ps. 97:1–5). It then records the response, first of the heavens (v. 6), then of idolaters, and of their gods (v. 7). The Greek has construed an indicative (השתחוו) as an imperative, and understood the original psalm's reference to 'gods' (אלהים), to be to the angelic hosts. The author of Hebrews presumes that reading and adds his own twist, the construal of the pronoun 'him' to be the Son, not Yahweh.

The introduction, 'Again, when he introduces the firstborn into the world, he says', raises in an acute form the temporal reference of the action envisioned in the catena. Some commentators have construed the whole catena as a consistent reference to the exaltation.[17] If so, then the 'world' (οἰκουμένη) is the heavenly world, or perhaps the 'world to come' (cf. 2:5). Alternatively, the verse alludes to the incarnation, and perhaps to traditions like that of Lk. 2:13–14 that describe angelic song at the Messiah's birth. Given the high christological perspective of the exordium of Hebrews, the latter possibility seems the more likely. If so, then the author has probably adapted a collection of some psalm texts used as testimonies for Christ's exaltation, expanded and reinterpreted them in the light of his own christological framework.

Two more citations from the Psalms follow, providing more evidence for the Son's superiority to angels. The first citation is Ps. 104:4, with a minor variation from our Greek witnesses.[18] The psalm praises the work of the Creator by describing the marvels of the natural order. This verse described how God made winds and flame his servants.[19] Our homilist quite

---

[16] On the form of the citation and its use in other liturgical contexts, see Kenneth J. Thomas, 'Old Testament Citations in Hebrews', *NTS* 11 (1964–65), p. 304; Kistemaker, *Psalm Citations*, p. 22. On a Greek psalter as possible source, see Friedrich Schröger, *Der Verfasser des Hebräerbriefes als Schriftausleger* (BU 4; Regensburg: Pustet, 1968), p. 49.

[17] For literature, see Attridge, *Hebrews*, pp. 54–55.

[18] Hebrews reads πυρὸς φλόγα instead of πῦρ φλέγον, perhaps reflecting liturgical language, as Kistemaker, *Psalm Citations*, p. 23, suggests.

[19] The verse perhaps alludes to passages such as Exod. 3:2; 13:21; Job 40:6.

reasonably[20] hints at an alternative construal of the syntax. The psalm then is taken to say that God has made his messengers and servants to be mere elements of the created order. The verse serves as a foil for the next citation, another address to the Son. Heb. 1:8 derives from another royal psalm (45:7–8), a celebration of a royal marriage. The verses first selected praise symbols of royal authority, the throne and sceptre. They proceed to hymn the king's virtue, suggesting that it was for such qualities that Yahweh anointed him. All of this, says our author, is directed at (πρός)[21] the Son.

Psalm 45 at the very least offers evidence of the superiority of the addressee, anointed with the 'oil of gladness beyond your fellows'. In the argument of the chapter, they must be 'angels' rather than the other candidates for kingship or other royal personages envisioned by the original psalmist. Yet the psalm offers more.

The most significant contribution rests on syntactic ambiguity in its reference to God. It is possible to construe the whole citation, in the light of its original sense, as a description of the king's majesty. Hence, the first verse (ὁ θρόνος σου ὁ θεὸς εἰς τὸν αἰῶνα τοῦ αἰῶνος) would offer a bold assertion that God functions as the king's throne. The second verse (διὰ τοῦτο ἔχρισέν σε ὁ θεὸς ὁ θεός σου) would involve a mere apposition, 'God, your God, has anointed you'. Another construal of the syntax is possible. The nominative form ὁ θεός could be used as a vocative, as is frequent in the LXX and New Testament.[22] In fact, there is evidence in Jewish tradition that the reference to God was so construed.[23]

If there is any doubt that our homilist wants to have Ps. 45:7–8 construed as an address to the Son as θεός, the next citation, from Ps. 102:27–29, dispels that doubt. The poem's lament contrasts the pitiable condition of the psalmist, whose 'days pass away like smoke' and whose 'bones burn like a furnace' with the Lord who 'remains forever',[24] whom the psalmist begs for assistance. In construing the addressee of the psalm as the Son, Hebrews relocates the affirmations once made about Yahweh's majesty. Four elements in the citation are important in the overall context of Hebrews. The citation initially (Heb.

---

[20] The definite nouns τοὺς ἀγγέλους αὐτου and τοὺς λειτουργοὺς αὐτου would normally be construed as first objects and the indefinite πνεύματα and πυρὸς φλόγα as second or predicate accusatives.

[21] There is some ambiguity in the preposition, which could be construed to mean 'about'. Such a construal is possible for the parallel in v. 7, but difficult in v. 13, where the preposition clearly involves a direct address to the Son (Ps. 110:1). The citations in vv. 8–12 all involve a second-person addressee. The introductory comment highlights that fact, while it identifies the addressee.

[22] Cf., e.g., Ps. 2:8; 5:11; 7:2; 40:9, cited in Heb. 10:7; and in the NT Mk 15:34; Lk. 18:11, Jn 20:28; Rev. 4:11; 11:17; 16:7.

[23] For the targum on the psalm, see Attridge, *Hebrews*, p. 58, n. 93.

[24] The MT reads 'But you, O Lord, *are enthroned* forever'. If the Greek had translated literally, one might have suspected a catch-word association between this psalm and Ps. 44 (LXX), cited in the previous verses of the catena.

1:10: 'In the beginning, Lord, you founded the earth') evokes the affirmation of the exordium that the Son was the instrument of God's creation (Heb. 1:2). It continues by contrasting the transitory character of creation with the Son's abiding character (Heb. 1:11: 'they will perish but you will remain'). The eternal quality of the Son as high priest will constitute a major part of what it means to be 'in the order of Melchizedek'.[25] By contrast, the ephemeral character of creation that will be 'rolled up' like a cloak and 'changed', foreshadows the allusions to eschatological transformation that will sound more loudly as the text reaches its conclusion.[26] Finally, the acclamation in v. 12 that the Lord addressed in the psalm remains always 'the same' (ὁ αὐτὸς) will re-echo in the final solemn declaration that Jesus Christ is 'the same, yesterday, today and forever' (Heb. 13:8).

The homilist concludes the catena (Heb. 1:13), as already noted, by citing Psalm 110. The citation seems almost anticlimactic, given the dazzling christological readings of the two previous psalm citations. Yet in addition to sounding its note of heavenly session, important for the homily's overall structure, the second clause, 'until I make your enemies a footstool for your feet', plays a role in the immediate context. By introducing a note of opposition to the Son, it sets the stage for the next chapter and a new christological play on the psalms, focusing on the suffering Son.

Whatever the traditional inspiration for this collection of scriptural testimonies among messianic florilegia, our homilist has carefully chosen his texts to highlight elements of his own christological portrait. The catena, in demonstrating the superiority of Christ to the angels paints a portrait of the eternal Son, who bears the imprint of God's own fundamental reality.

A Psalmodic Reminder of the Son's Suffering

The first two chapters of Hebrews offer a reflection on Christology in the form of a diptych, hinged on the first of the text's warnings (Heb. 2:1–4). While the initial focus was on the exalted or heavenly character of the Son, attention now shifts to his very human suffering and death. As in the initial half of the diptych, the Psalms again play a major role in ch. 2.[27]

The key text is Ps. 8:5–7, cited in Heb. 2:6–8. The homilist follows the text of the LXX closely, with the omission of one clause 'you have set him over the works of your hands'.

This psalm of praise offers joyful thanks for the graciousness of the Creator. In contrast to the majesty of creation, asks the psalmist, of what significance is

---

[25] Cf. 7:24–25, as well as the image of entering the eternal realm in Heb. 9:23–24.

[26] Cf. 10:30–31; 12:26–27.

[27] For a recent treatment, see C.P. März, "'...nur für kurze Zeit unter die Engel gestellt" (Hebr 2,7): Anthropologie und Christologie in Hebr 2,5–9', in E. Coreth, ed., *Von Gott Reden in säkularer Gesellschaft. Festschrift für Konrad Feiereis zum 65. Geburtstag* (Leipzig: Benno, 1996), pp. 29–42.

humankind? His answer notes the position of authority within the created order that Yahweh has given to humankind: a little lower than the angels, crowned with honour and glory and sovereign over all creation.

Our homilist picks up the notion of sovereignty, and, ostensibly continuing the argument about the superiority of the Son to angels,[28] asks who it is to whom God has subjected the 'world to come'. When the question is posed in that way, the answer is almost inevitable, but getting to 'Jesus' requires several exegetical moves. While exegesis in the catena of ch. 1 was implicit, it is here explicit, and the verses immediately following the citation of the psalm constitute a brief midrash on the text.

The homilist begins by contrasting the affirmation of the text that 'you have subjected all things under his feet' with experience. 'We see,' he says, that all things have not been subjected to 'him'. The antecedent of the pronoun is clearly the pair of nominal elements of the first two clauses: 'What[29] is *man* that you remember him, or the *son of man* that you should watch over him?' In the psalm, the phrases in synonymous parallelism clearly refer to all of humankind.[30] The fact that the words, and the pronouns referring to them, are singular in number, allows for the possibility of another reading.[31]

The homilist does not elaborate on the observation that all things have not been subjected. It is possible that he is reflecting on the fact that all things are not subjected to human beings generally. Wind, wave and wild beast indeed do not obey mankind. Yet of equal importance is the testimony of scripture. Ps. 110:1, cited at Heb. 1:13, had asked the Son to be seated until God put all under his feet. It may have been the verbal similarity between that verse and Ps. 8:7 that led the homilist to associate them. In any case, the 'him' to whom all things have not been subjected will soon be identified as Jesus.

Verse 9 provides new data from the homilist's experience, what he has seen with the eyes of faith. The homilist wraps this experience in the terms of the psalm, construed in a fashion different from the obvious meaning of the original text. This move offers a new christological reading to the psalm, reminiscent of the first chapter.

The psalm originally presented a static tableau, an image of humankind at an exalted place in the created order, only a bit lower than heavenly beings, above

---

[28] The reference to 'angels', serving as a link to the immediate context, depends upon the Greek translation of the Hebrew *elohim*.

[29] Some mss of Hebrews read τις, 'who' rather than τι, 'what', probably understanding the phrase 'Son of Man' as a christological title. For a similar question, cf. Matt. 16:13.

[30] Some exegetes have been tempted to find here some play on the 'Son of Man' title used widely of Jesus in the Synoptic Gospels. If the audience knows that title, the christological reading of the psalm would have even more resonance.

[31] This element of the exegetical play becomes obscure in the NRSV: 'What are human beings that you are mindful of them, or mortals, that you care for them'. The translation, both for the original psalm and Hebrews, eliminates a potential source of gender offence but obscures the christological exegesis of Heb. 2:8–9.

all things earthly. Our homilist instead drives a wedge between the two parallel affirmations 'you have made him a little less than the angels' 'with glory and honor you have crowned him'. Instead, he reads these affirmations as two temporally discrete stages in the history of the Son. Being made lower than the angels was only for a 'little while'[32] and had a salvific function, 'that, by God's grace,[33] he might taste death for everyone'. Being crowned with 'glory and honour' now describes not a position in the created order but the Son's post-mortem exaltation.

In our homilist's hands Psalm 8 offers not a reflection on humanity, but a portrait of the Son, now not in heavenly glory, but in subjection, suffering death for the benefit of others. The following verses (Heb. 2:10–18) continue to reflect on the salvific work of the Son, using another text from the Psalms, but that usage is part of a larger pattern that merits separate attention.[34]

A Psalmist's Call to Fidelity

Hebrews grounds its appeal for renewed fidelity to the covenant community in a vision of the reality that shaped the community, the action of Christ as High Priest. The first four chapters of the text replicate *in nuce* the overall strategy of the whole work. The first two chapters, deftly using texts from the Psalms, depicted the exalted Son who made low for the sake of his brethren. The next section, Heb. 3:1–4:13, offers a preliminary appeal, foreshadowing the elaborate summons to 'faith' in chs 11 and 12. The appeal to fidelity does so using Psalm 95, cited at Heb. 3:7–11.

The appeal takes the form of a well-rounded exegetical homily within the larger homiletic context of Hebrews. The homily opens with an introduction (Heb. 3:1–6) to the theme, comparing Moses and Christ as examples of fidelity. This introduction also integrates the homily on Psalm 95 into the larger programme of the text, with its series of *synkriseis*, or comparisons, typical of encomiastic rhetoric.[35] Following the exordium, the homilist (3:7–11) cites the text, Ps. 95:7–11, on which the exhortation is based. There follow three exegetical comments, each focused on a verse of the psalm: 3:12–19, focusing on the citation of v. 7 (Heb. 3:15); 4:1–5, focusing on v. 11 (Heb. 4:3), and 4:6–10, focusing again on v. 7 (Heb. 4:7). Exegesis culminates in exhortation, 'Let us strive to enter the rest' (Heb. 4:11). A festive reflection on the power of God's living and active word (4:12–13) functions as a postlude.

The text of the psalm is, as normal in Hebrews, from a Greek translation. The most significant difference from the Hebrew is the etymological translation

---

[32] There is no change in the Greek expression βραχύ in v. 7 and v. 9. The diachronic reading of subjection and exaltation in v. 9 forces a temporal construal of the adverb.

[33] On the variant, 'apart from God', see Attridge, *Hebrews*, p. 69, n. 5.

[34] See the final section of this chapter.

[35] The comparisons are: Christ and the angels, chs 1–2; Christ and Moses, 3:1–6; Christ and Joshua, 4:8; Christ and ordinary high priests, 4:14–7:28.

of the place names Meribah and Massah as adverbial phrases: 'in the rebellion' (ἐν τῷ παραπικρασμῷ) and 'with scrutiny' (ἐν δοκιμασίᾳ). There are, however, several minor deviations from the LXX.[36] These may simply be due to the manuscript tradition available to our homilist, although it is possible that he is responsible for the association in vv. 9–10 of 'forty years' with the rebellion of the Exodus generation rather than with the divine anger.

The psalm as a whole is a song of thanksgiving, calling upon the congregation to 'make a joyful noise to the rock of our salvation' (Ps. 95:1). It proceeds to celebrate the kingship of God (vv. 3–5) and summons the congregation to worship (vv. 6–7). It concludes with a note of warning. The congregation is urged to avoid the negative example of the Exodus generation, when God, enraged at the way the Israelites tested him, swore that they would not enter 'my rest'.

By the first century, the psalmist's exhortation had become a homiletic commonplace. Another prominent example is found in 1 Cor. 10:1–22, where Paul uses the desert generation as a negative example of the idolatry which the Corinthians should avoid.[37] In issuing that warning, he reads the sacramental experience of his congregation into the biblical story and finds in the biblical account 'types' (1 Cor. 10:6, 11) of contemporary behaviour.

The homilist of Hebrews adopts a more complex exegetical strategy to actualize the text. Each portion of his exposition introduces another scriptural passage and uses a variety of appeals to the addressees. He begins by identifying the problem that the psalmist has in mind as 'lack of faith' (ἀπιστία, 3:12, 19) and suggests that the psalm calls for a community response to the problem. He calls upon his addressees to offer mutual 'exhortation' (παρακαλεῖτε, 3:13[38]), by repeating the call of the psalm not to harden hearts ('If today you hear his voice do not harden your hearts as in the rebellion', 3:15). To reinforce the appeal he evokes (3:17) the full account of Yahweh's wrathful oath in Num. 14:26–35, in which Yahweh predicts that the dead bodies of the rebellious generation would lie in the desert. A parenthetical phrase at 3:14 encapsulates the parenetic thrust of the exegesis. Being fellows with or 'partakers' in Christ

---

[36] The most significant are (1) the reading ἐν δοκιμασίᾳ, 'by testing', at v. 9, instead of the ἐδοκίμασαν, 'they tested', of the LXX; and (2) the insertion of a particle, διό 'therefore', in v. 10, which leads to the association of 'forty years' with the rebellion of the Israelites and not with the divine wrath. Cf. Num. 14:33. The mss of Hebrews show a tendency to bring the citation into conformity with the LXX. For details, see Attridge, *Hebrews*, p. 113 and A.H. Cadwallader, 'The Correction of the Text of Hebrews towards the LXX', *NovT* 34 (1992), pp. 257–92.

[37] On the two passages see H. Löhr, ' "Heute, wenn ihr seine Stimme hört…" Zur Kunst der Schriftanwendung im Hebräerbrief und in 1 Kor 10', in M. Hengel and H. Löhr, eds, *Schriftauslegung im antiken Judentum und im Urchristentum* (WUNT 73; Tübingen: Mohr/Siebeck, 1994), pp. 226–48.

[38] The verb echoes Hebrews' self-description. See n. 11 above.

(μέτοχοι γὰρ τοῦ Χριστου) is conditional. One must hold fast one fundamental commitment[39] to the end.

The second portion of the exposition insists on the contemporary relevance of the promise of 'rest' in the psalm. In order to make that point, the homilist draws on Gen. 2:2 in a *gezera shawa* argument. The two verses are linked through a common word, which they share only in the Greek Bible. Ps. 95:11 ('As I swore in my wrath, they shall not enter my rest') concluded the divine oath with a reference to 'rest' (κατάπαυσίν μου). The end of the creation account in Genesis (2:2) reported that on the seventh day God 'rested' (κατέπαυσεν). Juxtaposing the two verses (Heb. 4:4–5) the homilist suggests that the 'rest' to which God was referring in the psalm was not the 'resting place' of the land of Canaan, but something more basic, and more transcendent, that place or state into which God himself entered after the work of creation.[40] It is to that goal that a way lies open for the addressees (4:6).

The brief final portion of the homily returns to the same verse featured in the initial segment, the call to hear God's voice today and not harden one's heart (Heb. 4:7). Focusing on 'today' (σήμερον), the homilist insists that the psalm must be referring to his own day, not some day in the past. He argues now on the basis of the assumed Davidic authorship of the Psalms (v. 7), and, since David lived long after Joshua entered the land of Canaan (v. 8), another day must be in view. He finally hints at what that day must be, labelling it a 'Sabbath festivity' (σαββατισμὸς). The argument reinforces the point of the second segment of the exegesis, and draws on the point made there that the 'rest' of the psalm is equivalent to the heavenly 'rest' into which God himself entered at the end of his creative work. The hortatory conclusion then follows naturally, 'Let us enter that rest, so that no one may fall in the same type of disobedience' (Heb. 4:11).

The festive summary on God's 'living and active word' (Heb. 4:12–13) in effect celebrates what the homilist has done in his little homily on Psalm 95. The task was simplified by the fact that the text made a direct appeal to listen and not 'harden the heart'. Yet the relevance of the historical precedent to which the text appealed required clarification. Unlike Paul, who had seen the 'typological' significance of the Exodus in 1 Corinthians 10, the homilist of Hebrews found in the psalm a more direct reference to the eschatological hopes by which his congregation might be moved. Scriptural exegesis, using an intertextual play, enabled him to do so. While he did not define those hopes in

---

[39] The verse uses pregnant phrasing, particularly in τὴν ἀρχὴν τῆς ὑποστάσεω, paraphrased here as 'fundamental commitment'. For the complex associations of the phrase, see Attridge, *Hebrews*, pp. 117–18.

[40] For a recent treatment, see Judith Hoch Wray, *Rest as a Theological Metaphor in the Epistle to the Hebrews and the Gospel of Truth: Early Christian Homiletics of Rest* (SBLDS 166; Atlanta: Scholars Press, 1998).

detail, his allusive play on the divine Sabbath rest was apparently enough to evoke what his addressees expected from God.

The Psalms as the Voice of Jesus and his Followers

The treatment of Psalm 95 indicates the efforts of our homilist to enable his addressees to encounter the vital presence of God's word in the text of scripture. One further use of the Psalms in Hebrews takes the 'actualizing' project to a new and distinctive level. In this device, the Psalms give voice to the aims and aspirations of Jesus himself, in a dialogue with the God who made him High Priest. That prayerful exchange, which perhaps evokes a liturgical practice of antiphonal recitation of the Psalms, embraces all of the sons and daughters who follow in the covenantal footsteps of the Son.

The initial verses of Hebrews prepared the way for this dialogue, with the focus on God's speech, in manifold ways of old and finally through a Son (Heb. 1:1–2). The homilist introduces the catena of scriptural citations at 1:5 by asking whether God had ever spoken to one of the angels as he did to the Son in Psalm 2. The catena ends as it began, with God speaking to the Son, this time in the words of Ps. 110:1 at Heb. 1:13. Such an address deserves a response and the Son finally gives one in ch. 2.[41] That is the first of two clusters of sayings through which the Son finally speaks to God and to the audience. Appropriately enough, in each case he speaks the words of scripture.

The Son's response in ch. 2 continues the reflection on his suffering and death which began with the exegesis of Psalm 8 (Heb. 2:5–9). In what follows (Heb. 2:10–18) the homilist considers the soteriological significance of the Son's death, as the act by which he was 'perfected' and made a model suitable to lead other children of God to heavenly glory (Heb. 2:10). In order to show the solidarity between the one Son and his siblings, the homilist cites three brief statements of the Son. The first (Heb. 2:12) derives from Ps. 22:23, a key text in the passion narratives (cf. Mk 15:24, 34 and parr.). The second and third citations both come from contiguous verses in Isaiah (8:17–18), but the formula introducing the third indicates that the two verses are to be construed as independent utterances. The resulting chiastic pattern frames a simple statement 'I will put my trust in him' (Isa. 8:17 at Heb. 2:13), with two characterizations of the 'many children' for whom the Son serves as 'pioneer' or 'forerunner' (ἀρχηγός, 2:10). The first utterance, 'I will proclaim your name to my brothers and sisters; in the midst of the congregation I will praise you' (Ps. 22:23 at Heb. 2:12) establishes the solidarity between the Son and other children, which is the surface argument of the text at this point. It also

---

[41] Pamela M. Eisenbaum, *The Jewish Heroes of Christian History: Hebrews 11 in Literary Context* (SBLDS 156: Atlanta: Scholars Press, 1997), pp. 90–133, calls attention to the use of the Psalms as direct divine speech.

efficiently scores three points significant for the text's theology. It first defines an important element of the Son's work, to proclaim the name of God, emphasizing the text's ultimate focus on God.[42] It also defines the sphere where the response to the proclamation of God's name takes place, the congregation or *ekklesia*, a pregnant term in Hebrews, which will appear again at 12:23 referring to the community of 'firstborn ones' enrolled in heaven. Heb. 2:12 finally describes how the Son responds to God's call: by singing God's praise. The final verse of the triptych, 2:13b from Isa. 8:18, 'Here I am and the children whom God has given me', also scores two points. The actions that Jesus claims for himself in the previous verses are not his alone, but are to be shared with his 'brothers and sisters', who also must trust in God and sing God's praise. Furthermore, those siblings are, like all else in the salvific process, also a gift of God.

The Son's comments here, though framed in the homilist's argument, in effect, answer the divine address of the first chapter. The dialogue and response established in these chapters forms a pattern at work throughout the text. The next instance of such dialogue, in the homiletic midrash of chs 3 and 4 discussed above, reveals a passionate God who appeals to all who hear scripture 'today' not to harden their hearts (Heb. 3:8). The response in that context consists of the homilist's exhortations, echoing the divine call, to take heed (Heb. 3:12; 4:1), exhort one another (3:13), and make bold to accept the promise of divine rest (4:11). As already noted, this exhortation is a preliminary version of the more comprehensive appeal that concludes the text. The one major element that will be added to the appeal is the homilist's high-priestly Christology that is yet to be developed. The homily hints that being committed 'participants' (μέτοχοι) with Christ is the key to achieving the divine promise (Heb. 3:14), but how that 'participation' works remains to be seen.

Chapters 7 to 10 develop the image of the heavenly High Priest, effecting final and permanent atonement for sins by his unique sacrifice. We have already noted the anticipation of that development by the citation of a scriptural verse, Ps. 110:4 at Heb. 5:6. It is noteworthy that the context of that citation echoes the opening of the homily, by referring again to God's speech (5:5, λαλήσας) and by repeating the address to the Son in Ps. 2:7. Like that verse, Ps. 110:4 is construed to be a direct address of God to the Son: 'You are a priest forever according to the order of Melchizedke'. The verse appears to be a performative utterance, the act by which God makes the Son a High Priest. If the words of the initial scriptural catena addressed to the Son merited a response, one might expect that this word of installation would similarly require an answer, but the audience is kept in suspense for some time before hearing it.

---

[42] For emphasis on the point, see David Wider, *Theozentrik und Bekenntnis: Untersuchungen zur Theologie des Redens Gottes im Hebräerbrief* (BZNW 87; Berlin/New York: W. de Gruyter, 1997).

Chapter 7, as already noted, teases out the significance of the Son's priesthood 'after the order of Melchizedek'. Chapters 8–10 describe his priestly act, through a comparison between the death of the Son and the ritual of Yom Kippur. The exposition is a complex play on yet another scriptural text, Jer. 31:31–34, cited at Heb. 8:8–12. The key point for our purposes is to note that the death of Christ is understood to be a covenant-inaugurating sacrifice (Heb. 9:15–31), which fulfills the promise of a new covenant in Jeremiah.[43]

This exposition culminates in a quotation of the Son's words, which ultimately constitute the response to his appointment by God as High Priest at Heb. 5:6. These words also show how Christ's death fulfills the promise of Jeremiah 31, how, that is, God makes a new covenant by inscribing laws onto human hearts. The Son's words in Heb. 10:5–6, similar to his comments in ch. 2, come from Ps. 40:7–9.

As usual, the homilist cites the Greek version, which differs from the Hebrew in two significant details. In Hebrew the second clause reads: 'Ears you have dug for me'. The Greek instead offers what is probably an interpretative paraphrase: 'A body you have prepared for me'. Although the homilist's interpretation of the citation would be possible without that phrase, the connection to the overall exposition depends on the psalm's reference to 'body'. The second detail appears in v. 7, where the Hebrew reads 'in the scroll of the book', while the Greek reads 'in the head of the scroll' (ἐν κεφαλίδι βιβλίου).

The original psalm offers thanks for divine deliverance and a prayer for further assistance against the psalmist's enemies. The verses cited record the psalmist's fidelity, contrasting the externals of 'sacrifice and offering' that God does not desire, with obedience to the divine will. The psalmist declares that he put himself at God's disposal saying (Heb. 10:7) 'Behold, I have come' (ἰδοὺ ἥκω). The obscure parenthetical phrase that follows, 'In the scroll of the book it is written of me' (ἐν κεφαλίδι βιβλίου γέγραπται περὶ ἐμοῦ), makes perfect sense for our homilist, with his conviction that 'the book' of Scripture is replete with allusions to Christ. The passage ends with the indication of the purpose of the speaker's coming, 'to do your will, O God'.

The homilist's exegetical comment (Heb. 10:8–10) draws implications from the opposition of the text. The traditional contrast between external sacrifices and an obedient heart distinguishes the promised new covenant. Of equal importance is the exemplary function of the Son's response to the divine initiative. Just as the Son's earlier words in ch. 2 modelled the kind of behaviour expected of all God's sons and daughters, this final comment of the dutiful, priestly Son models the fidelity that his siblings should exhibit. Crucial

---

[43] For exploration of the themes of covenant and sacrifice, see J. Dunnill, *Covenant and Sacrifice in the Letter to the Hebrews* (SNTSMS 75; Cambridge: Cambridge University Press, 1992).

for the way in which Christ establishes a covenant community in this text is the fact that he functions as a model of the virtue of fidelity.[44]

Hebrews presents Christ as a model of faith, as is abundantly clear from the description of Christ as 'initiator and perfecter of faith' (Heb. 12:1–3). Of equal importance, Christ is a model of one who prays, as is clear from Heb. 5:7: 'In the days of his flesh, Jesus offered up prayers and supplications with loud cries and tears to the one who was able to save him from death, and he was heard because of his reverent submission'. Although an appeal to the Gethsemane stories known from the Synoptic Gospels is unlikely, the passage does evoke in a dramatic way the imagery of faithful prayer in the psalms, in passages such as Ps. 6:5–8: 'Turn, O Lord, save my life: deliver me for the sake of your steadfast love ... I am weary with my moaning; every night I flood my bed with tears; I drench my couch with my weeping'.[45] The crucial point is the inference that Hebrews makes from this allusion to the language of the psalms: that because of his faithful obedience Jesus became 'the source of eternal salvation for all who heed him' (Heb. 5:9). One way in which he so functioned is as a model of faithful prayer. A verse in the concluding admonitions underscores the point. Heb. 13:15 indicates one important consequence of its homiletic advice: 'Through him, then, let us continually offer a sacrifice of praise to God, that is, the fruit of lips that confess his name'.

There is one final way in which our homilist, in a more subtle fashion, makes the point that prayer, indeed, the prayer of the psalms, is the appropriate response of the covenant community. After his remarks at Heb. 10:5–7, the voice of the Son falls silent. Yet the voice of God continues to speak. Speaking in manifold and various ways, it speaks words that threaten judgement (Heb. 10:30), 'Vengeance is mine, I shall repay' (Deut. 32:35), words that console, 'My child, do not regard lightly the discipline of the Lord ...' (Prov. 3:11–12, at Heb. 12:5–6), words of warning, 'Once more I shall shake not only the earth but also the heaven' (Hag. 2:6, 21, at Heb. 12:26), and words of comfort, 'I shall never leave you or forsake you' (Deut. 31:6 and Gen. 28:15, at Heb. 13:5). Although the homilist assures his audience that the blood of Jesus, the mediator of the new covenant, cries out in a better fashion than the blood of Abel (Heb. 12:24), he does not make explicit what Jesus says. The voice of God would seem to be unanswered.

The homilist finally breaks the silence at Heb. 13:6, with something that 'we' make bold (θαρροῦντας ἡμᾶς) to say: Ps. 118:6 'The Lord is my helper; I will

[44] The use of the psalm to express christological convictions may be more widespread. Margaret Daly-Denton, *David in the Fourth Gospel: The Johannine Reception of the Psalms* (AGJU 47; Leiden: Brill, 2000), pp. 252–53, hears echoes of Psalm 40 in the Johannine motif of Jesus as the one sent to do the Father's will.

[45] Cf. also Ps. 116:4–9. The importance of the psalms in this context was long ago highlighted by A. Strobel, 'Die Psalmengrundlage der Gethsemane-Parallele Hebr. 5,7ff', *ZNW* 45 (1954), pp. 252–66.

not be afraid. What can anyone do to me?' By the finale of Hebrews, the followers of Jesus, in the person of the homilist and his audience, have assumed the role of Jesus in his dialogue with God. Their prayer of the psalm is what Heb. 13:15 calls for, an acknowledgement of God. Their prayer affirms their faith in God's fidelity, a faithfulness that trumps all threats of judgement.

Conclusion

Hebrews uses Psalms in many and diverse ways, as a structuring element for the discourse as a whole, articulating its major segments and serving as an essential ingredient in its innovative Christology, as evidence along the way for various contentions that the homilist wants to make about the person and work of Christ and the kind of response required of his followers. Most intriguing is the use of the Psalms to give voice to Jesus. Ironically, the one who delivers the final word of God to the world speaks in Hebrews only in the words of scripture, and principally in the words of the Psalms. In portraying that speech of the Son, Hebrews suggests that it is part of a dialogue of prayer between God and Christ, both of whom address one another in the text with the words of scripture. By the end of the text, the Son has fallen silent, but the dialogue continues as his followers pick up his voice, and reply to the continued voice of God with their own confession of trust in God. Their prayer, appropriately enough, is from the Psalms.

Our homilist is at pains throughout the text to see how the word of God in scripture can speak to the reality of his addressees. Imaginative exegesis helps him along the way to find fresh meaning in old texts, but the crucial move that he makes at the conclusion of his homily is to invite his audience into the world of the Psalms as a world of prayer to make their own, in imitation of the 'initiator and perfecter' of their faith.

11

The Psalms in 1 Peter

Sue Woan

Introduction

Even a casual reader of 1 Peter could hardly fail to be aware of the 'lavish use of OT quotations and allusions'[1] and would not be surprised at W. Schutter's assessment of its dependence on the Old Testament: 'Few early Christian documents incorporate as much of its material in proportion with their size'.[2] In this often overlooked letter there are a considerable number of quotations and allusions to Isaiah, plus occasional citations from other prophetic writings, the Torah and wisdom literature. It is against this background of other Old Testament citations, allusions and echoes that we seek to identify the particular role that the Psalms play within the text of 1 Peter.

Identifying Quotations and Allusions

Much has been written about how to recognize quotations (explicit and implicit) and allusions. Based largely on the approach adopted by M. Thompson[3] and S. Porter,[4] quotations are here defined as those substantial portions of scripture that have been used in the New Testament where there is a more or less exact reproduction of the original text.[5] Those that are introduced by a citation formula are termed explicit quotations, thereby distinguishing them from the implicit quotations, where there is no such formula. Applying these criteria to 1 Peter, explicit quotations from the psalms

---

[1] R. Bauckham, 'James, 1 and 2 Peter, Jude', in D.A. Carson and H.G.M. Williamson, eds, *It Is Written: Scripture Citing Scripture* (Cambridge: Cambridge University Press, 1988), p. 309.

[2] W.L. Schutter, *Hermeneutic and Composition in 1 Peter* (WUNT 2, 30; Tübingen: Mohr-Siebeck, 1989), p. 3.

[3] M. Thompson, *Clothed with Christ* (JSNTSup 59; Sheffield: JSOT Press, 1991), p. 30.

[4] S.E. Porter, 'The Use of the Old Testament in the New: A Brief Comment on Method and Terminology', in C.A. Evans and J.A. Saunders, eds, *Early Christian Interpretation of the Scriptures of Israel* (JSNTSup 148; Sheffield: Sheffield Academic Press, 1997), pp. 79–96.

[5] Most commentators agree that the author of 1 Peter follows the LXX rather than the Hebrew text. Throughout this chapter the psalms will be numbered according to the Hebrew Scriptures and quoted in the NRSV, unless indicated otherwise.

can be seen at 2:7 (Ps. 118:22) and 3:10–12 (Ps. 34:13–17).[6] There are no implicit quotations from the psalms in 1 Peter.[7]

Arriving at a universal set of criteria against which potential allusions can be measured is difficult. Some commentators avoid the issue, preferring to list those verses that owe something of their form and content to a text in the Old Testament.[8] Indeed the dividing line between allusion and echo is often a subjective one, and even within the category of allusion, many different technical terms have been used to denote different types. For example, Schutter coins the terms 'iterative' and 'incipient'; the former he defines as an Old Testament pericope, dependent for its recognition upon 'an exegetical tradition associated with that pericope' – the latter as an instance where 'an Old Testament text, cited elsewhere by the author, is anticipated or resumed'.[9] Thus he ends up with a hierarchy of what he considers to be the most obvious allusions.

On the other hand R. Hays and C. Stanley emphasize the need to have in mind the original hearers of a text, rather than just the perceived exegetical skill of the author. By their criteria it would seem more valuable to attempt to rank all allusions and echoes solely in terms of their blatancy, regardless of how the allusion is effectively making the link in the readers'/hearers' minds between the text and the source.[10]

---

[6] Many commentators regard the presence of διότι περιέχει ἐν γραφῇ ('for it stands in scripture') in 2:6 as also applying to the psalm verse and the γάρ ('for') of 3:10 as acting as an introductory formulae. See P.J. Achtemeier, 1 Peter (Hermeneia; Philadelphia: Fortress Press, 1996), p. 12; E. Best, 1 Peter (London: Oliphants, 1971), p. 28; Bauckham, 'James, 1 and 2 Peter', p. 310; Schutter, Hermeneutic, pp. 36–37.

[7] Commentators generally agree that there are quotations from the Old Testament at: 1:16; 1:24–25a; 2:6,7,8; 3:10–12; 4:18; 5:5b and (implicit) 2:22. See Thompson, Clothed, p. 40; W.A. Grudem, The First Epistle of Peter: An Introduction and Commentary (Tyndale NT Commentaries; Leicester: Inter-Varsity Press, 1988); E. Best, '1 Peter II, 4–10: A Reconsideration', NovT 11 (1969), p. 273. However, there are some variations; P.H. Davids adds 1 Pet. 2:9 as a quotation from Isa. 43:20, Exod. 19:6 and Isa. 43:21, but it more properly should be regarded as a series of allusions (The First Epistle of Peter [Grand Rapids, MI: Eerdmans, 1990], p. 24). Schutter includes 1 Pet. 4:8 on the basis of the presence of ὅτι (Hermeneutic, p. 37). However, I am not convinced that this belongs anywhere other than as a 'significant allusion' – type B, on the grounds of poor replication of the text from Prov. 10:12. Achtemeier, 1 Peter, p. 12 and J.R. Michaels, 1 Peter (WBC 49; Waco: Word Books, 1988), p. xl count only 1:16; 1:24–25; 2:6 and 3:10–12 as true quotations. Michaels then presents an unnamed category of citations that are neither quotations nor allusions. In this latter group he lists 2:3; 2:7–8; 2:22–25; 3:14–15; 4:18 and 5:5b.

[8] Davids, Peter, p. 24 and Best, '1 Peter II, 4–10', pp. 270–93, both take this approach.

[9] Schutter, Hermeneutic, p. 36.

[10] R.B. Hays, Echoes of Scripture in the Letters of Paul (New Haven and London: Yale University Press, 1989), pp. 28–29. Hays develops his own seven 'Hearing Tests'. C.D. Stanley, '"Pearls before Swine": Did Paul's Audience Understand his Biblical Quotations?', NovT 41 (1999), pp. 124–44. This latter article raises important questions about the extent to which Paul's audiences understood the biblical quotations he used.

For the purposes of this study, I consider allusions to be shorter phrases (even single words, if they are particularly unusual, or there are other grounds for thinking that the author has reflected on the passage in mind). Allusions have no introductory formula, tend to appear mid-sentence rather than as a distinct item, and probably refer back to one or more Old Testament sources. They are not usually cited as accurately as quotations (comparisons will be made initially with the LXX) and may require the original reader to have knowledge of the wider context of the Old Testament source (as might quotations), though not all would agree with this. Though scientific objectivity is impossible, I propose the following classification of allusions as a means of broad differentiation.

- Type A – a strong allusion, where there is only one clear contender for the source, which is well replicated in the text (Ps. 34:9 in 1 Pet. 2:3 meets these criteria).
- Type B – a significant allusion, one that is clearly from one Old Testament source, though not well replicated, or one that *is* well replicated, but where two or more texts could have been the source (Ps. 34:14 in 1 Pet. 2:1; Ps. 39:13/Gen. 23:4 in 1 Pet. 2:11; Ps. 118:22 in 1 Pet. 2:4 meet these criteria).
- Type C – a weak allusion, one where given the context and the particular source, it is *more likely than not* that the author had some Old Testament reference, character, theme or event in mind, though there is insufficient evidence to pinpoint the location precisely.[11]

The Psalm Quotations

Psalm 118:22 in 1 Peter 2:7

The first quotation from the Psalms appears as part of the group of 'stone' texts in 1 Pet. 2:6–8. At 1 Pet. 2:6 and 2:8 are two quotations from Isaiah, 'See I am laying in Zion a stone, a cornerstone chosen and precious, and whoever believes in him will not be put to shame' (Isa. 28:16), and 'A stone that makes them stumble and a rock that makes them fall' (Isa. 8:14). The Isaiah texts also appear in Paul's writings:[12]

---

[11] Space forbids a full discussion but we will comment on the possibility of psalm allusions in 1 Pet. 1:17; 3:22 and 5:7–8, as well as the ubiquitous presence of Ps. 34.

[12] W. Bornemann, 'Der erste Petrusbrief – eine Taufrede des Silvanus?', *ZNW* 19 (1920) claimed the presence of many other allusions in 1 Peter including those at 1:14, 15; 2:16; 3:14, 17 and 4:10.

1 Peter 2:6–8	Romans 9:33	Romans 10:11	LXX (trans. author)
⁶See I am laying in Zion (τίθημι ἐν Σιών) a stone, a cornerstone (ἀκρογωνιαῖον) chosen and precious, and whoever believes in him will not be put to shame	See I am laying in Zion (τίθημι ἐν Σιών) a stone (... *that will make people stumble, a rock that will make them fall*) and whoever believes in him will not be put to shame	No one who believes in him will be put to shame	See I am laying in Zion (ἐμβαλῶ εἰς ...Σιών) a foundation stone, a tested stone, a precious cornerstone (ἀκρογωνιαῖον), a sure foundation: 'Whoever believes will not be put to shame' (Isa. 28:16)
(οὐ μὴ καταισχυνθῇ)	(οὐ καταισχυνθήσεται)	(οὐ καταισχυνθήσεται)	(οὐ μὴ καταισχυνθῇ)
⁷ᵇThe stone (λίθος) that the builders rejected has become the very head of the corner (εἰς κεφαλὴν γωνίας)			The stone (λίθον) that the builders rejected has become the chief cornerstone (εἰς κεφαλὴν γωνίας) (Ps. 118:22)
⁸A stone that makes them stumble (λίθος προσκόμματος) and a rock that makes them fall (καὶ πέτρα σκανδάλου).	...that will make people stumble (λίθον προσκόμματος) a rock that will make them fall (καὶ πέτραν σκανδάλου).		He will become... a stone one strikes against (λίθου προσκόμματος),... a rock one stumbles over (πέτρας πτώματι). (Isa. 8:14)

1 Pet. 2:6 replicates part of the LXX of Isa. 28:16, and although ἐγὼ ἐμβαλῶ εἰς ...Σιών in Isa. 28:16, is replaced with τίθημι ἐν Σιών it is clearly a substantial quotation of that text.[13] W. Bornemann, however, identified the latter part of the verse, 'And the one believing in him will not be put to shame' as a quotation from Ps. 34:6 ('... so your faces will never be ashamed'). He acknowledged that 1 Pet. 2:6 is a quotation from Isa. 28:16 but at the same time conjectured that the writer chose this quotation and also Ps. 118:22 because of the degree of thematic agreement with Ps. 34:6. This allowed him

---

[13] The phrase, 'a sure foundation' is omitted along with the adjective 'costly', and two words, cornerstone (ἀκρογωνιαῖον) and ἐκλεκτόν (chosen) appear in reverse order compared with the LXX. The only other reference to a cornerstone (ἀκρογωνιαῖον) in the New Testament is to be found in Eph. 2:20, 'Christ Jesus himself as the cornerstone'.

to list 1 Pet. 2:6 as a point of contact with Psalm 34 as part of his overall thesis that Psalm 34 plays a pivotal role in the letter (see below).[14]

The citation of Isa. 8:14 at 1 Pet. 2:8 differs significantly from the LXX, but is virtually identical to Rom. 9:33, where Paul has combined it with words he drew from Isa. 28:16.[15] In between these two citations from Isaiah we find the explicit quotation from Ps. 118:22, 'The stone that the builders rejected has become the head of the corner'.

Textual Affinities

All three quotations in 1 Pet. 2:6–8 are collectively introduced by the phrase 'for it stands in scripture' (διότι περιέχει ἐν γραφῇ)[16] and the citation at 1 Pet. 2:7 consists of a quotation from the LXX version of Ps. 118:22 with only one minor alteration (λίθος instead of the accusative); the LXX is here a close rendering of the Hebrew.[17] Both κεφαλὴν γωνίας and לראש פנה mean 'head of the corner' and could be used to describe either a foundation stone stabilizing the two adjacent walls or a keystone. However, the use of ἀκρογωνιαῖον ('cornerstone') in the quotation from Isa. 28:16 suggests that the author of 1 Peter had a foundation stone in mind and reinterpreted Ps. 118:22 accordingly.

The Meaning of Psalm 118 in the Context of the Psalter

Within the Psalter, Psalm 118 is presented as a royal song of thanksgiving for military victory, set in the context of a processional liturgy.[18] As the participants make their way into the Temple courts, the stone gateway (v. 20) provides the setting for the exclamation about the stone in v. 22. Most scholars date the psalm as post-exilic, looking back to and giving thanks for the Davidic dynasty and Yahweh's goodness to Israel. With its themes of deliverance after humiliation, and a majestic triumphal entry, Psalm 118 (like other royal

---

[14] Bornemann, 'Der erste Petrusbrief', p. 147. In other words, his argument is that it was Psalm 34 that came first. He reasons that it was in the process of reflecting on the themes contained within it that the author made the connection with Isa. 28:16, which also has reference to 'will not be ashamed' and then, having stumbled almost accidentally on stone imagery, went on to link his thoughts with Ps. 118:22 and Isa. 8:14.

[15] Against most commentators, Achtemeier (1 Peter, p. 161) consigns this to the category of allusion (of Isa. 8:14) on the dual grounds of lack of quotation indicator and significant variations from the citation in the LXX. This is an over-cautious response to what is clearly a direct attempt to quote from the scriptures.

[16] Davids, Peter, p. 89 notes that the expression 'for it stands in scripture' is not used elsewhere in the New Testament, but it does occur in the LXX (1 Macc. 15:2; 2 Macc. 11:16, 22) and other Jewish literature (Josephus, Ant., 11.104; T. Levi 10:5).

[17] By contrast, the vocabulary of the citation of Isa. 28:16, while still that of the LXX, is not an exact quotation, nor does it agree with the Hebrew text. The citation from Isa. 8:14 appears to have closer affinity to the Hebrew (Davids, Peter, p. 89; Achtemeier, 1 Peter, pp. 154–61).

[18] It is not clear when such a thanksgiving might have taken place. The Talmudic tradition links it to the Feast of Tabernacles (Sukk. 45a, 45b) but see L.C. Allen, Psalms 101–150 (WBC 21; Waco: Word Books, 1983), p. 123 for a short, but useful summary of other suggestions.

psalms) probably came to be imbued with messianic import; this may explain why it was used as the climax to the Hallel Psalms (113–118).

The Role and Function of Psalm 118 in 1 Peter

Much has been written concerning the catena of 'stone' citations at 2:6–8.[19] This unique confluence is triggered by the allegorical reference to Christ as the 'living stone' in 2:4, which is developed in 2:5 to feature Christians as themselves also being 'living stones'.[20] Thus the stage is set for the introduction of the three stone citations, which therefore conclude the previous section, rather than introduce a new theme.

Why does the author of 1 Peter quote these texts together here? In 1916 J. Rendel Harris proposed that the early church made use of a book of messianic passages and other 'composite quotations' drawn from the Old Testament.[21] He noted some recurring New Testament and patristic quotations agreeing with each other in contrast to any extant Old Testament text; at times they represented a combination of the same Old Testament passages, supported the same arguments and were grouped around some common keywords. The 'stone testimonia' of 1 Pet. 2:6–8 were a case in point. Rejecting Petrine dependence on Paul, Harris suggested that each separately and severally had access to a 'Testimony Book', consisting of anti-Jewish polemic.[22] Certainly Cyprian's *Testimonies* revealed that the tradition of equating Christ with 'the Stone' was an ancient one, and both that writing and the *Epistle of Barnabas* cite similar passages from Isaiah and the Psalms (Isa. 28:16 then Ps. 118:22) to substantiate their arguments. Furthermore, both sets of quotations reveal the same variations in tense and other endings compared with the LXX, variations identical with those described above in 1 Peter. Harris' thesis was criticized but the discovery of 4QFlor has given it new life and a number of scholars now believe that lists of proof texts may well have been current in the early church.[23]

To my mind, R. Bauckham convincingly demonstrates that the literary unit 1 Pet. 2:4–10 is essentially midrashic, 'a particularly complex and studied piece

---

[19] This section of 1 Pet. 2:4–10 has generated considerable debate and an enormous body of scholarly literature. J.H. Elliott concluded that 2:6–10 was composed entirely to provide justification for the assertions in 2:4–5 (*The Elect and the Holy: An Exegetical Examination of 1 Pet 2:4–10 and the Phrase βασίλειον ἱράτευμα* [NovTSup 12; Leiden: Brill, 1966], pp. 16–49). Best, '1 Peter II, 4–10', p. 278 takes a diametrically opposite view. L. Goppelt, *A Commentary on 1 Peter* (Grand Rapids: Eerdmans, 1982), p. 152 incorporates discussion on these verses within a more general exploration of 'typology'.

[20] See, for example, K.R. Snodgrass, '1 Peter ii 1–10: Its Formation and Literary Affinities', *NTS* 24 (1978), p. 97.

[21] J.R. Harris, *Testimonies* (2 vols.; Cambridge: Cambridge University Press, 1916), I, p. 4.

[22] Harris, *Testimonies*, I, pp. 29–31.

[23] A.T. Hanson, *The Living Utterances of God* (London: Darton, Longman & Todd, 1983), p. 33 has a useful summary of the debate, but a more detailed treatment of the subject may be found in M.C. Albl, *'And Scripture Cannot Be Broken': The Form and Function of the Early Christian Testimonia Collections* (NovTSup 96; Leiden: Brill, 1999).

of exegesis, resembling ... the thematic pesharim of Qumran'.[24] The twin allegorical themes of Jesus as elect stone and the church as living stones are introduced in vv. 4–5 and then supported and expanded by Old Testament citations and interpretation in vv. 6–10, perhaps drawn from the author's store of Old Testament texts, or perhaps from some external *testimonia*. However, unlike a true rabbinic midrash, the author's intention was not primarily to provide further illumination for any particular text, but to show how the election of Christ leads to the election of those who believe in him as the holy people of God. Certainly Psalm 118, while clearly prominent, appears here in a supportive and collective role among the other fulfilment citations from Isaiah.[25] It seems likely that early in the life of the Church, this psalm (among others) was understood as providing a prediction both of Jesus' exaltation at the right hand of God and of his sufferings and atoning death. It also serves to illustrate the theme of reversal in God's activity and the contrast between those who believe and those who do not. The placement of ἀπιστοῦσιν just before Ps. 118:22 has the effect of making this text primarily a preface to Isa. 8:14 in v. 8 – in itself it makes no statement about the fate of the unbelievers.

Psalm 34:13–17 in 1 Peter 3:10–12

The most extensive Old Testament quotation in 1 Peter occurs at the heart of the epistle, in 3:10–12:

1 Peter 3:10–12	Psalm 34:13–17
For those who desire life (ὁ γὰρ θέλων ζωὴν ἀγαπᾶν) and desire to see good days,	Which of you desires life (τίς ἐστιν ἄνθρωπος ὁ θέλων ζωὴν ἀγαπῶν) and covets many days to enjoy good?
let them keep their tongues from evil and their lips from speaking deceit;	Keep your tongue from evil, and your lips from speaking deceit.
let them turn away from evil and do good; let them seek peace and pursue it.	Depart from evil, and do good; seek peace and pursue it.
For the eyes of the Lord are on the righteous and his ears are open to their prayer.	The eyes of the LORD are on the righteous, and his ears are open to their cry.
But the face of the Lord is against those who do evil	The face of the LORD is against evildoers, to cut off the remembrance of them from the earth.

---

[24] Bauckham, 'James, 1 and 2 Peter, Jude', p. 310. See also Elliott, *Elect*, p. 38; Davids, *Peter*, p. 90; Hanson, *Living Utterances*, p. 34; Schutter, *Hermeneutic*, p. 138; Michaels, *1 Peter*, p. 95. J. de Waard actually concludes that the quotation of Isa. 28:16 must be referred to as 'a midrash concerning the "stone", based on a verbum Christi, since we now have an excellent example of such a midrash in 1QS' (*A Comparative Study of the Old Testament Text in the Dead Sea Scrolls and in the New Testament* [Leiden: E.J. Brill, 1965,] p. 58).

[25] B. Lindars agrees that 1 Pet. 2:4–10 is indeed pesher-like, but holds that Ps. 118:22 is the decisive text with additional texts (Isa. 8:14 and 28:16) being introduced on the strength of their verbal tallies in order to provide a commentary on Ps. 118:22 (*New Testament Apologetic: The Doctrinal Significance of the Old Testament Quotations* [Philadelphia: Westminster, 1961], pp. 169–74). For a critique of this view see Schutter, *Hermeneutic*, pp. 132–6.

Textual Affinities

The Greek text of 1 Pet. 3:10–12 closely follows the LXX which in turn is an almost word for word translation of the Hebrew text.[26] There are a few obvious differences[27] but none are particularly important in terms of the function of the quotation in 1 Peter. The LXX (and so 1 Peter) preserves many of the poetical features of the psalm (parallelism, repetitions) but there is no attempt to reproduce its original acrostic form.

Some of the differences between 1 Pet. 3:10–12 and LXX Ps. 33:13–17 can easily be explained as accommodations of the psalm to the content of the letter. For example, the omission of the words τίς ἐστιν ἄνθρωπος is necessary for the flow of the argument and the addition of γάρ in 1 Pet. 3:10 gives a smooth transition from the text of the Old Testament psalm to that of the letter. The question, 'Which of you desires life?' has been changed into the statement, 'Those who desire life' in 1 Pet. 3:10 and the second person imperatives throughout the psalm have been changed into the third person.[28] Taken together, these alterations all make the quotation fit the context and adhere to the logic of the passage: 'He that would love life ... let him ...' The omission of Ps. 34:17b, about the extinction of those who do evil can be similarly explained. The author of 1 Peter is addressing the Christians of Asia Minor who are the 'righteous'; he does not need to threaten them.

One change is less easily explained on the basis of the author's editorial activity. Instead of ἀγαπῶν, 1 Pet. 3:10 has an infinitive. Michaels explains this variation by positing a variant Greek text but Eriksson considers it another example of deliberate editing.[29]

The Meaning of Psalm 34 in the Context of the Psalter

Psalm 34 is generally regarded as a carefully crafted psalm using many intricate poetic devices in addition to its acrostic feature.[30] In terms of *Gattung* it defies

---

[26] Schutter, *Hermeneutic*, p. 144.

[27] For example v. 5b in the Masoretic text includes a Hebrew word מגורותי that literally means 'my fears'. The LXX has seen it as a form of another word meaning 'a place of residence' and so renders the word in question as τῶν παροικιῶν (my sojournings). See L.O. Eriksson, *'Come, Children, Listen to Me!': Psalm 34 in the Hebrew Bible and in Early Christian Writings* (Stockholm: Almqvist & Wiksell, 1991), p. 99.

[28] J. Piper, 'Hope as the Motivation of Love: 1 Pet 3:9–12', *NTS* 26 (1980), pp. 226–28 sees the change from a rhetorical question and a second person, to a conditional participle and a third person imperative, as highly significant. From this, and other examples drawn from 1 Peter, Piper deduces that the author is 'not primarily *commanding* in vv. 10–12, but rather *arguing* for the command of v. 9 and its motive' (p. 226, emphasis original). In other words the way that 1 Pet. 3:9–12 motivates enemy-love is by showing that it is a condition for inheriting the eschatological blessing.

[29] Michaels, *1 Peter*, p. 180; Eriksson, *Come, Children*, pp. 117–18.

[30] Eriksson notes that, unlike Psalms 37, 111, 112 and 119, Psalm 34 is not a perfect acrostic psalm, having an additional פ- line and missing a ו- verse. However, he suggests that these changes may be deliberate in order to enhance the teaching function of the psalm (*Come, Children*, pp. 45–46).

easy classification, being neither purely a psalm of thanksgiving nor solely a Wisdom Psalm. Despite the psalm's title, which alludes to the time when David feigned madness in the presence of Achish king of Gath (1 Sam. 21:10–15), there is no consensus as to its *Sitz im Leben* or date. However, most commentators cautiously allow a setting in which teaching and poetic skills are valued, perhaps just before or at the beginning of the exile.[31] What is clear is that the psalm as a whole lays emphasis on listening and learning, specifically that the readers may learn 'the fear of the Lord' (34:11). The portion quoted in 1 Pet. 3:10–12 lies immediately after this key admonition and encapsulates the major thrust of the teaching of the psalm.

The Use of Psalm 34 in the New Testament and Rabbinic Literature

This is the only substantial occurrence of Psalm 34 in the New Testament, though NA[27] lists a few others, the most significant of which is the quotation in Jn 19:36 ('none of his bones shall be broken'). A further quotation is found in 1 Clem. 22:16 and allusions in 2 Clem. 10:2 and Barn. 9:2.[32] When the rabbis dealt with this passage they identified 'doing good' (Ps. 34:15) with observing the Torah as one might expect; they also equated 'life' (Ps. 34:13) as 'life in the world-to-come'. With its references to the deliverance of the righteous sufferer, this psalm may have acquired a Messianic significance.[33]

The Role and Function of Psalm 34 in 1 Peter – Bornemann's Thesis

In an early and influential article, published in 1920, Bornemann argued that 1 Peter was a baptismal sermon written by Silvanus to a group of late first-century Christians.[34] However, in the same piece of writing he suggested that, despite the clear existence of quotations and allusions to many parts of the Old Testament, this sermon was a development of Psalm 34, later 'published' as 1:3–5:11 with the addition of '*through Silvanus*' (5:12); and still later, a beginning and ending were added to form the apostolic letter as we know it today. Beare dubbed it a 'fascinating but wholly fanciful reconstruction'[35] and Elliott and Schutter gave it scant regard.[36] However, Snodgrass is more positive and suggests that 'the author of 1 Peter attempted to convey the consolation and exhortation of the righteous sufferer in Ps xxxiv to his readers and that he used explicit quotations, allusions and themes from Ps xxxiv to do so'.[37] In exploring afresh the psalmic sources that the writer of 1 Peter drew

---

[31] See for example P.C. Craigie, *Psalms 1–50* (WBC 19, Waco: Word Books, 1983), pp. 276–82.
[32] B.H. McLean, *Citations and Allusions to Jewish Scripture in Early Christian and Jewish Writings through 180 CE* (New York: Edwin Mellen, 1992), p. 70.
[33] Craigie, *Psalms 1–50*, p. 282.
[34] Bornemann, 'Der erste Petrusbrief', pp. 143–65.
[35] F.W. Beare, *The First Epistle of Peter: The Greek Text with Introduction and Notes* (Oxford: Blackwell, 3rd edn, 1970), p. 212.
[36] Elliott, *Elect*, pp. 184–208. Schutter, *Hermeneutic*, pp. 44–9.
[37] Snodgrass, '1 Peter ii 1–10', p. 102.

on, both consciously and unconsciously, Bornemann's claims will have to be re-examined alongside other possibilities.

Allusions to Psalm 34

Strong/Significant Allusions

1 Pet. 2:1 says, 'Rid yourselves, therefore, of all malice (κακίαν), and all guile (δόλον), insincerity, envy, and all slander.' Although not immediately apparent in an English translation, Ps. 34:14 is the most likely source of this allusion since the LXX not only agrees in *evil* (κακοῦ) and *deceit* (δόλον), but there is also a strong thematic resonance.[38] As part of an exhortation to live in the 'fear of the Lord' (Ps. 34:12), the readers are enjoined to keep themselves from evil and deceitful speech ('Keep your tongue from evil, and your lips from speaking deceit'). In 1 Pet. 2:1, the close proximity to the very strong allusion at 2:3 adds weight to the probability that Psalm 34 is in mind.

1 Pet. 2:3 reads, 'if indeed you have tasted that the Lord is good' (εἰ ἐγεύσασθε ὅτι χρηστὸς ὁ κύριος). This is clearly derived from Ps. 34:9, 'Taste and see that the LORD is good' (γεύσασθε καὶ ἴδετε ὅτι χρηστὸς ὁ κύριος).[39] A few Greek manuscripts of 1 Pet. 2:3 read εἴπερ instead of εἰ (strengthening the particle) but this does not alter the meaning significantly.

As was discussed earlier in connection with 1 Pet. 2:6–8, the whole of 1 Pet. 1:13–2:10 is a delightful medley of metaphors and words of the author mingled with words and expressions culled from the Old Testament. Some have described the phenomenon as midrash or midrash-like;[40] others point to the similarity between this and the pesher of the Qumran community.[41] In the context of 1 Peter it is clear that the author has seen the (LORD) of the psalm as Christ. No explanation, argument or apology is given for this; it is natural and self-evident for the author and his church, and the overall effect is to provide from the scriptures an authoritative conclusion to the admonitions of 1 Pet. 2:1–2.

Bornemann laid great emphasis on *verbal parallels*, however tenuous, and concluded that Psalm 34 is found throughout 1 Peter in the form of quotations, allusions and echoes. What he failed to consider, however, was the significance of the *setting* of the possible allusions and echoes. In order to get a full picture of how the author of 1 Peter has utilized Old Testament texts

---

[38] Bornemann elevated several allusions to the status of quotations from Psalm 34, including those at 1 Pet. 2:1, 3, 4 and 6, but the evidence is insufficient to support that position ('Der erste Petrusbrief', p. 147).

[39] Eriksson classifies this as a quotation (*Come, Children*, p. 111) as does Bornemann ('Der erste Petrusbrief', p. 147).

[40] For example J.N.D. Kelly, *A Commentary on the Epistles of Peter and Jude* (London: A & C Black, 1969), p. 82.

[41] Schutter, *Hermeneutic*, pp. 130, 168.

(including the psalms) we must ask questions about how these quotations and allusions contribute to the structure and argument of the letter. What function do they serve within the overall text? Do they serve as foundations from which to launch different strands of the argument of the letter? Or are they proof-texts, giving scriptural weight at the conclusion to each section and subsection?

The Role and Function of Psalm 34 in 1 Peter – 'Janus Behaviour'

It can be demonstrated that all but one of the explicit Old Testament quotations in 1 Peter, whether they are employed in a typological, midrashic or other role, act as a *summary* to the previous section.[42] The exception is at 1 Pet. 3:10–12. Here is an extensive quotation from Ps. 34:13–17 which is unlike the other quotations. Apart from being the longest, it stands as a summary of the theme that has persisted throughout the letter to this point: the kind of behaviour expected from someone who has entered the 'new life' of the Christian. But it also seems to act as a springboard to the section that follows, a section that begins in 1 Pet. 3:13, with a paraphrase of the same thoughts from Psalm 34. The section continues with a positive reference to the kind of speech Christians should be engaged in (3:15b) and the theme of Christian suffering, while at the same time behaving in a holy manner and doing good, pervades much of the rest of the letter. These themes, on closer inspection, also have their roots back in the quotation at 1 Pet. 3:10–12.

It could be said, then, that this quotation seems to exhibit 'Janus' behaviour.[43] Like the god of Roman mythology it has two faces, one looking forward and one looking back; it both summarizes *and* introduces material. The phenomenon exists at both a linguistic and thematic level and is best illustrated diagrammatically:

Themes of 1 Peter	*Key words in each section*	*and in 3:10–12*
1:1–2 Greetings		
1:3–12 Contrast between present circumstances and the new life begun (and eternal life to come)	ἐλπίδα ζῶσαν (living hope) (v. 3) ἰδόντες (have seen) (v. 8)	ζωήν (life) (v. 10) ἰδεῖν (to see) (v. 10)
1:13–16 Therefore be holy		
1:17–25 Contrast between perishable/ imperishable		
2:1–3 Therefore be holy	κακίαν (malice/evil) (v. 1) δόλον (deceit) (v. 1)	κακοῦ (v. 10) δόλον (v. 10)
2:4–10 Contrast between what you were/what you are becoming		

---

[42] There is broad agreement across the commentators. See, for example, Schutter, *Hermeneutic*, pp. 5, 64; Achtemeier, *1 Peter*, pp. 12, 150, 221.

[43] This proposal forms part of a PhD submission by the author.

2:11–20 So there are implications for how you behave	κακοποιῶν (evildoers) (vv. 12, 14) κακίας (v. 16) ἀγαθοποιοῦντες (doing right/good)(v. 20)	κακοῦ (v. 11) ποιησάτω ἀγαθόν (do good)(v. 11)
2:21–25 Christ's example. His activity contrasted with our need	δόλος (deceit)(v. 22) δικαίως (justly/righteously) (v. 23)	δικαίους (v. 12)
3:1–9 Further examples of how to live the holy life	κακὸν ἀυτὶ κακοῦ (evil) (v. 9)	κακὰ (v. 12)

The identification of common words and their order of appearance is only part of the picture; much of the duplicated vocabulary is not surprising given that this is in all probability a letter encouraging the recipients to make firm their change of lifestyle.[44] However, it is probably more significant that these key words are to be found occurring progressively throughout 1:1–3:9 *in the same order* as they appear in 3:10–12. In addition, what cannot be shown on a diagram is how the *thematic progression* of 1:1–3:9 also mirrors very closely the format of 3:10–12, even when there is no verbal agreement. For example, at first glance there seems to be no parallel for the injunction at 3:11, 'Let them seek peace and pursue it', until we realize that the whole of section 2:11–20 is saying much the same thing, about pursuing a deliberate lifestyle of turning away from evil and from any activities not commensurate with their new status in Christ. Such activities are described in 2:11 as 'waging war'; the implication being that renouncing them is equivalent to 'seeking peace'. Similarly 3:12 refers to 'prayer' using the word δέησιν. If there is indeed a pattern of thought throughout the first part of 1 Peter as described above, one might expect such an important word to appear in the section 3:1–9. It does not, but at 3:7 the same idea *is* expressed using προσευχάς.

So much for the way in which 3:10–12 concludes the extensive section 1:1–3:9. But what about the other factor of the 'Janus' phenomenon; does the quotation have a forward-facing dynamic? It is clear that many of the words of 3:10–12 also appear in 3:13–17.

Themes of 1 Peter	Key words in each section	and in 3:10–12
3:13–17 How to behave under persecution (v. 11)	κακώσων (v. 13) δικαιοσύνην (v. 14) ἀγαθοποιοῦντας (v. 17) κακοποιοῦντας (v. 17)	κακὰ (v. 12) δικαίους (v. 12) ποιησάτω ἀγαθόν (v. 11) κακοῦ (v. 11)

---

[44] Not all scholars would agree that 1 Peter is a letter, but this is becoming the consensus, as demonstrated by Achtemeier, *1 Peter*, p. 62; Best, *1 Peter*, p. 13; J.H. Elliott, 'The Rehabilitation of an Exegetical Step-Child: 1 Peter in Recent Research', *JBL* 95:2 (1976), pp. 243–54, not least because 1 Peter broadly follows the form of a Pauline letter and is in keeping with other general, circular letters known to be in circulation at the time from Jewish, Christian and secular sources.

There is a significant degree of correspondence in vocabulary, notably in the early stages immediately after the citation at 3:10–12, but also in the section 4:12–19 (v. 15 has κακοποιός and v. 19 ἀγαθοποιΐᾳ paralleling κακοῦ and ἀγαθάς of 3:10). In addition it can be seen that the common words appear *in reverse order* to their use in 1 Pet. 3:10–12 (and hence in Psalm 34). Taking these two tables together, it is at least a plausible suggestion that the quotation from Psalm 34 is being used in a broadly chiastic pattern.[45]

But there is more to it than a word-analysis alone can reveal. For example, there are no references in this second section of the letter which convincingly match Ps. 34:10, 'Those who desire life and desire to see good days ...', yet the eschatological section of 4:7–11 (the end of all things is near) and more specifically 4:13 (referring to the time when followers will be glad and shout for joy when Christ's glory is revealed) and 5:1, 4, 6 each focus on the 'good days' which are to come for those who are faithful. This, then, is both in keeping with, and reinforces the likelihood of, the proposed chiastic pattern of 1 Peter where the quotation from Psalm 34 lies at its fulcrum.

Weak Allusions

Bornemann suggested a whole host of allusions to Psalm 34, many of which are too speculative to consider. The following, however, are worthy of consideration and could have cumulative value. 1 Pet. 1:14 recalls the idea of 'obedient children' and may be an allusion to Ps. 34:12. This is strengthened by noting that the following verse (1 Pet. 1:15) speaks of being holy, a possible allusion to Ps. 34:10. In 1 Pet. 1:17b, the author urges his readers to 'live in reverent fear, during ... exile', which may reflect Prov. 23:17, Jer. 46:27–28 or Ps. 34:5, 8, 10. Verbal links are not strong but the psalm does speak of 'my sojournings' (34:4b LXX). 1 Pet. 2:16 shares the image of the 'servants of God' with Ps. 34:23. Not much can be deduced from the command to fear God in 1 Pet. 2:17b but it is interesting that in 1 Pet. 3:6, the readers are exhorted not to fear what others may do to them. Such a variation is also found in Psalm 34, specifically in v. 5, but implicitly also in vv. 6–8 and 18–20. Finally, the term 'blessed' in 1 Pet. 3:14; 4:10 might have originated in Ps. 34:9 and the injunction in Ps. 34:15 to 'do good' may be behind 1 Pet. 3:17.

If Psalm 34 is indeed fundamental to 1 Peter, then the argument for at least some of these allusions is strengthened by noting their location in the letter. For example, the possible allusions to Psalm 34 at 1:14, 15, 17b serve to strengthen the impact of the quotation from Lev. 19:2 at 1 Pet. 1:16 'You shall be holy, for I am holy' and the stronger allusions in 2:1 and 2:3 form part of the outworking of the quotation at 1:24, 25 from Isa. 40:6–8. Careful scrutiny of

---

[45] Best observed, but did not demonstrate in detail, that 'the themes of verses 8,9 re-appear in reverse order in verses 10–11 in the quotation' (*1 Peter*, p. 129). Michaels, *1 Peter*, p. 174 finds the idea unconvincing.

the use of each of the allusions does not reveal any intricate schema equivalent to that described above with the Ps. 34:13–17 quotation. This suggests that, in the case of allusions at any rate, it was an *unconscious* rather than a *deliberate* usage of familiar scriptures that was at work in the mind of the writer of the epistle.

Taking both the word parallels and the chiastic pattern in which they fall, there seems to be cumulative evidence to show that the quotation from Psalm 34 at 3:10–12 is indeed pivotal to the thinking of the whole letter. This quotation not only stands at the climax of the letter; it not only concludes one section and introduces another; it also contains vocabulary and themes that pervade the entire letter.

Psalm Allusions Other than to Psalm 34

1 Pet. 1:17 ('If you invoke as Father...'). While God is described as *like* a father in both Pss 68:6 and 103:13, appealing to God *as* Father is a theme found only in Ps. 89:27 and Jer. 3:19.

1 Pet. 2:4 ('stone ... though rejected by mortals' – ὑπὸ ἀνθρώπων μὲν ἀπο-δ εδοκιμασμένον) is clearly a precursor to the use of Ps. 118:22 at 2:7, 'The stone ... that the builders rejected' (ἀπεδοκίμασαν οἱ οἰκοδομοῦντες) where the theme is amplified as part of the 'stone catena'.

1 Pet. 2:11 ('aliens and exiles'). This combination of words (παροίκους καὶ παρεπιδήμους) is only found in Ps. 39:13 and Gen. 23:4 and, despite appearing in those texts in the singular rather than the plural, one or other is almost certainly the source of the allusion in 1 Peter.[46]

1 Pet. 3:22 ('At the right hand of God'). There are many possible contenders for the source of this allusion, including Pss 20:7, 48:11, 60:7, 108:7, 110:1 or 118:15, 16 where mention of the right hand of God or of the LORD appears. While only Ps. 110:1 specifically refers to someone/ something being '*at* the right hand of God', Ps. 8:6 (only in the LXX) carries a similar thrust to 1 Pet. 3:22 in acclaiming 'the son of man' to be set over all things, while the threefold usage in Psalm 118, coupled with that psalm's appearance already in 1 Peter 2, makes it another likely candidate.

1 Pet. 5:7 ('Cast all your anxiety on him because he cares for you') has some significant verbal links with LXX Ps. 54:22 but, as has already been mentioned, the theme of fear/anxiety is a common feature of several verses of Psalm 34.

1 Pet. 5:8 ('Like a roaring lion ... the devil prowls around looking for someone to devour'). This imagery is close to and evocative of Job 1:7, but Ps.

---

[46] M. Chin, 'A Heavenly Home for the Homeless: Aliens and Strangers in 1 Peter', *TynBul* 42 (1991), pp. 96–112 provides a useful exploration of the terms παροί κους καὶ παρε πιδήμους. See also J.H. Elliott, *A Home for the Homeless: A Sociological Exegesis of 1 Peter, its Situation and Strategy* (London: SCM Press, 1981).

22:14 ('as a ravening and roaring lion') and Ezek. 22:25 ('like a roaring lion tearing the prey') have closer linguistic parallels.

Summary of the Role and Function of the Psalms

Since each of Psalms 8, 22, 39, 54, 89 and 110 is found only as a 'weak allusion' at best, it is unwise to make great claims as to how the author of 1 Peter consciously used them within the letter as a whole. However, it is fair to say that the images contributed by the psalm allusions seem to enhance statements that the author has already made. Thus 1:17, 'If you invoke as Father...' (Ps. 89:27), picks up the image of 'obedient children' from v. 14. At 2:11, the allusion to 'aliens and exiles' (Ps. 39:13 or Gen. 23:4) relates to the substance of the previous verse. Similarly, Jesus' status at the 'right hand of God' in 1 Pet. 3:22 (LXX Ps. 8:6 or Ps. 110:1) continues the dynamic of the resurrection, referred to in 3:18 and 21. At the end of the letter, 1 Pet. 5:7 'Cast your anxiety on him...' reaffirms the injunction in v. 6 and, as with 1:17, may in fact be derived from Psalm 34. In the following verse the author introduces a vivid analogy – that of the devil as a roaring lion (Ps. 22:14) in response to his own injunction that his readers should be alert. These psalms therefore provide a source of words and images which the author draws on to reinforce his message, but the level of allusion is such that it is impossible to be sure how far the dependence was conscious and deliberate, and how far a reflection simply of the language and phraseology with which the author was generally familiar.[47]

Psalm 118, on the other hand, appears selectively, principally in and around 2:6–8 as part of the 'living stone imagery' of 2:4–10. As we have seen, there is evidence that Psalm 118 has been used midrashically, in combination with two well-known citations from Isaiah. If this is indeed a midrash, or a pesher, then it is one with a very firm christological focus. Hanson, referring to 1 Pet. 2:1–10 writes:

> Thus our author in these densely packed ten verses has clothed the Christian church in all the attributes and responsibilities of Israel of old, and has extended salvation history to cover not only the history of Israel but also God's culminating action for salvation in Jesus Christ. This is surely a brilliantly successful use of scripture in a christological sense.[48]

But what of Psalm 34? The message of that psalm that God will protect and vindicate the righteous sufferer has been warmly embraced by the author of 1 Peter in his presentation of both Christ as the archetypal 'suffering servant' of Isaiah and also the Christian church as called to the *imitatio Christi*.[49] Christ

---

[47] Hanson describes this use of scripture as being 'simple, non-typological, illustrative' (*Living Utterances*, p. 61).

[48] Hanson, *Living Utterances*, p. 143.

[49] Michaels, *1 Peter*, p. lxx.

suffered and was vindicated by resurrection to the right hand of God; so too will his righteous followers be exalted if they maintain their godly behaviour and their steadfast discipleship of Christ. In the midst of afflictions the readers are encouraged to focus on the one who has given them an example (1 Pet. 2:21). Here is an instance where a significant portion of scripture makes a central contribution to the structure and content of the letter and gives authority to a pastoral message.

Conclusions

From what has been presented above, it does not seem possible to cast the author of 1 Peter firmly into the role of one particular type of interpreter of the psalms of the Old Testament. Using explicit quotations of scripture, allusions and echoes (which are nearly always from the LXX and show no knowledge of the Hebrew) he incorporates them in a variety of exegetical patterns, using allegory (1 Pet. 2:7), *testimonia* and catchword links (1 Pet. 2:1–10). However, the primary aim of the author is not to focus on providing further illumination to the psalm texts themselves, but to make sense of the Christian gospel and particularly the example of Jesus Christ.[50] The extensive use of Psalm 34 demonstrates that the author was conscious of a continuity between the ethical demands of the scriptures he was handling and the lives of the Gentile Christians to whom he was writing, yet in the stone passages (2:1–10) there is also a desire to reinterpret images from the past and give them a new focus.[51]

This study suggests that, in 1 Peter, two of the quotations and possibly as many as eleven allusions emanate from the Psalms. The psalms clearly represented are Psalms 34 and 118, with Psalms 8, 22, 39, 54, 89 and 110 as likely. Bornemann made the extravagant claim that there are seven quotations and around seventy allusions made to Psalm 34.[52] This is very over-stated but it should not detract us from taking seriously the importance of Psalm 34 in the epistle. Perhaps Bornemann's major fault was that his circle of investigation was not drawn widely enough. His focus was the genre of 1 Peter and his evidence drawn almost exclusively from perceived linguistic parallels with the Old Testament, without due regard for the underlying structure of the document and the role that the quotations and allusions played. It is, perhaps, ironic that Bornemann failed to appreciate the structural significance of the major quotation from Psalm 34, which is the key to understanding the whole letter.

---

[50] Goppelt claims that it is by the help of scripture that the author of 1 Peter understands the Christian message (*1 Peter*, p. 55).

[51] It is, of course, arguable as to whether the author of 1 Peter provided this new interpretation or whether this was provided by the *testimonia*.

[52] Unlike Schutter who, using a slightly different accounting system, allows for three citations, with six other instances of what he terms 'iterative allusions' grouped around the quotation at 3:10–12 (*Hermeneutic*, p. 44).

I am convinced that, uniquely among the quotations in 1 Peter, the citation of Psalm 34 at 1 Peter 3:10–12 exhibits '*Janus*' type behaviour. The treatment by the author of the epistle of the *quotation* from Ps. 34:13–17 is commensurate with midrashic techniques of the day even though the result may have been too subtle for the readers to appreciate. While the entire letter seems to have been crafted around that central citation, the *allusions* to Psalm 34 probably appear unconsciously, the result of the author having reflected on that particular psalm while preparing to address the specific concerns of the potential readership.

If this is correct, then why was *Psalm 34* chosen? As a general letter of encouragement and challenge, probably to Christians in Asia Minor who were largely Gentile, 1 Peter focuses on Christ Jesus as the archetypal righteous sufferer who is both their saviour and their example. Psalm 34 contains many features that would make it an ideal scriptural source for imagery about a righteous sufferer.[53] However, one has to wait until the writings of Origen and Tertullian for conclusive evidence that this psalm (along with Psalm 133) was popularly in use during the eucharistic liturgy. In this psalm the LORD is the central figure, hearing, rescuing and redeeming his people, especially those who are crushed in spirit (Ps. 34:6, 18, 19, 23). The reference to bones not being broken (Ps. 34:21) would have resonated, for author and readers alike, both with the Passover (Exod. 12:46) and, christologically, with the crucifixion of Christ.

---

[53] Hanson misses the christological potential of this citation from Psalm 34 at 1 Pet. 3:10–12 (*Living Utterances*, p. 145).

12

The Psalms in the Book of Revelation

Steve Moyise

Introduction

As has frequently been pointed out, John's style is not to cite scripture using introductory formulae and no explicit quotations are recognized by the United Bible Societies' *Greek New Testament* (*UBSGNT*). This chapter will therefore be concerned with allusions and echoes. However, this does not mean that John's use of the psalms is less important than that of the other writers of the New Testament. Indeed, there are a number of allusions which would qualify as unmarked quotations in terms of verbal affinity to known sources. But John's technique is not to introduce them with an introductory formula or even a break in syntax. For example, the messianic promise to rule the nations with an iron rod in Ps. 2:8–9 is cited as a promise to the Christians in Thyatira in Rev. 2:26–7:

> Ask of me, and I will make the nations your heritage, and the ends of the earth your possession. You shall break them with a rod of iron, and dash them in pieces like a potter's vessel (Ps. 2:8–9).
> To everyone who conquers and continues to do my works to the end, I will give authority over the nations; to rule them with an iron rod, as when clay pots are shattered (Rev. 2:26–7).

Agreement in the means ('iron rod'), result ('authority over the nations') and analogy ('when clay pots are shattered') makes it clear that John has Psalm 2 in mind. Furthermore, he cites it in two other places. In Rev. 12:5, the male child born to the woman will 'rule all the nations with a rod of iron'; and in Rev. 19:15, the rider of the white horse will 'strike down the nations, and he will rule them with a rod of iron'. As we will see later, John even uses the same verb ποιμαίνω ('rule, shepherd') that is found in the LXX text, even though it is commonly regarded as a mistranslation of the Hebrew verb רעע ('shattered'). There are three other psalm texts (Pss 2:1–2; 86:8–10; 89:28, 38) that can similarly be regarded as unmarked quotations.

A second category is where a particular psalm text has contributed the leading idea in a passage, though certain aspects could also have come from elsewhere. For example, the letter to the church at Sardis contains the warning, 'If you conquer, you will be clothed like them in white robes, and I will not *blot* your name out of the *book of life*' (Rev. 3:5). This could come from

Exod. 32:32, where Moses asks to be *blotted* out of the *book* if God will not forgive Israel. Or it might owe something to Dan. 12:1, which offers the promise that 'your people shall be delivered, everyone who is found written in the *book*'. But the closest parallel is Ps. 69:29, for it not only speaks about being blotted out, it also uses the compound 'book of life' and the context is a warning. There are eight other psalm texts that can be included in the category, 'Psalms that contribute the leading idea in a passage' (Pss 75:8; 99:1; 106:48; 115:4–7, 13; 137:8; 141:2; 144:9).

A third category is where a particular psalm text appears to have contributed *one* of the ideas in a passage. For example, the images of salvation in Rev. 7:15–17 are drawn mainly from Isa. 49:10 ('They will hunger no more . . . for he who has pity on them will lead them, and by springs of water will guide them') but the specific use of ποιμαίνω in the positive sense of 'shepherd', along with the image of being led by still waters suggests that Ps. 23:1–2 is also in mind. There are a further seven psalm texts that we might categorize as contributing at least *one* of the ideas in a passage (Pss 7:10; 47:9; 62:13; 78:44; 79:1; 96:13; 119:137).

A final category are those psalm texts that could be in the background but verbal agreement is minimal and thematic links slight. Jon Paulien[1] has compiled a list of the most likely allusions in the book of Revelation, based on the suggestions of ten scholars or editions of the *Greek New Testament*. All but five of them have been included in the above three categories, and the remaining five belong to a final category of 'Faint echoes' (Pss 7:10; 10:16; 17:15; 19:9; 104:2; 111:2; 135:1; 139:14; 141:2; 145:17 etc.). For reasons of space, we will not be able to discuss these in this chapter.

Four Unmarked Quotations from the Psalms

Psalm 2:1–2 in Revelation 11:15,18

With the sounding of the seventh trumpet comes the announcement that, 'The kingdom of the world has become the kingdom of our Lord and of his Messiah, and he will reign forever and ever' (11:15). A few verses later, the 24 elders praise God for his victory, mentioning that the 'nations raged'. These two ideas, the 'rage of the nations' and 'the Lord and his *christos*' go back to the LXX of Ps. 2:1, which rendered the Hebrew verb רגש ('conspire', 'plot') with φρυάσσω ('rage'). The text is quoted in this form in Acts 4:25–26 but John uses the more common verb ὀργίζω, perhaps through the influence of Exod. 15:14,[2] where the nations are enraged (ὠργίσθησαν) or Ps. 99:1. As we will

---

[1] Details of his method can be found in J. Paulien, 'Criteria and the Assessment of Allusions to the Old Testament in the Book of Revelation', in Steve Moyise, ed., *Studies in the Book of Revelation* (Edinburgh: T & T Clark, 2001), pp. 113–30.

[2] So D. Aune, *Revelation 6–16* (WBC 52B; Nashville: Thomas Nelson, 1998), p. 643.

see later, the latter is more likely since John also uses the unusual aorist ἐβασίλευσεν for God's reign. Thus the threat of Psalm 2 is now seen to have taken place; the nations raged against the Lord and his anointed and were defeated.

Psalm 2:8–9 in Revelation 2:26–27; 12:5; 19:15

Ps. 2:7 is quoted extensively in the New Testament but John makes use of the verses that follow on three separate occasions. The central idea is sovereignty, expressed as 'rule with a rod of iron', and is applied to Christians who overcome in Rev. 2:27, the male child born of the woman in Rev. 12:5, and the rider of the white horse in Rev. 19:15. The allusion to Ps. 2:8–9 is strengthened in Rev. 2:27 and 19:5 with the addition of the 'authority over the nations' clause and additionally in 2:27, with the analogy of 'smashing clay pots'. In order to understand John's use of this psalm, it is necessary to discover what John understood by the Greek verb ποιμαίνω. In Rev. 7:17, he uses it in the entirely positive sense of 'shepherding' or 'guiding' the saints to springs of living water.[3] As will be seen in Section 12.4, the verse owes something to Psalm 23, where ποιμαίνω is also used.

The verb takes on a negative sense in Rev. 12:5, where it refers not to God's people but to the nations, and is accompanied by the expression 'with a rod of iron'. The meaning appears to be 'rule' in the sense of 'subdue'. However, in Rev. 2:27 and 19:15, the word is paralleled by a phrase that indicate 'destruction' rather than 'rule'. In Rev. 2:27, it is the analogy used by Psalm 2 ('as when clay pots are shattered') and in Rev. 19:15, a phrase drawn from Isa. 11:4 ('strike down the nations'). This raises two questions: (1) Does Psalm 2 predict a 'subjugation' or a 'destruction' of the nations? (2) Does John understand ποιμαίνω in 2:27 and 19:5 to mean 'rule' or 'destroy'? The first question is complicated by the fact that the Hebrew consonants could derive from רעע (an Aramaic loan word corresponding to the Hebrew רצץ) meaning 'shatter', as in MT or רעה (meaning 'shepherd' or 'rule'), and good reasons can be offered for both. In favour of רעע is the fact that it stands in parallel with the analogy of 'smashing' clay pots and this is how it was understood by Symmachus, Aquila and the later Masoretes.[4] The LXX is in this case a mistranslation, which John follows. On the other hand, Wilhemi[5] has argued for the originality of רעה, citing the evidence of the LXX and the parallel with Mic. 5:4–6, where רעה is first used of 'shepherding' the sheep and then of

---

[3] Most English translations turn the verbal expression 'will shepherd them' into a noun clause 'will be their shepherd' (so NIV, NRSV, NJB).

[4] So M. Dahood, *Psalms 1–50: Introduction, Translation and Commentary* (Garden City: Doubleday, 1966), p. 13; H.-J. Kraus, *Psalms 1–59: A Continental Commentary* (trans. H.C. Oswald; Minneapolis: Fortress Press, 1993), p. 124.

[5] G. Wilhemi, 'Der Hirt mit dem eisernen Szepter: Überlegungen zu Psalm II 9', *VT* 27 (1977), pp. 196–204, and cited with approval by Aune.

'ruling' the land of Assyria with a sword. A further factor is that the previous verse (Ps. 2:8) says, 'Ask of me, and I will make the nations your heritage, and the ends of the earth your possession'. Now unless this is a promise of a wasteland full of corpses, it would appear that the next verse must be an exaggerated expression for the *completeness* of the victory rather than the annihilation of the nations. It is their futile resistance that will be utterly smashed, not the people themselves. As Kraus says:

> the picture of the smashing of the earthen vessels has the signification of pointing out the absolute judicial power of the 'son' as the heir of the world and its nations by means of a metaphor that was well known in the ancient Near East.[6]

Thus the psalm speaks of the sovereignty of the anointed over the nations and uses a violent metaphor for the smashing of all resistance. The only question is whether this metaphor is present in the last line only or is also to be found in the 'iron rod' saying.

As for the second question, the main issue is whether the Greek word ποιμαίνω can bear the otherwise unattested meaning, 'destroy'. It is certainly not *required* in Rev. 2:7, since like the psalm, it is preceded by a promise of authority over the nations. The victory will be like the shattering of clay pots, but the nations remain as an inheritance. Rev. 19:15 is more difficult in that it is followed by an account of destruction, where 'the rest were killed by the sword of the rider on the horse...and all the birds were gorged with their flesh' (Rev. 19:21). There appears to be nothing left for the rider of the horse to rule over; the enemy has been completely destroyed. On the other hand, in the next chapter, we have a vision where Satan is bound and the saints reign with Christ for a thousand years. It is of course a well-known difficulty as to how this 'millennial rule' is related to the various battles in Revelation[7] but one thing is clear; the 'rule' is intended to correspond to the promise of 'rule' in Rev. 2:28. Thus it would appear that John has not only borrowed the language of Psalm 2 to describe the messianic victory; he has also borrowed its paradoxical exaggeration, whereby 'rule' means 'subjugation' but is described in the language of 'destruction', presumably the destruction of all resistance. This seems more likely than the subtle sophistication proposed by Beale, that the LXX translator deliberately chose ποιμαίνω to echo the ambiguity of the Hebrew consonants.[8]

---

[6] Kraus, *Psalms 1–59*, p. 134.

[7] See R.J. McKelvey, 'The Millennium and the Second Coming', in Moyise, ed., *Studies in the Book of Revelation*, pp. 85–100.

[8] Beale thinks that John understood ποιμαίνω in the dual sense of 'shepherding' believers but 'destroying' unbelievers and cites Mic. 5:5; Jer. 6:3, 22:22 as evidence that ποιμαίνω can mean 'destroy' or 'devastate'. However, the dual sense in these verses is between 'shepherd' and 'rule' not 'shepherd' and 'destroy'. See G.K. Beale, *The Book of Revelation* (NIGTC; Grand Rapids: Eerdmans, 1999), pp. 266–67.

Psalm 86:8–10 in Revelation 15:3–4

In Rev. 15:3, John says that those who conquered the beast sing 'the song of Moses, the servant of God, and the song of the Lamb'. The title has puzzled commentators for the words that follow have little verbal similarity with the song of Moses, either in Exodus 15 or Deuteronomy 32, but are drawn from various psalms, notably the universalistic sounding Psalm 86:

> There is none like you among the gods, O *Lord*, nor are there any *works* like yours. *All the nations* you have made *shall come and bow down before you*, O *Lord, and shall glorify your name*. For you are *great* and do wondrous things; *you alone* are God (Ps. 86:8–10).
>
> *Great* and amazing are your *deeds*, *Lord* God the Almighty! Just and true are your ways, King of the nations! *Lord*, who will not fear and *glorify your name*? For *you alone* are holy. *All nations will come and worship before you*, for your judgments have been revealed (Rev. 15:3–4).

Bauckham argues that John *is* thinking of the song of Moses in Exodus 15 but has been led by verbal association from Exod. 15:11 ('who is like you, O Lord, among the nations?') to three other texts, namely, Ps. 86:8–10, Jer. 10:7 and Ps. 98:1–2. From these three texts, by the 'skilful use of recognized exegetical methods', John has composed a new song 'in line with the most universalistic strain in Old Testament hope'.[9] As an example of John's skilful strategy, Bauckham suggests that John changes the Hebrew text of Ps. 86:10 ('you alone are God') to 'you alone are holy', because like the LXX before him, he found the statement of uniqueness somewhat at odds with, 'There is none like you among the gods'. However, the verbatim agreement between John's Greek and the LXX of Psalm 86 runs to 16 or 17 words, making it virtually certain that John is dependent on a Greek source. It is therefore more likely that John changed the LXX's 'you alone are great' to 'you alone are holy', perhaps because he has already used the epithet 'great'.

Beale agrees with Bauckham that John *is* alluding to the Song of Moses and is not arbitrarily composing the song himself. He acknowledges that the 'actual contents of the song itself come not from Exodus 15 but from passages throughout the OT extolling God's character'[10] but suggests that more attention needs to be given to Deuteronomy 32. Thus he notes that Deuteronomy 32 is specifically called a 'song' in Deut. 31:30, and is applied to judgement and reward in the world to come in *b. Ta'anith* 11a. He also makes the astonishing suggestion that the opening words, 'Great and amazing are your deeds', come from the LXX of Deut. 28:59–60, where Israel is threatened with a judgement like God's 'great and amazing plagues'. The reason for this is that Beale wishes

---

[9] R. Bauckham, *The Climax of Prophecy: Studies in the Book of Revelation* (Edinburgh: T & T Clark, 1993), p. 306.
[10] Beale, *The Book of Revelation*, p. 794.

to challenge Bauckham's view that John's use of scripture here is in the service of universalism. He admits that 'the OT allusions in Rev. 15:3–4 have a kind of universalist strain' but insists that the emphasis of the song is judgement, which is 'supported by the broad OT context of the song of Moses in Deuteronomy 32 and especially Exodus 15, which underscores the idea of judgment of Israel's enemies leading to Israel's redemption'.[11]

Beale is quite correct that 'universalism' does not summarize all that John has to say about the fate of the nations but his argument here is quite tendentious. The obvious sources for his opening phrase, 'Great and amazing are your deeds', are positive psalm texts like 111:2 ('Great are the works of the Lord') or 139:14 ('Wonderful are your works'),[12] not the threat of God bringing upon Israel 'great and amazing plagues'. In fact, Beale's point that the general context of Revelation 14–16 is judgement makes the extensive quotation of Psalm 86 even more remarkable. Verbatim agreement with the LXX runs to 16 or 17 words (τὰ ἔργα, σου, πάντα τὰ ἔθνη, ἥξουσιν καὶ προσκυνησουσιν ἐνώπιόν σου, κύριε καὶ δοξάσουσιν τὸ ὄνομά σου).[13] This is strong evidence that John wishes to highlight the importance of this text (much more than Exodus 15 or Deuteronomy 32) and contrary to Bauckham, John appears to be dependent on a Greek source.

Psalm 89:28, 38 in Revelation 1:5

In the opening greeting, John parallels the three-fold description of God ('who is and who was and who is to come') with a three-fold description of Jesus as 'the faithful witness, the firstborn from the dead, and the ruler of the kings of the earth' (Rev. 1:5). This could be a functional-chronological description of the death, resurrection and ascension of Jesus, taking 'faithful witness' and 'firstborn from the dead' as backward references and 'ruler of the kings' as essentially future. Alternatively, the three titles might have christological intent and be purposely mirroring God's description. Aune, for example, thinks that 'faithful witness' is not a backward reference but refers to the 'exalted Jesus who guarantees the truth of the revelation transmitted through John'.[14] A third alternative is that John is deliberately alluding to Psalm 89, where it is said of David:

> I have found my servant David; with my holy oil I have anointed him; my hand shall always remain with him; my arm also shall strengthen him ... I will make him the firstborn (πρωτότοκον), the highest of the kings of the earth ... I will not lie to David. His line shall continue forever, and his throne endure before me like the sun. It shall be established forever like the moon, an enduring witness in the skies (ὁ μάρτυς ἐν οὐρανῷ πιστος) (Ps. 89:21, 28, 36b–38).

---

[11] Beale, *The Book of Revelation*, p. 799.

[12] Or Tob. 12:22 ('They kept blessing God and singing his praises, and they acknowledged God for these marvelous deeds of his, when an angel of God had appeared to them').

[13] Seventeen if we include John's use of the singular δοξάσει for δοξάσουσιν.

[14] D. Aune, *Revelation 1–5* (WBC 52A; Dallas: Word Books, 1997), p. 37.

Grace to you and peace ... from Jesus Christ, the faithful witness (ὁ μάρτυς ὁ πιστός), the firstborn (ὁ πρωτότοκος) of the dead, and the ruler of the kings of the earth (Rev. 1:4–5).

There is some evidence that the psalm was regarded as messianic (*Midr. Rab.* Exod. 19.7) and according to *UBSGNT*, the New Testament alludes to ten of its verses. However, there are no quotations of Psalm 89 in the New Testament and most of the suggested allusions are of a very general nature, seldom listed as the primary source. There are three major differences between the psalm and Rev. 1:5: (1) The psalm speaks of the moon as 'faithful witness' to God's covenant but John applies the phrase directly to Christ; (2) The psalm speaks of 'firstborn' but John has 'firstborn of the dead'; (3) The psalm has 'highest of the kings of the earth' but John has 'ruler of the kings of the earth'. This raises an important question as to whether John implants this psalm in the mind of the reader or hearer because it says what he wants or because he wants to highlight the changes he is making. Caird opts for the latter, arguing that the change from 'firstborn' to 'firstborn of the dead' makes it clear that the only victory recognized by Christians is Jesus' victory on the cross. Thus 'firstborn, instead of being an honorific title, is the guarantee that others will pass with him through death to kingship'.[15] In Caird's view, John is not pointing to Psalm 89 because he *agrees* with its 'aggrandisement of the Messiah' theme, but in order to *challenge* it with the cross of Christ.

Aune, on the other hand, thinks that the most likely source of 'firstborn from the dead' is the tradition that underlies Col. 1:15, 18 ('firstborn of all creation ... the beginning, the firstborn from the dead'). If this is correct, then John already has the phrase 'firstborn of the dead' in mind and uses Psalm 89 in order to enhance it by combining it with other functions and titles. As I have argued elsewhere, the relationship between Rev. 1:4–5 and Psalm 89 is best described as 'dialectical' rather than replacement.[16] John does not think that Psalm 89 says all that there is to say about Christ but neither is he contradicting it. It is more that he wishes to bring old and new into a dialectical relationship where each affects the other. As Aune says, a 'theology of glory' has been deftly combined with a 'theology of the cross'.[17] This certainly leads to transformation but not to replacement. For John, Jesus is 'first born of the dead' *and* 'Lord of lords and King of kings' (Rev. 17:14).

Summary

It is striking that each of these four unmarked psalm quotations offers a particular perspective on the fate of the nations. Psalm 2 emphasizes their rage and subsequent conquest by the Lord and his anointed. Psalm 89 focuses more

---

[15] G.B. Caird, *The Revelation of St John the Divine* (London: A & C Black, 2nd edn, 1984), p. 17.
[16] S. Moyise, *The Old Testament in the Book of Revelation* (JSNTSup 115; Sheffield: Sheffield Academic Press, 1995), pp. 116–18.
[17] Aune, *Revelation 1–5*, pp. 37–41.

on the character of the Davidic king but includes the thought that God will make him 'highest of the kings of the earth', which John changes to 'ruler of the kings of the earth'. The change shifts the emphasis towards the fate of the nations (who are 'ruled') rather than the person of the Messiah (who is 'highest'). Lastly, Psalm 86 offers the more positive promise that the greatness of God's deeds will cause the nations to come, bow down and glorify his name. Thus these four psalm texts contain the seemingly contradictory themes that (1) the nations will be utterly destroyed by the Messiah; and (2) the Messiah will rule over them as his inheritance. It is perhaps significant that this same paradox is also found at the climax of John's book:

> When the thousand years are ended, Satan will be released from his prison and will come out to deceive the nations at the four corners of the earth, Gog and Magog, in order to gather them for battle; they are as numerous as the sands of the sea. They marched up over the breadth of the earth and surrounded the camp of the saints and the beloved city. *And fire came down from heaven and consumed them . . .* And the city has no need of sun or moon to shine on it, for the glory of God is its light, and its lamp is the Lamb. *The nations will walk by its light, and the kings of the earth will bring their glory into it* (Rev. 20:7–9; 21:23–24).

As for the text used by John, despite the consensus view that John favoured Semitic texts,[18] there is little to suggest that here. Verbatim agreement with the LXX of Psalm 86 runs to 16 or 17 words and is strong evidence for John's dependence on a Greek text. The key words taken from Psalm 89, namely, ὁ μάρτυς ὁ πιστός and πρωτότοκον appear in the LXX and Beale has argued that John deliberately preserved the nominatives ὁ μάρτυς ὁ πιστός (ἀπό should be followed by a genitive) in order to highlight this.[19] John does of course change 'highest of the kings' to 'ruler of the kings' but this is a change of meaning, equally applicable to the Greek or Hebrew text. Finally, the use of ποιμαίνω has often been cited as evidence for the LXX, since the MT means 'shatter' not 'rule'. This would of course lose its force if the LXX is evidence for a more original Hebrew text and it is probably true that ἐν ῥάβδῳ σιδηρᾷ ('with an iron rod') is the obvious rendering of בשבט ברזל. Nevertheless, the evidence that can be gleaned from these four psalm texts points to Greek rather Hebrew sources, though it is clear that John only takes what he wants and feels free to modify certain words and expressions to suit his purpose.

---

[18] Begun by R.H. Charles, *A Critical and Exegetical Commentary on the Revelation of St. John* (ICC; Edinburgh: T & T Clark, 1920) I. pp. 1, lxii–lxxxvi, and (supposedly) confirmed by C.G. Ozanne, 'The Influence of the Text and Language of the Old Testament on the Book of Revelation' (PhD Thesis, University of Manchester, 1964) and L.P. Trudinger, 'The Text of the Old Testament in the Book of Revelation' (ThD Dissertation, Boston University, 1963). I have attempted to refute this consensus in S. Moyise, 'The Language of the Old Testament in the Apocalypse', *JSNT* 76 (1999), pp. 97–113.

[19] Though it should be noted that John does change the case of πρωτότοκον. See Beale, *The Book of Revelation*, p. 192.

Psalms that Contribute the Leading Idea in a Passage

Psalm 69:29 in Revelation 3:5 (13:8; 17:8; 20:14–15; 21:27)

One of the metaphors of salvation in the book of Revelation is whether one's name is written in a book of life. The idea of a special enrolment has a long history, from city registers, censuses for war or settlement, records of an individual's good and bad deeds and books of heavenly destiny. In the majority of cases in Revelation, the metaphor emphasizes the divide between the saved (whose names are written in the book) and the damned (whose names are not). If we are looking for a biblical text, the most likely source is Dan. 12:1 ('But at that time your people shall be delivered, everyone who is found written in the book'). However, in Rev. 3:5, the promise to the church at Sardis is framed as a warning:

> If you conquer, you will be clothed like them in white robes, and I will not blot (ἐξαλείψω) your name out of the book of life; I will confess your name before my Father and before his angels.

The most likely source here is either Exod. 32:32 (where Moses asks to be blotted out of the book) or Ps. 69:29 ('Let them be blotted out of the book of the living; let them not be enrolled among the righteous'). Beale is unhappy with the interpretation that Christians might be erased from the book of life and suggests that the warning is directed at false-Christians, who only *think* their names are written in the book. In terms of John's use of scripture, he says, 'The metaphor from Exodus 32 and Psalm 69 is read in the light of Daniel rather than the other way around or even that on an equal footing with Daniel'.[20] However, it is difficult to see why this is so for (1) John's use of 'erasure' (ἐξαλείφω) and 'book of life' points to Ps. 69:29 more than any of the other suggested texts; (2) one would expect such false-Christians to be warned of exposure rather than erasure; and (3) there is no *textual* evidence that John read Exodus 32 and Psalm 69 in the light of Daniel 12. Just as the church at Ephesus is threatened with the removal of its lampstand (Rev. 2:5), so those at Sardis must overcome or risk being erased from the book of life.

Psalm 75:9 in Revelation 14:9–11

The fate of the wicked in Rev. 14:10 is that they will 'drink the wine of God's wrath poured unmixed into the cup of his anger'. The idea of a 'cup of wrath' is frequent in the Old Testament (e.g. Ps. 75:9; Isa. 51:17; Jer. 25:15; Ezek. 23:31; Hab. 2:16) but the unusual expression κεκερασμένου ἀκράτου (literally, 'mixed unmixed') points specifically to Ps. 75:9 (Jer. 25:15 only has ἄκρατος). The seemingly contradictory phrase is explained by noting that the verb generally refers to mixing wine with spices to bring it to full strength,

---

[20] Beale, *The Book of Revelation*, p. 281.

while 'unmixed' means 'undiluted', that is, unmixed with water. The expression therefore means 'mixed in full strength'. John finds in Ps. 75:9 a graphic description of the fate of the wicked, which is almost certainly taken from the LXX.[21]

Psalm 99:1 in Revelation 11:17–18

When the seventh angel blows his trumpet in Rev. 11:15, we hear of the victory of the Lord and his anointed and the rage of the nations. As we have seen, this draws on Psalm 2 but the unusual expression καὶ ἐβασίλευσας καὶ τὰ ἔθνη ὠργίσθησαν is commonly thought to be an allusion to the LXX of Ps. 99:1 (κύριος ἐβασίλευσεν ὀργιζέσθωσαν λαοί). The Hebrew acclamation מלך יהוה is rendered κύριος ἐβασίλευσεν in four psalms (93:1; 96:10; 97:1; 99:1) but only in Ps. 99:1 is it followed by a reference to its negative consequences for the peoples of the earth. Swete[22] used this verse as one of his key examples of John's dependence on the LXX, noting that the Hebrew verb רגז means 'tremble' rather than 'angry'. This argument is somewhat weakened by the fact that the anger of the nations could derive from Psalm 2 or indeed from Exod. 15:14, but the unusual aorist, generally taken as inceptive ('begun to reign') confirms Swete's intuition. John borrows from Ps. 99:1 the twin ideas of 'God's reign' and the 'rage of the nations' but finds in Psalm 2 the specific mention of 'the Lord and his anointed'.

Psalm 106:48 in Revelation 19:4

Not surprisingly, the language of the psalms is frequently echoed in the hymns and praises of Revelation. In Rev. 19:4, there is an acclamation of 'Amen, Hallelujah', which could simply be John's combination but many commentators regard it as an allusion to Ps. 106:48. The call to praise God with the words הללו־יה occurs 23 times in the psalms (and nowhere else) but Ps. 106:48 is the only place where it occurs with אמן. Beale calls it an echo but insists that it is not 'haphazard, since in the Psalm, as here, it functions as part of the people's thanksgiving to God for gathering them to himself after delivering them from "their enemies" who "oppressed them"'.[23] The Greek is of course a transliteration of the Hebrew letters, the LXX generally rendering אמן with γένοιτο. This could be evidence of John's use of a Hebrew text, though it is perhaps more likely that the phrase came to John through liturgical repetition.

Psalm 115:4–7 in Revelation 9:20

Rev. 9:20 says that those who were not killed by the plagues 'did not repent of the work of their hands or give up worshipping demons and idols of gold and

---

[21] The MT reads חמר, 'foaming' (RSV, NRSV, NIV) and is unlikely to be the source of John's phrase.
[22] H.B. Swete, *The Apocalypse of St John* (London: Macmillan, 3rd edn, 1991), pp. cxl–clviii.
[23] Beale, *The Book of Revelation*, p. 930.

silver and bronze and stone and wood, which cannot see of hear or walk'. The list of materials comes from Dan. 5:4, 23 (Beale) but the phrase 'work of human hands' and the sequence 'see, hear, walk' (Daniel has 'see, hear, know') points to the more comprehensive list in Ps. 115:4–7 ('speak, see, hear, smell, feel, walk'). This suggestion is strengthened by the use of Ps. 115:13 in Rev. 11:18; 19:5 (see below).

Psalm 115:13 in Revelation 11:18, 19:5

Twice in Revelation, John refers to God's servants as 'those who fear him' and adds 'both small and great'. Now μικρός ('small') and μέγας ('great') occur together some 67 times in the LXX but there are only five texts where this is combined with some form of φοβέω ('fear'), namely, 2 Kgs 25:26; Est. 1:1; Judg. 16:16; Ps. 113:21 = MT 115:13; Jer. 49:1). Only Ps. 115:13 bears any contextual similarity to Rev. 11:18. Thus it would appear that John found in Psalm 115 both a denouncement of idolatry, the work of human hands, and a blessing on those who fear God, small and great alike.

Psalm 137:8 in Revelation 18:6

That Babylon will be punished according to her works occurs several times in Jeremiah (27:15; 27:29; 28:24) but it is Ps. 137:8 which speaks of rendering to her what she rendered to you, using different tenses of the same verb. John uses the imperative and the aorist of ἀποδίδωμι; the psalm uses the future and aorist of ἀνταποδίδωμι. Charles categorizes this as based on the Hebrew text but offers no reasons. It is more likely stylistic variation, since John uses ἀποδίδωμι on three occasions but never uses ἀνταποδίδωμι. Indeed, the proportion of occurrences of ἀποδίδωμι to ἀνταποδίδωμι in the LXX is 2.4:1 but 14.8:1 in the New Testament. John has simply used the more common word. John finds in Psalm 137 a graphic description of the fate of God's enemies, namely, that the punishment will fit the crime.[24]

Psalm 141:2, 144:9 in Revelation 5:8–10

The song of praise in Rev. 5:8–10 draws on a number of passages but the analogy of prayer rising like incense is only found in Ps. 141:2 and, in a somewhat different context, Wis. 18:21.[25] The idea of angels presenting prayers to God is found in Tob. 12:12, 15, while the 'new song' occurs in a number of passages, but only combined with harps in Ps. 144:9. It is difficult to deduce much about the text used as the agreement is only in a few isolated

---

[24] Actually, the next phrase appears to contradict this by declaring that Babylon will receive double for her sins, though Kline thinks the expression can mean 'make a duplicate' and hence render what was rendered (M.G. Kline, 'Double Trouble', *JETS* 32 [1989], pp. 171–79).

[25] 'For a blameless man was quick to act as their champion; he brought forward the shield of his ministry, prayer and propitiation by incense; he withstood the anger and put an end to the disaster, showing that he was your servant.'

words. John calls the instrument a κιθάρα instead of the LXX's ψαλτηρίον, but as the latter does not occur in the New Testament, not much can be deduced from this. John finds in these psalm words a description of eschatological victory for the people of God.

Summary

Many of the psalms in this second category fill out the idea of God's judgement of the nations. Thus Ps. 137:8 supplies the idea that the punishment will fit the crime, while 75:9 provides the graphic description of drinking the cup of God's wrath, mixed in full strength. Ps. 99:1 combines with Psalm 2 to speak of the rage of the nations, adding the thought that God has taken up his reign. Psalm 115 supplies a description of the sin of the nations, namely, the worship of dumb idols.

This leaves the acclamation of praise from Ps. 106:48, the analogy of prayers ascending like incense from Ps. 141:2, the faithful singing a new song from Ps. 144:9, the description of God's people as those who fear him, both small and great, from Ps. 115:13 and the warning to avoid being erased from the book of life from Ps. 69:29. Thus based on our first two categories, we may summarize John's use of the psalms thus:

(1)   Judgement of the idolatrous nations by God (Pss 2:1–2, 8–9; 75:8; 99:1; 115:4–7; 137:8)
(2)   The salvation of the nations (Ps. 86:8–10)
(3)   Images of salvation for the people of God (Pss 69:29; 106:48; 115:13; 141:2; 144:9)
(4)   Attributes of God's anointed (Ps. 89:28, 38)

Psalms that Contribute One of the Ideas in a Passage

Psalm 7:10/62:13 in Revelation 2:23

The idea that God 'searches' or 'examines' the human heart is a stock idea in the Old Testament but the particular expression 'kidneys and hearts' only occurs in Jer. 11:20; 17:10; 20:12 and Ps. 7:10. None of these texts uses John's word for search (ἐραυνάω), which perhaps comes from Christian tradition (e.g. Rom. 8:27; 1 Cor. 2:10). John follows the statement that God searches 'kidneys and hearts' with the statement that he will render to everyone according to their works. This suggests that Jer. 17:10 is the key passage, which continues, 'to give to all according to their ways', though Ps. 7:10 may also be in the background. It is also possible that John has Ps. 62:13 in mind ('For you repay to all according to their work') since Jer. 17:10 speaks of 'ways' rather than 'works'.[26]

---

[26] *UBSGNT* lists the Old Testament sources for the first phrase as Ps. 7:9; Prov. 24:12; Jer. 11:20; 17:10, and for the second phrase, Ps. 62:13; Prov. 24:12; Jer. 17:10.

Psalm 23:1–2 in Revelation 7:17

Whether John has taken the idea of the Lamb 'shepherding' (ποιμαίνω) and guiding (ὁδηγέω) his people to springs of living water from Psalm 23 is a matter of debate. The surrounding verses ('They will hunger no more, and thirst no more; the sun will not strike them') certainly come from Isa. 49:10, which continues, 'for he who has pity on them will *lead* them, and by springs of *water* will guide them'. It does not, however, use the word ποιμαίνω, which would appear to derive from Ps. 23:1. Aune is not convinced and suggests that John probably took the idea of 'shepherding' from Christian tradition (e.g. Matt. 15:24; Jn 10:2; Heb. 13:20; 1 Pet. 2:25) or perhaps from Ezek. 34:23.[27] Nevertheless, the specific use of ποιμαίνω to mean 'shepherd' rather than 'rule', in conjunction with the fact that Psalm 23 does speak of guiding to water, suggests that Psalm 23 lies in the background.

Psalm 47:9 in Revelation 4:2–3, 9–10 and others.

Some commentators include Ps. 47:9 as one of the Old Testament verses that speak about God sitting on a throne (cf. 1 Kgs 22:19; Isa. 6:1; Dan. 7:9; Ezek. 1:26). Aune notes that it is rarely used as an epithet for God in the Jewish tradition but is frequent in Graeco-Roman magical formulae. John uses the expression 'seated on' some 27 times, of which 12 are a circumlocution for God. That Jesus also occupies the throne (22:1) was perhaps suggested by the promise in Matt. 19:28/25:31 that the 'Son of Man' will 'sit on the throne of his glory'.

Psalm 78:44 in Revelation 16:4

The pouring out of the third bowl evokes the Egyptian plague where God tells Moses to stretch out his hand over the 'waters of Egypt – over its rivers, its canals, and its ponds, and all its pools of water – so that they may become blood' (Exod. 7:19). The double mention of 'rivers and springs of water' (Rev. 16:4) may also evoke Ps. 78:44 ('He turned their rivers to blood, so that they could not drink of their streams'). John's word for 'springs' (πηγὰς) differs from any of the words used in Exodus 7 or the rare ὄμβρημα (*hapax legomenon*) used in Ps. 78:44. John is simply using the common word for 'streams'.

Psalm 79:1 in Revelation 11:2

The trampling (πατέω) of the holy city is probably based on the trampling of the sanctuary from either Dan. 8:13 (συμπατέω – Theodotion) or Isa. 63:18 (καταπατέω). Neither text, however, speaks of the trampling of the holy city. A number of texts refer to Jerusalem as the holy city (e.g. Neh. 11:1; Isa. 48:2; Dan. 3:28) but not in a context of 'trampling'. Thus no text is all that close to John's 'they will trample on the holy city'. It is possible that the thought of Ps.

---

[27] Aune, *Revelation 6–16*, pp. 477–79.

79:1 is in the background ('they have defiled your holy temple; they have laid Jerusalem in ruins') but there is little verbal similarity.

Psalm 96:13 in Revelation 19:11

In Rev. 19:11, the rider of the white horse is called 'Faithful and True, and in righteousness he judges and makes war'. Charles suggests Isa. 11:4 ('but with righteousness he shall judge the poor'). However, the negative focus ('and makes war') makes it more likely that John is drawing on a number of psalms where this phrase occurs (e.g. 96:13: 'He will judge the world with righteousness').

Psalm 119:137 in Revelation 15:3; 16:7

In Rev. 15:3, John says that God's ways are 'just and true', and in Rev. 16:7, that his judgements are 'true and just'. Beale thinks this comes from Deut. 34:2, which according to the LXX, says, 'his work is true, and all his ways are just. A faithful God, without deceit, just and upright is he.' However, if we are looking for a source for the specific statement that God's 'judgements' (κρίσεις) are just, it is probably Ps. 119:137 (along with Ps. 19:9) that is in mind ('You are righteous, O Lord, and your judgments are right').

Summary

The allusion to Ps. 78:44 adds to our first category ('Judgement of the idolatrous nations by God') the idea that judgement will mimic the Exodus plagues and their rivers will turn to blood. Ps. 23:1–2 adds a theme to our third category ('Images of salvation for the people of God'), namely, being led to springs of living water. The remaining psalms require us to expand the category of 'Attributes of God's anointed' to 'Attributes of God and his Anointed'. Thus based on our first three categories, we can now offer a summary of John's use of the psalms in the book of Revelation:

(1) Judgement of the idolatrous nations by God

- the nations raged and were defeated (Ps. 2:1–2)
- the nations' opposition is smashed like clay pots (Ps. 2:8–9)
- judgement is according to works (Ps. 62:13)
- the wicked are forced to drink the wine of God's wrath (Ps. 75:8)
- as in the Exodus plagues, their rivers will turn to blood (Ps. 78:44)
- the nations raged and God took up his reign (Ps. 99:1)
- idolatry, the work of human hands, is denounced (Ps. 115:4–6)
- 'Babylon' is repaid for her cruelty (Ps. 137:8)

(2) The salvation of the nations
- all nations will come and worship God (Ps. 86:8–10)

(3) Images of salvation for the people of God
- being led to springs of living water (Ps. 23:1–2)
- not being erased from the book of life (Ps. 69:29)

- a blessing on those who fear God, great and small alike (Ps. 115:13)
- prayers rising like incense (Ps. 141:2)
- singing a new song (Ps. 144:9)

(4) Attributes of God and his Anointed
  - searches the human heart (Ps. 7:10)
  - he judges in righteousness (Ps. 96:13)
  - his judgements are just and true (119:137)
  - God's anointed is firstborn of the dead (Ps. 89:28)
  - God's anointed is ruler of the kings of the earth (Ps. 89:28)

In terms of the type of text used by John, the presence of 'Amen, hallelujah' and some of the variations from the LXX, such as κιθάρα for ψαλτηρίον and ἀποδίδωμι for ἀνταποδίδωμι, might be evidence for John's use of a Hebrew text. But the majority of verses discussed above supports our earlier conclusion that John knew and used Greek sources. Since this is contrary to the consensus, it is clearly a subject worthy of further study.[28] Despite the difficulties of obtaining concrete evidence from allusions rather than explicit quotations, there is enough to affirm that John knew and used a Greek translation of the psalms.

Conclusion

Can we say anything about John's hermeneutical stance towards the psalms? It is clear that he regards them as prophetic. He thinks that Psalm 2 speaks about the victory of Jesus the Messiah; Psalm 89 offers a description of him as firstborn, faithful witness and ruler of the kings of the earth; and Psalm 86 describes the eschatological conversion of the nations. It is interesting that our four themes are very close to Fekkes's summary of John's use of Isaiah, which suggests that John did not distinguish between what we would call prophetic oracles and liturgical songs.[29] They were both viewed as prophecies awaiting fulfilment in the new age. On the other hand, John does not seem to think that each text has one single fulfilment in the new age, for he uses some texts more than once. Thus the prophecy of 'ruling the nations with an iron rod' (Ps. 2:8–9) is applied first to the Christians in Thyatira (Rev. 2:26–7), then to the male child born of the woman (Rev. 12:5), and finally to the rider of the white

---

[28] It is interesting that the most convincing examples of John's use of a Hebrew text all come from the book of Ezekiel (Rev. 1:15; 18:1; 18:19; 22:2). Perhaps John was familiar with some books in Greek and some in Hebrew. See further, Moyise, 'The Language of the Old Testament in the Apocalypse'.

[29] Fekkes speaks of (1) visionary experience and language, (2) christological titles and descriptions, (3) eschatological judgement and (4) eschatological salvation. We have not found an example of the psalms used to describe visionary experience but then Fekkes only finds one example in Isaiah (6:1–4). Our theme of the salvation of the nations is included in his theme of eschatological salvation (e.g. Isa. 60:3, 5, 11).

horse (Rev. 19:15). Whether this involves ascribing new meanings to texts or simply giving them new significance is an ongoing debate.[30]

John feels free to make certain changes to his sources or apply them to different subjects. Thus Jesus is 'ruler of the kings' rather than 'highest of the kings' and the 'faithful witness' of the moon has become a title for Christ. In Revelation 15, despite the arguments of Bauckham and Beale, John has drawn on a number of scriptures, notably Psalm 86, rather than the song of Moses in either Exodus 15 or Deuteronomy 32. Aune goes too far when he describes it as a 'pastiche of stereotypical hymnic phrases'[31] but it is clear that Revelation 15 is not intending to offer an exposition of Exodus 15 or Deuteronomy 32 or discover its 'original meaning'.[32]

What about the term 'typology'? Texts that spoke of judgement against Israel's enemies are freely applied to the church's enemies. Their rivers will turn to blood, they will be forced to drink the 'unmixed mixture' and like Babylon of old, they will be repaid in kind. Indeed, John calls the new enemy 'Babylon'. However, typology suggests a one-to-one correspondence between new and old, which does not do justice to John's creative reconfiguration of his sources. It is perhaps best to avoid trying to summarize this complexity in a single designation. In John's own words, he was 'in the Spirit on the Lord's Day' (Rev. 1:10) and what he has given us is a complex reconfiguration of scripture in the light of his Christian experience. And as we have demonstrated above, the psalms played an important part in that.

---

[30] See S. Moyise, 'Does the Author of Revelation Misappropriate the Scriptures?', *AUSS* 40 (2002), pp. 3–21.

[31] Aune, *Revelation 6–16*, p. 874.

[32] Murphy makes the astounding statement that Exod. 15 and Rev. 15:3–4 are 'broadly similar' but admits (1) the song is full of the language of the Hebrew Bible, citing 14 different texts; and (2) the enemies in Exod. 15 are either destroyed (Egyptians) or in terror (inhabitants of Canaan) and their conversion is not contemplated. I would suggest that these two points show that Exod. 15 and Rev. 15:3–4 are *not* 'broadly similar'. See F.J. Murphy, *Fallen is Babylon: The Revelation to John* (Harrisburg: Trinity Press International, 1998), pp. 329–32.

Index of Quotations and Allusions – New Testament Order

Index of Quotations and Allusions –
Psalm Order (MT)

Index of Modern Authors

Lightning Source UK Ltd.
Milton Keynes UK
UKOW06f2308270316

270998UK00001B/15/P